OPERA IN THE DEVELOPMENT
OF GERMAN CRITICAL THOUGHT

OPERA
in the
Development
of German
Critical Thought

GLORIA FLAHERTY

PRINCETON UNIVERSITY PRESS

Copyright © 1978 by Princeton University Press

Published by Princeton University Press, Princeton, New Jersey
In the United Kingdom: Princeton University Press,
Guildford, Surrey

All Rights Reserved

Library of Congress Cataloging in Publication Data will be
found on the last printed page of this book

This book has been composed in linotype Baskerville

Clothbound editions of Princeton University Press books
are printed on acid-free paper, and binding materials are
chosen for strength and durability.

Printed in the United States of America by
Princeton University Press, Princeton, New Jersey

To
JEAN BACENAS FLAHERTY
and
in memory of
JOHN ROBERT FLAHERTY

CONTENTS

CONTENTS

PREFACE

OPERATIC forms dominated the seventeenth- and eighteenth-century stage in Germany. They generated a long line of controversies between academic critics espousing universally valid standards of beauty and theater people upholding their freedom to experiment with a vast array of untested possibilities. This volume deals with those controversies. When I began my research, I hoped to provide information contributing to a historical reappraisal of early German criticism. My intention at the time was merely to show that writings defending opera against rationalistic condemnation anticipated the artistic values, philosophical points of view, and critical methodologies prominent in the early nineteenth century.

As I discovered more and more material and attempted to assess it historically, I realized that the significance of early operatic writings was far deeper than I had at first suspected. They illuminate the classical, patriotic, and romantic tendencies that became manifest during the Renaissance and developed uninterruptedly thereafter. And, most importantly, they reveal how the continuing interaction of those tendencies prepared the ground for the artistic flowering during the age of Goethe.

Opera's failure as a revival of Greek tragedy, its success as a uniquely modern theatrical form, and its seemingly unrealized potential as a fusion of the arts fascinated generations of German poets, composers, artists, philosophers, critics, and scholars. In seeking to justify their own artistic interests and tastes, they transformed the viable critical ideas of the past and applied them to the present. Their operatic writings enriched German criticism with new vocabulary, provided theoretical justification for the epic tendencies of older European theater, promoted the study of the performing arts, and emphasized music and spectacle as essential components of theater. By encouraging further consideration of "melosdramaturgy," opera's exponents helped shape a version of the classical ideal that was distinctively German and, as they saw it, divorced from the Roman, Italian, and French conceptions of Greek antiquity.

The ever widening scope of my study required limitation, and for this reason I often had to refrain from pursuing discursive matters latent in the subject. Several of those matters are indicated in the notes. I believe additional work on them could prove valuable for our understanding of eighteenth-century artistic developments and could contribute significantly to the much needed reappraisal of the early history of critical thought in Germany.

The bibliography is designed to assist those who would continue the study of German criticism within its greater European context. In addition to the works discussed in the text and mentioned in the notes, I have included other librettos with literary critical prefaces, useful reference books from the period, and other publications that warrant closer attention than my study allowed.

The translations of quoted materials are intended to be utilitarian glosses rather than demonstrations of my ability to render into English the exact flavor of the originals. I hope they will be helpful to readers in all fields, but especially in those where the nuances of seventeenth- and eighteenth-century style are not of primary importance.

Over the years I have sought advice and assistance from many people. The generosity and good will with which they responded made my research possible. I am deeply grateful to all of them. In particular I should like to thank the many dedicated librarians of Bryn Mawr College, the Johns Hopkins University, the Music Division of the Library of Congress, the Newberry Library, the New York Public Library, Northwestern University, the University of Pennsylvania, Princeton University, Yale University, and the libraries in Göttingen, Hamburg, Marburg, and Wolfenbüttel. I owe thanks of a special sort to the friends who shared their time and ideas with me.

My greatest debt is to Harold Jantz. He granted me unlimited access to his collections of rare books. He read drafts of several chapters, discussed them with me, and offered invaluable suggestions for improvement. He encouraged me to follow my own intuition, but not without first teaching me how to test it in the realm of fact. Should that intuition have been left untested in any sections of this volume, the fault is mine alone.

OPERA IN THE DEVELOPMENT
OF GERMAN CRITICAL THOUGHT

INTRODUCTION

DURING the late eighteenth and early nineteenth centuries, the German-speaking lands experienced one of the most active periods of artistic creativity in their long history. The works of Goethe and Schiller stand as glorious monuments to that period when German artists sought in the ideal realm the natural unity of culture their real world lacked. Having learned to distinguish rationally devised pseudo-classical notions from the genuine spirit of classical antiquity, they strove to recapture that spirit and harness its powers. Like countless generations before them, they sought the aesthetic secrets of the ancients and, in so doing, discovered hitherto unsuspected ones. Those newly found secrets made them fully conscious of the spirit of their own era and the past out of which it had evolved. Schiller analyzed the phenomenon and described it with the word "sentimental." Friedrich Schlegel used the word "romantic." And Goethe depicted it symbolically through Faust's marriage to Helena.

The advances in literary criticism and aesthetics that accompanied the artistic creativity of the Goethean age have long been subjects of scholarly interest. Time and time again students of the period have sought antecedents for the new artistic attitudes. The English garden, the bourgeois tragedy, the sentimental novel, the fairy tale, the poetic descriptions of primordial nature, and the poetic adoration of ruins are regularly considered symptomatic of changes in the premises of taste. The coining of the word "aesthetics" by Baumgarten, the affirmation of the wondrous by Bodmer and Breitinger, the rejection of predetermined rules by Lessing, and the demand for creative freedom by the *Sturm und Drang* writers are always mentioned as significant indications of the changes that were taking place.

3

One of the best indicators of changing aesthetic premises and critical attitudes is never, or hardly ever mentioned in works discussing the evolution of German criticism or the artistic flowering of the Goethean age. And that is opera: the theatrical form that innumerable German poets, critics, and philosophers considered the ultimate artistic possibility.[1] Because their operatic ideas have been overlooked, we are not only deprived of information about German theatrical history, we are also left with a distorted picture of an important phenomenon in the history of criticism.

One example of such distortion is George Saintsbury's outdated, but nevertheless useful *History of Criticism and Literary Taste in Europe.* In addition to underestimating the richness of German literature, he overlooked the ongoing discussions about opera and erroneously suggested that the Germans "possessed little critical starting-point" in the eighteenth century because they had suffered a long period of "drowsy inertia." The Germans, unlike the English, he maintained, lacked an "abundance of really great writers upon whom to fix practical and real critical examinations."[2] René Wellek perpetuated this kind of value judgment by contending that there could not have been any influential indigenous contributions to criticism because Germany failed to produce any immortal masterpieces until after mid-eighteenth century. He therefore concluded that "poetic theory remained an abstract academic exercise."[3]

Perhaps seventeenth-century Germany did not produce a dramatic genius of international stature. It did, however, produce writers whose works and ideas inspired later generations to develop modern critical habits. If we consider the quality of what was subsequently written by Germans, we cannot disregard their earlier indigenous backgrounds. Nor can we pass over their works as too speculative, fumbling, and immature to warrant careful attention. In addition to reviewing the repositories of traditional dramatic theory—the often reprinted poetic handbooks—we must seek out the less accessible writings about theatrical forms

4

cultivated and discussed since the Renaissance. Those writings were usually produced in the milieu of living theater where playwrights sought to explain or defend their own practices to a general, nonacademic audience. I have chosen opera precisely because it grew out of Renaissance attempts to revive Greek tragedy and because it gained the kind of flexibility that permitted change as the mood and style changed from Baroque to Enlightenment, to classicism, and then on to romanticism.

Writings for and against opera, which remained the most vital force in seventeenth- and eighteenth-century German theater, provide invaluable information about the artistic temper of their times and prove that pre-Goethean criticism was much more than just "an abstract academic exercise." There were many unknown, minor figures among the librettists, performers, composers, and opera enthusiasts who wrote them, but there were just as many major figures. As Paul Oskar Kristeller has pointed out about the history of aesthetics in general:

> The basic questions and conceptions underlying modern aesthetics seem to have originated quite apart from the traditions of systematic philosophy or from the writings of important original authors. They had their inconspicuous beginnings in secondary authors, now almost forgotten though influential in their own time, and perhaps in the discussions and conversations of educated laymen reflected in their writings. These notions had a tendency to fluctuate and to grow slowly, but only after they had crystallized into a pattern that seemed generally plausible did they find acceptance among the greater authors and the systematic philosophers.[4]

The ideas advanced, supported, and perpetuated by opera's exponents had lasting effects on theatrical practices and far-ranging implications for critical thought. These writings help to illuminate the developments that took place between the Renaissance and the age of Goethe, the two greatest turning points in the history of modern European culture. This study intends to examine such writings as documents in the history of German criticism and theater.

Opera originated in Italy at the turn of the seventeenth century. Its invention in Florence by the poets and musicians of the Camerata came at the height of Renaissance dramatic experimentation, production, and discussion. Audiences all over western Europe were deriving great delight from pastoral plays, spectacles, intermezzos, performances of the commedia dell'arte, and other decidedly unclassic theatrical entertainments. Guarini and Tasso had reached the pinnacle of their fame, and Lope de Vega, Shakespeare, Ben Jonson, and Tirso de Molina were approaching maturity. The dramatic practices of these playwrights already stood in sharp contrast to the neoclassical code that was beginning to form out of the writings of theorists like Antonio Sebastiano (Minturno), Lodovico Castelvetro, and Julius Caesar Scaliger. Their attempts to reconcile the traditional views of Horace, Cicero, Quintilian, and Donatus with the recently rediscovered ones of Plato and Aristotle had provided the formulations of the three unities, the concept of verisimilitude, the theory of decorum, and the dogma of drama's pedagogical function.

While more and more dramatists, theorists, and critics focused on such standards for reproducing classical drama, the members of the Florentine Camerata concentrated their efforts on rediscovering the musical means used in antiquity. The question of music's role in ancient drama had arisen earlier as increasing attention was given to the fifth of Vitruvius's *Ten Books on Architecture* and the second book of Aristotle's *Poetics*. Vitruvius's ideas on the musical and visual nature of ancient drama together with Aristotle's treatment of music and spectacle as two of Greek tragedy's six essential components helped lay the theoretical foundation for subsequent practical experimentation. Music had long been a significant component of Renaissance drama, but the polyphonic tendencies of the age precluded dramas

6

comprehensibly set throughout to music. It was left to the Camerata to invent the kind of music that could be adapted to a text without obscuring the meaning of the words.

The classicizing theories of the Renaissance gave birth to opera. But it was the continuing interaction of those theories with modern theatrical practices and aspirations that sustained opera and determined its future. As the Camerata's successors developed monodic music still further and incorporated the all-important visual component, opera lost its resemblance to the ancient forms it was intended to restore and became a thoroughly independent form of theater that continued to spawn new variants as well as influence older ones. It was so compatible with seventeenth-century tastes, sensibilities, and habits that it quickly gained widespread acclaim and developed into one of Europe's leading cultural institutions. By the end of the seventeenth century, however, it had also become a subject of widespread controversy.

Theologically oriented adversaries decried opera's power over the fancy of man and condemned its excessive emphasis on the senses, while neoclassical literary men denounced its failure to comply with the dramatic rules and mocked what they considered its artistic inanities. For some of them, opera was comparable to Gothic architecture, medieval doggerel, chivalric romances, Chinese plays, harlequinades, and assorted varieties of baroque exotica. It represented to them either the return of the barbarous irrationality of past ages or the advent of alarmingly relativistic attitudes. They therefore objected not only to operatic practices, which sometimes left much to be desired, but also to the very idea of opera.

Such objections were vigorously opposed by a continuing line of writers who rose in opera's defense. Those who defended the idea of opera as a revival of classical drama recalled the aims of the Camerata and stressed the need to reform current practices by simplifying and ennobling the relationship of word, music, and spectacle. Those who believed opera excelled the dramas of classical antiquity defended it as a modern theatrical form with almost limitless artistic potentialities. They found the sensual appeal of contemporary operatic practices irresistible and sought to explain their own reactions and justify their own tastes. Like Guarini, Lope de Vega, Tirso de Molina, and François Ogier, whose ideas on tragicomedy and modern drama they often shared, they supported the tendency to derive critical theory from actual practices. From its inception and throughout most of its history, opera was closely associated not only with the resuscitation of ancient drama and the evolution of modern theater but also with the development of modern critical thought.

Although opera figured importantly in the French Quarrel of the Ancients and the Moderns and the English discussions of heroic tragedy, it was in Germany that its role in the development of criticism and aesthetics was most pronounced. The early defenses of opera contributed immeasurably to the refinement of German critical genius. In seeking arguments to disprove opera's opponents, German writers became increasingly aware of certain basic problems in critical theory, practical criticism, and aesthetics. When they applied their common sense to neoclassical dramatic theory, they discovered erroneous assumptions and methodological inconsistencies. Authoritarian claims about the universal validity of the ancient standards were illogical to them, for it seemed obvious that times changed, and what was good for one age was not necessarily good for the next. And since each age developed its own art forms to satisfy its own needs, no one corpus of rules could possibly, in their opinion, account for the new and different theatrical forms that human ingenuity and talent were constantly devising. Furthermore, their reexamination of ancient dramatic theories failed to disclose any specific sources for such normative, prescriptive standards. The battle these defenders of opera gave to the self-styled authorities retarded the acceptance of neoclassicism in Germany and encouraged further inquiry into the essence of the genuinely classical.

It also led to the formulation of more liberal critical principles and the affirmation of Romantic premises of taste. Preferring what could be demonstrated empirically to what was derived from theoretical speculation, opera's defenders established the primacy of the individual artistic product. They carefully scrutinized the writings of earlier European playwrights who had maintained that newly developed theatrical forms were justified by usage; they selected and made their own only those ideas whose validity could be tested in the theater and substantiated by live audiences. From observing audience reactions, they learned that the highly stylized, make-believe world of opera appealed directly to the imagination and emotions. In addition to analyzing the sources and effects of theatrical pleasures, opera's German defenders investigated the doctrine of mimesis and contemplated the kind of reality presented in the arts. Because their studies indicated that the arts were neither methodical nor predictable, they insisted on the kind of liberty that would allow for continuing artistic progress.

As time passed, their terminology became less awkward and their argumentation more sophisticated. Eventually opera came to exemplify certain aesthetic ideas and was mentioned more and more often in works dealing primarily with theatrical history or the criticism of spoken drama. By the end of the eighteenth century, the premises and principles contained in operatic writings had permeated all branches of criticism and aesthetic theory. Opera's exponents had helped to transmit the viable ideas of the past and to transform them so that they could be employed meaningfully in the future. As a result, German criticism gained its own distinctive character and began to exert considerable influence on European letters.

ONE

ANCIENT OR MODERN

QUINTESSENTIAL THEATER

THE Holy Roman Empire comprised over three hundred territorial states at the turn of the seventeenth century. Its universal authority, like that of the church it supported, had already been irrevocably destroyed by the Lutheran Reformation and the accompanying cataclysmic events. Habsburg attempts to regain control over the German-speaking states met with increasingly violent opposition from within as well as from without. Politically ambitious German princes feared that centralized power would threaten their own sovereignty. To combat imperial encroachment, they promoted decentralization, banded together along religious lines, and solicited foreign assistance. The precarious balance created by the Peace of Augsburg (1555) was shortly to be upset by a civil war that would involve most European states for at least three decades.

It was on the eve of the Thirty Years' War that the newly developed Italian opera was introduced to the German-speaking lands. The first opera was performed in Salzburg in 1618 by the predominantly Italian group of musicians and singers assembled by Archbishop Marx Sittich von Hohenems (1574-1619).[1] German princes, whether ecclesiastical or secular, were particularly receptive to the arts. They collected paintings, maintained musical ensembles, supported poets, and spent fabulous sums of money all for the greater glory of their office and, of course, themselves. German burghers were also interested in keeping up with the very latest foreign fashions. They might of necessity have been less extravagant than their rulers, but they too

loved pageantry, music, and theatrical entertainments. Theater flourished in multifarious forms before, during, and
after the Thirty Years' War. And so did interest in theatrical history, dramatic theory, poetics, philology, bibliography, and criticism.

Martin Opitz (1597-1639) stands out at the beginning of
the seventeenth century as the most notable German consolidator of current European critical thought. Having immersed himself in the poetic theories of the Italian, the
French, and the Dutch Renaissance, he strove to make them
the basis for purifying and ennobling indigenous literature.
His *Buch von der deutschen Poeterey* (1624) synthesized
those theories and outlined important metrical, linguistic,
and generic reforms. The numerous works he either wrote,
translated, or adapted were to serve as examples of what
Germans could do to bring their country up to the artistic
level of other polite nations. It was no coincidence that he
was commissioned to prepare the first opera libretto in the
German language. The history of German operatic criticism
as well as opera begins with him.

Opitz's adaptation of Ottavio Rinuccini's (1562-1621)
Daphne, the earliest of the Florentine Camerata's musical
dramas, was set to music by Heinrich Schütz (1585-1672)
and successfully performed in 1627 during the festivities attending the marriage of the daughter of the Saxon elector
to the landgrave of Hesse-Darmstadt. The preface Opitz
wrote for this pastoral tragicomedy shows that he did not
share the Camerata's views about restoring ancient drama.
Far more important to him were the dramatic standards
that Renaissance theorists had purportedly derived from antiquity. Opitz explained that he would have preferred to
construct his libretto according to such standards but had
had to deviate from them in order to satisfy the tastes of his
modern audience.[2] In the dedicatory preface to *Judith*
(1635), a heroic opera also adapted from an Italian source,
Opitz again compared his work to pseudo-Aristotelian rules

and offered excuses for its divergence. The main excuse this time was that it fulfilled a useful didactic function by reinforcing Christian beliefs and stimulating patriotic feelings.

Although Opitz never resolved the conflict between contemporary theatrical demands and so-called ancient dramatic theories, he set important precedents for his contemporaries and for those who followed. They carried out his verse reforms, continued his investigation of the Germanic past, elaborated on his poetic manual, and experimented with many of the genres he had sanctioned. His ambivalent attitude toward opera did not hinder some of his disciples from trying their hand at it. August Buchner (1591-1661), one of the most loyal of the Opitzians, recognized music's importance for the new metrics and collaborated with Schütz on a *Singballet* treating the Orpheus motif (1638). Like most early seventeenth-century operas, it too was performed during an aristocratic wedding celebration. Such celebrations generally included some form of musical theatrical extravaganza, which afforded ample opportunity for praising the lord of the principality, his family, or his visitors, in grand style.

As Italian opera grew more and more fashionable in courtly and patrician circles, a steadily increasing number of German poets and playwrights became involved in operatic productions. While some translated or adapted Italian texts, others wrote original librettos. For many, it was a patriotic matter to vie with the Italians and stem the tide of their influence. Opposing current tendencies to ape other countries and produce *Alamode* works, these writers strove to renew ancient Germanic virtues by cultivating their own language and the indigenous forms that mirrored such virtues. Songs, ballads, and various kinds of musical accompaniment had long been popular in German moralities, Shrove Tuesday shows, farces, and plays. With the arrival of the englische Komödianten in the closing decades of the sixteenth century, music became the medium for the comic figure's jigs and antics. Jakob Ayrer (1543-1605), the Nuremberg dramatist who took as his model the low interpretation of English Renaissance drama provided by the englische Komödianten, wrote several plays based on folksong tunes and called them *singets spiele*. Sight and sound were the main elements of these plays as well as of the *Liederspiele*, marionette plays, *pièces à machines*, and intermezzos that were enthusiastically welcomed by German audiences. Some seventeenth-century librettists disavowed such popular traditions as too coarse and naturalistic. Nevertheless the newly imported operatic form gradually merged with them and, in so doing, satisfied contemporary demands for contrast, pageantry, suspense, excitement, and colorful spectacle.

By mid-seventeenth century, despite the Thirty Years' War, German operatic forms and their Italian counterparts had become so successful that they began receiving more and more critical recognition. It was a time of active inquiry and debate, for the recently founded literary societies (*Sprachgesellschaften*) labored to reconcile Germany's artistic practices, traditions, and needs with the ideas of ancient theorists, Renaissance scholars, and contemporary English writers. The membership of such societies, which often included musicians as well as poets, theorists, and critics, studied the German language, applied the Opitzian metrical reforms, discussed the significance of the so-called ancient rules, and analyzed the various poetic genres. Because of their high estimation of music, they were particularly concerned with the lied and the operatic form. Though frequently mentioning the intentions of the Florentine Camerata, they affirmed those tendencies to fuse word, action, spectacle, and music that were already latent in German theater. Many of them thought opera surpassed ancient drama in its manner of portraying actions.

Georg Philipp Harsdörffer (1607-1658), a leading member of the Nuremberg society known as the Shepherds of the Pegnitz, was one writer who believed that modern theatrical works were far superior to those of antiquity. In his

Frauenzimmer Gesprächspiele (1641-1649), eight volumes of conversations about the artistic aims, concerns, and ideas of the society, he unequivocally rejected the notion of Aristotle as the incontestable lawgiver and proudly asserted that Euripides, Aristophanes, and Sophocles as well as Terence and Plautus would have much to learn if they returned to life in the modern world (VI, 164). Imitating them or observing the unities could not, he contended, be of any importance when the primary aim was effectiveness in modern living theater. What was important, in his opinion, was the playwright's ability to command the arts of dancing, stage design, painting, music, and poetry, and to bring them into one grand synthesis.

Harsdörffer's own attempt to produce just such an artistic synthesis was *Seelewig*, a spiritual pastoral set to music by Sigmund Gottlieb Staden (1607-1655). The fourth part of the *Gesprächspiele* contains both the libretto and the score (IV, 76-209 and 533-666). Harsdörffer had his speakers present the text line for line and then had them comment on the various artistic theories and problems that those lines suggested. This running commentary on the text not only provided detailed stage directions for musicians, actors, and designers, but also contained Harsdörffer's clearest explanation of opera as the quintessential theatrical form. The speakers first discuss Italian opera and compare it to a plant too tender and precious to strike root when transplanted into arid, infertile soil. Because they consider it incompatible with the hardy Germanic spirit, they suggest the cultivation of genuinely German operas presenting heroic deeds and Christian virtues. Their attention then turns to *Seelewig*, its German names, and its attempt to synthesize widely divergent arts.

To elucidate the concept of artistic synthesis, Harsdörffer had his speakers consider Pythagorean ideas of world harmony. After accepting music as an echo of the eternal verities radiating from heaven, they proceed to Simonides' distinction between poetry as a speaking picture and painting as a mute poem. Finally they conclude that opera is the supreme art form because its music blends poetry and painting into one entity just as divine music harmonizes the dissonances of the universe.[3] As if unconsciously sensing the deficiencies of the libretto, the speakers bemoan the fact that there are too few human beings talented enough in all three arts to effect a perfect synthesis. Although Harsdörffer had earlier described this synthesis with the image of inseparably conjoined links in a great chain (III, 304), here he referred to it as being like the surveyor's level, an equally proportioned circle with three points (IV, 202). The use of images from surveying, architecture, or construction was not unusual because he, like numerous other writers since the Renaissance, considered the artist comparable to the divine architect of the universe.

In addition to opera's theoretical background, more practical matters like acting techniques, costuming, and staging are discussed by the speakers. Their comments about the kind of stage necessary for performing *Seelewig* reveal Harsdörffer's penchant for visualization as well as his complete disavowal of the unities and other restrictive rules. They claim the frequent scenic changes would be best facilitated with a revolving disk-shaped stage quartered off to display in proper perspective coastal, mountainous, meadow, and urban landscapes (IV, 208-209). Because the operatic medium allowed for greater novelty, variety, and change, Harsdörffer considered it a distinct advance over spoken drama. To him, musical theatrical works represented the greatest kind of poetic masterpieces possible.

Harsdörffer's fellow Pegnitz Shepherds shared his high evaluation of such artistic syntheses and, in addition to experimenting with various types of poetic sound painting, wrote operatic texts and investigated the backgrounds of what had come to be known as the sister arts. Sigmund von Birken (1626-1681), who prepared two operatic librettos, considered music the oldest of the sisters. In *Teutsche Redebind- und Dicht-Kunst*, a poetic manual that was published

in 1679 after circulating since the 1650s, he explained that
the noble art of poetry originated out of the songs primordial shepherds had sung in praise of their gods (sig.):(
vij^r). Birken also credited those shepherds, who had presumably understood the fundamental relationship between
music and poetry, with inventing musico-poetic plays (p.
314). He agreed with Scaliger (1484-1558) that such simple
pastoral plays were the sources of other dramatic genres, and
in explaining their evolution, applied rather primitive notions of progression to conventional ideas of decorum.
Comedy, he explained, resulted after city dwellers imported pastoral plays and adapted them to portray common
people; when courtiers and aristocrats subsequently transformed them to depict their milieu, they created tragedy
(p. 322). Birken's interpretation of tragicomedy's origins,
which omitted mention of Euripides or Plautus, places him
in the same tradition as those sixteenth-century German
humanists who believed that Christianity's promise of heav-
enly rewards for earthly pains precluded pure comedy or
pure tragedy and justified the creation of new, modern
mixed dramas.[4] Like them, he rejected the concept of generic purity, arguing that modern sacred plays should not
be created or judged according to ancient pagan standards.
While accepting Opitz's *Daphne* as a revival of the early
pastoral, Birken emphasized that modern musical theatrical
plays should replace ancient pagan superstitions with
Christian values (pp. 315-316).

Questions of opera's origins and historical development
were equally important in North German cities, where
operatic plays and semioperatic spectacles were enthusiastically produced and fostered by members of local literary
societies. Some theorists and handbook writers continued
relating opera to their own interpretations of the ancient
pastoral, but others compared it to what they knew of
Greek drama.

Konrad von Höveln (ca. 1630-1670), member of two
Hamburg literary societies, considered opera a special kind

16

of theatrical play in his *Eren- Danz- Singe Schauspile-Ent-wurf*, a discursive, often contradictory little treatise that appeared in 1663 under the pseudonym Candorin. He thought it comparable to spoken drama in that it portrayed certain human actions in a poetic manner; however, he found it differed in many respects. After vainly trying to apply Ciceronian ideas to what he claimed were actual practices, Höveln contended that opera must be a highly developed, modern version of the Greek dithyramb. To support his contention that the prototype of operatic song dated from remotest antiquity, he explained that Aristotle had divided all poetic works into epic, lyric, and dithyrambic categories and had included all dramas in the last one (pt. 2, pp. 23-24). The musical theatrical form that had recently originated in Italy was, Höveln concluded, a more elevated kind of drama because it portrayed actions with the divine gift of modern music. He was one of the first theorists to grant composers primary control over the construction as well as production of operas (pt. 3, p. 19). He did so because he hoped they would know how to employ the recitative style in a way that would not interfere with easy comprehension of the words, which, after all, were most important for presenting the necessary "copy of life, mirror of custom, and reflection of truth."

Much more sophisticated was the treatment of opera by Daniel Georg Morhof (1639-1691), professor of poetry and rhetoric at Kiel and one of Germany's best known polyhistors. It reflected his wide learning and his concern about discovering the historical interrelationships between all branches of knowledge. Opera was just one of the many topics included in his influential *Unterricht von der Teutschen Sprache und Poesie* (1682), an encyclopedic work outlining the stages of German literary development within a general European framework. Morhof was as familiar with European theatrical practices as he was with the various schools of theoretical thought. Instead of speculating about them, he attempted to view them in historical perspective, and he developed a descriptive approach that was admired until Goethe's (1749-1832) day. The mimes and older theatrical traditions merited just as much of his attention as Cardinal Richelieu's attempt to rid French theater of *drame libre* by strictly enforcing neoclassical rules. If Morhof claimed that modern writers still had much to learn from Greek and Roman poetics, then he suggested they do so not only by studying the ancients but also by reading the criticism of Italians like Francesco Patrizi (1529-1597) who opposed pseudo-Aristotelian tendencies.

According to Morhof's own research, verse, music, pantomime, and dance had all been combined in antiquity. The art had been lost, he explained, with the decline of ancient civilization, but the idea of such combinations remained and inspired modern artists to attempt to create similar ones (p. 737). Among the first he could find who made attempts at revival were the poet Ottavio Rinuccini and the composer Emilio de' Cavalieri (ca. 1550-1602). In Morhof's opinion, it was precisely their use of the more highly developed music of the present that had prevented their actually restoring ancient musical drama. He affirmed the results of their efforts because he believed their failure to achieve their goals had produced an equally excellent theatrical form. Like others who thought this form had become something completely new, he referred to it with the word *opera*, translating it into German as *Werck* (p. 738).

Opera Diabolica

Opera had gained such overwhelming acclaim by the last quarter of the seventeenth century that it all but conquered the theatrical scene. While critics and theorists continued to investigate its aims, essence, origins, and background, playwrights prepared librettos that captivated German audiences. Depending on the occasion and circumstances, they provided what they called musical allegories, pastorals, farces, representations, comedies, tragedies, tragicomedies, festival plays, *Singeballette, Danzspiele*, and *Singspiele*. Comic figures, along with shepherds, fairies, and flying gods were standard elements in their works, which usually were presented in sophisticated settings simulating grandeur and infinite space. Dances and elegant processions by richly costumed performers helped to intensify the fabulous atmosphere of the highly illusionistic stage. Machines, devices, sets, and props that allowed for quick scene changes and spectacular embellishments also contributed to the aura of unreality. The effect of make-believe was heightened still further by the musical underscoring of dialogues and monologues and by the aria, an especially important aspect of early German opera.

Not aiming for concentrated dramatic interest and well-drawn, three-dimensional characters, these highly stylized musical theatrical works appealed directly to the senses. The rational faculties were subordinated to the emotions, which were shocked or soothed by mixtures of tragic and comic elements. Pastoral or grandiose heroic actions dominated in plots woven together of complicated intrigues, amorous affairs, and political schemes. German librettists shaped mythology and history to their works; they also borrowed from contemporary novels and adapted Italian librettos as well as French, Dutch, Spanish, or indigenous plays. Some repertoires also included biblical subjects, satires on urban life, and plots dealing with robbers, pirates, and other socially undesirable characters.[5]

The cumbersome equipment and large casts indispensable for baroque opera tended to preclude performances by itinerant companies; consequently opera was conducive to the construction of theater buildings in Germany and to the concomitant development of theatrical techniques.[6] By the end of the seventeenth century, opera had become firmly established in all the German lands. It was being performed in permanent theaters, while spoken drama was still being presented either in makeshift structures by troupes of wandering players or in schools by young students.

Opera's impact was so great that several German dramatists began incorporating some of its elements into their spoken dramas. The Jesuits, whose plays served as instruments of the Counter-Reformation, had long recognized the potentialities of the operatic medium and successfully employed it to depict divine majesty, omnipotence, and otherworldliness. For them and for most others, opera had come to epitomize modern theater.

Some Protestant clergymen in Germany's northern and central principalities, however, interpreted opera as the most visible manifestation of modern dissoluteness. Consequently they made it the focal point of their campaign to abolish public theatrical spectacles. Such campaigns were nothing new in Europe. Originating in patristic writings against the decadent Roman theater, this hostile attitude was reinforced in the seventeenth century by religious zealots who staunchly opposed all theatrical genres. In England, for example, Puritans like William Prynne (1600-1669) worked assiduously to stamp out theater. In order to comprehend the success of their campaign, one need only remember that the English theaters remained officially closed from 1642 to 1660.

The Calvinistic and Pietistic theologians were not quite as successful on the continent although they joined the battle with the same righteous indignation as their English colleagues.[7] They judged both operatic form and content according to theological criteria, and they concluded that opera's use of pagan mythology and lustful themes was blatantly anti-Christian. They also insisted that opera was destructive to the Christian way of life because of its costly extravagance, which they thought overemphasized the material world and titillated the senses. Orthodox Lutherans frequently disapproved of opera, but they did not condemn it as virulently and steadfastly as did the Pietists, those reformers who, in their attempt to revive religious devoutness, shunned all worldly amusements. In the opinion of the Pietists, opera could not be considered among the *adiaphora*, that is, those neutral affairs, or matters of individual conscience, neither forbidden nor supported by Holy Scriptures. They punned on the word "work," which had come to subsume all musical theatrical plays, and referred to opera as *opera diabolica* or *Teufelswerck*. Since opera's stress on externals contradicted the basic tenets of their belief and threatened their theological position, they became increasingly militant as it gained ever greater popularity.

Pietistic leaders like Philipp Jakob Spener (1635-1705) regarded opera as a "temptation of the devil" and worked diligently to abolish it. Although he and his followers fought against it wherever it had secured a foothold, Hamburg was the scene of their most intensive battle. The permanent opera company at the Gänsemarkt had been founded in 1678 by prominent citizens, presumably after a Venetian model, and had achieved such resounding success that it began attracting actors, singers, musicians, and librettists from near and far.[8] It also attracted numerous supporters. The controversy that developed because of their support quickly assumed such major importance that both church and government became involved.[9] The leading member of the Hamburg antiopera faction and the man who best epitomizes its position was Spener's friend and colleague, Anton Reiser (1628-1686). When this unfaltering advocate of Pietism became pastor of Saint Jacob's, he denounced opera in his sermons, asserting that it was not an *adiaphoron* or nonessential, "indifferent" thing upon which the Church had given no decisions. The writings of the church fathers supplied him with what he considered indisputable proof of its evil, and he quoted from them extensively in order to support his views in *Theatromania oder die Werke der Finsternis in den öffentlichen Schau-Spielen* (1681).

In the course of defending opera against such condemnations, Hamburg writers honed their critical faculties and perpetuated the theatrical attitudes of earlier theorists like Harsdörffer. Christoph Rauch (fl. 1680), a Roman Catholic actor, was among the earliest to refute the ideas propounded by Reiser and his fellow Pietists. In *Theatrophania, Entgegen gesetzet Der so genanten Schrifft Theatromania* (1682), he pointed out the fallacies in their critical method: first of all, they had failed to realize that the patristic writings dealt only with the theatrical practices current in their own time and that theater had developed considerably in the interim. Second, they had never attended any performances to see for themselves whether opera was indeed comparable to the orgiastic Roman spectacles condemned by the church fathers. Third, they had provided no tangible evidence that modern musical theatrical works were in any way sacrilegious or diabolical. Fourth, their denunciation of contemporary actors and singers was pure calumny.

Because of his firsthand experience with the Hamburg theater, Rauch considered himself better qualified to discuss opera than the Pietists. He claimed that it should be called a work of the nine Muses instead of a "work of the devil," for it combined the liberal arts of painting, music, sculpture, history, ethics, poetry, and rhetoric (p. 17). By describing this combination in terms of a Gymnasium, he gave currency to an image that was to recur often in subsequent Hamburg operatic writings. Although Rauch defined opera as a representation of something that had happened or could happen, he did not discuss it according to the conventional critical notion that tragedy was based on fact and comedy on fiction. He maintained that opera resembled other theatrical forms in general but differed from them in specifics. For Rauch, opera was neither a school of morality nor an idle, purposeless diversion; it was a very useful form of entertainment that amused, moved, and educated its spectators by offering them the kind of sensual pleasure that ultimately induced spiritual peace (p. 47).

Opera's worthwhile contributions to Christian society were also pointed out by Gottfried Wilhelm Leibniz (1646-1716) when asked for his opinion by Johann Christoph Marci's son. Writing from Stockholm on August 17, 1681, the younger Marci complained that his opera *Vespasian* might involve him in the controversy then raging in Hamburg. He sought reassurance from Leibniz that such plays were not the "works of the devil" that Reiser called them. The philosopher replied encouragingly in a lengthy letter dated January 13, 1682 that the patristic writings referred only to those ancient entertainments that were cruel, licentious public spectacles. As far as he himself could determine, opera was something entirely different; it was a new kind of amusement which had developed out of Christian church music and which in itself was neither good nor evil. Leibniz believed its purpose, like that of rhetoric, could only be determined by those who used it; if they wielded it correctly, it could serve a commendable moral function. According to Leibniz, opera was spiritually very effective because its combination of word, "insight," rhyme, dance, music, and spectacle appealed to both the internal and the two external senses. He even went a step further and suggested that opera be cultivated as an instrument for the regulation of the common man.[10]

Opera's notable effect on the common man's soul was the main concern of Pastor Johann Winckler (1642-1705), who succeeded Reiser as the Pietists' chief spokesman in Hamburg. Reiterating their standard arguments, he unreservedly condemned opera because of what he considered its dangers to the accepted moral code. Its depiction of depraved actions on an illusion-filled stage could only, he claimed, encourage flagrant disregard for Christian virtues. Pastor Johann Friedrich Mayer (1650-1720), patron of the arts and anti-Pietistic exponent of Lutheran orthodoxy, disagreed and encouraged his colleagues to join him in defending opera. In their sermons they objected to the attacks against the Hamburg theater, thus inducing Winckler and his colleagues to stronger and more authoritarian condemnations. As the agitation continued, the two points of view became more and more irreconcilable. Fearing the consequences of what could become a dangerously disruptive

23

situation, the municipal government intervened. When a mutually satisfactory solution did not present itself, the faculties of theology and jurisprudence of the universities of Wittenberg and Rostock were consulted. The questions for the disputation were formulated by one of the Hamburg opera's original founders, Gerhard Schott (1641-1702), in *Vier Bedenken von der Oper*.[11]

The university faculties debated the questions posed by Schott and in 1687 concluded that opera was a legitimate entertainment even though it had many faults requiring reform. While the Wittenberg theologians declared that it was not a "work of the devil" that prohibited performers from being good Christians, the jurists of that university clearly distinguished between the religious and secular "things of this world." They granted the Hamburg government sole jurisdiction over the opera, maintaining that it alone had the right to allow performances. The theologians and jurists of Rostock supported the defense even further when they concluded that the patristic writings were inapplicable to the current situation because they dealt solely with ancient pagan spectacles and pagan actors. After the universities acquitted opera, the battle subsided in Hamburg, only to be continued in Saxony, Thuringia, and Brandenburg, where polemical treatises appeared well into the 1730s.

During the battle in Hamburg, Pastor Heinrich Elmenhorst (1632-1704) was one of the Pietists' main irritants. He not only defended opera in his sermons but also prepared several librettos, among them an adaptation of Pierre Corneille's (1606-1684) *Polyeuct*. His *Dramatologia Antiqvo-Hodierna, Das ist: Bericht von denen Oper-Spielen* (1688) was such a comprehensive presentation of the arguments in opera's defense that it became the manifesto for several generations of operatic theorists. In order to refute theological objections, Elmenhorst investigated significant historical, artistic, and critical considerations. His studies had convinced him that the church fathers condemned specific works of Roman antiquity because of the physical as well as spiritual harm they did to early Christians. According to his observations, Hamburg operas did not martyr helpless Christians, nor did they mock Christ or subvert his teachings by presenting shameful sensual pleasures, provocative dances, and bloody fights. Relying on an argument that had become increasingly important since the Renaissance, he maintained that Christianity's victory over paganism had brought forth new forms of entertainment which fully supplanted pagan ones and, as time passed, developed to greater excellence. He viewed opera as one of those modern forms and consequently classified it among the *adiaphora*, which were subject to change depending on time, place, custom, and circumstance (p. 178). In attempting to prove that opera could not justifiably be condemned on either moral or ecclesiastical grounds, he stressed its modernity and also its secular nature. Operas, he repeatedly stated, came under civil jurisdiction, and as long as the secular government permitted their production, the clergy had no right to demand their abolition.

Another indication of Elmenhorst's desire to distinguish the relevant issues as exactly as possible was his philological explanation of the word "opera." Expanding Morhof's interpretation, he claimed it derived from the Latin word meaning work in German but pertained only to the kind of musical poetic work called *melodramma* or *dramma per musica* by the Italians (p. 99).[12] He explained further that the German word *Singspiel* was frequently used synonymously, even though it was a more general term that could also mean a nontheatrical combination of vocal and instrumental music.

Elmenhorst's defense of modern musical drama emphasized its wide-ranging salutary effects. Like Rauch and Leibniz, he believed that its poetic presentation of Christian ethics provided the spectator with the kind of spiritual pleasure that conditioned him for righteous daily living. And, in his opinion, secular as well as religious topics could provide such conditioning. He also thought opera gave the Germans more opportunity for cultivating poetry in their mother tongue and for experiencing depictions of their own stable, healthy customs.

In addition to allowing opera a wide range of subject matter, Elmenhorst discussed its particular artistic form as precisely that which distinguished it from other entertainments. The requirement he considered most fundamental was a kind of musical verse that could be sung in an elevated tone and cadence; ordinary prose recited with normal intonation did not suffice. He also included stage properties and machines among the essential parts of operatic form since he believed they helped make the representation of extraordinary or miraculous actions seem probable.

Elmenhorst's defense remained qualified by a Christian-didactic interpretation of art, yet it is important because he viewed Church authority in historical perspective and repudiated its misapplication by special-interest groups. He insisted that opera be judged within the context for which it was created. Subsequent writers who agreed that intrinsic standards were necessary for judging opera as an art form often lauded Elmenhorst for describing it so aptly and for affirming its vast thematic possibilities. His contributions were heartily acknowledged, for example, by Georg Bertuch (1668-1743) in *Disputatio juridica de eo quod justum est, circa ludos scenicos operasque modernas, dictas vulgò "Operen"* (1693). However, Bertuch differed from Elmenhorst in that he refused to deny opera's similarity to ancient drama. He distinguished the theatrical forms of late antiquity from those of the classical period and concluded that operas were works comparable to what the Greeks had called dramas because they also moved, taught, and refreshed or recreated audiences by using gestures, music, and certain devices to represent either true, fictitious, or fabulous facts (pp. 14-16). Like Pastor Mayer and the Wittenberg and Rostock scholars, from whom he quoted extensively, Bertuch contended that all of nature was a divinely designed play for man's observation, imitation, and improvement, and that the opera house presented on a small scale what the theater of the universe presented on a large scale. In his opinion, the Pietists along with Prynne and the English Puritans, had failed to understand this and consequently had misinterpreted the Scriptures, the Fathers, and Martin Luther, who himself had encouraged the cultivation of theater.

Epic versus Dramatic

Late seventeenth-century German librettists were much less given to doctrinal investigation and philosophical speculation than Bertuch. They were more concerned with defending their avocations and, in some instances, vocations. Their libretto prefaces show, however, that they were not merely hack writers anxious to gain fame by creating fantastic spectacles with mass appeal. They were aware of contemporary critical opinions but refused to accept any of them without careful examination. Although not all librettos were printed with prefaces, those that were usually contain remarks that not only pay lip service to Christian morality or flatter local audiences, but also reveal certain significant critical tendencies. Their authors questioned the literary as well as the religious authorities, disputed the validity of rules like the unities, and sought standards that would do justice to opera as a musical theatrical form. They also proclaimed opera's poetical essence and asserted that it was the poet's privilege to determine what was most suitable for his work.

The critical theories of Harsdörffer and Morhof were as important as theological considerations for librettists like Lucas von Bostel (1649-1716), who became Hamburg's mayor in 1709. In prefatory remarks to *Der Glückliche Gross-Vezier Cara Mustapha* (1686), he explained that he failed to understand why zealous clergymen and learned scholars were so resolute in their condemnations of opera when it fostered good citizenship and individual morality. Their claims, in his opinion, had been more than sufficiently refuted during the numerous controversies over theater in France and elsewhere, and there was no need to belabor the matter (p. 3). As far as his own libretto was concerned, he believed it accomplished its instructional purpose with the kind of diversions that Luther himself would have enjoyed.

Bostel's insistence on the importance of opera's didactic purpose actually resulted in a liberal interpretation of the normative, prescriptive rules for drama that were becoming more and more closely associated with emergent French neoclassical theory. Emphasizing theatrical effectiveness, he questioned the practicality of the Horatian rule about five acts and rejected the feasibility of observing the unities of time and place. Only those rules that facilitated rapid comprehension of the moral lesson or increased its poignancy were valid to him. Since he thought the unity of action did so, he encouraged his fellow librettists to abandon their convoluted Italianate style in order to combine the elements of their plots appropriately and convincingly (p. 6).

Though disputing the prescriptive authority of the French neoclassical theorists, Bostel emphasized the need to give opera dramatic focus by avoiding the *ab ovo* or panoramic type of plot favored by his German forebears, the English, and the Chinese (p. 7). Opera, he contended, was in many respects like painting; both required selecting various elements and concentrating them within a certain framework. It was not uncommon among European critics to compare painting and poetry. Bostel stands out, however, as one of the earliest Germans to do so specifically with reference to operatic verisimilitude. According to him, operas had to be interpreted as figurative or poetic representations rather than as distortions of the truth.

The librettists of Braunschweig-Wolfenbüttel, whose works were sometimes produced in Hamburg, also probed such ideas although they paid even less attention to theological objections. Ever since the days of Duke Heinrich Julius (1564-1613), who engaged englische Komödianten and borrowed their techniques for his own plays, the Braunschweig sovereigns had encouraged the cultivation of theater. In the middle of the seventeenth century, their court was one of the many affected by the operatic fervor sweeping the land. Musical theater became such a major attraction in Wolfenbüttel that a special building was erected in 1688 solely for opera performances.[13] Because of increasing local demands for operas during the semiannual fairs, a commercial house, modeled after Hamburg's, was constructed in Braunschweig in 1690.[14] Though overshadowed at the beginning, it soon outshone Hamburg's and went on to become one of the eighteenth century's most active and eminent musical theatrical centers.[15] Duke Anton Ulrich (1633-1714), himself a poet, music enthusiast, actor, singer, director, and librettist, was the man most responsible for its early success.

Friedrich Christoph Bressand (ca. 1670-1702), his court poet, also contributed to its success. Bressand's duties included writing librettos, supervising the printing of texts, and arranging everything associated with performances, from stage settings to salary disbursements. These practical experiences taught him that theater demanded a certain amount of freedom from preordained restrictions. Consequently, he considered it the librettist's prerogative to treat subjects as he saw fit. In his preface to *Hercules Unter denen Amazonen* (1694), for example, he explained that he had manipulated mythology in order to construct a plot suitable for musical theatrical production. His comments show that he acknowledged opera as a presentation of poetic truth, not actual truth, and that he recognized its inherent dramatic aspects.

In the preface to *Die Plejades Oder das Sieben-Gestirne* (1693), Bressand emphasized that the physical necessities of the stage took precedence over any other requirement and determined the amount of altering any given source would have to undergo. He realized the importance of delimiting epic extension for the sake of dramatic focus. And he, along with others who subscribed to Castelvetro's (1505-1571) ideas about the ignorance and unimaginativeness of audiences, eventually identified the so-called necessities of the stage with the French neoclassical dramatic rules. His introduction to *Arcadia, oder Die Königliche Schäferey* (1699) explained that he had altered his source, an Italian operatic adaptation of Sir Philip Sidney's work, because it did not agree very well with those rules.

Gottlieb Fiedler (fl. 1690), who was to become Bressand's successor as court poet, also believed that treating historical subjects operatically required deviation from known factual truths. However, he was less concerned with rules than with devising intriguing subplots whose final resolution would astound audiences. His prefatory comments to librettos about Alexander and Roland implied that such novelty, variety, and abundance served to increase rather than decrease operatic quality. In the preface to *Der Grossmüthige Scipio Africanus* (1694), he stressed the importance of making all adjustments necessary to produce a good, enjoyable show. Fiedler also used this preface to bemoan the absence of great living German poets since the death of Christian Hofmann von Hofmannswaldau (1617-1674) and Daniel Casper von Lohenstein (1635-1683), both of whom, he believed, used diverse sources to the best possible poetic advantage (sig. (a)2ᵛ).

Fiedler's Hamburg colleagues also admired the exotic, often erotic imagery of those two older poets and praised their vast erudition, rhetorical savoir faire, and proud concern for Germanic antiquities. They felt Hofmannswaldau had fully demonstrated the poetic capabilities of the German language, both in his own verse and in his translation of what was to become a poetic source book for generations, Giovanni Battista Guarini's (1537-1612) *Pastor fido*. And they believed Lohenstein had shown how to create dramatic tension by ingeniously weaving subplots into plots and by carefully depicting intense passions. To late seventeenth-century librettists, these writers represented a rich poetic heritage that was to be cherished and sustained.

As the French version of literary rationalism became better known, writers like the epigrammatist Christian Wernicke (1661-1725) attacked that heritage and singled out the Hamburg opera as the most offensive example of what it had brought forth. The ensuing dispute was one of the earliest clashes between liberal baroque attitudes and the neoclassical theories that had crystallized into a fixed set of normative, prescriptive standards. Christian Heinrich Postel (1658-1705), who was at the height of his career as one of Hamburg's most popular and prolific librettists, became embroiled in the dispute when he composed a sonnet rejecting the basic assumptions of Wernicke's attack on Hofmannswaldau and Lohenstein. Postel himself then received the main brunt of Wernicke's satirical wrath in *Ein Helden-Gedichte Hans Sachs genannt* (1702), which was presumably inspired by John Dryden's (1631-1700) *Mac-Flecknoe*.[16] When Postel did not reply, his adversary began attacking other librettists for the out-and-out absurdities they perpetrated on local audiences. Hamburg's citizenry, however, did not mind at all, for they sided with their librettists in favor of the baroque poets, forcing the infuriated Wernicke to make devious political threats in an attempt to gain satisfaction.

Although Postel was known as a capable advocate, learned man, and poet, his fame derived primarily from his numerous librettos, many of which were set to music by Reinhard Keiser (1674-1739). They well suited the conservative tastes of his Hamburg contemporaries and continued to be admired by following generations. Several of them were revived during the thirty years or so after his death when efforts were made to restore the declining Hamburg theater to its former glory.[17] According to the eminent scholar of German baroque literature, Curt von Faber du Faur, Hamburg writers who revered their indigenous traditions regarded Postel as one of their "poetic ancestors." Postel's lengthy, erudite prefaces also attracted the attention of other writers, among whom was one of Hamburg's most renowned theater poets. Gotthold Ephraim Lessing (1729-1781) claimed in his notes to the Hamburg theater that he was easily able to recognize and identify Postel's anonymously published librettos by their introductory remarks.[18]

Those remarks show that Postel intended to create what Faber du Faur aptly called "a world of pure opera, with nothing—neither characters nor action—naturalistic."[19] With arguments somewhat more precise than those of his fellow librettists, Postel disavowed all attempts to reproduce historical, religious, or mythological sources exactly. He believed something always had to be invented, omitted, or changed in order to produce a splendid dramatic effect. His preface to *Bajazeth und Tamerlan* (1690), for example, reported that some of the situations and intrigues had originated with him and therefore had to be accepted as the kind of fictions that generations of writers had recognized as inherently necessary in poetry. In his introduction to *Die Verstöhrung Jerusalem* (1692), he relied on Horace's suggestion about blending the false with the true and informed his Hamburg public that opera was neither pure fact nor pure fiction but a special mixture of both. According to its foreword, *Pygmalion* (1694) had many elements that had been invented according to that freedom which distinguished poets from historians.

Postel objected to those caviling critics who compared his operas to their historical sources and then invariably disputed the accuracy of the plot or rejected the delimitation of the subject. Claiming they failed to comprehend the very essence of dramatic poetry, he argued that the beginning, middle, and end of any plot depended entirely on the poet's choice. In his opinion, anyone who preferred historical verity should read the historians as well as the explanations he gave in his prefaces. And anyone who wanted religious themes depicted according to strict biblical sequence should read the Bible or go to the proper place for such things, namely to church, instead of to the opera. He emphasized the need for dramatic concentration and focus and, like Lucas von Bostel, explained what he meant by favorably comparing opera to the Chinese plays whose depiction of a man's life story, from childhood through adulthood to old age, required days and days of performing.[20]

Postel considered the Chinese manner one extreme, the other being the French with its literal interpretation of the unities. He agreed with Lope de Vega (1562-1635), whom he admired, that observing preestablished rules was of minor importance when one aimed to write plays effective in the living theater. Furthermore he disapproved of the uniformity that resulted from such regularity; variety was much more important to him. The preface to *Cain und Abel* (1689) shows especially well that he felt completely free to interpret the dramatic rules to suit his own purposes. According to his interpretation, opera was a fictional kind of reality that was governed by the laws of poetic fancy. Since it presented imaginary time and space, he argued, characters could travel from earth to hell and back as quickly as necessary to avoid transgressing against the unities of time and place. The unity of action, however, was important to him as a means for reproducing the "simplicity" of the biblical story (sig. B[r]). In the introduction to *Thalestris* (1690), Postel again claimed that a libretto could observe the rules only as much as the nature of opera —a theatrical play comprised of poetry, music, and other arts—would allow. Here he explained that he had not followed his novelistic source slavishly because he had had to condense its extensive elements in order to bring them into operatic form. He then added that the story itself precluded strict adherence to the rules (sig. b4[v]).

Postel's attitude toward his contemporary operatic sources was similar. In the foreword to *Porus* (1694), a Bressand libretto which he had reworked for Hamburg, he explained that he had shortened the plot, adjusted the verse, and added the all-important comic figure in order to suit the tastes of local theatergoers. Although not so bold as to reject the idea of conveying a moral lesson, he did not conceive of opera as just another school of morality that pleasantly imparted the concepts of Christianity. For him it was a thoroughly secular form of entertainment that aimed to give suitable pleasure to respectable citizens. Postel's deference to the audience as the supreme arbiter in operatic matters indicates not only his showmanship but also his acceptance of the Horatian dictum about appealing to the entire range of spectators by making as many concessions as artistically feasible.

Postel also believed that the poetic masterpieces of classical antiquity had to be adapted to modern circumstances in order to be comprehensible to contemporary audiences. He was fascinated by ancient Greek culture and regarded himself as one of its most competent interpreters. When he quoted Greek passages in his prefaces, he generally accompanied them with German translations, thus displaying to his Hamburg readers his linguistic skills as well as his erudition. He also sought to impress them with *Die Listige Juno* (1700), which was actually less a literal rendition of the fourteenth book of Homer's *Iliad* than an illustration of his views on literary adaptation and a demonstration of his familiarity with the epic tradition. In tracing Homer's poetic descendants, he named Virgil, Tasso, and John Milton (1608-1674), whom he quoted and whom he defended warmly as "der grosse Englische Poet."[21] It was decades later that the Swiss critics Johann Jakob Bodmer (1698-1783) and Johann Jakob Breitinger (1701-1776) praised Milton's style, recommended it to Friedrich Gottlieb Klopstock (1724-1803), and defended it against the criticism of Johann Christoph Gottsched (1700-1766). In the 1740s nonaligned observers recommended to the Swiss that they acknowledge Postel if not as a poet in his own right then at least as a critic (*Kunstrichter*) who had known enough to defend Milton.[22]

One of Postel's earliest explanations of operatic adaptation came in the preface to *Adonis* (1697), a libretto in which he had hoped to reproduce in modern terms the spirit of the ancients. His intention, as he explained it, was not merely to treat the gallantry of Venus and Adonis but rather to reveal the underlying secrets of nature they represented and the particular manner in which the ancients portrayed those secrets (sig.)( )(2ᵛ). In the preface to *Der Aus Hyperboreen nach Cymbrien übergebrachte Güldene Apfel* (1698), Postel again emphasized the importance of getting at what he called the hidden meaning or mythological sense of antiquity (sig.):(4ʳ). He believed those who strove to copy the Greek dramatists failed to understand not only antiquity and its dramatic forms but also their own era and its artistic prerequisites. To improve their understanding, he urged that they study such works and, after assimilating them, emulate only their strengths. This was what he claimed to have done and what he hoped Hamburg audiences would graciously accept and enjoy.

The preface to *Die Wunderbahr-errettete Iphigenia* (1699), indicates that Postel continued to reflect upon the relationship between ancient and modern theatrical forms and upon the methods of adaptation. He agreed with opera's other defenders that cultural and historical changes had brought forth new theatrical works and different artistic tastes. He went a step further, however, when he attempted to develop this idea so that it could be applied to the operatic adaptation of Greek dramas. He considered their subject matter of less importance than their formal elements, for he believed they provided better clues showing "wie man die köstlichen Erfindungen der Alten wiederum zu unseren Zeiten gebrauchen könne" (sig.):(2ᵛ; "how the precious inventions of the ancients could be used once again during our times"). Shortening Euripides' long monologues in order to adapt them for singing was, for example, far more important to him than Christianizing the content of the Greek dramatist's works.

35

Whether constructing a libretto about the Greek Iphigenia, the Frank Charlemagne, the Pole Sigismund, or the Vandal Gaiseric (Genseric), Postel was less concerned with details than with translating into modern musico-poetic form what he considered the spirit of the times. In attempting to explain his intentions and ideas, he developed a concept of opera that was to serve as the foundation upon which his younger Hamburg contemporaries built. And he transmitted a critical approach that served them well as opera came under increasing attack from those who sought to impose rationalistic restraints not only on it but on all art forms.

RULE BY PRECEDENT OR BY CODE

Saint Evremond and French Neoclassicism

At the turn of the eighteenth century, the Holy Roman Empire still comprised approximately three hundred territorial states. The political fragmentation resulting from the steady dissolution of imperial control had precluded the emergence of one capital city for the entire German-speaking world. The lack of a major center that could compete with Paris or London in establishing the fashion or setting the tone was not, however, quite as disastrous as many cultural historians would have us believe. In fact the decentralized political situation encouraged the independence, diversity, and individualism that had long been characteristic of the Germanic peoples and that after five more decades were to produce one of Western Europe's greatest artistic flowerings.

Although German theater at the turn of the eighteenth century brought forth no immortal dramatic geniuses, it was remarkably active and as diverse as the numerous localities that allowed productions. There was a little something for everyone, whether peasant, burgher, or aristocrat. Despite attempts to keep up with new foreign fashions, audiences remained rather conservative, oftentimes old-fashioned in their tastes. They thoroughly enjoyed the baroque showmanship involved in Faust plays, *Haupt- und Staats-Aktionen* (grand political plays), pyrotechnic productions, harlequinades, festival pageants, musical plays, and operas. And they worried little about the artistic implications or lasting values of spectacular display, complex form, wondrous content, and eccentric improvisation.

An increasing number of German intellectuals viewed

this situation with great disdain and even greater discomfort. They believed their country had cultural potentialities but was sadly lagging behind France. In their opinion, France had become the pacesetter in theatrical matters because its political unity allowed for an academy that enforced observance of a rationally comprehensible code of dramatic rules. Since they attributed the sophisticated level of French drama to that neoclassical code, they believed introducing it and demanding observance of it would help to dignify German theater and thereby improve public tastes. Consequently they rejected all archaic and provincial traits and condemned most of the popular baroque theatrical forms. In contemporary operatic productions, early German neoclassicists like Christian Wernicke, Gottlieb Stolle (1673-1744), and Johann Burkhard Mencke (1674-1732) saw the most shocking disregard for everything they were trying to make sacred.[1] They agreed with the French writers, whom they had come to view as authorities, that opera was as artistically disruptive as it was morally dangerous.

The French statement of the antiopera position most often cited by German writers was "Lettre sur les Opera à monsieur le Duc de Buckingham" (1677) by Charles de Marguetel de Saint-Denis, Seigneur de Saint Evremond (1610-1703), an active man of letters, well known for his essays on diverse literary and moral topics. According to his analysis, opera was one of the "most impossible" things that mankind had ever produced; it was a bizarre mixture of music and poetry which allowed neither art to do itself full justice because each was hopelessly limited by the other. He believed opera's inordinate sensuality rendered any appeal to the mind ineffectual, thus making it indisputably nothing more than "magnificent folly." Even though its marvelous elements as well as its music could be enticing at first, he found they gradually grew tedious and eventually induced fatigue.

Saint Evremond did not exclude song as a possible component of drama, especially in prologues and epilogues, for he thought the Greeks had been able to use it sensibly and effectively. He did, however, unequivocally condemn the continuous singing of modern opera. In his opinion, it was so unnatural and contrary to reason that intelligent spectators could never become reconciled to it as a sensible means of communicating anything. Since his description of opera's lack of *vraisemblance* was to become one of the cardinal points upon which German defenses as well as condemnations hinged, it is worth quoting at length:

> Il y a une autre chose dans les Opera tellement contre la nature, que mon imagination en est blessée; c'est de faire chanter toute la Pièce depuis le commencement jusqu'à la fin, comme si les personnes qu'on représente, s'étoient ridiculement ajustées pour traiter en Musique, et les plus communes, et les plus importantes affaires de leur vie. Peut-on s'imaginer qu'un maître appelle son valet, ou qu'il lui donne une commission en chantant; qu'un ami fasse en chantant une confidence à son ami; qu'on delibere en chantant dans un conseil; qu'on exprime avec du Chant les ordres qu'on donne, et que mélodieusement on tuë les hommes à coups d'épée et de javelot dans un combat? C'est perdre l'esprit de la représentation, qui sans doute est préferable à celui de l'harmonie.*[2]

As far as operatic characters were concerned, Saint Evremond summed them up as "un assemblage confus de Dieux, de Bergers, de Héros, d'Enchanteurs, de Fantômes, de Fur-

*There is another Thing in *Operas* so contrary to Nature, that I cannot be reconciled to it; and that is the singing of the whole Piece, from beginning to end, as if the Persons represented were ridiculously match'd, and had agreed to treat in Music both the most common, and most important Affairs of Life. Is it to be imagin'd that a Master calls his Servant, or sends him on an Errand, singing; that one Friend imparts a Secret to another, singing: That Men deliberate in Council singing; That Orders in time of Battle are given, singing; and That Men are melodiously kill'd with Sword and Darts. This is the downright way to lose the Life of Representation, which without doubt is preferable to that of Harmony (*The Works of Monsieur De St. Evremond*, II, 86).

ies, de Démons" (III, 163; "a confused Assembly of Gods, Shepherds, Heroes, Enchanters, Apparitions, Furies, and Devils," *The Works of Monsieur De St. Evremond*, II, 93). He claimed persons of good taste would be terribly offended by such outlandish figures and by the extraordinary contraptions used to portray them. Decorations and theatrical properties, he explained, could be important in any play, but the machinery used in opera simply served to satisfy the idle curiosity of people with no taste who merely sought amusing diversion. Repeatedly he referred to the sensible, well-cultured spectator who, he thought, would react adversely to such operatic nonsense.

His main objection to opera was its tendency to destroy genuine appreciation for tragedy, and this he found particularly distressing since the tragic genre "est la plus belle chose que nous ayons, la plus propre à élever l'ame, et la plus capable de former l'esprit" (III, 164; "the finest Thing we have, I mean Tragedy, than which nothing is more proper to elevate the Soul, or more capable to form the Mind," *The Works of Monsieur De St. Evremond*, II, 94). To reform opera and make it charm the mind, soul, and spirit as well as the senses, he insisted that the composer subordinate himself completely to the poet and follow his orders unquestioningly. Because Saint Evremond did not think that music and the other arts could be integral parts of a theatrical work, he insisted on treating opera as a dramatic form that had to be brought into line with the rules of the stage.

Although German critics thought of Saint Evremond as the leading spokesman for the antiopera position, they also referred to the works of other French neoclassicists with similar views. Among them were Jean de la Bruyère (1645-1696), François de Callières (1645-1717), Nicolas Boileau-Despréaux (1636-1711), and Jacques Bénigne Bossuet (1627-1704). They all tended to interpret contemporary opera as an aberrant dramatic form and to criticize its defects without acknowledging its basic assumptions or intentions. For the most part, they agreed that opera's nondramatic components should be considered accessory decorations with no artistic rights of their own.[3]

As such views received more and more attention in Germany, those involved with operatic productions began to scrutinize the assumptions from which they derived. In Hamburg, where the precedent for such scrutinizing had already been established, opera's defenders rejected those assumptions, preferring to support their indigenous traditions, views, and practices against foreign critical domination. This support, which sometimes included attempts at sorely needed reform, helped to counteract acceptance of neoclassicism in the French version and to insure further inquiry into the essence of theater. The increasing number of disputes over opera first in Hamburg and then in Leipzig, Braunschweig, Berlin, and elsewhere, shows that the two points of view (the French criticism by code and the Germanic criticism by precedent) were clashing with greater frequency. The continuing interaction of those two points of view is one of the most significant factors in the history of German criticism, aesthetics, and literature. It is to the modifications and reforms brought about by this interaction that we owe the critical thought of the Goethean age.

HAMBURG'S TRADITION AT THE TURN OF THE EIGHTEENTH CENTURY

The city of Hamburg is famous as a stronghold of Germanic independence. It has enjoyed a long history of democratic governments, economic successes, and cultural activities. One of the highpoints in that history came in the eighteenth century when the city reestablished the wealth and cosmopolitan flavor it had lost after the decline of the Hanseatic League. Hamburg burghers were generally shrewd, down-to-earth business people. They instinctively knew what would or would not sell. They also knew what they did or did not like as regards social affairs and public entertainments. The fervent support they gave theater resulted from a mixture of wealth, instinctive reactions, common sense, and artistic pretensions. Although their theater suffered from financial vicissitudes as well as changing artistic tastes, Hamburg burghers have, from the seventeenth century to Lessing's time and even into the present, demanded one or another form of music in stage productions. Opera was, is, and perhaps, will continue to be one of their favorites.

In the first decade of the eighteenth century, the opera house at the Gänsemarkt was an overwhelming success. It could boast of a varied German-language repertoire, professional singers, and distinguished composers, among whom were Reinhard Keiser, Johann Mattheson (1681-1764), Georg Friedrich Händel (1685-1759), and Christoph Graupner (1683-1760). The Pietistic clergy's denunciations had served to liberate opera from religious jurisdiction and to make it all the rage. Furthermore, their denunciations had unwittingly led to the development and cultivation of the kind of arguments that could be used to refute the anti-opera charges made by admirers of French dramatic ideals. Though still clumsily, if not tortuously expressed, and though often dependent on a host of other authorities, the arguments advanced by Hamburg's defenders of opera eventually gained greater independence and sophistication. While some early writers continued to cite Morhof, Harsdörffer, Guarini, and Patrizi, others sought support in the writings of the Jesuits, who were noted for successful theatrical works and for practical suggestions about their construction.

One of the best examples of this tendency is the preface to *Störtebecker und Jödge Michaels* (1701), a libretto about a favorite subject of Low German ballads. It was written by a man named Hotter, about whom all we know is that he was an opera singer in Hamburg around 1701 and then later cantor in Jever.[4] Hotter claimed that there had been many Hamburg operas about people of high as well as low station, but that no one had yet attempted to present anything about the disorderly and preposterous conduct of the two famous local pirates who came to such a terrible end. After discussing his work's content, which even amused Lessing when he read it, Hotter turned to its form and justified its neglect of the unities of time and place (sig. A3ʳ). He refused to accept the French neoclassical code because he thought it consisted of impractical rules whose universal validity had already been disproved by numerous earlier writers.

Hotter preferred the critical ideas of the Jesuit Jakob Masen (1606-1681) and cited the third part of his *Palaestra Eloquentiae Ligatae* (1654-1657), which dealt specifically with drama.[5] Arguing that a play's quality depended solely on its artistic organization, Masen singled out unity of action as the only valid dramatic rule. He interpreted it as allowing only the most relevant subplots and episodes but demanding neither unity of time nor unity of place. Although Masen might not have fully comprehended Aristotle's explanation of plot or fable, he at least maintained an independent position in regard to the unities when other German handbook writers either did not come to grips with them or accepted them unquestioningly. His dramatic theory was definitely colored by the baroque Jesuit context for which it was written, yet its emphasis on a workable approach to living theater found acknowledgment not only in Hamburg but in other Protestant areas as well. To the chagrin of German neoclassicists, many playwrights were still relying on it in the 1750s and reinforcing the critical attitude it represented.[6]

Hinrich Hinsch (d. 1712) was another of the Hamburg librettists who believed observance of the unities of time and place detracted from operatic quality. His prefaces are noteworthy because they reveal the increasingly important tendency to affirm opera as a sensual play (*Spiel der Sinnen*). In the one to *Der irrende Ritter D. Quixotte de la*

43

Mancia (1690), Hinsch explained that he had condensed Cervantes' novel and restructured some of its adventures in order to produce a comedy suitable for musical theatrical production (sig.)(2ʳ). Opera's pleasure-giving function was more important to him than anything else, and consequently he considered himself free to treat his source as he saw fit. He hoped his audience would understand that he had chosen such a ridiculous subject because it had what he rather grossly described as the cathartic possibilities of satire (sig.)(2ᵛ).

In the preface to *Claudius*, first printed in 1703 and then reissued in 1726, Hinsch claimed opera provided a pleasurable poetic type of experience precisely because it titillated the senses of its audience without attempting to address their reason or understanding (sig. a4ᵛ). He believed it was impossible to simulate actual reality or reproduce factual details in historical sequence because he thought the very nature of opera required artificial or different laws of probability. Tantalizing the ear and seducing the eye remained his ultimate objectives.

Christian Friedrich Hunold (ca. 1680-1721) agreed with him and contributed even more to the persistence of such ideas. His best-selling novels, published under the pseudonym Menantes, had catapulted him to fame in Hamburg, where he quickly found close contact with opera's proponents. He shared their doubts about the validity of those normative, prescriptive French rules that were being used with greater frequency to denounce opera as an aberrant dramatic form. And he joined with his new Hamburg colleagues in opposing Wernicke's application of such rules to Postel's operas as well as to earlier German baroque poetry.[7]

Hunold's own musical dramatic interests ranged from the theoretical to the practical, for, in addition to writing two operas and preparing several cantatas and serenatas at Johann Sebastian Bach's (1685-1750) request, he often defended the operatic form and discussed its artistic possibilities.[8] His lengthiest discussion appeared in the essay "Theatralische Gedichte," which he published with his *Theatralische/ Galante und Geistliche Gedichte* (1706). At the time Hunold believed opera surpassed all other theatrical forms, and he often called it the principal one, because it combined verse, action, and music. Since he, like Johann Gottfried Herder (1744-1803) and later German writers, considered music the soul or essence of all poetry (p. 4), he harbored no misgivings about the possibilities of writing verse that easily lent itself to musical instrumentation. Though tending to interpret opera as a kind of lyrical theatrical work, Hunold did not overlook its dramatic aspects. He considered its plot or action the all-important superstructure on which everything else depended, and he insisted that it be devised so as to permit an artistically interesting portrayal of true events.

Comments about opera's stageworthiness had been made by many writers before Hunold. He consolidated them, however, and used them as the basis for his entire interpretation. Again and again he emphasized the importance of producing operas in theaters before live audiences and of judging the entire production rather than the libretto alone. He claimed that opera's combination of several arts gave it the kind of vitality that precluded its ever becoming anything like a closet drama. He thought the incomparable dramas of Lohenstein and Guarini had become closet dramas because they lacked the components for theatrical effectiveness in the contemporary world. In Hunold's opinion, opera had replaced tragedy and tragicomedy as the foremost theatrical form precisely because of its ability to make full use of all the possibilities of the stage.

He maintained that theater poets learned through practice just how to use the stage, but, as we would expect from a writer of his era, he did not consider firsthand experience sufficient. Certain talents, learned or otherwise, were prerequisites for doing so. Hunold was one of the earliest to describe the ideal librettist in detail. His description emphasized the importance of contriving interesting plots, but omitted mention of erudition, rhetorical principles, ethical aims, and thorough knowledge of the dramatic rules (pp. 87-88). Though aware of such rules, he disputed their universal validity, asserting that they often prevented the construction of a successful opera. His objection to the unity of time is especially clear in the paragraph introducing the libretto he offered as a model, his own *Nebucadnezar*. He stated that excuses were not at all necessary for his selection of a story (*Historie*) which could not possibly have happened within twenty-four hours. If, he continued, that were an unavoidable requisite, then the histories of excellent emperors and heroes could not be presented (p. 135).

Hunold's opposition to constructing librettos according to the rules—though somewhat eclectic, if not contradictory—led to his disavowal of the rules as the basis for judging operatic productions. He did, however, believe some kinds of standards were necessary. The main one, he claimed, was that an excerpt or an entire work should be well received and popular with audiences, and by this he meant approbation from an experienced, knowledgable public, for he purported to be concerned primarily with the serious connoisseur and repeatedly expressed objections to the unsympathetic, stupid spectator who considered himself a competent judge.

Hunold thought that standards allowing for the particular beauties of the individual work were needed. In the preface to his edition of Erdmann Neumeister's (1671-1756) manual on poetics, *Die Allerneueste Art / zur Reinen und Galanten Poesie zu gelangen* (1707), he stressed the importance of humility, tolerance, and reverence, especially in regard to evaluating works of the past: "Denn wann so edle Verfasser von langen Jahren her mit grossem Beyfall gelesen/ und ihrer Schätzbarkeit wegen in die besten Bibliothecken genommen/ von keinen als eigensinnigen Leuten aber verachtet worden/ weil es überall verkehrte Köpffe gibet: so wäre es alsdenn nicht allein eine Verwegenheit/ sondern eine Thorheit/ an den Meriten dieser Scribenten zu zweifeln. Siehet man nicht allezeit die Schönheit an solchen Verfassern/ so muss man nicht schliessen/ dass keine vorhanden/ sondern dass man keinen Verstand davon besitze" (sig. b5ʳ; "For, if such noble authors, read for many years with great approbation and included in the best libraries on account of their value, have been despised by none other than the self-willed because there are wrong-headed persons all over, it would be not only presumptuous but also foolish to doubt the merits of these writers. If one does not always notice beauty in their works, one must not conclude that none is present, but rather that one possesses no understanding of it"). In this same vein, Hunold affirmed the imperishable quality of works by dramatists like Pierre Corneille and voiced a negative opinion about the Quarrel of the Ancients and the Moderns; he believed that each point of view had its defects as well as its merits and that critics should not take sides so unequivocally.

Hunold's whole treatment of opera centered on discovering those factors that ensured success. In addition to citing sections of his own librettos, he presented and discussed in "Theatralische Gedichte" examples culled from the repertoire of the Hamburg theater. He praised Postel for his outstanding achievements and, though not uncritically, more or less viewed them as models. The works of other librettists provided what he considered consistently mediocre examples, and he used them for the sake of contrast. Hunold cited specific passages, analyzed them as individual units, and passed judgment on them, but he recognized the necessity for appreciating the totality of a work. Although he himself was not always able to do so, he urged his readers to view each opera with understanding and to see what it actually accomplished in the theater instead of paying attention to what he called the petty rules of the self-appointed authorities. He spoke of allowing oneself to be emotionally transported by the artistic product when he ex-

47

plained: "Hieraus wird die Meynung vieler klugen Leute bekräfftiget/ wie der Enthusiasmus in Einrichtung der Poesie und des Theatri tausendmahl mehr Approbation verdiene/ als was ein Criticus von dem Caracter der Personen/ von der Kenntniss des Theatri, von guten Intriguen und dergleichen sagen mag" (sig.)(5^r; "Hence the opinion of many clever people is corroborated that enthusiasm in the production of poetry and theater deserves a thousand times more approbation than what a critic may say about the character of the persons, about theatrical knowledge, about good plots and the like"). Throughout his writings, Hunold continued to maintain that any opera, no matter how far it deviated from the orthodox standards of spoken drama, could be considered good as long as it effectively produced its desired results. He even upheld this liberal critical point of view when discussing the comic figure, which he himself opposed in theory but accepted in practice as long as it was handled cleverly enough to provide a good diversion (p. 119).

Hunold's preface to his edition of Neumeister's manual on poetics reiterated many of these same ideas and developed some of them even further. He continued to advocate a nonnaturalistic, lyrical, yet dramatic opera and once more touched upon the question of verisimilitude which, because of Saint Evremond, was becoming a key issue in operatic discussion. Hunold believed that the portrayal of everyday happenings in an ordinary manner would be pointless and therefore insisted that opera portray other kinds of happenings in an elevated poetic manner. In "Theatralische Gedichte" he had compared poetry and painting in order to prove that no art presented unadulterated reality (p. 29). In his preface to Neumeister's work, he used a similar comparison, hoping to clarify the effects of operatic illusions. He also alluded to art's relationship to reality when he discussed poetic style and versification: "Viele urtheilen nach ihrem schlechten Vermögen in der Rede-Kunst auch so schlecht: je gemeiner man rede/ je natürlicher sey es

48

gesagt. Dahero sind sie in ihren Gedancken und Redens-Arten so niedrig und gemein/ dass wenn ich solche lese/ ich mich eher auff dem Marckte unter Krähmern/ Höckern und solchem Zeuge/ als auff dem Parnass unter Musen glaube. Nicht was niedrigen Leuten von niedrigen Professionen, sondern was erhabenen Musen gemein/ das wird hier vor natürlich geachtet" (sig. d6ʳ; "Many also judge so poorly by their inferior ability in rhetoric: the more vulgarly one speaks, the more naturally it be said. Therefore they are so base and mean in their thoughts and expressions that when I read them, I sooner believe myself to be at the market place among tradesmen, junkmen, and such rabble than on Parnassus among the Muses. Not what common people of lowly professions but what sublime Muses share, that is to be regarded as natural here"). To support his idea that poetry was interesting only because it was unlike reality, he gave the example of the parrot which, he claimed, human beings noticed and cultivated as a pet only because it differed so much from the birds they normally experienced in nature (sig. d7ʳ). Hunold would have considered a detailed examination of the question of artistic verisimilitude a belaboring of the obvious, but some of his contemporaries went on to analyze it in greater depth in order to use it as one of their main arguments in defense of opera.

When we view Neumeister's poetic manual, we understand more clearly why Hunold would choose to edit it and see to its publication.[9] Neumeister also considered success the most important standard for evaluating the common literary conventions of the day. This Lutheran clergyman, who firmly opposed his Pietistic colleagues, was well versed in literature, having won his master's degree with an annotated index of seventeenth-century German poets that is still of value to scholars today.[10] His wide ranging interests included theater as well. He presumably gained some first-hand experience by producing several librettos for the court at Weissenfels.[11] Like some of the earlier German writers whom he studied (and like many who followed him), Neumeister was fascinated by the operatic aria and what it seemed to have achieved as regards the relationship of ideas, metrics, and music. Many of his own attempts to revitalize the religious song with forms borrowed from opera were, interestingly enough, arranged by Georg Philipp Telemann (1681-1767) and printed in eighteenth-century hymn books.

For Neumeister, the aria was opera's most essential element; it was plainly and simply, its "soul" (p. 408). This had not always been the case, he explained, for in earlier days operatic form had consisted merely of recitatives and choruses. The momentous change, he insisted in his not altogether accurate historical description, had come about with Guarini's *Pastor fido*, which he regarded as the first notable sign of progress because it not only used a different kind of recitative but also developed the aria and suggested further avenues for experimentation. He considered this work an important "source of all operas" and praised Hofmannswaldau and Hans Assmann von Abschatz (1646-1699) for providing Germany with translations (p. 395).

Neumeister's penchant for lyric poetry and his understanding of music as well as theater produced a very significant suggestion for synthesizing opera's two main components. Instead of using long, unmusical alexandrines like Andreas Gryphius (1616-1664), Lohenstein, and the French, he thought German librettists should use a shorter iambic verse form that would lend itself more readily to musical arrangement (p. 73). The shorter the line, he claimed, the easier it would be for the composer to do a good job.

Many of Neumeister's other suggestions derived from baroque stage conventions and the typical rhetorical distinctions. Occasionally, however, they contained the kind of ideas that slightly younger Hamburg writers were to take up and develop further. His ideas on style were among them, not necessarily because of his devoted adherence to the principle of decorum but certainly because of what he made out of that principle. In explaining it to his readers, he used the argument that had steadily evolved since the Renaissance and that had been particularly effective during the Pietistic attacks against the Hamburg opera. He maintained that whole countries differed in ways of expression depending on the specific times and circumstances.

Another idea his handbook helped to keep alive for future generations had to do with operatic verisimilitude which he, unlike Hunold, related to the age-old concept of poetic fiction. Neumeister contended that one should not expect to see things happen on the stage as they would in ordinary nature: "so wird wohl nimmermehr jemand so närrisch seyn/ dass er sich einbilde/ es wäre wahrhafftig also geschehen. Welches daher denn der Probabilität zimlich zuwieder scheinet; Gleichwohl aber muss es ebenfalls die Opinion, und weil es einmahl von den Alten so eingeführet ist/ entschuldigen" (p. 399; "No one would ever be so foolish as to imagine that it had truly happened thusly. This is a fact that therefore seems to contradict probability considerably. Nevertheless opinion must excuse it in a similar way, and because it was once so introduced by the ancients"). Although he thought fundamental discrepancies with nature were inherent to opera, he cautioned librettists against totally neglecting theatrical probability.

Like Masen and Hotter before him and like Lessing and so many after him, Neumeister doubted that the unity of time contributed to probability: "Nun ist nicht ohne/ dass etliche so rigorös sind/ und nur eine Zeit von einem oder ein Paar Tage haben wollen. Allein es scheinet an sich selber fast unmöglich/ dass so vielerley Dinge/ welche in einem Dramate vorkommen müssen/ sich in einem eintzigen Tage zutragen können" (p. 399; "Now there is a good deal to be said about some being so rigorous and wanting only a duration of one or a couple of days. But it seems in itself almost impossible that the many kinds of things that have to happen in a drama can occur in one single day").

Operatic splendor and magnificence were more important to him than artificially compressing the action into one day, for they helped to portray things as they could actually have happened (p. 412).

Neumeister also considered them important means for preventing boredom among spectators. While in itself not very innovative, his concern for audience welfare did support a strange mixture of traditional and rather progressive ideas. He suggested, for example, that the librettist limit his plot to eight or, at most twelve characters if his source did not predetermine the number. Though considering opera a serious matter that should avoid the frivolous, he condoned the ever popular comic figure as long as it appeared in varied forms. Like Horace, Neumeister worried about spectators having something to look at and therefore demanded that one actor be present to keep the stage from being left completely empty. Changing the scenery once every half-hour in addition to frequent ballets and other displays, he thought, helped to sustain interest but should be considered artistically improper unless meaningfully related to the particular context (p. 405). Without mentioning organic dramatic necessity, he suggested a primitive kind of unity of action which rejected intermezzos (*Zwischenspiele*) and required each of the opera's individual parts to be connected: "Die gröste Kunst bestehet in der Connexion, dass/ wenn keine Verwandlung darzwischen kömmt/ die neue Scene mit der vorhergehenden/ oder doch mit der folgenden allemahl eine Verwandniss haben muss" (pp. 403-404; "The greatest art lies in the connection so that, when no transformation of the stage set intervenes, the new scene must always be related to the preceding or at least to the following one").

Neumeister selected only the dramatic rules he considered pertinent for opera. But, like the consolidator of baroque operatic ideas that he was, he asserted that even they could be disregarded whenever necessary. According to him, it was senseless to hold them up as absolute laws: "Jedoch

weil alle Theatralische Sachen in der Opinion beruhen/
darff man eben in einem und andern Dinge kein Distel-
Kopff seyn/ sondern muss dem Theatro, der Materie/ der
Zeit und andern Circumstantien eine Freyheit lassen" (p.
412; "However, because all theatrical matters are based in
opinion, one must avoid being a thistlehead [critically
prickly or picayune] in one or the other matter, and grant
the theater, the material, and other circumstances a certain
freedom"). The practical demands of contemporary theater
were always what influenced his choice.

Feind's Preference for English Dramatic Style

The fullest expression of contemporary Hamburg operatic
attitudes came in the libretto prefaces and other writings
of Barthold Feind (1678-1721). He was an independent
character whose satire against a libretto-writing theologian
involved him with the municipal authorities and eventually
brought about his temporary but nevertheless painful banishment to Stade. His jurisprudential training at the University of Wittenberg, where he defended his dissertation in
1700, had obviously whetted his appetite for forensic debate
and political controversy. Feind could never keep quiet
about anything, nor could he couch his objections in gentle
terms. Because of his outspoken stand on local matters,
Hamburg's city fathers several times censored and burned
his publications. He enraged the neighboring Danes so
much by favoring their Swedish enemy that they imprisoned him in Schleswig in 1717. The imprisonment did not,
however, last very long, for he was soon back in Hamburg
where he easily resumed his barristerial duties and artistic
investigations.

Like some of his contemporaries, Feind thought the arts
in the German-speaking lands were steadily declining. He
blamed "das sterbende Seculum der Poëten" ("the perish-
ing century of poets") on the failure of his fellow citizens
to support aspiring young writers. Without support he be-

lieved the reattainment of a golden age comparable to the one ushered in by Opitz would be impossible. What Feind meant by support is particularly important. He meant not only the patronage and financial backing mentioned by other intellectuals but also honest, perceptive criticism. Like Lessing, he suggested that the critic be friendly, tolerant, and understanding rather than hostile, dogmatic, and sanctimonious toward the object of his criticism. The critical theory Feind espoused was definitely conditioned by liberal seventeenth-century baroque ideas, but its combination of those ideas with his own insight, learning, common sense, and artistic experience provided his successors with something they could polish and apply.[12]

In "Von dem Temperament und Gemühtsbeschaffenheit eines Poeten" (1708), an essay sadly neglected by modern scholars, Feind rejected the dogmatic kind of judgment advocated by the handbook writers, whose spirit as well as methodology he found negative, petty, and rigid. He claimed: "Es wäre besser/ dass ein Poet von Poeten raisonnirte."[13] ("It would be better if a poet reasoned about [studied] poets.") The critical method he considered most conducive to improving indigenous talents combined the comparative with the historical. If we are to believe his comments in "Gedancken von der Opera" (1708), he attended performances at many major European theaters with the express purpose of comparing their stages (p. 89). Unlike opera's other defenders, who used the idea of historical change to prove the superiority of their own times and works, he maintained that all forms of art differed according to time, nation, and climate without necessarily being better or worse because of such differences. His interest in distinguishing the temperaments stimulated him to consider the effects of climate as well as cultural variables in both the Western and Eastern Hemispheres (pp. 23-24). (It was not until 1721 that Bodmer, in the first part of *Die Discourse der Mahlern*, thought of relating climate to artistic productivity [sig.)(3ᵛ].) Feind's position is clearly expressed in the preface to *La Costanza Sforzata* (1706), where he explained that "Eigenschafften nach der Gewon-heit der Zeiten bey einer jeden Nation variiren; denn unsre Schau-Spiele/ insonderheit die Musicalische/ sind von den alten Tragoedien und Comoedien des Euripidis, Sophoclis, Senecae, Plauti, Terentii, auch schon von den jüngern Teutschen des Lohensteins/ Gryphii und Hallmanns/ weit abgesondert/ die Frantzösische wiederum in vielen Stücken/ so wohl wegen der Composition der Musique als Poësie, von den Italiänischen und Teutschen" (sig.)(4ʳ; "Charac-teristics vary with each nation according to the custom of the times, for our plays, especially the musical ones, are vastly different from the ancient tragedies and comedies of Euripides, Sophocles, Seneca, Plautus, Terence, and by now also from the later German ones of Lohenstein, Gryphius, and Hallmann. The French in turn differ from the Italians and Germans in many works because of the composition of the music as well as the poetry").

Feind's dislike of abstract reasoning and theorizing led to practical approaches for applied criticism. He wanted to elucidate the main points of his critical theory empiri-cally with actual works, and to do so he chose those of Homer and Virgil. Comparing the two poets, which had begun during Roman antiquity itself, became especially popular among critics of the Italian Renaissance who strove to demonstrate Virgil's superiority. Such comparisons were crucial to the evolution of French neoclassicism and to the appreciation of classical antiquity. With Scaliger's attack against the Greek tradition in his *Poetices libri septem* (1561), many French writers viewed Virgil as the epitome of good taste and Homer as an illiterate, dishonest, uncouth barbarian.[14] Like so many other German writers who were aware of the debates raging in France, Feind disputed this view without actually aligning himself with the opposition. He contended that Homer and Virgil were poets whose works could not be judged with exactly the same standards because their different societies and different historical periods had required different artistic treatments. He agreed with his older contemporary Postel that Homer was no less great than Virgil (sig.)(4ᵛ). A few years later, when Feind tried to explain in "Gedancken von der Opera" (1708) that singing stories about heroic deeds and historical events had never been unnatural, absurd, or useless, he described Homer with superlatives. His words are worth quoting at length because of his reference to the poets of other ancient tribes: "Von den alten Barden und Druyden ist bekandt/ dass sie alle Heroische Thaten ihrer berühmten Generalen und Helden in Versen abgefasset/ und solche öffentlich bey der Taffel abgesungen. Dass der grösseste und vollkommenste Poet der Welt/ der blinde *Homerus*, auf dergleichen Art durch seine Gedichte sein Brodt sich erworben/ weis ich nicht/ ob es eine Pasquinade, oder ein warhafftes Vorgehen" (p. 82).[15] ("It is known of the ancient bards and druids that they composed in verse all the heroic deeds of their famous generals and heroes and sang such verses publicly at table. I do not know whether it is a pasquinade or a true happening [story] that the greatest and most perfect poet of the world, the blind Homer, earned his bread this way with his poems.")

Feind's historical perspective led him to urge his contemporaries to cultivate newly developed art forms rather than vainly attempt to imitate those of the Greeks or the Romans. The art form he felt most strongly about was opera. He considered it a modern creation, something brand new in the history of theater. Even its designation, as he explained in his preface to *Simson* (1709), proved this: "das Wort Opera ist bey weiten noch keine hundert Jahr alt" (sig. aᵛ; "The word opera is by far not yet one hundred years old"). Feind knew about the dramas of antiquity, but he believed tastes had changed so radically that such dramas would not be suitable for contemporary audiences unless considerably altered. He thought Postel had given better directions than the French for translating the spirit of antiquity into modern terms and repeatedly lauded him for doing so.

Feind shared many of the older writer's other views, often carrying them several steps further and adding other dimensions. In "Gedancken von der Opera" he explained that opera was a musico-poetic drama that portrayed certain actions. Since he considered the dramatic aspect crucial, he proposed that the composer subordinate himself to the text and design his score so as to bring into sharper focus the passions (*Affekten*) outlined by the librettist. He believed close and sympathetic collaboration was necessary if the proper emotions (*Gemüths-Beschaffenheiten*) were to be roused in the audience. Feind's concept of opera as musical drama evolved from a consideration often ignored or rejected by operatic theorists as well as handbook writers, namely the relationship between acting techniques and the construction of theatrical works. Here and elsewhere Feind, who was one of the first of a long line of Hamburg writers interested in acting theory, maintained that actors should not just be static figures who do nothing on stage except mouth artificially contrived expressions and beautiful sayings; the playwright must give them something to do, something to enact.

Feind supported his argument by juxtaposing what he understood of French and English dramatic styles. He claimed he could never accept the French style because it consisted of too many lyrical descriptions and long dialogues without any real action. His affinity for the English was actually an affinity for the typically baroque style:

Wo sonst keine Affecten sind/ da sind auch keine Actiones, und wo keine Actiones sind/ da wird es auf dem Theatro sehr frieren. Je natürlicher der Poet sich eine Idée von der vorzustellenden Sache und Affect macht/ und je genauer er denselben in dem nohtwendig dazu erforderten mouvement d'esprit bey sich überleget/ die

Umstände reiflich erweget/ und wo keine sind/ welche erdichtet/ je besser wird der Affect sein. Aus dieser Uhrsache bin ich mit den Frantzösischen Tragicis, die darinnen die alten Griechen und Lateiner imitiren/ nicht einerley Meynung/ dass sie in den Tragedies die fürnehmsten Thaten nur erzehlen lassen/ so/ dass die fürnehmste Action des Acteurs in einer wehmühtigen Erzehlung allein besteht/ hauptsächlich wenn es den Untergang einer Person betrifft/ worinnen die Engelländer abermahl von ihnen gantz different.* (p. 106)

Feind believed the theater in England was excellent because its playwrights knew precisely how to hold the attention of modern audiences. The best representative of this gripping dramatic style he thought must surely be Shakespeare. From Sir William Temple's (1628-1699) essay on poetry, he had learned "dass etliche/ wenn sie des renommirten Englischen Tragici *Shakespear* Trauer-Spiele verlesen hören/ offt lautes Halses an zu schreyen gefangen/ und häuffige Thränen vergossen" (p. 109; ("that some, when they heard recited the tragedies of the renowned English tragedian Shakespeare, often began to scream at the top of their voices and shed copious tears").[16] Shakespearean dramas had, of course, been known in Germany and had elicited similar responses ever since the traveling troupes of englische Komödianten began their performances in the late sixteenth century. What makes Feind's analysis signifi-

---

* As a rule where there are no passions, there are also no actions, and where there are no actions, it will be very frigid on stage. The more naturally the poet forms an idea of the matter to be presented and the more precisely he reflects upon the passion in the mood necessarily required for it, thoroughly weighing the particulars and devising some where there are none, the better the passion will be. For this reason I am not of the same opinion as the French tragedians, who imitate the ancient Greeks and Romans and let the most eminent deeds be narrated in their tragedies so that the actor's best action consists only of a melancholy report, mainly when it has to do with the fall of a person. In this the English are once again completely different from them.

cant is not just that he cited Shakespeare by name but that he wrote of him in admiring terms and used his work as a definitive contrast to French neoclassicism and the style of the Comédie française. Yet Feind wrote long before Bodmer referred to the "Engelländische Sasper," and half a century before Lessing advised his countrymen to look to England rather than France for theatrical guidance.[17]

Feind's other comments on libretto writing reveal his strong concern for the dramatic. He rejected the diffuseness characteristic of so many contemporary operas in favor of a unified plot. Like Neumeister, he meant strict scenic continuity rather than any central dramatic necessity out of which the main plot developed (p. 91). Feind considered it the librettist's job to see to this unity while taking full advantage of the possibilities of the stage. Suspense and surprise, he maintained, should develop from the actions of the characters and not from the desire to use a particular theater's sophisticated machines and technical devices. As far as topics were concerned, he believed in careful selection, for not everything could be presented on the stage, and even fewer things were suitable for genuine operatic portrayal. As he explained in the preface to *Masagniello furioso* (1706), "Es mangelt auf dem grossen Schau-Platz der Welt an Begebenheiten zwar nicht, sie sind alle aber nicht dem kleinen Theatro convenable" (*Deutsche Gedichte*, p. 255; "On the great stage of the world there is indeed no lack of events; they are, however, not all suitable for the small theater [operatic stage]"). He suggested that librettists, for variety's sake, select different kinds of topics instead of relying on the standard ancient ones.

Although Feind recognized opera's dramatic potentialities and tried to explore them, he combatted those who wanted to treat opera as a traditional genre. His main objections were to their interpretation of the rules. In "Gedancken von der Opera," he insisted that observing rules was a matter of individual choice: "Methodus ist und bleibt, allemahl arbitraria, und wer einem andern so grosse Aucto-

rität geständig seyn wil/ dem wird es niemand verwehren"
(p. 87; "Methodology is and will always remain arbitrary,
and he who wants to grant someone else such great authority will be hindered by no one"). Furthermore he doubted
the usefulness of the rules and repeatedly inserted comments like "Alle Regeln sind auch nicht gleich Gesetze"
(p. 92; "All rules are not also simultaneously laws").
Feind was primarily concerned with what resulted from observing the rules; as long as they did not hamper an opera's
successful reception, he found no quarrel with them. As he
stated throughout his writings but especially clearly in the
preface to *Das Römische April-Fest* (1716), opera's ultimate purpose was "dem Auditorio zu gefallen/ weil demselben ein Plaisir zu machen die Opern geschrieben werden/
deshalb man sich an die Regeln des Altherthums gar nicht
so genau allemahl binden darf/ wie sonsten wol die Curi-
ösität in andern Stücken erfodert" (sig. a4^v; "to please the
audience because operas are written to provide them pleasure; therefore one must not always tie oneself down to the
rules of antiquity so very closely as curiosity may demand
in other works").

This did not mean that he considered opera a mere form
of amusement or idle diversion; on the contrary, he considered it an art form with stature. Feind's comments about
the playwright's relationship to the public were quite perceptive given the period in which he lived. Sometimes they
state implicitly that audience preferences had to be taken
into account so that drama could remain vital to the people
instead of becoming the exclusive property of scholars.
Feind advocated working within the restrictions imposed
by the spectators; however, he refused to submit to their
wishes unconditionally. Whenever he disagreed with Hamburg tastes, he did not hesitate to make his opinion known.
His writings are filled with remarks, for example, deploring
the popularity of the comic figure whose coarse, vile antics
he thought degraded theatrical works. The preface to *Lucretia* (1705) indicates that he sought a practical solution

to the conflict between the demands of the audience on the one hand and opera's artistic integrity on the other. Originally, he had intended to make the libretto completely serious but was able to concede to public tastes by learning to view the comic figure as a kind of ancient satyr rather than a decadent mime (sig.):( ):(ᵛ).[18]

If Feind did not always agree with audiences, he agreed even less with those self-styled authorities who claimed the theatrical rules were time-honored, absolute standards for everyone to follow. His research had shown that the ancient theorists, with whom those rules supposedly originated had never been explicit. It had also shown that there was scholarly disagreement about what the ancients actually wrote and that eminent modern dramatists, including Pierre Corneille, questioned their validity as well as their authenticity; furthermore, Jakob Masen had supplied sufficient proof of their worthlessness. Masen's views on the unity of time were especially memorable to Feind who explained in "Gedancken von der Opera": "Die Observance des Spatii XXIV horarum ist heute zu Tage nicht mehr im Gebrauch/ und hat der Jesuit *Masenius* dessen Nichtigkeit sattsam erwiesen. Man weis auch nicht einmahl/ ob *Aristoteles*, in Vorschreibung der Zeit von einem Tage/ einen natürlichen Tag von 24 Stunden/ oder einen künstlichen/ von 12 Uhr/ wolle verstanden haben/ worüber sich so viele die Köpffe gebrochen" (p. 86; "The observance of the space of twenty-four hours is nowadays no longer in use. The Jesuit Masen has proven its invalidity sufficiently. One does not even know whether Aristotle in prescribing the duration of one day wanted to have understood a normal day of twenty-four hours or an artificial one from 12 o'clock, about which so many have racked their brains").

Feind subscribed to other ideas that can be found in Masen's *Palaestra Eloquentiae Ligatae*. Along with his Hamburg colleagues, he obviously relied on the baroque theoretical work because it supplied him with encouragement and support for his own liberal tendencies. Like the Jesuit theorist, Feind was willing to accept three acts as well as the five prescribed by Horace. His comments in "Gedancken von der Opera" reveal his attitude: "Was die Observance dieser Regel für einen wahren Grund habe/ ist mir unbewust: Dieses aber wohl bekandt/ dass man noch ungewiss sey/ ob die alten Griechen 3/ 4 oder 5 Actus gehabt/ weil sie derselben Eintheilung am Margine nicht bemercket/ sondern man nur solches aus den Chören schliest/ so aber nicht allemahl Stich hält" (p. 93; "What the real reason for the observance of this rule is, I do not know. I do know, however, that it is still uncertain whether the ancient Greeks had three, four, or five acts, because they did not note the division on the margin, but that such is only concluded from the choruses, which, however, does not always hold true").

This same skeptical attitude colored Feind's defense of opera against Saint Evremond's condemnation of its inherent lack of verisimilitude. That defense, which was a culmination of Hamburg critical thought, struck a chord that resounded throughout the eighteenth century and even beyond. To dispute the French critic's objections, Feind used his common sense and decided to compare opera with ordinary reality. There was, indeed, he admitted, a vast difference, but it was not a valid reason for such abusive criticism. The work the librettist had imaginatively invented could not, Feind argued in the preface to *Simson*, be interpreted literally because it was feigned reality or a kind of make-believe; it dealt in figurative truths rather than factual or natural ones, and it consisted of imaginary actions (*Actiones imaginire*, sig. a2^v). Since opera did not intend to be nature, he continued, it could not justly be compared to nature, nor could it be judged according to nature's standards. Opera, he concluded, required the kind of standards that accepted its illusion of reality as an artistic convention. In "Gedancken von der Opera" Feind pointed out the fallacies in Saint Evremond's concept of *vraisemblance* while giving his own interpretation:

Mich daucht/ ein Knabe/ wenn er zum erstenmahl eine Opera lieset und siehet/ fället gleich ein solches Urtheil/ wenn man ihn/ wie alle Zuschauer/ zu überreden trachten würde/ dass solches wahr/ und der Poet durch seine Acteurs solches für etwas gantz natürliches ausgeben wollte/ was eine Fiction seyn soll. Die Warheit wird in den Schau-Spielen durch Fictiones vorgestellet/ denn sonst müsten es keine Verse seyn/ die man redet und absinget. Man ahmet nur der Natur einiger massen nach/ und wer was ganz natürliches sehen will/ dem giebt der grosse Schau-Platz der Welt täglich neue Praesentationes, nicht aber der kleine/ in Opern und Comödien. Ein Schauspiel ist/ so zu sagen/ nur ein Schatten-Spiel/ allwo man zwar etwas siehet/ aber kein Fleisch und Bein berühret/ und wenn man bey hellem Tage einige hundert Lichter anbrennet/ und der Zuschauer im Finstern in die Opera tritt/ wer will ihn überreden/ dass die *Acteurs* verlangen/ er solle glauben/ dass es Nacht sey/ da noch die Sonne übern Horizont stehet? Statuen, Fontainen, Cascaden &c sind und bleiben deshalb etwas Natürliches/ ob sie gleich kein Geist beseelet/ und die Natur dahin verordnet.* (pp. 77-78)

* It seems to me that a boy, when reading and seeing an opera for the first time, would make exactly such a judgment if one tried to persuade him, like all spectators, that it were true and that the poet wanted through his actors to pass off for something completely natural that which is supposed to be a fiction. Truth is presented in plays through fictions, for otherwise there would not have to be any verses to be spoken and sung. One imitates nature only a little, and to him who wants to see something completely natural the great stage of the world gives new presentations everyday, not, however, the small one in operas and comedies. A play is so to speak a shadow play, a phantasm; everywhere one does indeed see something but touches no flesh or bone. And when several hundred candles are burned during broad daylight and the spectator steps into the darkness of the opera house, who wants to convince him that the actors demand he believe it be night when the sun is still above the horizon? Statues, fountains, cascades, etc. are and therefore remain something natural although no spirit animates them and nature orders thus.

This idea was even more vividly stated in the preface to *L'amore ammalato* (1708): "So wird keiner leicht die Thorheit begehen/ dass er jemanden auf dem *Theatro* in Backofen stecken und verbrennen/ . . . geschweige/ wenn sich nichts destoweniger einer der Welt als einen grossen *Criticum* aufwerffen wolte" (sig.)(3ʳ; "So nobody will easily commit the folly of putting someone into an oven on stage and burning him . . . not to mention, if a man of society nevertheless wanted to proclaim himself a great critic"). The need for theatrical make-believe seemed so obvious to the Hamburg librettist that he could not understand why a thinker with Saint Evremond's background and knowledge had not immediately perceived it. In addition to rejecting what he considered the French writer's naive assumptions, Feind pointed out the logical inconsistencies in his criticism. Saint Evremond did not, for example, consider through-composed prologues and epilogues unnatural, yet he objected to plays that were entirely sung, although they used music in the same way and consisted of the same kinds of conversations, pleas, orders, and declarations of love and war. In Feind's opinion, Saint Evremond failed to appreciate the fact that verisimilitude could be achieved with a musical medium in theatrical works of any length.

Feind's other publications consistently defended artistic truth and mentioned the techniques for producing it. Although he never suggested making up the story out of thin air, he demanded, as a playwright, the freedom to add, omit, or change whatever his sources contained and to invent whatever was necessary. In the preface to *Lucretia* (1705), he made the conventional distinction, attributed to Aristotle, between the factual truth of the historian and the artistic truth of the poet and explained that the latter necessitated inventing some things. He also referred to Pierre Daniel Huet's (1630-1721) treatise of 1670 which explained how the fictitious fables of the ancients had originated through poetic invention (sig.):( ):(ʳ). Again and again throughout his writings Feind distinguished poetry from

64

reality by the kind of probable truth it used. As long as the epic or heroic poet had the freedom to alter the established facts and use poetic devices (*fictiones*), he felt the dramatic poet deserved the same freedom, for drama's poetic essence also necessitated fabricating certain things.

Feind's disagreement with Saint Evremond represented a definite advance in clarifying the idea of operatic verisimilitude at a time when basic questions of aesthetics were becoming increasingly important in Hamburg. His objections to the French neoclassical code upheld the ancient Germanic idea of establishing rules by precedent. And his admiration of Homer, curiosity about Shakespeare, and interest in acting produced seminal ideas that his younger Hamburg contemporaries cultivated and in some instances began to harvest.

THREE

CONTINUITY IN CHANGE

STRUGGLE AGAINST DECLINE

HAMBURG retained its prestige in the 1720s as one of the eminent cultural centers in the German lands. No territorial power had been able to subjugate it, and despite the ravages of the plague, commerce quickened, civic pride increased, and the arts flourished. The city's artistic life was also affected by an unexpected kind of import-export trade. Poems, plays, oratorios, and operas (as well as poets, scholars, performers, and composers) were exported north to Denmark, east to the Baltic states and Russia, west to England, and even south to Vienna. On the import side of the ledger were French theatrical works, Italian operas, and English prose and poetry. Hamburg's age-old commercial and political ties with England had been strengthened by the Great Northern War and by the understandably active German interests of the English kings from Hannover.[1] Hamburg's citizens were as receptive to the latest foreign fashions as they had always been. Their spirit, however, was too competitive and their reverence for the past too strong for them to accept these fashions without question or substantial alteration. They therefore selected from the newest fashions and transformed the ones congenial to their local needs and their North German identity.

The problem of identity was especially worrisome to Hamburg librettists who began to feel threatened by the increasing popularity of operas sung throughout in Italian. While some of them undoubtedly worried about their earning power, others were more concerned with the German operatic tradition that had developed uninterruptedly since Harsdörffer's day. There had been some bilingual texts and,

66

of course, many translations, but they had always been adapted in one way or another to give a distinctly German if not Hamburg flavor. Reinhard Keiser, the distinguished composer and longtime manager of the Theater am Gänsemarkt, had recognized the advantages of using German folk types, local legends, and popular folksongs as the basis for entire operas. And he did so decades before John Gay (1685-1732) and the Berlin-born composer Johann Christoph Pepusch (1667-1752) combined indigenous English materials with Italianate forms to create the sensationally successful *Beggar's Opera* (1728). In addition to writing the music for Hotter's *Störtebecker* (1701), Keiser had collaborated with another otherwise unknown librettist, Weidemann, to produce *Le bon Vivant oder die Leipziger Messe* (1710). Its preface defended what it termed the "natural style," explaining that plots based on events from common, everyday life were more relevant and therefore should be more successful than those from mythology or remote history.[2]

Johann Philipp Praetorius (d. 1775) was of a later generation, but he shared many of these views and supplied Keiser with *Der Hamburger Jahr-Marckt* and *Die Hamburger Schlacht-Zeit* in 1725. These librettos also employed dialect although they were too unflattering in their sarcastically naturalistic portrayal of local customs to please Hamburg burghers. Praetorius's other librettos, many of which were translated and adapted from French as well as Italian sources, were much more popular. The introductions, analyses, and apologies prefacing them contributed greatly to the preservation of German theatrical and critical traditions.

The preface to Praetorius's *Tamerlan* (1725), a discussion of the differences between poetry and other kinds of literature, reveals his concept of opera. He considered it less straightforward and prosaic than other art forms because it combined lyric poetry and drama. Like opera's earlier proponents, he emphasized that the essence of opera was dramatic rather than epic. And like them, he alluded to Aristotle's distinction between poetry and history in order to explain that librettists required the freedom to change or omit known facts. Without failing to acknowledge the operatic achievements of the Italians, Praetorius often derided their diffuse, undramatic style. He had been commissioned to translate an Italian *Amphytrion* and, as he explained in the preface to his translation (1725), did just that even though he thought its rambling plot needed to be condensed and given focus.

Even more significant are the views he expressed in the preface to another translation from the Italian, *Die geliebte Eigensinnige Und der Leicht-gläubige Liebhaber* (1725). He opposed the kind of convoluted style that obfuscated the communication of ideas, whether in Italian or any other language, and he upheld clarity of expression with half the phrase that was to be made famous through Johann Joachim Winckelmann's (1717-1768) characterization of classical art: "Ich halte vielmehr dafür/ die Reinlichkeit/ nebst einer edlen Einfalt gebe allen Sprachen die gröste Zierlichkeit" (sig. A2ᵛ; "I am much more of the opinion that purity together with a noble simplicity gives all languages the greatest elegance"). The concept of "noble simplicity" was indeed an old one when Winckelmann took it up from Adam Friedrich Oeser (1717-1799), an artist, who, interestingly enough, designed operatic stage sets. Its frequent use, however, in Hamburg in the 1720s—decades before Winckelmann, and before Christoph Willibald Gluck (1714-1787) mentioned "une belle simplicité" in the dedicatory letter to his *Alceste* score—indicates that those involved in the cultivation of German opera were concerned, consciously or not, with the means, style, and form that would revive the intentions of opera's Florentine originators and reproduce the spirit of the ancient Greeks.[3] None of them quite succeeded, not Postel, nor Feind, nor Praetorius, but their attempts served to strengthen such interests and such inquiries.

The fate of German opera was among Praetorius's main concerns in the preface to *Calypso* (1727). He believed the musical theatrical forms that not only had been but also would be invented by his own countrymen were threatened by the increasing fashionableness of singing in Italian. He urged careful cultivation of indigenous forms because he felt they alone did justice to "die sinnreiche Gemühts-Beschaffenheit der Teutschen *Nation*" (sig.)(3^{r-v}; "the ingenious character of the German nation"). He also defended the musicality of the German language by claiming that it differed from the Italian but was nonetheless fully capable of expressing all the emotions. Performance in the native language of the audience seemed absolutely necessary to him, and in giving his explanation, he touched on the subject of operatic pleasure. According to him, pleasure derived from the union of ideas expressed simultaneously by the words and the music. If the words were in a foreign language, he argued, the audience would get only half the pleasure because it could then not possibly experience that all-important union (sig.)(3^v).

Another of his concerns had to do with verisimilitude. Opera differed from tragedy, he maintained, because it relied on the kind of unnatural things that had a greater poetic quality and thus a stronger appeal to the imagination of the audience which the librettists wished to captivate: "Die übernatürliche und allegorische Persohnen/ welche bey gewisser Gelegenheit in Opern gar füglich eingeführet/ und in Tragedien nicht geduldet werden können/ sind der Einbildung ein angenehmer Zeit-Vertreib: Und obgleich diese Caracteren ausser den Gräntzen der Natur und der Warheit formirt werden/ so ist demnach darinnen eine gewisse Poetische Eigenschafft/ wornach sich der Poet/ sowohl in der Erfindung als Ausführung seines Werkes/ zu richten hat" (sig.)( )(^v; "The supernatural and allegorical persons, which can at certain opportune moments be quite appropriately introduced in operas, and not tolerated in tragedies, are a pleasant amusement for the phantasy. And although these characters are formed outside the limits of nature and truth, so there is consequently therein a certain poetic quality by which the poet has to guide himself in the invention as well as in the execution of his work"). Along with other Hamburg writers, Praetorius contended that art was based on its own laws rather than those of real nature. Any work of art, he explained, resulted from the artist's recognizing a certain undefinable poetical quality, using it, and developing it to its fullest advantage without necessarily conforming to any preestablished rules. Since that work, he continued, was not made according to such extrinsic rules, it could not be held up to them and judged by its observance of them; it could only be evaluated from the point of view of its own accomplishments.

As popular support for Hamburg's German-language opera waned in the late 1720s, other librettists began explaining and defending their efforts not just in their prefaces but in actual operatic works as well. One such example is the anonymous *Critique des Hamburgischen Schau-Platzes* (1725).[4] This comic prologue portrays a mock trial of the Hamburg opera. Before Apollo's judicial bench on Mount Parnassus, Momus, known since antiquity as a pedantically carping critic, and the Audience present accusations while the Muses, a Technician, and a Painter offer evidence in Opera's defense. Momus repeatedly complains that Opera lacks verisimilitude and is inferior in every other respect, but he is quite favorably impressed by the wondrous scenes Apollo's daughters join together to enact. This in itself, they contend, is sufficient proof of Opera's power and consequently high value. After numerous petty criticisms which are quickly refuted by the witnesses for the defense, Momus becomes convinced that Opera's problems really originate with the fickle Audience whose illogical demands and stupid grievances even he cannot condone. After Momus agrees to direct his taunting powers against the Audience instead of against the greatly misunderstood Opera, the prologue ends with a happy aria sung by all.

Audience support also seemed essential to Christoph Gottlieb Wend (ca. 1700-1745), a private tutor, poet, and translator, who prepared twelve librettos for the opera during his stay in Hamburg. One of the most original prefaces is his "Zuschrifft" to *Die Last-tragende Liebe/ Oder Emma und Eginhard* (1728), a libretto based on the relationship of Charlemagne's daughter to his secretary, a relationship that was made famous by many writers, among them Hofmannswaldau, who wrote a heroic epistle on the theme. Instead of dryly repeating what had become the standard arguments, Wend imitated the earlier poet's style and used a love letter from the Hamburg opera to her audience to explain what he thought the art form really was and what it aimed to do. In this fictitious bid for approval, opera describes her main characteristics as those inherent in any woman—change, variety, and beauty. She further explains that she is capable of giving unsurpassed pleasure because she has at her disposal the enticing charms of music, architecture, painting, and poetry.

Opera claims she may do whatever she likes with her chosen subject and with the form in which she presents it, because, and she emphasizes the fact, she has "Poetische und Theatralische Freyheit" (sig.)(4^r). Pedestrian rules are irrelevant to her, for she assumes the right to create fabulous situations, intrigues, characters, or whatever as long as they serve her ultimate goal, which is pleasing her lover, the audience. Although earlier writers like Hinsch had referred to opera as a "sensual play," Wend singled out its sensually seductive abilities and emphasized them without paying any lip service whatsoever to a moral didactic purpose. In his opinion, opera was a theatrical form that in truth aimed mainly at providing enjoyment. Like many of his immediate predecessors, he believed the best opera was a successful one (sig.)(3^r).

The following year Wend collaborated with Telemann on a work celebrating the reopening of the theater after an eight-month pause caused by financial and managerial difficulties. *Die aus der Einsamkeit in die Welt zurückgekehrte Opera* (1729) is a musical allegory, which gently points out the fickleness of the Hamburg audience. A personification of Opera is reunited with saddened figures that represent poetry, vocal music, instrumental music, painting, and dancing. Having found no faithful patrons, Opera retired from the Hamburg stage so that the individual arts were forced to go their independent ways. Because the arts miss this friend who was able to unify their group into a meaningful whole, they go in search of her and convince her to return with them. In the seventh and final scene, an Opera who is again together with her friends prepares to serve and honor Apollo in the Hanseatic city. The piece concludes with her warning that she can remain only if she continues to receive sufficient support.

The subsequent decade saw even more defenses of opera in operatic form. In 1737, the year before the last German baroque opera was produced at the Gänsemarkt, *Prologus der Musen* celebrated the theater's new management by allegorizing current conditions. It explains that Opera had died because there had not been enough doctors to cure her many afflictions. Unable to forget her, however, her devotees bestrew her grave with flowers and honor her with memorable verses chosen from Hamburg librettos. Among those saddened by the absence of Opera is Apollo who is so lonely that he sends Mercury to awaken her. Asserting that the synthesis of the Muses' efforts is worthy of admiration and support, this emblematic prologue urged the public not to remain insensitive to the divine operatic art. Hamburg's citizens, it suggested, should show gratefulness to the new managers who revived one of their city's greatest glories.

RESEARCH, REVIVAL, AND REFORM IN THE 1720S

As cultural and artistic imports increased in the early decades of the eighteenth century, prominent Hamburg citizens became more and more concerned about their German heritage and especially their city's contributions to it. In 1715 the senator and poet Barthold Heinrich Brockes (1680-1747) joined with his Hamburg associates to found the Teutschübende Gesellschaft. Michael Richey (1678-1761), teacher of history and Greek, formulated its bylaws and outlined its program of German studies. Members were to submit original pieces or translations of worthwhile works. While all were responsible for translating from French, Richey was specifically assigned Dutch, Brockes Italian, Samuel Triewald (fl. 1720) English, Johann Albert Fabricius (1668-1736) Greek, and Johann Ulrich König (1688-1744) Latin. Reports about theoretical issues, philological problems, historical questions, and Germanic antiquities had high priority.[5]

One form of German art given special attention was the Hamburg opera. Most of the members had musical inclinations and, in addition to writing lyric poetry, prepared at one point or another operatic texts or experimented with other possibilities like the oratorio, serenade, and "operetta." The last was a term used by Johann Hübner (1668-1731) in his *Poetisches Hand-Buch*, which appeared in five editions between 1696 and 1742. Hübner was a latecomer to the society, apparently drawn to it because he shared its interests. He considered opera an irregular form of comedy or tragedy in which the performers communicated in the elevated medium of song. If it is short, he explained, "das wird eine Operette genennet; oder es ist mittelmässig, so heisset mans eine Operine; oder es ist ein vollstandiges Werck, so wirds eine Opera genennet."[6] ("It is called an operetta; or if it is middling, one calls it an *operine*; or if it is a full-fledged work, it is called an opera.") Like his fellow members, Hübner did not think these were the only possibilities. He predicted the continuing invention of other musical theatrical forms by Germans as well as by other nationalities.

The society acknowledged the possibilities of such future development, but it was much more concerned about documenting and even reviving what it considered the glorious past of Hamburg's theater. Its efforts in that direction marked the beginning of bibliophilic interest in German-language opera and historical research into the subject. The society's proceedings mentioned the need for a chronological list naming the librettist as well as the composer of each work, discussing its reception, and indicating whether it was a translation, adaptation, or original. Fabricius and König were appointed to organize the project since it was hoped their theatrical connections would enable them to obtain such facts easily. König began his assignment with a review of the first opera produced in the theater at the Gänsemarkt in 1678, Christian Richter's (fl. 1680) *Adam und Eva*.[7] When neither he nor Fabricius submitted anything else that could be published, Richey himself took up the idea, collected Hamburg librettos, and worked on an index. Publication of an annotated list was left to another man who later became more closely associated with the Brockes circle.

Of all the members of the Teutschübende Gesellschaft König was the one most directly involved with opera. Before leaving in 1716 to become court poet at Weissenfels and then later Dresden, he prepared numerous librettos for the Hamburg theater and began expressing his views on the state of the arts. He disapproved of seventeenth-century German literature because he thought it lacked discretion, clarity, elegance, and good taste, the cardinal points in his artistic theory, which he subsequently summarized in the essay, "Von dem guten Geschmack in der Dicht- und Rede-Kunst" (1727). According to König, good taste was that inborn combination of the intellect and the emotions that perceived the true, the good, and the beautiful and instinctively preferred them over the false, the bad, and the ugly.[8] He maintained that those not born with good taste could develop it only through intensive training.

The bombastic, excessively ornate style of some older German poets indicated to him that they had not received any training. König rejected such style in all literary works,

especially in opera. The only older librettist who command-
ed his respect was Bressand. While in Hamburg König paid
lip service to the operatic achievements of Postel and Hunold, but he considered Wernicke's negative criticism of
them and what they represented cogent. Eventually he
openly supported the epigrammatist's satire against Postel
and mentioned it in his letter of March 28, 1724 to Johann
Jakob Bodmer, whom he lauded for a courageously outspoken stand against the belabored and unnatural style of
Lohenstein and Hofmannswaldau.[9] König's Hamburg colleagues, who were annoyed by his attack against their heritage, refused to accept the critical absolutes he tried to
thrust upon them. He lost patience, turned on them, and
decided to fight them in the journal he and Bodmer were
planning to publish. Their plans for collaboration, however, failed to materialize.[10]

König did not endorse the French neoclassical code unconditionally; nevertheless his position differed from that of
his Hamburg colleagues. Some modern scholars claim that
König was at first dependent on Postel and Feind for his
theory of opera but then changed his point of view under
the direct influence of Johann von Besser (1654-1729), who
made him aware of French ideas on naturalness and elegance.[11] König's operatic theory, however, was from the very
beginning determined by traditional Horatian and rhetorical notions. What we notice in his writings is the gradual
association of such extrinsic criteria with those of the
French neoclassical theorists and the attempt to apply them
to opera in order to transform it into musical drama. Although rationalistic aesthetic ideas, especially as regards
formal correctness, gained greater importance in his concept of art, König never learned to think in terms of strict
artistic classifications according to pure genres like Boileau
or his German followers. Nor did he, like many other theorizing librettists, ever learn to put all of his theories into
practice.

König's complaints about contemporary opera centered

on its mixture of languages and its continual lapses from good taste. Instead of rejecting it because of such faults, he resolutely defended it against those rationalists who strove to abolish it. He considered opera a worthwhile form of art with potentialities worth developing, and in his estimation, he was the best qualified to lead it to new and greater heights. He even liked to think of himself as a German Corneille or Molière (1622-1673), whose operatic endeavors would improve the quality of spoken drama and thereby raise Germany's level of taste.

König's introduction to *Theatralische, geistliche/ vermischte und galante Gedichte* (1713) clarified his position and outlined his ideas for reform. In it, he stressed the fact that opera was a dramatic form supplemented by several other arts. It differed from spoken drama and was the most impressive of all art forms, he explained, because it used a variety of literary genres, as well as elaborate stage effects, ballets, music, and machinery. Considering opera essentially drama, he insisted that it observe the unities and all the other rules he thought had been handed down from antiquity. Consequently he asserted that it was the librettist's duty "auf die eingeschränckte Zeit einer theatralischen Vorstellung/ auf die Beybehaltung oder wenigstens wahrscheinliche Erdichtung aller Umstände/ auf eine geschickte Eintheilung der Abhandlungen und Auftritte; auf das Decorum um die absurda Comica zu vermeiden/ auf die Gebräuche des Alterthums bey allen vorkommenden Gelegenheiten/ . . . zu dencken" (sig. **r; "to think about the limited duration of a theatrical performance, about the retention or at least probable fabrication of all the details, about an adroit division of the acts and scenes, about decorum, so as to eschew the *absurda comica*, about the customs of antiquity for all the occasions to be presented"). König assigned the composer a subordinate role because he believed that music served a purely decorative function predetermined by the librettist, the one who coordinated all the collaborating arts "als in einem Circul" (sig. *5^r) and controlled the entire production.

Opera's moral-didactic purpose was of the utmost importance in König's theory, which suggested that the librettist adjust his topic in order to make the lesson clearer and more readily understandable. As long as the action did not seem too improbable, he allowed that the known facts of the story could be altered for the sake of the lesson. Throughout his writings he cited Horace and sometimes even quoted whole passages from him as authoritative justification for his views.

König also advocated altering contemporary works to make them more effective for local audiences. In the preface to *Die getreue Alceste* (1719), his rendition of the libretto Philippe Quinault (1635-1688) wrote in 1674 for Jean-Baptiste Lully (1632-1687), he explained that he had increased its dramatic quality by combining Italian taste with the French. Quinault, he maintained, had written "nach der Gewohnheit seiner *Nation*" ("according to the custom of his nation") and that had meant lyrical descriptions of off-stage action. Instead of having Alceste's voluntary death described, König continued, he preferred to portray it on stage, "um durch die sichtbare Vorstellung einer so *heroischen Action* und die von mir hinzugefügte zärtliche Gedanken die Herzen der Zuschauer desto kräfftiger zu rühren/ welches zwar das schwerste/ aber auch das vornehmste Kunst-Stücke der threatralischen Poesie" ("so that the visible enactment of such a heroic action and the tender thoughts added by me affect the hearts of the spectators all the more powerfully, which is the hardest, yet grandest feat of theatrical poetry"). Unlike Postel before him and Gluck and Christoph Martin Wieland (1733-1813) after him, König did not think of opera in terms of Euripidean drama, nor did he carefully study the Greek *Alcestis*.

To the other members of the Brockes circle, however, understanding the genuine spirit of antiquity, rather than any Frenchified versions of it, was as important as cultivating the Germanic past and present. Perhaps it was precisely their close familiarity with the ancient classics that made them so skeptical of the neoclassical code. Richey continued teaching Greek, Fabricius investigated Greek philology, literature, and culture; and Christian Friedrich Weichmann (1698-1770) studied Postel's interpretation of Homer and Euripides. The older Hamburg librettist's *Iphigenia* (1699) seemed so outstanding to him that he edited it and included it in the first part of his anthology *Poesie der Nieder-Sachsen* (1721).

It was the anthology's only example of a libretto, and in a brief preface Weichmann explained his choice. Agreeing about the effect of different national and historical factors, he reiterated Postel's comments about the necessity of adaptation. He too believed that ancient dramas like Euripides' *Iphigenia in Aulis* would be meaningful for contemporary audiences only if they were revitalized and suited to modern operatic form instead of being merely copied or imitated (p. 327). The widespread popularity of the libretto (which, incidentally, was set again in 1710, in 1728, and in 1731) indicated to Weichmann that Postel had succeeded in doing just that.

Weichmann's defense of Postel—indeed his whole anthology—was published with the patriotic intention of proving that the Germans, especially the North Germans, had their own esprit and their own particular artistic capabilities. The preface to the first part contained his careful rebuttal of the ideas of Abbé Dominique Bouhours (1628-1702) on the superiority of France and French culture. Weichmann considered it illogical and impertinent for any one nation to set itself up as a model for others to follow. He argued that each had something worthwhile of its own to offer. Bouhours, he concluded, had made wildly exaggerated assertions, for he could not possibly have been familiar with so many of the world's cultures (sig. ***4^{r-v}). Unlike other writers who shared his national pride, Weichmann rebutted Bouhours in order to oppose the absolutist French code and not to prove that Germans could follow it equally well. The preface to the second part of *Poesie der Nieder-Sachsen* (1723) engaged the emerging Swiss school and disputed its censure of rhyme as well as its apparent misunderstanding of German metrics. Weichmann's defense of rhyme followed what had become the tradition with Hamburg writers. He questioned the nature of art and upheld the artistic conventions. His argument went as follows: if rhyme is foolish, then all poetry must be nonsensical, and if this is so, then all the arts are absurd because each uses media that are strange and unreal when compared to nature (sigs. ++3^v − ++4^r).

Such critical attitudes were strengthened by the Patriotische Gesellschaft which was founded by the Brockes circle in 1722. Weichmann, along with Richey, participated in the planning and editing of *Der Patriot*, the moral weekly through which they made their views known from 1724 to 1726. On June 1, 1724, it lauded the theater's valuable contribution to the quality of Hamburg life and promised a lengthier article in the near future. The June 22, 1724 issue supplied such an article. It comprised the written report of a fictitious young visitor to Hamburg, who had never seen an opera before, and the comments of his more experienced cousin.

Although opera had at first seemed unnatural, the young visitor reported, it was so pleasing that any comparisons to reality or to the rules were quickly forgotten. Despite its disregard for the theatrical rules and the traditional concept of verisimilitude, he wrote, the operatic performance had totally absorbed him and transfixed him because it had seduced his rational faculties and appealed directly to his imagination. He claimed to have thought "dass ich entweder bezaubert, oder in dem Lande wäre, wo die Verwandlungen Ovidii in der That vorgingen" (p. 240; "that I were either bewitched or in the land where Ovid's *Metamorphoses* in fact happened"). Opera's continuous singing, use of rhymes, and dances, he discovered, were necessary means for making the wondrous, strange, and unexpected stage events seem probable. Elaborate costumes, stage sets, and machinery, he continued, were also necessary because they helped to transform the fabricated situation into another reality, one that was based on special cause-and-effect relationships and that could only be probable within its own context.

During a discussion of this report, his cousin advised him to read the operatic writings of Saint Evremond and the *Spectator* before attending any more performances.[12] He dutifully complied, and, instead of accepting or rejecting them unequivocally, he purported to use his common sense to evaluate them in light of what he himself experienced in the theater. Although he found many of their comments quite applicable to the operas of inconsistent quality produced in Hamburg, he refused to reject the whole idea of opera because of them. If the librettos, he added, were the sources of so many deficiencies, then they should, by all means, be reformed.

His cousin responded by blaming librettists for their failure to provide texts that satisfied the intellect as well as the eye and the ear. The visitor agreed with this and then presented further comments from his cousin's notes. The singers' acting ability, the cousin pointed out, as so many later writers were to do, was crucial for making an opera seem probable. He believed a talented singer without that ability would be superb in concert but disastrous on the operatic stage, for he would "nicht allein die Zuschauer nicht rühren, sondern sie auch leicht zum gähnen bringen" (p. 245; ("not only fail to touch the spectators but also very easily cause them to yawn"). Opera's unique features, the cousin maintained, "scheinen zwar die Gedancken etwas zu zerstreuen, und von dem Haupt-Wercke fast zu sehr abzuziehen; doch vermehren sie auch das wahrscheinliche in den erdichteten Umständen, und unterstützen bey den Zuschauern die sanfte Einbildung, dasjenige vor sich zu sehen, was sie doch wircklich nicht sehen. Sie machen den Eindruck in unser Gemüthe desto lebhafter, und geben der gantzen

Sache ein gehöriges, wichtiges und majestätisches Ansehen"
(p. 246; "do indeed seem to distract one's thoughts somewhat and divert [one's attention] almost too much from the
main work; yet they increase the probable in the fabricated
situations and sustain amongst the spectators the mild fantasy of seeing before them that which they really do not see.
They make the impression in our soul all the more lively
and give the whole matter a fitting, important, and majestic
appearance").

   As befitted the moral weekly in which it was contained,
the cousin did not omit mention of opera's relationship to
morality. Although he maintained that opera was not designed specifically to teach a moral lesson, he thought it
could aid in the betterment of spectators by reinforcing
good rather than evil habits and customs. He believed its
wholesome pleasures had an ethically beneficial effect on
the individual, and this, in turn, contributed to the general
well-being of society. He also stated that opera provided
employment and attracted businessmen as well as tourists
and, in so doing, brought about more directly beneficial results, which were, needless to say, important considerations
in the northern commercial city.

   This and other issues of *Der Patriot* indicate that its contributors viewed the French as far from perfect, indeed not
even good models for emulation. Futhermore the neoclassical code was considered just another fashion that had already outlived its importance. The subsequent editions of
Der Patriot and, in addition, the many adaptations of its
format as well as its attitudes and style, attest to the fact
that other German writers agreed with the members of the
Brockes circle.

Johann Mattheson

Mattheson, a schoolmate of Brockes, began his association
with the Hamburg opera as a child in 1690 and remained
patriotically devoted to it throughout his lifetime. He was

a singer, musician, composer, and, in its years of trouble, its exegete, champion, and benefactor. His acquaintance with the Brockes circle and the international diplomats stationed in the city proved as fruitful for the opera as for his own intellectual development. In 1704 he was appointed tutor to Cyrill Wich, son of Sir John Wich, the English Resident in Hamburg. This appointment, which allegedly occasioned a duel with Händel, whom he had supplanted in the position, was the first in his long career in the English foreign service. With it also began his study of history, literature, international law, and English culture.[13] He was eventually promoted to secretary of the legation and remained in favor when Cyrill Wich assumed his father's post in 1714. Mattheson continued serving the English even after Thomas Lediard (1685-1743) was sent from England to take the position of secretary in 1725.[14]

Both Englishmen shared Mattheson's active interest in the Hamburg theater. Cyrill Wich, along with other diplomats, assumed responsibility for its management when it was threatened by bankruptcy in 1722. They revived older works, commissioned new ones, and brought the theater at the Gänsemarkt to renewed eminence before its dissolution.[15] Lediard, who became an active member of the Patriotische Gesellschaft, contributed to the opera's cause by serving as one of its directors and one of its staunchest defenders. In addition to producing works and designing stage sets, he actually prepared librettos in German. One of them was *Julius Caesar in Aegypten* (1725), his adaptation of an Italian libretto that had had its premiere the year before in London with Händel's music. When it became the object of attack, Lediard countered with the parody "Democriti Antwort auf Hans Sachsens Schreiben und einfältige Kritik," which defended other librettos as well as his own. Some of Lediard's comments in his preface to the *Collection Curieuser Vorstellungen in Illuminationen Und Feuer-Wercken* (1730) show not merely his familiarity with contemporary Hamburg theatrical notions but his wholehearted acceptance of them. The twelfth letter of *The German Spy*, the work he published in 1738 after his return to England, described the Gänsemarkt theater and its operatic productions in glowing terms.[16] Lediard agreed with the Hamburg patriots of his acquaintance that German was a harmonious language and even more suitable than Italian for naturally expressing the passions. Like them, he preferred German to Italian opera.

Mattheson was as much a transmitter of English culture as Lediard was of German. Long before Bodmer and Breitinger, Gottsched, or even Richey and Weichmann, he published a moral weekly in the English fashion; he adapted and changed parts of the *Tatler* and the *Spectator* to suit Hamburg circumstances. It appeared under the title *Der Vernünfftler* from June 30, 1713 to May 26, 1714, when censorship forced it out of existence. Although it often referred to English literature in general, on April 4, 1714 it spoke specifically of *Henry IV* and the *Merry Wives of Windsor*, without, however, mentioning Shakespeare by name.[17] Mattheson, who could not subscribe to the traditional derision theory of laughter, probed what he termed "die Gemühts-Bewegung des Lachens" (sig. Nnnn^r; "the emotion of laughing"). He examined the history and effectiveness of the comic figure or fool and found that Sir John Falstaff was indeed the most successful example. Unlike Joseph Addison (1672-1719) and Richard Steele (1671-1729), Mattheson affirmed the importance of opera and included in his suggestions for a Hamburg lady's library several librettos, among which were Postel's *Iphigenia* and Feind's *Octavia*.

He also admired König. He thought highly enough of his poetic capabilities to collaborate with him on a serenata and illumination in 1714 to celebrate the coronation of George I of England. Mattheson shared many other interests with the Brockes circle and the societies it founded to cultivate things German. He presumably contributed one-fifth of the articles in the second edition of Richey's *Idioti-*

con/ Hamburgense/ oder Wörter-Buch (1754), and he completed the long-planned index of Hamburg librettos printed
between 1678 and 1728. He published it in 1728 in his
journal *Der Musikalische Patriot* (pp. 117-195).

Mattheson's lifelong critical concern for musical theater
manifested itself in numerous writings beginning with *Das
Neu-Eröffnete Orchestre* in 1713. Here he explained that
opera was more than a libretto alone. It was a theatrical
play that provided "einen Confluxum aller Musicalischen
Schönheiten" ("a confluence of all musical beauties") and
that had to be acted out by living performers on a stage
equipped with scenery, decorations, and machines.[18] This
he realized had made some critics view it as aberrant drama
in need of being brought into line with the time-honored
rules. Instead of commenting on the pertinence of the rules,
however, Mattheson took a practical approach. He examined several regular operas and concluded that their mediocrity proved beyond a doubt the worthlessness of those rules.
Postel's librettos, by contrast, provided what he considered
excellent examples. He published a review of Weichmann's
revival of Postel's *Gensericus* in 1722 in his *Critica Musica*,
which was Germany's first musical periodical, and praised
the older Hamburg librettist as "gewiss einer der gelehrte-
sten/ richtigsten/ feurigsten/ sinnreichsten Poeten" ("certainly one of the most erudite, most correct, most ardent,
and most talented poets").[19]

Mattheson frequently referred to opera as "eine musicalische Universität." A more complete definition appeared
in *Der Vollkommene Capellmeister* (1739). He related opera
to other theatrical genres and tried to explain that it "fasset
gleichsam einen Zusammenfluss von allen übrigen Schönheiten des Schau-Platzes in solcher Maasse in sich, dass es
bisweilen zu viel wird" (p. 219; "comprises as it were a fusion of all the other beauties of the stage to such a degree
that it sometimes becomes too much"). As he saw it, the
special function of music in this great artistic fusion was to

underscore and intensify the drama. Therefore, he maintained that composers should avoid excessively ornamental musical forms and should "sich einer edlen Einfalt im Ausdrucke befleissigen" (pp. 141 and 211; "take great pains with a noble simplicity in expression"). Mattheson explained what he meant by noble simplicity: "Edle Gedancken haben immer eine gewisse Einfalt, etwas ungekünsteltes, und nur ein eintziges Augenmerck. Wer sich nun dergleichen ohne allen Zwang, nach den blossen Natur-Gesetzen vorstellet, der wird am besten fortkommen" (p. 149; "Noble thoughts always have a certain simplicity, something unaffected, artless, and only a single aim. He who conceives of them unconstrainedly according to pure natural laws will succeed best"). Although he believed the dramatic plot determined the type of music, he did not assign music a subordinate role.

Again in *Die neueste Untersuchung der Singspiele* (1744) Mattheson contended that poetry and music were equals that had to cooperate in order to produce a well-unified opera. Because he considered them sister arts, he wrote, "man sollte vielmehr auf ihre beständige Einigkeit bedacht seyn, und lieber von beyden Seiten etwas nachgeben" (p. 32; "one should be much more intent upon their constant unity and preferably yield a little from both sides"). Repeatedly he emphasized artistic integration. A good opera theater, in his opinion, was "eine hohe Schule vieler schönen Wissenschaften, worinn zusammen und auf einmal Architectur, Perspective, Mahlerey, Mechanik, Tanzkunst, Actio oratoria, Moral, Historie, Poesie und vornehmlich Musik, zur Vergnügung und Erbauung vornehmer und vernünftiger Zuschauer, sich aufs angenehmste vereinigen, und immer neue Proben geben" (pp. 86-87; "a high school of many beautiful sciences in which all at once and together architecture, scenography, painting, mechanics, dancing, acting, moral philosophy, history, poetry, and above all music unite in the most pleasant manner, and always give new demonstrations for the pleasure and edification of distinguished and sensible spectators").

Mattheson claimed that this artistic fusion had to fulfill a moral-didactic purpose because he, along with writers like König, believed that only such a purpose could justify its existence. Accepting pleasure as the ultimate goal he viewed as both unwise and dangerous. On the other hand, he thought opera took cognizance of the importance of pleasure insofar as it enveloped its lessons in an enjoyable theatrical experience, making them more palatable and therefore more readily acceptable.

Some of Mattheson's ideas were very conventional while others were quite progressive. Living a little longer than most members of his generation, this versatile man retained the same critical outlook for over forty years. He continued to defend the baroque theatrical form throughout the period of change when German opera in Hamburg was being replaced by Italian, when confirmed neoclassicists were waging their verbal warfare against it, and when younger critics began defending opera as well as other art forms that did not conform to stringent rationalistic prescriptions. Frequently there was mutual borrowing between the generations.

Mattheson's most progressive ideas developed out of his opposition to Saint Evremond's condemnation of opera's lack of verisimilitude. He began disputing the French writer in 1713 in *Das Neu-Eröffnete Orchestre*. The argument he offered was a version of the one that had already become standard in Hamburg. Instead of holding opera up to reality like Feind, he followed Bostel and compared it to painting; he found that neither opera nor painting could imitate nature exactly because both were man-made fabrications which merely employed certain natural elements. Although the comparison of painting and poetry had long been a commonplace in European criticism, Mattheson's is particularly significant because it came in a discussion of

operatic verisimilitude eight years before Bodmer and Breitinger even founded *Die Discourse der Mahlern* (1721) in
order to examine the significance of such comparisons. The
argument, which was to become more sophisticated as
Mattheson and others used it to defend opera, ran as follows:

> Ferner ist es in diesem Stück mit dem Theatro als wie
> mit einem Gemählde beschaffen. Denn wer in der Mah-
> lerey der blossen Natur gar zu genau folgen will/ der wird
> nimmer reussiren/ ja nicht einmahl eines Mahlers/ son-
> dern nur eines Copisten Nahmen verdienen: also/ wer in
> Scenicis nichts vorstellen wolte/ als die simple Natur/
> ohne einigen Zierrath/ der würde blutschlecht ankom-
> men/ und wenige Surprisen machen. Leidet nun nicht
> allein beydes Mahlerey und Theatrum/ sondern erfordert
> ausdrücklich/ und auff alle Weise/ hier eine Versteckung
> und Verbergung derjenigen Sachen/ die zwar natürlich
> sind/ oder nicht à propos kommen/ dort ein Additamen-
> tum oder Zusatz solcher Dinge/ die/ ob sie gleich nicht
> so gar natürlich/ als eine Pfeiffe Toback/ sind/ sich doch
> sehr wolschicken und zur ungemeinen Zierde dienen.*
> (p. 166)

Mattheson agreed with Feind that only the person lack-
ing artistic knowledge would misinterpret the kind of truth
portrayed in opera. Such an inexperienced person, he continued, would be inclined to understand things literally in-

---

* Furthermore in this point it is with theater as with a picture.
For, whoever wants to follow bare nature entirely too closely in painting will never succeed, forsooth will not even deserve the name of
painter but rather of copyist. Hence, whoever wants to present on
stage nothing but simple nature without any embellishments would
succeed wretchedly and make few surprises. Both painting and theater
not only tolerate, but they expressly and in every way require here
a secretion and a concealment of those things that are in fact natural
or inappropriate, there an addition or an insertion of such things
that, though not so completely natural as a pipe of tobacco, nevertheless conform well and serve as unusual ornamentation.

stead of figuratively. In Mattheson's opinion, anyone familiar with opera had the right "sich über den sonst superklugen St. Evremont in diesem Fall weidlich zu mocquiren. Uber dem weiss ja ein jeder dass Opern und dergleichen nur Schertz- und Lust- aber keine Ernst-Spiele/ und kan dannenhero nicht böse werden/ dass man zu der Zuschauer Vergnügen/ auch alles was Menschen schönes und künstliches haben/ hervor suche" (p. 165; "to sneer in this case to his heart's content at the otherwise superclever Saint Evremond. Moreover, everyone knows that operas and the like are only entertaining and delightful plays but not serious ones, and therefore cannot become angry that everything beautiful and artificial which human beings have is sought out for the spectators' pleasure").

In 1728 Mattheson again poked fun at Saint Evremond in *Der Musikalische Patriot*. The words he used to explain operatic reality this time deserve particular attention, for they closely resemble those used by countless German philosophers, critics, and poets throughout the eighteenth century: "Das Opern-Theatrum an sich selbst nun ist eine kleine Kunst-Welt, auf einer ansehnlichen Schau-Bühne von allerhand Bau-Materialien errichtet, und mit vieler Wissenschafft dazu gemacht" (pp. 117-118; "The opera theater is in itself a little art world, constructed from various building materials on an imposing stage and made with much learning"). When theorizing about novels, Mattheson's contemporary, Christian Wolff (1679-1754), wrote that they presented "another world with different relationships." In 1735 Alexander Gottlieb Baumgarten (1714-1762) compared the poet to a maker or creator and wrote that "the poem ought to be like a world." It was several years later that Bodmer and Breitinger began contemplating the implications of such ideas and referring to an "ideal world" or a "poetic world."[20] And it was in 1798 that Goethe described opera as "eine kleine Kunstwelt."

Mattheson tried his utmost to distinguish operatic reality from ordinary reality. In so doing, he struggled to explain the essence of the artistic medium. He began by stating that whatever depicted nature or explained natural phenomena with artificial means was theatrical: "Theatralisch ist nichts anders, als künstlich, was künstlicher Weise, in Nachahmung der Natur, zur Schau gestellet wird, i.e. etwas gemachtes, und einigermassen durch Fleiss erzwungenes, doch so, dass es weder gemacht, noch gezwungen heraus komme oder lasse" (p. 118; "Theatrical is nothing other than artificial, something that is displayed artificially in imitation of nature, i.e. something made and to some extent contrived with industriousness without, however, appearing either made or contrived"). Rhetoric, logic, and geometry as well as painting, music, and opera, he continued, all used artificial means to accomplish a particular purpose. Mattheson argued that those means were by definition always foreign to ordinary reality but that some of them seemed less so than others. The degree of foreignness, or what other theorists came to call natural and arbitrary signs, was of little interest to him. He merely wanted to prove that opera only seemed to be more like nature because it was a three-dimensional portrayal by living performers.

Mattheson continued his investigation into the essence of theater and in 1739 wrote in *Der Vollkommene Capellmeister* that opera presented a fictitious reality which spectators accepted because "ein jeder weiss, dass die Sache erdichtet ist. Hiebey kan ein Aussenschein, oder etwas gläntzendes und funckelndes, obs gleich kein Gold ist, mehr ausrichten, als etwas dichtes, festes und ein mühsames Wesen" (p. 86; "Everyone knows that the matter is fabricated. An external appearance, or something glittering and sparkling, though not gold, can hereby accomplish much more than something impervious, solid, and a hard substance"). He even suggested that spectators willingly and automatically suspended their disbelief in order to enjoy the performance.

Mattheson's abiding interest in defending operatic probability led to the publication in 1744 of *Die neueste Unter-*

suchung der Singspiele, an essay indicative of the crosscurrents and interacting forces in contemporary German criticism. He wanted not only to defend opera against Johann Christoph Gottsched's attacks but also to clarify his own position in light of new critical developments. In order to do so he acknowledged and adopted Johann Elias Schlegel's (1719-1749) recently (1740) published arguments justifying comedy in rhymed verse. Schlegel's arguments were, he thought, logically developed and perfectly applicable to opera (p. 69). They were, indeed, actually what he himself had striven to articulate for several decades. It is quite significant for the history of early German criticism that Johann Elias and his brother Johann Adolph Schlegel (1721-1793), along with some of their contemporaries, subsequently discussed operatic probability in exactly the same terms.

In this essay Mattheson explained that opera used artificial media, or conventions, to create its effect, and that this was precisely what prevented an exact simulation of reality. Discussing artistic media, he contended in Schlegelian fashion:

Wieder die Unwahrscheinlichkeit und Unmöglichkeit, auf dem Theatro in Versen zu reden, wird uns gezeiget, dass alle künstliche Nachahmer sich eine gewisse Materie, um darauf zu arbeiten, mit völliger Freyheit wehlen mögen. Der Bildhauer z.E. nimmt Stein oder Holz dazu; der Mahler eine ebene Tafel, ein Tuch, eine glatte Wand &c. Einige thun es der Natur mit Farben nach; andre nur mit Licht und Schatten. Viele verrichten es in Lebensgrösse; viele ins kleine u.s.w. Wer verbietet solches? Und wo stehet es im Buche der Vernunft geschrieben, dass der Musikus und Poet seine Nachahmung nicht mit harmonischen Klängen, mit Melodien, mit Versen und Reimen anstellen, mithin dazu diese besagte Materie erkiesen dürfe?

Wenn ein nachgeahmtes Bild in allen und jeden Stücken seinem Vorbilde oder Original gänzlich gleichte, so wäre es mit demselben einerley; und das solls eben nicht seyn: ja, es kann nicht einmal seyn. Denn in der ganzen Welt ist kein Ding dem andern völlig ähnlich.* (pp. 70-71)

Mattheson pointed out other characteristics of theatrical works differentiating them from actual reality. One was that daytime actions were portrayed in the evening with the aid of artificial illumination. This did, he admitted, make them contrary to nature, but, he quickly added, that was no logical reason to condemn them. Opera, like any other play, he continued, was intrinsically different from the real world because it was art, and as such presented "eine neue Art angenehmer Ordnung" (p. 77; "a new sort of pleasant order"). It was perhaps for this very reason, he contended, that people went to the opera in the first place. He claimed they derived pleasure from observing how the performers made the new order seem probable; otherwise they would stay home and just read the libretto (p. 81).

Consequently Mattheson considered fatuous those critics who maintained that pleasure resulted from comparing the artistically probable with the naturally true. Although he believed there were limits to what could be done on stage in a probable fashion, he thought those limits should not be too narrow or arbitrary, "absonderlich kann und mag

---

* We have been shown as regards the improbability and impossibility of speaking in verse on the stage that all artificial imitators may select with complete freedom a particular material in order to work on it. The sculptor, for example, takes stone or wood for that purpose, the painter, an even panel, a canvas, a smooth wall, etc. Some imitate nature with colors, others only with light and shadow. Many execute it life-size, many smaller, etc. Who forbids such? And where is it written in the book of reason that the composer and poet may not undertake his imitation with harmonious tones, melodies, verses and rhymes, and therefore may not choose this aforementioned material for it?

If an imitation resembled its model or original in each and every point, then it would be one and the same with it, and that it is just not supposed to be. To be sure, it cannot even be. For in the whole world no one thing can be completely similar to another.

solche Einsperrung in melopoetischen Werken am aller-wenigsten geschehen" (p. 105; "especially in melopoetic works such confinement can and may happen least of all"). A decade later he vehemently disagreed with Charles Bat-teux's (1713-1780) theory that opera could only be prob-able if it imitated wondrous nature. The Hamburg baroque writer thought that limiting the arts to a common denomi-nator and bringing them into a rigid system was absolutely senseless. In *Plus Ultra* (1755) he maintained that only a laissez-faire system was appropriate: "Die Künste sollen keine reducirte, abgesetzte, oder verrufene Münzarten vor-stellen: ihr Preis soll vermehret und gesteigert; nicht vermindert, nicht devalvirt werden. Es wird hier nichts eingeschränkt" (II, 275; "The arts should represent no reduced, recalled, or discredited types of coins: their price should be increased and strengthened, not decreased, not devalued. Nothing is to be curbed here").

The writings of Mattheson and his Hamburg contem-poraries clearly illustrate the continuity of critical attitudes in the early decades of the eighteenth century. It was a pe-riod of constant change and active debate. Many new artis-tic rules were introduced, and many self-styled authorities came forth to support and codify them. By maintaining a position of nonalignment and by refusing to accept without question the pronouncements of Gottsched, Bodmer, and Breitinger as well as Saint Evremond, Boileau, and Bat-teux, the Hamburg writers perpetuated their heritage and transformed it to suit their own times. They tempered the new with the old and the foreign with the indigenous. As a result, they set important precedents for the future, which was to witness the evolution of still other art forms and styles.

COLLISION AND CONCESSION

GOTTSCHED'S ATTACKS

FRENCH neoclassicism reached its culmination in Germany with the ardent support of Johann Christoph Gottsched. He had studied theology and philosophy in Königsberg where he received his master's degree in 1723. Soon thereafter he evaded conscription into the Prussian army by leaving for Leipzig. There he was indoctrinated into rationalistic views and French tastes by the editor, historian, and poet Johann Burkhard Mencke, whose children he tutored. Because of his connection to Mencke, he joined the local scholarly society and gave occasional philosophical as well as literary lectures at the university. Hoping to ensure his academic career, he courted favor from Johann Ulrich König, who had already become quite influential with the Saxon rulers in Dresden, and dedicated the first volume of his moral weekly *Der Biedermann* (1727) to him.[1] König helped him obtain a professorship in 1729, but the friendship soon deteriorated, for Gottsched began a vehement attack against opera. When Gottsched refused to rescind his condemnation or modify his attitude, König attempted to discredit him first in Dresden and then elsewhere. Virtual warfare broke out between the two. König's campaign was so intense that liberal Hamburg writers, who had looked on with great amusement, wondered who would come forth to replace him as the news of his death spread in 1744.[2]

Gottsched's ultimate goals were similar to those of the Brockes circle and were all basically quite admirable. He too wanted to cultivate German history, poetry, and theater and thereby prove that his country was as great as France. His historical and bibliographical methods resembled theirs, but his critical theory and methodology differed considerably. Gottsched advocated the rationalistically founded neoclassical code because he wanted his countrymen to demonstrate that they had enough good taste and politeness to follow it just as well as the French. Consequently he rejected whatever contradicted that code. Opera, along with the baroque historical drama and the largely improvised harlequinade, was one of the popular theatrical abominations that he strove to eliminate.

In Leipzig, which had a long, rich musical tradition, operatic performances began in mid-seventeenth century and became so popular by the 1690s that they were given regularly during the major trade fairs.[3] A commercial venture, the Leipzig opera was frequently beset with financial problems and other troubles. Despite many vicissitudes, however, it rose to prominence under the leadership of composers like Nicholas Adam Strungk (1640-1700) and Telemann, who served as its director from 1701 to 1704 while studying law at the university. The opera house often employed singers, musicians, and composers from the city's musical academies and was viewed by some as an adjunct where invaluable musical knowledge could be gained firsthand. Except for operas given in concert form by the music students, there were no public performances after the house closed in 1720 until traveling companies began visiting the city in 1732.[4] In 1734 a cantata by one of the city's most famous composers, Johann Sebastian Bach, was performed as a "*dramma per musica*" by students. After 1744 Italian operas became the main staple and were produced during the local fairs.

Gottsched's antiopera campaign began in 1728 with the eighty-fifth number of *Der Biedermann*. It was occasioned by one of those abusive attacks against all theatrical spectacles that came in the aftermath of the Pietistic onslaught. Gottsched wished to distinguish the infamous opera from the regular dramatic genres that he was prepared to defend. In a later issue published that same year, he presented a more developed critique. Saint Evremond had already supplied what he felt was the consummate description, and he simply adopted it: opera was "ein ungereimter Misch-masch von Poesie und Musik, wo der Dichter und Kom-ponist einander Gewalt tun, und sich überaus viel Mühe geben, ein sehr elendes Werk zu Stande zu bringen" ("a non-sensical hotchpotch of poetry and music where the poet and the composer violate each other and take exceedingly great pains to bring about a very miserable work").[5] Since opera's failure to observe the dramatic rules prevented his classify-ing it as either comedy or tragedy, he insisted that it could have no place within the legitimate system of arts. Opera's improbability and total lack of naturalness made it the kind of nonsense that he could only approach in one of two ways: "Man muss seinen Verstand entweder zu Hause lassen und nur die Ohren mitbringen, wenn man in die Oper geht; oder man muss sich Gewalt antun, und alle Unmög-lichkeiten, die uns darin vorgestellt werden, verdauen kön-nen."[6] ("One must either leave one's intellect home and only bring one's ears along whenever one goes to the opera, or one must violate oneself and tolerate all the impossibili-ties which are presented in it.") He further maintained that its voluptuousness, marvels, stunning splendor, and indeco-rous content, and the questionable character of its perform-ers all added up to make it a dangerously seductive form of entertainment as well as a nonsensical one.

When Gottsched's *Versuch einer Critischen Dichtkunst* appeared in 1730, it contained an even more extensive ex-position of this dangerously sensual theatrical form. Gottsched again concurred with Saint Evremond that opera was "das ungereimteste Werck, so der menschliche Verstand jemahls erfunden" (p. 604; "the most nonsensical work the human mind ever invented"). Unable to understand why it enjoyed such great popularity, he tried to analyze the reasons for its persistence. It sustained itself, he concluded, only because of that current trend which considered matters of taste arbitrary and relative. Opera's defenders "halten derowegen in Sachen, die auf die Lust ankommen, alles vor willkührlich, und meynen man müsse es damit nicht so genau nehmen. Was nur den Augen und Ohren gefiele, das wäre schon gut; und man müsse die Vernunft hier schweigen heissen, wenn sie uns dieses Vergnügens durch ihre critische Amerckungen berauben wollte" (p. 606; "therefore consider everything arbitrary in matters that have to do with pleasure and think one must be rather liberal with them. What pleases only the eyes and the ears would be good enough, and one must silence reason when it wants to deprive us of this pleasure with its critical remarks"). This statement, which implies that liberal critical tendencies remained quite strong throughout Germany, shows clearly how Gottsched himself viewed the arts. For him they were governed by absolutes that could not be challenged: "reason" was the infallible guide and "nature" the indisputable basis.

In examining opera closely Gottsched found that it was neither based in nature nor guided by reason. As far as he could determine, it was based in the realm of magic and wonder since there was no natural prototype for its continuous singing; the technical complexity of its machines and devices removed it still further from ordinary reality, and its frequent mixture of languages reinforced its already high degree of irrationality. Following the long line of authorities, who demanded that art imitate nature rationally, Gottsched disavowed the marvelous as an acceptable foundation for any art. He confused natural truth with artistic probability and therefore upheld a literal concept of verisimilitude: "Eine Nachahmung aber, die der Natur nicht ähnlich ist, taugt nichts: denn ihr gantzer Werth entsteht von der Aehnlichkeit" (p. 604; "An imitation, however, that is not similar to nature is worthless, for its total worth arises from the similarity"). Contemporary opera, he correctly explained, failed to imitate nature according to any rationalistic laws of probability; it was more like a fantastic novel than a drama, "ein gantz nagel-neues Stück in der

Poesie, davon sich bey den Alten wohl niemand hätte träumen lassen" (p. 604; "a totally brand new piece of poetry, which nobody among the ancients would ever have dreamt possible"). The possibility that it lacked precedents in antiquity made Gottsched all the more suspicious. Although he himself had demonstrated that contemporary opera was something unique, he could not accept it as such because his scheme of clearly defined arts was just too rigid to permit any new "kinds."

Gottsched's subsequent antiopera writings indicate that his efforts did not decrease and, furthermore, that his views did not change. In 1734 he published "Von dem Bathos in den Opern" together with Johann Joachim Schwabe's (1714-1784) *Anti-Longin, oder die Kunst in der Poesie zu kriechen.* Sublimity, which was often cited to excuse irregularity, pathetic sentiments, and subjective emotional transport, had become increasingly important in literary critical discussion since Boileau's translation of Longinus in 1674. Gottsched permitted no such irrational excuses; he used this concept of the sublime as ammunition against opera.

He also pulled out what he thought were his big guns to meet the defiant pro-opera challenge of other writers in the mid-1730s. His 1735 rebuttal of Johann Friedrich Uffenbach (1687-1769) warned about what would ultimately result if such old-fashioned, baroque liberal critical assumptions were allowed to persist and develop. His prediction of future developments was actually quite accurate, for later eighteenth-century criticism affirmed such assumptions, refined them, and made them applicable to all artistic products. Gottsched wrote:

Der Geschmack muss den Regeln der Vernunft gemäss seyn, sonst ist er ungereimt. Wäre dieses nicht: So müste auch die Gothische Baukunst eben so viel Schönheit haben, als die alte Griechische und Römische. Ja es müsten die altdeutschen Knittelverse, die nach dem Geschmacke

97

unsrer Vorfahren recht schön klungen, eben so schön seyn, als die Virgilianischen, oder unsre heutigen Verse. Ich kan mirs nimmermehr einbilden, dass der Herr U. diess in Ernste behauptet habe: sonst müste er auch einer barbarischen Janitscharen-Musik, eben so viel Lob zugestehen, als dem besten italienischen Concerte. Es nimmt mich auch Wunder, dass er glaubt, dass man sich in der Poesie nach dem Geschmacke der eingeführet ist, richten solle; und darvor hält, dass sich die Welt wohl schwerlich nach etlicher weniger critischer Liebhaber ihrem Sinne richten werde.*[7]

Despite German grand opera's disappearance, Gottsched persisted in trying to corroborate the validity of his position. In his 1740 German version of Saint Evremond's play, *Les Opéras* (1677), the locale was changed, and the comments about French operas were adapted to those that had been produced in Hamburg.[8] The preface he wrote for W.B.A. von Steinwehr's 1742 translation of Saint Evremond's letter on opera is another indication of his continuing allegiance to the French critic.[9]

Gottsched's continuing negative attitude toward all musical theater is best illustrated by his review of Voltaire's (1694-1778) works for the July 1745 issue of *Neuer Büchersaal der schönen Wissenschaften und freyen Künste*. Gottsched concentrated on Voltaire's opera *Samson* and expressed astonishment that the eminent French writer had

---

* Taste must conform to the rules of reason, otherwise it is nonsensical. If this were not so, then even Gothic architecture would have just as much beauty as the ancient Greek and Roman. To be sure, old German doggerel, which sounded right beautiful according to the taste of our ancestors, would have to be just as beautiful as Virgil's or our contemporary verses. I absolutely cannot believe that Mr. U. maintained this in earnest, otherwise he would have to grant the barbaric music of the Janissaries as much praise as the best Italian concerto. I also wonder about his believing that one should guide oneself in poetry according to the taste that has been introduced and about his thinking that the world would with difficulty guide itself according to the opinion of some few critical admirers.

even considered working with an art form condemned by so many of the leading literary authorities (pp. 31-32). Then he proceeded to explain in his typical fashion that *Samson*, like any opera, failed to observe the unities and other time-honored poetic rules.

The last major engagement in Gottsched's crusade was precipitated by Christian Felix Weisse's (1726-1804) *Der Teufel ist los oder die verwandelten Weiber*, a free adaptation of Charles Coffey's (d. 1745) *The Devil to Pay, or the Wives Metamorphosed* (1731). Successfully produced in Leipzig in 1752, Weisse's operetta had those characteristics Gottsched hated most—irregularities in form, distracting music, and English origins. His vehement fight to have it suppressed, however, simply helped to increase its popularity, for Leipzig, like late seventeenth-century Hamburg, rallied to the defense of musical theater. Although Gottsched's attempt to abolish the newly developed operetta was as much a failure as his attempt to abolish grand opera, he remained steadfast in his stand against all such theatrical forms. His subsequent suggestions for reform sometimes seemed to indicate a change in tactics, but they did not constitute a change in his fundamental ideas. The kind of musical theater he would have accepted would have been one so extensively reformed that it would no longer have been a fusion of the arts; it would have been drama with incidental music. He insisted that operatic music, which he adjudged the main source of the irregularities, be written "mehr auf eine edle Einfalt" ("more with noble simplicity") and made completely subservient to the drama.[10]

Gottsched attempted to inculcate his rationalistic artistic views and his admiration for French dramatic style on students and colleagues in Leipzig. As to be expected, not all of them responded favorably in this city, where Johann Sebastian Bach served as Thomas Cantor. Whether in Leipzig or elsewhere, many questioned Gottsched's assumptions as well as his authority. Even those who became enamored of his views hesitated to accept his neoclassical code in its entirety. While some of his followers opposed the very idea of opera, others merely condemned current abuses, which in the 1730s were considerable.

Christian Gottlieb Ludwig (1709-1773) shared his teacher's negative opinion of opera but, analyzing it more perceptively, came closer to explaining its essence as an art form in "Versuch eines Beweises, dass ein Singespiel oder eine Oper nicht gut seyn könne" (1734). If sensuous pleasure were the sole purpose of theatrical works, then, Ludwig had to admit, opera could justifiably be called "das Meisterstücke der Schaubühne" (the masterpiece of the stage").[11] He quickly added, however, that the authorities had firmly established theater's didactic purpose and had clearly outlined the necessary rules for accomplishing this purpose. Although Ludwig held music responsible for opera's defiance of the rules, he realized that it was such an essential component that it could not be eliminated altogether; even a reformed opera would not solve the fundamental problem of its fusion of the arts.

Opera's continuous singing was drawn into the critical spotlight and denounced by another Gottsched student, Jacob Friedrich Lamprecht (1707-1744), in *Schreiben eines Schwaben an einen deutschen Freund in Petersburg von dem gegenwärtigen Zustand der Opera in Hamburg* (1736). This fictitious report resembled the one published earlier in *Der Patriot* but expressed exactly the opposite opinion. It described a sojourn in Hamburg and, focusing on the opera, turned into an abusive critique. Lamprecht, who was a native of Hamburg, had his correspondent explain that while music could usually delude one into forgetting opera's unnaturalness, nothing could disguise the disturbing deficiencies of the older baroque works that were being revived. He claimed their texts were inferior to begin with and were made still worse by their incomprehensible mixture of languages. The fact that they were sung throughout, he added, made them not only ridiculous but also potentially dangerous: "Die Italiänische Sing-Art muss nothwendig wieder die

Natur seyn, weil sie den Mund in die unnatürlichsten Stellungen bringet. Gewiss mein Herr, es ist gut, dass die Opera hier so wenig besucht wird: denn, sollte ein eintzigesmahl eine schwangere Frau diese Verdrehungen ansehen, so wäre ein unersetzlicher Schade zu befürchten. St. Evremond sagt, dass die Italiäner keine Leidenschaft natürlich ausdrücken, und ich bin nunmehr vollkommen davon überzeugt." ("The Italian style of singing must necessarily be contrary to nature because it forces the mouth into the most unnatural positions. Certainly, sir, it is good that the opera here is being frequented so little, for should a pregnant woman see these contortions a single time, there would be an irreparable injury to be feared. Saint Evremond says that the Italians express no passion naturally, and I am by this time completely convinced of it.") The correspondent interpreted opera's failure to attract large audiences as a sign that good taste was finally replacing "die Barbarey in Niedersachsen" ("barbarity in Lower Saxony").[12]

THE DISSIDENTS

Johann Georg Hamann (1697-1733), known to modern scholars as the uncle of the "Magus des Nordens," was one Leipzig scholar whom Gottsched influenced very little. Hamann joined the professor's Deutsche Gesellschaft and contributed to the moral weekly, *Die Vernünftigen Tadlerinnen*, but his interests lay elsewhere. He liked seventeenth-century German literature and in 1724 published a continuation of Heinrich Anselm von Ziegler und Kliphausen's (1663-1696) *Asiatische Banise* (1698), though he later regretted having done so.[13] For him opera was not just a valid form of art but an extraordinary one. Agreeing with its earlier exponents, he wrote in his *Poetisches Lexicon* (1725): "Eine Opera oder Singspiel wird nicht unfüglich das Meisterstück der ganzen Poesie genennet" (p. 61).[14] ("An opera or musical play is not misleadingly named the masterpiece of all poetry.") Because the nature of the manual precluded

more detailed treatment of opera and its variants, he encouraged readers to consult the works of Brockes, König,
Richey, Weichmann, Feind, and the theories of Hunold and
Neumeister. He claimed that these examples, some of which
had appeared approximately twenty years earlier, were still
very cogent. Judging from the number of times his own
poetic lexicon was reissued, it must have been equally
popular with subsequent generations.

Hamann's views coincided very nicely with those of his
contemporaries in Hamburg. Arriving there in 1727, he
promptly gained entrance into prominent literary and social circles. He became tutor to the children of Minister von
Hagedorn, who was a patron of the arts and generous host
to Feind, Richey, and other intellectuals. Hamann strengthened his ties to that family when he later published an essay
by Friedrich von Hagedorn (1708-1754), whose literary
critical ideas were at the time as liberal as his.[15] Hamann
also frequented the home of Senator Brockes, who became
his friend and let him see several parts of *Irdisches Vergnügen in Gott* through the press. Hamann's other activities
included publishing a moral weekly, writing reviews for local journals, serving as editor of the influential newspaper
Der Hamburgische Unpartheyische Correspondent, and preparing for the Gänsemarkt theater four librettos, which
were set to music by Telemann. He was apparently proud
of his first one, *Margaretha* (1730), and sent a copy of it to
Gottsched in 1731. If he aimed at flattering him with it, he
failed, for his former Leipzig colleague ignored it, sending
neither an answer nor the requested evaluation.[16] Because
of essential disagreement over opera, Hamann, like König,
whom he admired greatly, enjoyed a rather brief literary relationship with Gottsched.

Hamann had begun to formulate his operatic opinions
several years before writing *Margaretha*. When he reviewed
Mattheson's *Der Musikalische Patriot* in 1728, he affirmed
its treatment of operatic probability and its rejection of
Saint Evremond's criticism.[17] Hamann examined such ideas

more fully in the August 25, 1729 number of his moral weekly, *Die Matrone*. In it he spoke of his growing dissatisfaction with unsubstantiated judgments against the idea of opera as well as against contemporary practices. He found particularly untenable those assertions by Saint Evremond and his followers that operatic singing was unnatural. As far as he knew, no one had proven conclusively that through-composed theatrical works were contrary to reason. He also doubted that anyone ever would.

Following in the Hamburg tradition, Hamann claimed that his judgment of opera was based on his own experience and observations. In trying to describe his method, he wrote: "Ich urtheile nur aus den Würckungen dieser so herrlichen Kunst, und kan so wohl aus anderer vernünfftigen Leute, als aus meiner eigenen Erfahrung ein Zeugniss ablegen, wie offt wir die Proben davon empfunden" (p. 268; "I judge only from the effects of this so magnificent art and can give evidence from my own experience as well as from that of other sensible people, how often we felt the stamp of it"). An observation he considered especially important was that opera delighted its audiences. He interpreted its warm reception among cultivated people as an infallible indication of its artistic validity. Another of his observations had to do with opera's attempt to fuse diverse arts; it was, he explained with terms like Mattheson's, a "Zusammenfluss so vieler Vortreflichkeiten von so mancherley Künsten" (p. 266; "a fusion of so many excellent qualities of such diverse arts"). His adoption and frequent use of words like *Zusammenfluss* and *vereinbaren* suggest that he considered it more than just a combination of arts. Because he thought variety was a source of great enjoyment for the audience, he maintained that the more things an opera brought together, the better it was. As he later explained in his preface to *Margaretha*, meaningful diversity was so difficult to achieve that it should be recognized as great and praiseworthy.

Despite his acknowledgment of opera as a different type

of theatrical play, Hamann made no distinction between its purpose and that of spoken comedy or tragedy. He believed they all should present a moral lesson. However, he claimed opera surpassed other theatrical genres in didactic effectiveness because its greater ability to provide pleasure made the lesson more palatable, citing König's *Sancio, Oder die Siegende Grossmuht* (1727) as one of the most impressive examples. In his opinion, *Sancio* proved that an art form with little direct appeal to the mind could convey a moral lesson and, furthermore, that it was better suited to do so than other kinds of plays: "Ich leugne nicht, dass ich die Opera um einige Grad für erlaubter halte als die gemeinen Schauspiele. . . . Ich finde solche augenscheinlich ärgerliche Dinge in zwölff Opern nicht, welche ich in einem Schauspiele zuweilen hören muss" (p. 272; "I do not deny that I consider opera a few degrees more justifiable than the common plays. . . . I do not find in twelve operas such manifestly irritating things that I sometimes have to listen to in one play").

Hamann's attitude toward the rules was quite lenient even if seemingly inconsistent. He recognized a contradiction between theory and practice and tried to reconcile it by allowing for concessions from both. He honored the rules, but he claimed to attach far greater importance to their underlying principles: "Inzwischen ist es freylich nohtwendig, dass man, so viel möglich, wieder die Haupt-Regeln der Schauspiele, welche uns von den Alten übrig geblieben, bey Verfertigung einer Opera nicht sündige. Es gründen sich solche auf die natürliche Einfältigkeit, Ungezwungenheit und Vernunfft; ohne welche alles in der Dicht-Kunst, in der Mahlerey, in der Bau-Kunst &c. &c. Gothisch und ungestallt, verdrüsslich und abgeschmackt ist" (p. 271; "In the meantime, it is certainly necessary when writing an opera that one transgress as little as possible against the principal dramatic rules left us from the ancients. Such rules are based on natural simplicity, inartificiality, and reason, without which everything in poetry, in painting, in architecture, etc., etc. is Gothic, misshapen, unpleasant, and insipid"). Hamann doubted that slavishly observing the traditional dramatic rules made for good opera. He also questioned whether complete observance was necessary just because the rules were reputedly handed down from antiquity: "Dass sich endlich die Verfertiger der Opera nicht genau an die Vorschrifften der Alten, welche sie den Schauspiel-Verfassern vorgeschrieben, binden; das ist die Schuld der Opern-Schreiber. Vielleicht ist es auch nicht nöhtig, dass man den Regeln und Gewohnheiten dieser ehrlichen Leute allzu abergläubisch folget" (pp. 270-271; "It is the fault of opera's manufacturers that they do not adhere closely to the precepts prescribed for playwrights by the ancients. Perhaps it is not even necessary that the rules and customs of these honorable people be followed all too superstitiously"). Purporting to reinterpret the importance of the rules for contemporary theater, Hamann devalued those that directly contradicted his own observations and tastes.

Ludwig Friedrich Hudemann (1703-1770), another acquaintance of both Gottsched and Mattheson, did the same. The results of his thinking appeared in "Von den Vorzügen der Oper vor Tragedien und Comedien," which prefaced his first and only libretto, *Constantinus der Grosse* (1732).[18] Hudemann, who at the time advocated a critical approach based on experience and common sense, rejected the methodology of opera's foes, contending their hyperbolic assertions lacked adequate proof and even contradicted actual conditions. Since he thought Gottsched added to the confusion by dogmatically upholding and disseminating the unsubstantiated objections of Saint Evremond, Boileau, and La Bruyère, he made him the main target. Hudemann, a lawyer by profession, concentrated on Gottsched's treatment of opera in *Versuch einer Critischen Dichtkunst* and systematically tore it apart. He agreed that some contemporary operas lacked "eine edele und rührende Einfalt" (p. 168; "a noble and touching simplicity") because of their mixture of languages as well as their Italianate music, but he disagreed that such faults were generic and thus a reason for condemning the whole idea of opera. Gottsched, he claimed, had failed to realize that there were bound to be qualitative differences not only between individual works but also between specific performances by particular casts. It seemed obvious to Hudemann that textual and musical faults, as well as the ones that derived from bad performances, were superficial and easily removable.

Opera was, he insisted, far superior to the dramas of antiquity because modern German poetry had an inherently more musical rhythm. Although Hudemann respected the ancient Greeks and Romans, he disapproved of admiring them immoderately and regarding them as perfect models for emulation: "Allein so waren ihre Gemüther mit eben den sclavischen Vorurtheilen, die ihnen eine gar zu grosse Ehr-Furcht vor dem Alterthum gebahr, beschweret, mit denen wir uns bis auf diese Stunde, leyder! so starck schleppen" (p. 151; "But so their spirits were encumbered with just those slavish biases, which their inordinately great reverence for antiquity brought forth, biases with which we unfortunately still up to this moment burden ourselves"). Hudemann also explained why he thought opera far surpassed all other contemporary dramatic forms. Its language, he maintained, was neither coarse and vulgar as in comedy, nor pretentious and bombastic as in tragedy. He credited operatic music for that because it demanded "in den Worten eine edele Einfalt" (p. 150; "a noble simplicity in the words"). Another reason he gave for opera's superiority was the great and interesting variety its combination of arts permitted. Clever plots, machines, set changes, and dances in addition to music were what he thought made it so very effective. He also thought opera was much more probable. Because its characters, he explained, were elevated beings existing in a different realm, they never overstepped the boundaries of human possibility as did those in other dramas.

Gottsched's claims about operatic unnaturalness provoked Hudemann to expend a great deal of effort analyzing the question of probability. He first pointed out that all poetry consisted of artificial means which in themselves precluded an exact simulation of nature. Like opera's other defenders in Hamburg, he believed that art would no longer be art if it were exactly like reality. Opera's magical transformations, enchantments, and marvels, he explained, were the kind of fictions used throughout the ages in poetic works: "Werden aber Zaubereyen von geschickten Meistern in eine Oper gebracht, so schaffen sie ja dem Verstande das ihm sehr beliebte Unerwartete und Wunderbare, das man *fictionem* κατ' ἐξοχήν nennen mögte; ob sich zwar noch ein anderes (das keine eigentliche *fictionem* zum Grunde hat) in den Gedanken, und deren Ausdrucke, findet. Denn was sind Zaubereyen in einer Oper anders, als ausnehmende *fictiones poëticae*? es sey nun dass durch Geister, oder Menschen, sich mancherley ausserordentliche Kräfte und Zufälle eräugen" (p. 153; "If magical marvels, however, are presented in an opera by talented masters, they create the unexpected and wondrous that the mind so favors, which might be called fiction par excellence; although there is yet another [which has no actual fiction as a basis] in the ideas and their expression. Then what are magical marvels in an opera other than exceptional poetic fictions, be it that diverse extraordinary powers and events are made visible through spirits or human beings?").

Hudemann defended opera's continuous singing by comparing it to the verse forms used in spoken comedy and tragedy. He found them equally unnatural. Anyone, he maintained, who conversed in such a way in the real world would indeed be strange and abnormal. But, he added, this did not mean they would be strange and abnormal within the framework of a dramatic piece. Improbability resulted when the playwright failed to make them convincing, when the performers lacked talent, or when they disregarded the score and improvised at great length. As long as the opera was good and the performance effective, Hudemann contended, the spectator's reason would permit the deception for the sake of enjoyment: "Es ist dem Verstande angenehm auf eine sinnreiche Art betrogen zu werden; und er zürnet nicht, dass man ihm falsche Personen und Dinge vorbildet, wenn sie ihm Gelegenheit geben, etwas wahres durch sie zu erkennen und sich dabey wegen seiner Einsicht zu ergetzen" (p. 153; "It is pleasant for the intellect to be deceived in an ingenious way. And it does not become angry that artificial persons and things are represented if they give it opportunity to recognize something true and to take delight in the insight").

Hudemann considered Gottsched's reverence for the unities of time and place absurd. He believed they did not make a play more probable or rationally acceptable because place and time in dramatic works were always imaginary anyway. He agreed with Feind that stage sets painted to depict a certain place and illuminations to depict the time of day or night were in themselves make-believe. In Hudemann's opinion, the intellect or rational faculty (*Verstand*) pays no attention to such trifles "wenn nur das übrige ihm einen guten Eindruck verursachet. Denn er weiss mitten unter seinen Ergetzlichkeiten gar wol, dass ihn nichts als Erdichtetes rühret, wie sehr er sich auch bestrebet es für lauter Wahres zu halten. Daher lässet er auch den plötzlichen Zeit-Wechsel zu, ob er ihm gleich, wenn er genau urteilte, ungereimt scheinen würde" (p. 168; "as long as the rest causes a good impression. For it knows, quite well in the midst of such delights that nothing but a fabrication is affecting it, however much it strives to view it as pure truth. Therefore it also allows the abrupt change in time, although that change would appear absurd if judged precisely").

Another point he disputed was the Gottschedian claim about terror and pity (*Schrecken und Mitleid*). With no greater comprehension of Aristotle's explanation of catharsis, Hudemann maintained that opera lost nothing by failing to arouse such uncommendable feelings in its spectators.

They did not, he wrote, appreciate being terrorized, but they might not object to pitying distressed damsels and un-requited lovers. He thought opera accomplished something far more meaningful when it enthralled its spectators by appealing directly to their senses of sight and hearing. Al-though he claimed opera should at least endorse a moral axiom, he did not overemphasize didactic purpose.

The ultimate aim of Hudemann's essay was to justify his venture into libretto writing. Like the other lawyers who de-fended opera, he constructed a relatively airtight case based on the facts as he and his witnesses knew them. His system allowed for no outcome other than opera's acquittal.[19] When Gottsched publicly castigated him for using the wrong system and ignoring the neoclassical code, Hude-mann believed the very foundation of his case was de-stroyed. His conversion to the other system must have come about fairly quickly, for he wrote Gottsched on April 12, 1735 admitting that he had erred in denying the universal validity of neoclassicism.[20] The Leipzig professor, happy about this turn of events, even mentioned in the 1737 edi-tion of *Versuch einer Critischen Dichtkunst* that Hude-mann had yielded to logic and abandoned all desire to defend the insidious opera.[21] Hudemann thereafter emu-lated French drama and translated Racine (1639-1699). His preface to the volume of tragedies he published in 1751, *Diocletianus der Christenverfolger und Phädra*, outlined the dangers of the stage and provided suggestions for its improvement in such a stridently rationalistic way that we would hardly suspect the earlier supporter of opera as the author. Allegiances to certain critical methodologies fre-quently shifted in the first half of the eighteenth century—Hagedorn's change of heart would be another example. Hudemann's complete surrender to Gottsched, however, was a rarity among opera's proponents in Hamburg and else-where.

Johann Friedrich Uffenbach was similarly attacked by Gottsched but refused to surrender. His essay "Von der

Würde derer Singe-Gedichte" (1733) had been carefully formulated after years of reading, libretto writing, and preoccupation with artistic developments.[22] Uffenbach, whom Goethe remembered as a family acquaintance and patron of the arts in Frankfurt am Main, corresponded extensively with artists, performers, directors, and composers, many of whom he got to know on his frequent travels.[23] Like them he objected to Gottsched's condemnation of opera. He intended to prove that it was not only counter-productive but also illogical. His analysis of its methodology is yet another example of how enlightened reason was used to defend a vanishing baroque theatrical form.

After repeating some points made by Mattheson and Hudemann, whose essay he cited as excellent, Uffenbach concentrated on a point that was becoming increasingly important in operatic discussion.[24] He stated that opera met with adverse criticism because it was something so new in the history of poetry that it had no time-honored precedents. Therefore, he continued, critics like Gottsched lacked the proper means for evaluating it and simply closed their minds to its accomplishments as a modern art form completely unknown to antiquity. Uffenbach considered their system, in which the number and kinds of genres were predetermined, not only foolish but also potentially detrimental to artistic progress. He thought it would be better if "alle Künste und Wissenschafften immer wüchsen, und wir das sogenannte Meisterstück menschlicher Erfindungs-Kunst, den Zusammenfluss aller poetischen und musicalischen Schönheiten, den Sammel-Platz aller sinnlichen Ergötzlichkeiten nicht verlöhren oder untergehen liessen" (sig. c6ᵛ; "all arts and sciences always grew, and we would not lose or let perish the so-called masterpiece of human ingenuity, the fusion of all poetic and musical beauties, the assembly place of all sensuous delights").

Opera, Uffenbach explained, was a theatrical work in which music and poetry collaborated with other arts in order to form a synthesis. He concurred with Mattheson that

they were sisters who should cooperate rather than compete
with each other. Uffenbach believed the librettist had to
maintain the integrity of his own art while at the same time
trying to understand music's needs and, if need be, compro-
mising for the sake of the work as a whole. The composer,
he added, should be committed to the same goal and should
never try to steal the spotlight for his art.

Uffenbach considered this fusion of the arts so new and
different that he saw no reason why it should follow rules
formulated for older genres. Furthermore, he claimed his
thorough investigations of the tradition from Aristotle to
the seventeenth-century French had unearthed no proof
that the rules were valid even for the traditional genres.
Consequently he refused to apply to opera the standards set
up by any authorities, whether Aristotle or Gottsched: "ist
es aber nur darum recht, weil es Aristoteles Praeceptor-
mässig befohlen, so verbindet mich der blinde Gehorsam so
wenig dazu, als unsere heutige Welt-Weisheit seinen ver-
legenen Spinnen-Genisten überhaupt den Staub-Besen gegeben" (sig. b4^v; "If it is right, however, only because Aristotle preceptorially ordered it, then blind obedience binds
me to it as little as our current world philosopher has considered taking the dust broom to his confused nest of cob-
webs"). Blind obedience to rules was also objectionable to
him because he thought that often the result was not excellent. This, he pointed out, was best exemplified in the
poetry of Horace, for there was often a wide discrepancy between his theoretical regularity and his actual practices:
"Horatius beschriebe nach Anleitung alter Vorgänger die
Regeln der Dicht-Kunst, und triebe solche auch mit mehr-
mahliger Widersprechung seiner eigenen Poesien sehr hoch,
verschiedene seiner Nachfolger aber dichteten eben so gut,
ja zuweilen besser als er, ohne sich so gar genau an den
eigenmächtigen Gesetzgeber zu binden: nichts desto weniger
wurden, und werden ihre Schriften noch gelobet" (sig. a4^v;
"With the guidance of older predecessors Horace described
the rules of poetry and promoted them very far, even with

the frequent contradiction of his own poems. Various of his successors, however, wrote poetry just as well, sometimes even better than he without tying themselves down too closely to unauthorized lawgivers: nevertheless their writings were and still are lauded"). Uffenbach anticipated later critics like Lessing when he urged opera's opponents to realize that it was not strict adherence to predetermined rule that made the drama of antiquity so great: "Gesetzt auch, sie hätten die theatralischen Regeln so gar genau nicht beobachtet, so hätten sie das, was wir bey manchem alten Poeten sehen, gethan" (sig. b2r; "Even given the case that they had not observed the theatrical rules so very exactly, they would have done that which we see in many an ancient poet").

Uffenbach acknowledged the greatness of ancient art but disavowed slavish imitation of it because he believed that contemporary art could make worthwhile contributions on its own. He maintained that it was headstrong and foolish to judge either one by the standards of the other. If modern poetry, he explained, were criticized strictly according to the poetic rules of antiquity, then many things of exceptional quality would have to be rejected. One of them would be rhyme, and another opera. With this observation, Uffenbach brought together two closely related critical topics that were to be even more carefully scrutinized by subsequent generations who were interested in artistic media and verisimilitude.[25]

Uffenbach's own interpretation of verisimilitude resembled that of opera's other defenders but went a few steps further. He conceded that opera seemed highly improbable and unnatural when compared to reality. However, he suggested making the same comparison with the drama of antiquity, which critics somehow held up as the epitome of naturalness and probability. If they would do that honestly, he surmised, they would find it just as unnatural. This was so, according to Uffenbach, because all theatrical forms were hypothetical, a word he used throughout the essay to designate something that had to be assumed without proof.[26] Naturalistic forms, he implied, could be no more natural or real than those based in pure fancy. He even suggested—before Johann Elias Schlegel—that the greater the divergence from nature the better: "Alle sind Gedichte, das ist, Erfindungen, Vorgebungen &c. Schweiffet nun ein Poet in seiner Bemühung eine Geschichte recht natürlich vorzustellen, gegen die Wahrscheinlichkeit so übernatürlich aus, ja gereichet dieses ihm vielmehr zum Lobe als einem Vorwurff, und bemäntelt man es alsdann mit der so genann-ten hypothetischen Wahrscheinlichkeit, warum soll es in denen Sing-Gedichten allein eine Schande seyn?" (sig. c^{v}; "All of them are poems, that is, inventions, fabrications, etc. When the poet, in his endeavor to present a story right naturally, transgresses against probability so unnaturally, it does him much more credit than blame; and when one thereupon disguises it with the so-called hypothetical proba-bility, why should it be a disgrace only in musical theatrical poems?"). He concluded that it was logically inconsistent to reject only opera for a reason that held true for all the poetic arts.

While giving his views on the nature of art, Uffenbach referred to man's aesthetic reaction. With words like those of Feind, he explained that "jeder, der in eine Opera gehet, zum voraus weiss, dass er ein Gedichte sehen werde, so kan ihm auf seinem Platze sitzenbleibende nicht so ungereimt oder abentheuerlich fürkommen, wenn er in Gedancken aus einer Zeit in die folgende, von einem Lande in ein anderes derselben Nachbarschafft ohne sorgliche Gefahr versetzet wird" (sig. b4^{v}; "everybody who goes to an opera knows in advance that he will see a poem, thus it cannot seem so absurd or fantastic to him, who is sitting in his seat, when he is in thought transferred out of one time into the following and out of one land into another in the same vicinity without worrisome danger"). The intellect, Uffen-bach continued, obviously recognized incongruities but will-ingly adapted itself to the new order of things: "Mögte

man aber fragen: was kriegt der Verstand dabey zu gedencken? so erwiedert man: dasjenige, was er bey An-
schauung aller Künste zu dencken hat. Was bekommt doch
der Verstand bey dem Betrachten einer schönen verfertigten
Statue, eines annehmlichen Gartens, eines künstlichen Ge-
mäldes oder Gebäudes, einer meisterlichen Gold-Arbeit zu
gedencken? Dasjenige, dass es schön und hoch zu schätzen
sey, gleichwie es in allen Künsten auf kein anderes Dencken
angesehen ist" (sig. c3^r; "If one would like to ask: what
does the rational faculty thereby get to think about? one
answers thus: that which it has to think about while viewing all the arts. What does the rational faculty receive to
think about while viewing a beautifully executed statue, a
pleasant garden, an artful picture or building, a masterful
work in gold? This, that it is beautiful and to be esteemed
highly, just as all the arts are intended for no other thinking"). Later German writers who deliberated these operatic
questions continued to call upon the plastic arts to prove
that no art could be an exact imitation of nature because of
its very conventions and media.

Johann Andreas Fabricius (1696-1769), who is not to be
mistaken for the Hamburg writer with the same initials and
surname, was the kind of average scholar that abounded in
the early eighteenth century. Although he polemicized
against some of his fellow professors in Braunschweig, he
did not become involved in the battle over opera, and he
did not make any striking contributions to German philosophy, literature, criticism, or music. No one ever mentions him. I do so because of his poetic manual *Versuche
in der Teutschen Rede- Dicht- und Sprachkunst* (1737).
Such manuals, whether written in the seventeenth or eighteenth century, were by definition repositories of traditional thought. This one was no exception. The treatment
of opera it presented for all those students who might be
subjected to it summarized succinctly the views on verisimilitude upheld by Hudemann, Uffenbach, and the Hamburg patriots.

Fabricius classified opera, along with the fable, emblem, novel, pastoral, heroic epic, and spoken drama, as the most magnificent kind of poetry. It deserves that place, he explained, "weil sie einen hohen grad des dichtens erfodert, nemlich der sachen und umstände, mit welchen die sachen vorgestellet werden" (p. 9; "because it requires a high degree of poetic fabrication, namely, of the things and circumstances with which matters are represented"). In contending that its elevated ideas and subjects necessitated the very highest verse style, he borrowed from conventional rhetoric but outstripped Neumeister who assigned it the middle style. Fabricius' system, which was organized according to the degree of poetic fabrication (grad des dichtens), gave opera a higher rank than spoken tragedy.

He believed its continuous singing justified that rank. To dispute those who disagreed he examined the concept of verisimilitude: "Wenn man sagt, es sei wider die wahrscheinlichkeit, was man reden solte zu singen, so antworte ich, dass es gar falsch sei, dass die vorgestellten dinge auf dem schauplaze und bei lichtern geschehen sind, und doch erzürnen wir uns nicht darüber, wenn man sie also vorstellet. Schauspiele und opern sind begebenheiten aus einer andern möglichen welt, dergleichen man, wie bei den fabeln geschicht, wol dichten kan" (p. 36; "When one says it is contrary to probability to sing what should be spoken, I answer that it is completely false that the represented things happen on the stage and by candlelight, and nevertheless we do not get irritated when they are thusly presented. Plays and operas are events out of another possible world, of such kind one can fabricate, as in fables"). In distinguishing probability from possibility, he relied on his philosophical training and borrowed ideas from Leibniz and Wolff. According to Fabricius, the probable was whatever agreed with logic in all aspects, while the possible was merely whatever had no contradictions in and of itself (p. 17). His manual burdened its students with much deadwood, but it did transmit to them at least one seminal idea: art consists of events or situations out of another world that is governed by its own kind of logic. Those who subsequently wrote about opera, rhyme, or the fable cultivated that idea.

RATIONALISTIC REFORMERS

Gottsched's condemnation of opera also provoked antagonism from those who endorsed his attempt to dignify German theater with rationalistic principles. His stubborn refusal to admit that it was even possible for opera to have artistic merit forced many of his admirers to clarify their own understanding of the neoclassical code as well as their concept of musical theater. While rejecting his literal interpretation of generic purity, they suggested reforms that would bring operatic practices closer to the kind of regular drama he sanctioned. In so doing, they perpetuated the suggestions made earlier by König—and eventually carried out by Gluck.

Johann Adolph Scheibe (1708-1776), a professional musician who affirmed opera's potentialities, was so profoundly influenced by Gottschedian principles as a student in Leipzig that he spent almost his entire life adapting them for Germany's musical stage. His interest in operatic matters increased in Hamburg, where he arrived at the time the theater at the Gänsemarkt no longer needed any composers. The reason for its downfall seemed obvious to him as he studied its historical background and the disputes it had engendered. His studies of the past, observations of the present, and hopes for the future were all included in the journal he published there from 1737 to 1740, *Der Critische Musikus*.

Its first few issues were as patriotic as any of the other Hamburg writings. They urged the abandonment of foreign operatic styles, which Scheibe considered despicable and unnatural, and the cultivation of indigenous ones according to the principles of reason and good taste. As though poking fun at local efforts to adapt Euripidean drama for opera, this disciple of Gottsched wrote on March 9, 1737: "Es waren aber die Trauerspiele und Lustspiele der alten Griechen und Römer von weit anderer Beschaffenheit, als unsere Opern bisher gewesen sind, die doch eine Nachahmung der alten Schauspiele heissen wollen. Die überbliebenen Stücke der Alten beweisen unwidersprechlich, dass ihre Dichter edler und erhabener gedacht haben, als heut zu Tage unsere meisten Operndichter."[27] ("The tragedies and comedies of the ancient Greeks and Romans were of a vastly different character from what our operas, which claim to be imitations of the ancient plays, have hitherto been. The surviving works of the ancients prove incontrovertibly that their poets thought more nobly and more loftily than most of our librettists nowadays.") Most contemporary librettists, he explained, were inferior talents whose artistic ignorance and moral indifference produced the shamefully coarse and vile texts that led to the decline of German opera. The one exception Scheibe mentioned was König whose librettos he cited here and throughout the journal as sublime examples worthy of emulation.

Several issues later, on May 28, 1737, Scheibe blamed capricious, egotistical performers as well as careless composers and incompetent librettists for the sorry state of musical theatrical affairs (p. 74). Controlling performers, which has been problematic throughout theatrical history, remained one of his most serious concerns. In the preface to *Thusnelde*, the libretto he wrote in 1749 to demonstrate good operatic taste, he even outlined the means he thought would be most successful. He suggested that the theater poet preface each of his librettos with explanatory comments about the particular rules he had observed. That, Scheibe believed, would prevent singers, musicians, directors, and stagehands from giving a distorted presentation of the work and, furthermore, would enable critics to judge the work more easily and fairly (pp. 87-88).

Scheibe's other comments on May 28, 1737 indicate that he strove to find the means for regulating and systematizing

all the variables inherent in operatic productions, including its spectacular components (*die Pracht der Schaubühne*). Those components, he contended, would never
have become the major objection of opera's foes if they had
been used naturally and reasonably. He asserted that Postel,
Feind, and Hunold had been given to Lohenstein-type pom-
posity, unnaturalness, and outlandishness only because they
had lived in an era that knew nothing of good taste or
reason. Although they might have been much better in a
different era, Scheibe added, it could not be denied "dass
alle ihre Opern mehr gute Eigenschaften besitzen als alle
andere Singspiele, die ungefähr in den letzten zwanzig
Jahren, vor dem gänzlichen Verfalle derselben, auf der hamburgischen Schaubühne sind vorgestellet worden" (p. 70;
"that all of their operas possess more good characteristics
than all the other musical plays which have been performed
on the Hamburg stage in the last twenty years or so preceding its complete downfall"). Scheibe thought contemporary
composers were equally at fault, but he did not criticize any
of his colleagues by name. He merely suggested that they
carefully study Horace, apply his rules, and avoid "so viel
abgeschmackte Einfälle" (p. 73; "so many absurd notions").

Like other disciples of Gottsched, Scheibe interpreted art
as a rational exercise comparable to other branches of
knowledge. He believed it was governed by certain absolute
rules, which had been clearly defined and categorized so
that they could be studied and learned. François Hédelin,
Abbé d'Aubignac (1604-1676) had provided what he considered the best codification in *Pratique du Théâtre* (1657).
Scheibe merely transferred d'Aubignac's neoclassical code of
rules for spoken drama to opera. Careful observation of that
code, Scheibe contended, would eliminate opera's baroque
artificialities, absurdities, and complexities and make it a
probable imitation of nature that tastefully exemplified virtue rewarded and vice punished.

Many issues of *Der Critische Musikus* were devoted to
Scheibe's ideas on reforming opera according to the neo-

classical dramatic rules. The one that appeared on January 7, 1738, the year the theater at the Gänsemarkt closed down, presented a summation of those ideas. In this issue Scheibe stressed opera's dramatic essence and condemned the Hamburg tradition of adapting epics and novels for the operatic stage: "es war etwas ganz gemeines, die spanischen oder arabischen Romanen auf den Opernbühnen vorzustellen" (p. 224; "It was a very common thing to produce Spanish or Arabian novels on the operatic stages"). He thought such "verkehrte Träumereyen und Don Quischottenmässige Schwärmereyen" (p. 224 "perverse reveries and Don Quixote-like ravings") represented the very worst taste. The liberal tendency that allowed such taste became the object of his disdain and also his satirical wit. Scheibe's satire of his Hamburg contemporaries provides important information about the nature and popularity of their point of view. It shows that the rejection of rules and the assertion of individuality were not merely isolated ideas contained in the writings of a few unconventional critics but that they were part of a widespread and deeply embedded critical attitude. Furthermore, it helps to explain why Bodmer was so fiercely opposed to the circle gathered around Brockes. And it also helps to explain, in part at least, the failure in Hamburg of the stringent reforms Gottsched hoped would be carried out. Instead of Frenchified drama, Hamburg audiences preferred what they considered more stageworthy plays, like the Neuber acting company's rendition of the German tragedy, *Das ruchlose Leben und erschreckliche Ende des weltbekannten Ertzzauberers Dr. Johann Fausten*.[28] The words and phrases Scheibe mockingly quoted from his imaginary opponents anticipate the slogans and catchwords of the *Sturm und Drang* writers, who rose to prominence in German literature and criticism in the 1770s. Scheibe wrote:

> Man achtet in keiner Schreibart die Regeln weniger, als in der theatralischen. Es ist darinnen so sehr zur Mode geworden, eine selbst beliebige Freyheit anzuwenden,

ohne einige andere Absichten dabey zu haben, als nur seinem eigenen unumschränkten Willen zu folgen, der sich durch niemanden einschränken, oder sich etwa gewisse nothwendige Vortheile und Eigenschaften der Sachen vorschreiben lässt.

Regeln! was Regeln? spricht Schmirander. Was sollen die Schulfüchsereyen? die binden uns, und setzen unsern Gedanken gewisse Grenzen, die wir nicht überschreiten sollen. Sie machen uns zu Sklaven, und berauben uns der Freyheit, alles aufzuschreiben, was uns einfällt, und was wir für schön halten. Wenn man sich darnach bequemen sollte, so würde mancher vortrefflicher Einfall weg bleiben; wir würden auch bey weitem nicht so viel arbeiten können, als wir wohl ohne Regeln vermögend sind. Es sind also die Regeln nur Kinder des Eigensinns, welche die Thorheit zu Nachfolgern haben.

Was ist es nöthig, spricht ein anderer Held, dass man sich mit der Beobachtung der Regeln martern soll? Die Erfindung ist uns ja angebohren, und wir sollten uns freuen, wenn wir nur vielerley Gedanken hervorzubringen fähig sind. Es kömmt ja nicht darauf an, ob eben die Worte ausgedrucket sind, oder nicht; wenn nur die Melodie feurig und lebhaft ist.* (pp. 219-220)

---

* In no kind of writing does one respect the rules less than in the theatrical. It has become very much the fashion therein to make use of an arbitrary freedom without having any other intentions than following one's own unlimited will, which will be curbed by no one, nor dictated to by certain necessary interests and characteristics of matters.

Rules! What rules? says Scribbler. What is the use of those pedantries? They bind us and set certain limits for our thoughts, which we are not to overstep. They make slaves of us, rob us of the freedom to write everything that occurs to us and that we consider beautiful. If one were to comply with them, many a capital idea would be left out; we would not be able to produce by far as much as we can without rules. The rules are thus only children of caprice, who have folly as followers.

Why is it necessary, says another hero, for one to torment oneself with observing the rules? Our ingenuity is inborn, and we should re-

The following year, on March 17, 1739, *Der Critische Musikus* tried to underscore opera's legitimacy by codifying its rules and finding a place for it within the rationalists' system of arts. Instead of categorizing it as a specific kind under the greater generic heading of drama, as others were to do in the next decade, Scheibe made it a separate genre that could be subdivided into its own clearly defined dramatic kinds: "wenn das Singespiel aus lauter grossen u. erhabenen Personen besteht, so ist es entweder ein Freuden- oder Trauerspiel. Es hat aber allemal eine grosse Gleichheit mit der ordentlichen Tragödie. Besteht es aus mittlern Personen, so ist es insgemein ein Scherzspiel, und hat alsdann eine grosse Aehnlichkeit mit der ordentlichen Comödie, die moralisch, oder satyrisch ist. Ist es endlich ein Hirtengedichte, so hat man darauf zu sehen, ob der Inhalt scherzhaft, oder ernsthaft, traurig, oder freudig ist, imgleichen, ob die darinnen vorkommenden Personen wirkliche Schäfer und Schäferinnen, oder nur erdichtete, oder verstellte sind" (p. 276; "When the musical play consists of great and lofty persons, it is a play with either a happy or tragic ending. It always, however, has a great similarity with regular tragedy. When it consists of average persons [burghers], it is usually a comic play and then bears a great resemblance to regular comedy, which is moral or satirical. When it is a pastoral, one has to see whether the content is playful or serious, sad or happy, and at the same time, whether the persons appearing in it are real shepherds and shepherdesses, or only fabricated, or disguised ones").

This classification according to content and social class resembles the treatment of drama in baroque poetic handbooks so closely that one wonders why modern scholars like Torben Krogh and Eugen Reichel have called Scheibe's operatic theory revolutionary and modern.[29] He was not the first to reject the Italianate musical style or defend the

---

joice when we are able to bring forth many kinds of ideas. It does not matter whether the words are expressed precisely or not, as long as the melody is ardent and lively.

harmony of the German language. And even his application of the neoclassical dramatic code with its reverence for reason and good taste was something Bressand, Besser, and König had suggested, if not systematized, earlier. Perhaps his theory of opera has been confused with his theory of incidental music for spoken drama.[30]

Scheibe stopped publishing his journal in 1740, when he received the appointment from the governor of Holstein that eventually developed into a position as Royal Danish Kapellmeister. Danish patronage of opera had originated in the previous century with German companies which, visiting there as early as 1663, laid the foundation for future developments. They stimulated interest in musical theater as they knew it, and as a result, Danish versions of German librettos began to appear. Martin Opitz's *Judith*, for example, was published in Danish in 1666. Around the turn of the century, interest in opera increased still further with news of the flourishing theater in nearby Hamburg. German artists were invited to perform, and many accepted. Among them was Reinhard Keiser who directed a German troupe there in 1717 and again in 1722. Operas were prohibited during the reign of the pietistically oriented Christian VI, but the restrictions were lifted when Frederick V came to the throne in 1746.[31] Under the more liberal monarch, literary endeavors were revived, and a Danish society of fine arts was founded. Part of this tendency was the encouragement of German-Danish cultural relations which by mid-eighteenth century reached a high point. Scheibe was not the only German with operatic interests to find a haven in Denmark around this time. Johann Elias Schlegel arrived in 1745 and remained there until his death, and Gluck spent the winter of 1748-1749 in Copenhagen as conductor at the theater.

Copenhagen became one of the major centers of German cultural activity. The man largely responsible was Johann Hartwig Ernst von Bernstorff (1712-1772), a leading statesman in the Danish government and a patron of the arts.

Bernstorff hoped to further cultural developments in Denmark by encouraging immigration of German intellectuals. His offers of support did not go unheeded, for many Germans emigrated to the Danish capital in the 1750s and 1760s. Common interests led to their association in what came to be called the Copenhagen circle. One such interest was music, and Scheibe, who had preceded them, joined them in its cultivation. He composed for Heinrich Wilhelm von Gerstenberg (1737-1823), with whom he resided for some time. He supported the attempt to develop genuinely Germanic music that subsequently stimulated Klopstock to experiment with *Bardieten*, dramatizations of the musical form thought to be of ancient Nordic origin. And he continued to reiterate his earlier arguments in defending the possibility of musical drama.

Lorenz Christoph Mizler von Kolof (1711-1778) shared many of Scheibe's operatic views although he disliked him personally. While a student in Leipzig, Mizler attended Gottsched's lectures on poetry and at the same time studied under Johann Sebastian Bach. He became acquainted with Bach's friend, the organist and musical lexicographer Johann Gottfried Walther (1684-1748), and with others who hoped to restore music to its rightful place among the scientific disciplines. Mizler's zealous attempt to secure a mathematical foundation for music and make it once more a subject for university faculties of philosophy got him a Leipzig professorship, but it incurred the animosity of Mattheson who frequently polemicized against him.[32]

One of Mizler's more important critical endeavors was the *Neu-Eröffnete Musikalische Bibliothek*, an annotated anthology of articles on and related to music. He began it in 1736 during his Leipzig years and published it irregularly thereafter until 1754, including in it articles originally printed between approximately 1650 and 1750. Although Mizler claimed he aspired to make public all the pros and cons on the subject of opera, the predominance of articles representing the contra position indicates that he wanted to use his footnotes as vehicles for expressing his own critical views. His notes consistently defended the idea of an opera reformed according to rationalistic dramatic principles. They also treated music and poetry as sister arts, repeatedly drawing analogies between them and explaining their essence as the imitation of nature. In a 1738 note to an article by Gottsched, whom he considered a modern Opitz and regenerator of German poetry, he wrote: "Ja die Verwandschaft dieser zwey Wissenschaften ist so gar gross, dass auch die Regeln dieser in jener, und jener Regeln in dieser können gebrauchet werden. Kurz, sie haben viele Regeln mit einander gemein."[33] ("The consanguinity of these two sciences is so very great that the rules of the former can even be used in the latter and vice versa. In short, they share many rules with each other.") The interrelationships of the arts and the importance of opera became such fixed ideas in Mizler's critical theory that he even rendered Horatian precepts with the word "opera" in his prose translation of the *Ars Poetica* (1752).

Ludwig's "Versuch eines Beweises, dass ein Singespiel oder eine Oper nicht gut seyn könne" provided Mizler ample opportunity for comment when he included it in 1740. Opera would be as great as comedy and tragedy, he claimed, if all the obstacles to rational thought were removed. By that he meant avoiding artificial machines, observing the dramatic rules, and composing scores that reinforced the didactic purpose: "Denn wenn eine Oper lehren kan, so kan sie auch die Leidenschaften reinigen."[34] ("For, when an opera can instruct, it can also purge the passions.") Mizler objected to Ludwig because he believed he had, unlike Voltaire's teacher, the Jesuit Charles Porée (1675-1741), whose operatic article followed in the same issue, mistaken current abuses for inherent generic faults.

Gottsched, Mizler discovered, insisted on sustaining this kind of methodological error. His refusal to admit the possibility of a satisfactory opera when Mizler wrote him in 1740 provoked severely critical footnotes to "Gedanken von

Opern," the operatic section of *Versuch einer Critischen Dichtkunst* published in the collection in 1742. Mizler not only challenged his teacher's hypothesis, he also attacked his reliance on French authorities. Saint Evremond's personal prejudices against opera, he explained, had so beclouded his perception that he became irrational and threw out the baby with the bath. Another of Mizler's notes disputing Gottsched pointed out the inappropriateness of condemning opera because it was an art form unknown to the ancients: "Hätten die alten Griechen und Lateiner schon Opern gehabt, sie würden gewis zu unsern Zeiten nicht so angefochten worden seyn. Weil es aber was neues ist, so sind den Kennern der theatralischen Regeln so gleich die geringsten Kleinigkeiten in die Augen gefallen, worzu noch das Unglück gekommen, dass so wohl die Poeten als Componisten, so die ersten Opern gemachet, wenig Regeln, wie man der Natur nachahmen solle, verstanden."[35] ("If the ancient Greeks and Romans had already had operas, they would certainly not have been so attacked in our times. Because opera is, however, something new, the smallest details have caught the attention of the experts of the theatrical rules. There was the additional misfortune that the poets as well as composers who produced the first operas understood few rules about how nature should be imitated.")

In notes to the preceding article, Gottsched's translation of Lodovico Muratori's (1672-1750) condemnation of opera, Mizler had already suggested a more historically relevant approach by questioning the value of ancient drama as a modern critical standard. These notes imply that he espoused neoclassicism because of its rationalistic basis rather than because of its admiration for the Greeks and Romans: "Niemand wird zwar läugnen können, dass nicht die Alten bisweilen verschiedene Handlungen der Menschen singend vorgetragen, und drammatische Aufzüge öffters angebracht; Allein ihre Musik, ihre Schaubühne, ihre Aufzüge selbsten, waren, wie bekandt, von den unsrigen ziemlich unterschieden. Zweifels ohne haben sie auch öfters gefehlet . . . so wird es wohl am besten seyn, wenn man bey der Untersuchung unserer Opern, gar nicht an das dencket, was die Alten ähnliches mit solchen gehabt haben, indem es gar nichts zur Sache hilfft."[36] ("Nobody will be able to deny that the ancients did not occasionally present human actions through singing and often execute dramatic acts. But their music, stage, and even acts were, as is known, quite different from ours. Undoubtedly they also often erred . . . thus the best thing to do when examining our operas will be not to think about whatever the ancients had similar to them, since that contributes absolutely nothing to the matter.")

Mizler strove for years to prove that Gottsched had erred in his condemnation of opera. In so doing, he never disputed his teacher's rules for spoken drama; he merely superimposed them in toto on opera in order to make it over into musical drama. He departed from Gottsched's theory radically, however, when he analyzed probability in order to defend opera's continuous singing. One of the notes to the Muratori translation seems to indicate that he agreed with Hudemann and Uffenbach, whose essays he subsequently published:

eine Nachahmung, die der Natur vollkommen ähnlich ist, heisset keine Nachahmung mehr, sondern ist eine gleiche natürliche Handlung. Der Begriff der Nachahmung bringt es also schon mit sich, dass nicht alles im eigentlichen Verstande natürlich seyn kann. Bey dem allerbesten Trauerspiele bleiben noch viele Unwahrscheinlichkeiten, die aber leicht zu dulten und nicht zu heben sind, übrig. Z.E. es ist nicht wahrscheinlich, dass auf einem so engen Raum, als die Schaubühne ist, verschiedene Personen eine öffeters höchst wichtige Sache binnen 3. Stunden völlig zu Ende bringen. Es ist nicht wahrscheinlich, dass ein groser Herr in so kurtzer Zeit eine Armee versammeln, ins Feld stellen. . . . Doch dul-tet man dieses alles, warum wolte man denn auch nicht zugeben, dass man Personen mitten in ihren Beschäfftigungen singend auffüh014ret, da doch solches noch darzu nicht so gar unwahrscheinlich, sondern in der Natur gegründet ist?*[37]

Despite their derivative nature, Mizler's writings show how opera helped to induce closer scrutiny of authoritarian criticism. Even those of Gottsched's followers who wished to defend opera were forced to come to grips with questions about the nature of art neither asked nor answered by the code. They by no means wished to invalidate the code, but they did seek to adjust it so that opera would fit. This in itself indicates a change in focus, and once that change started, there was no stopping it. There were already too many nonaligned German writers who were strengthening the liberal critical tradition that had persisted uninterruptedly since the Renaissance and determined the attitude in Hamburg.

---

* An imitation that is completely similar to nature is no longer called an imitation but is a similarly natural action. The concept of imitation means that not everything can be natural in the true sense. In the very best tragedies there still remain many improbabilities that are easy to tolerate and not to be removed. For example, it is not probable that on such a narrow space at the stage various persons fully complete an often highly important matter within three hours. It is not probable that a great lord rallies an army in such a short time, takes to the battlefield. . . . But one tolerates all this, so why won't one then also allow that persons be presented singing in the midst of their pursuits, since such is moreover not so completely improbable but founded in nature?

FIVE

TRADITION, TRANSFORMATION, AND TRANSITION

OPERATIC IMITATION OF NATURE

THE 1740s are best characterized by the words "tradition," "transformation," and "transition." The Holy Roman Empire was still a political entity consisting of numerous free cities and territorial states with different laws on taxation, toleration, conscription, and censorship. A new threat to its already rather weakened viability came when Frederick the Great (1712-1786) ascended the Prussian throne in 1740 and challenged Maria Theresa's (1717-1780) power. Despite the years of war their political ambitions produced, both favored Italian opera and greatly honored the foreigners who served as their court poets, composers, and singers. Sovereigns of lesser states joined them in the cultivation of theater in the grandest of manners. Many of them commissioned new buildings just to suit the sights and sounds of their opera ensembles. Giuseppe Galli-Bibiena (1696-1756), whose father and uncle had designed distinctive settings for innumerable Viennese operas, perpetuated their dynamic baroque visual stage tradition in Vienna, Dresden, Bayreuth, and Berlin during the last decades of his life. The ruling princes were not alone in demanding ever grander operas in Italian. The burghers of once flourishing German operatic centers like Hamburg and Leipzig also demanded them. Except for a few isolated instances, musical theater in the German language was completely supplanted by its Italian counterpart in the 1740s.

In the same decade that German baroque opera vanished, however, German spoken drama began to feel new impulses. The emergence of aggressive native-born talent

128

was responsible. While Gottsched recognized some of the younger writers, he mistakenly thought they could be made to adhere to his prescriptions. They may have assimilated some of his intentions and goals, but they rejected most of his means as the kind of impractical, pedantic suggestions that only scholars divorced from reality could make. Caroline Neuber (1697-1760), manager of the troupe Gottsched hoped would carry out his theatrical reforms, was too great an actress and too wise in matters concerning living theater to remain his pawn or even agent for very long. She was only too happy to see Hanswurst rescued from the banishment Gottsched had ordered for him in 1737. She was also happy to include in her 1740s repertoire dramas by promising young playwrights like Johann Elias Schlegel and Christian Fürchtegott Gellert (1715-1769). It was in 1747, however, that she unwittingly made one of her greatest contributions to German theatrical history. She agreed to give two stage-struck Leipzig students free tickets in exchange for translating several French dramas. The translations Gotthold Ephraim Lessing and Christian Felix Weisse submitted revealed the kind of shrewd theatrical sense that Caroline Neuber understood and admired. In January of the following year (1748) Lessing's comedy, *Der junge Gelehrte*, was successfully staged under her aegis.

In 1740 another actor, Konrad Ekhof (1720-1778), began a career that was also to prove influential for the history of German theater. This native of Hamburg, where interest in histrionic techniques and styles had persisted since the seventeenth century, strove to combine literary value and audience appeal without losing artistic integrity on the one hand or theatrical vitality on the other. The idea of an academy to train actors had been germinating for some time. Ekhof, a friend of Weisse and an admirer of Johann Elias Schlegel and Lessing, was the one to bring it into reality thirteen years after his career had begun.

Many other ideas that had been germinating for a long time were cultivated during the 1740s. By the end of the decade some of them had already reached maturity and could be harvested to provide nourishment and energy for the future. The beginning saw Bodmer's treatise on the wondrous (1740), Gottsched's *Deutsche Schaubühne* (1740-1745), and an upsurge in translating activity. Bilingual editions of Longinus appeared (1738, 1742). Kaspar Wilhelm von Borck (1704-1747) published a German translation of Shakespeare's *Julius Caesar* (1741). And Mattheson, who had already translated Daniel Defoe's *Moll Flanders* (1723) and Elizabeth Rowe's *Friendship in Death* (1734), responded to Brockes's encouragement by producing a German rendition of Samuel Richardson's *Pamela* (1742-1743). It was the middle of the decade, 1744 to be exact, when Mattheson's *Die neueste Untersuchung der Singspiele* appeared. That same year the Leipzig intellectuals, who either ignored or passively resisted Gottsched, founded the journal that has since been known as the *Bremer Beiträge*. Gellert's *Fabeln und Erzählungen* (1746) contributed as much to the discussion of the fable as his *Schwedische Gräfin* (1747) did to discussions about the novel and the mood of sentimentality that was becoming pervasive. The publications that brought the decade to a close increased the excitement that had been generated and indicated a promising future: the opening three cantos of Klopstock's *Messias* (1748), the first of Lessing's *Beyträge zur Historie und Aufnahme des Theaters* (1750), and Baumgarten's *Aesthetica* (1750).

In the midst of this profusion of extraordinarily diverse ideas, styles, and techniques, there was growing historical awareness and continuing confrontation with the past. No matter what generation they belonged to—that of grandfather, father, or son—the German writers active in the 1740s did not view their past as a burdensome prison from which they had to escape. And least of all would they have wanted to escape their own past only to be yoked slavishly to the kind of foreign ideology Gottsched upheld. Whether it was because of Gottsched's belated neoclassicism or their ruling sovereign's lack of patronage and support, they felt stimulated to study their own rich heritage, seek their Germanic identity, and sort out their indigenous resources. While they examined, borrowed, and assimilated whatever foreign fashions were congenial to their interests, they investigated German medieval poetry, seventeenth-century drama, and Nordic as well as classical antiquities. They also continued to question what they liked and disliked. Opera became one of their important topics because it represented a convergence of so many trends and aspirations.

For the German writers in Frankfurt, Braunschweig, Copenhagen, and Hamburg who published operatic defenses in 1745, the year after Mattheson's *Untersuchung*, opera could be used to signify art per se. Joachim Christoph Nemeitz (1679-1753) was of the same generation as Mattheson. He had studied philosophy and law at the University of Rostock before becoming a private tutor, councilor, and then journalist in Paris and other European capitals. While in Frankfurt he did research for *Vernünfftige Gedanken Uber allerhand Historische/ Critische und Moralische Materien* (1739-1745). The sixth and last part contained a history of European musical theater with a short bibliography of critical works, among them, those of Elmenhorst and Feind (pp. 162-182). It also included Nemeitz's defense of contemporary actor-singers as virtuosos, whose life style and morality, he believed, had improved so much since late antiquity that excommunication and disenfranchisement were no longer warranted (pp. 182-188).

The origins of modern musical plays, Nemeitz contended along with Claude François Menestrier (1631-1705)—and not altogether incorrectly if we consider the evolution of European drama—lay in the religious services and other devotions of the early medieval church. He surmised that the tradition might have begun with the Jews, but he did not pursue it any further. He preferred to credit the Italians with having brought opera to its highest level of sophistication. Nemeitz claimed its ethically beneficial effect on modern audiences had motivated him to refute those who argued for its abolishment. His ideal judge of opera was someone familiar with its practice as well as its history and theory. He believed that person would not fail to accept its continuous singing as a necessary convention. The explanation he gave of operatic probability resembled Mattheson's more closely than Uffenbach's:

> Ich habe zuweilen mit Verwunderung angehört, wie Leute, die sonst nicht unvernünfftig sind, von diesen Schauspielen ein so gar verkehrt Urtheil haben fällen können. Opern sind Schauspiele, sprechen sie, worinnen eine Action vorgestellet wird, sie mag nun als eine Tragoedie oder als ein Ballet angesehen werden, und da kommts gar lächerlich heraus, wann ich singend einer Person eine Liebes-Erklärung thue, mich über etwas beklage, mich mit einem herumzancke, usw. Allein, diejenige, die solchergestalt urtheilen, haben keinen rechten Begriff von dieser Art Schauspielen. Wie wäre es, wann ihnen entgegen setzte: Solte dann das wohl wahrscheinlich seyn, wann in Comödien und Tragödien die Leute in Reimen und abgemessenen Sylben mit einander reden, Briefe wechseln, sich beklagen, sich zancken, sich schmeissen? usw. und doch hält man dasselbe nicht für ungereimt.* (pp. 162-163)

Such comparisons were considered particularly important in Braunschweig, which had become a leading operatic center under the musical direction of Georg Caspar Schür-

---

* I have sometimes heard with surprise how people who are otherwise not unreasonable have passed such a completely preposterous judgment on these plays. Operas are plays, they say, in which an action is presented, whether regarded as a tragedy or a ballet, and it appears quite ridiculous when I make a declaration of love to a person, complain about something, argue with someone, etc. singing. But those who judge in such a way have no correct concept of this kind of play. How would it be if I countered: is it then so probable when the persons in comedies and tragedies speak with each other, exchange letters, complain, argue, fight, etc. in rhymes and measured syllables? And one does not consider that absurd.

mann (ca. 1672-1751). The editors of the *Braunschwei-gische Anzeigen* hoped to stimulate critical discussion by asking their readers on May 12, 1745 to reply to the ques-tion: "Lässet sich die Frage entscheiden, ob Comödien den Opern, oder diese jenen vorzuziehen sind?" ("Can the question be resolved whether comedies are preferable to operas or the latter to the former?") Approximately one month later, on June 9th, two replies were printed. The one signed by an unidentifiable J.J. Camerer supplied reasons for opera's inferiority: first, it had no illustrious tradition because it had developed during the seventeenth century from comedy—both replies used the word "com-edy" as a synonym for drama. Second, it was totally un-natural because it consisted of singing that brutally ob-scured the text (p. 748). Camerer's remarks agreed with the orthodox Gottschedian point of view that regular drama was by far superior, yet they included no mention of abol-ishing opera.

The second reply was quite different in tone as well as in outlook. Its anonymous author—who described himself as "ein Verehrer des Schönen in beyderley Art, ohne für eine ins besondere eingenommen zu seyn" (p. 752; "an ad-mirer of the beautiful in both styles without being particu-larly partial to one of them")—considered the question not only unanswerable but also irrelevant. He purported that he nevertheless wrote to illuminate the foolishness of all such questions. Drama and opera, he began, were both theatrical plays but differed to such a great extent that they had to be judged according to their own specific merits. In order to do so logically and correctly, he continued, indi-vidual examples had to be examined. Such examinations, he explained, would uncover the different intentions of drama and opera: drama's was to delight through the in-tellect (*Verstand*), opera's to delight through the senses (*Sinne*). Because of this fundamental difference, he sug-gested that those desiring "Ergetzung durch den Verstand" choose spoken drama and those desiring "Ergetzung durch die Sinne," opera (p. 752). He stated that the choice of one over the other was contingent upon the spectator's own mood and had absolutely nothing to do with the artistic superiority of either. Amidst claims of impartiality, however, he reminded his readers that man lived not by reason alone and that the kind of sensuous pleasure opera provided was "eine zur Erhaltung des menschlichen Lebens höchstnöthige Cur der Seelen" (p. 752; "a cure of the souls, highly necessary for the preservation of human life").

This anonymous critic also tried to balance the similarities and differences when discussing verisimilitude. He maintained that the artistic media of both permitted a simulation but not a reproduction of actual reality. He admitted that opera's musical language was a degree less natural than dramatic verse but he insisted that neither medium had anything to do with sustaining artistic probability:

> Denket iemand, dis sey unnatürlich, so frage ich: ob es natürlich sey, dass einer in Versen rede? und ob, da die Comödie um mehrer Schönheit willen einmahl mit dem unnatürlichen angefangen hat, (wenn ichs dismahl alhie so nennen solle,) von seiten der Comödie der Oper ein Vorwurf gemacht werden könne, dass sie noch einen Schritt weiter gethan? und ob ich nicht, gleich wie ich die Poesie in den Comödien *durch die Fiction einer natürlichen Sprache entschuldigen muss,* auf eben die Art und mit eben dem Recht das Singen in den Opern (wann nemlich gar kein Wort dabey geredet wird) entschuldigen könne?* (p. 752)

* If someone thinks this be unnatural, I ask whether it be natural that one speak in verse? And, since drama began with the unnatural (if I should call it such here at this time) for the sake of greater beauty, whether it could reproach opera for having gone a step further? And, whether I could not in the same way and with the same justification excuse singing in operas (when namely not one word is spoken) just as I must excuse poetry in dramas through the fiction of a natural language?

The editors of the *Braunschweigische Anzeigen* were obviously well aware of the fact that the two alleged replies represented diametrically opposed schools of thought.

PAINTED STATUES AND LIFELIKE WAX FIGURES

Johann Elias Schlegel's untimely death at age thirty broke short what promised to be a remarkable career in literature and criticism. He had shown serious interest in the classics and modern European literatures while still a pupil at Schulpforta. His dramatic talent also revealed itself early, for one of his youthful works was performed by the Neuber troupe before he began his law studies in Leipzig in 1739. Schlegel participated in the activities of the Gottsched circle there but retained his own literary outlook and ideas. During nine semesters in Leipzig he developed his predilection for criticism and published seven essays indicative of his rare gift for sorting out and synthesizing ideas about the most troublesome artistic issues of the day. The precocious young writer then went to Copenhagen, via Berlin and Hamburg, as private secretary to an uncle who was a diplomat. In Denmark he wrote comedies, studied the country's language as well as culture, penned essays on the Danish theater, and published a weekly journal, *Der Fremde* (1745-1746). Eventually, with recommendations from Ludvig Holberg (1684-1754), the Danish playwright whose work he greatly admired, Schlegel was appointed professor at the academy in Soroe, where he spent the remaining years of his short life.

Among the troublesome issues Schlegel pondered as a Leipzig student was the imitation of nature. It was the subject of "Schreiben an den Herrn N.N. über Comödien in Versen" (1740), his first contribution to Gottsched's *Beyträge zur Critischen Historie*. Schlegel wanted to refute Gottlob Benjamin Straube (fl. 1740s), whose earlier essay had included a partial translation of Philippe Néricault Destouches's (1680-1754) *Le Glorieux* (1732) in its attempt to prove the inherent unnaturalness of comedy in rhymed verse.[1] Schlegel synthesized arguments that had been advanced singly and in various combinations since the late seventeenth century. Many closely resembled those of Uffenbach with whom he must have at least shared a similar line of antecedents.[2] Schlegel explained that the stage itself was make-believe, for one could not and would not build any real houses on it. He further explained that verse was simply the medium through which some writers imitated nature: it was to comedy what stone or wood was to sculpture, canvas to painting, and harmonious tones to music. Even if artists intended to reproduce nature, he argued, they would be prohibited from doing so by the very fact that all artistic media had their own distinctive limitations as well as features. Like any other artist, he continued, the writer selected certain aspects from nature and, approximating them as much as his chosen medium permitted, brought them into a new order. The ultimate purpose of art was, according to Schlegel, the sensuous pleasure that arose from perceiving the artificial new order. Exact imitations of nature could not by his definition be art because they would have natural order rather than the kind that produced artistic pleasure.

Schlegel's curiosity about the possibilities of artificial order was stimulated by examining actual dramas and by studying the writings of Longinus, d'Aubignac, and the other authorities Gottsched sanctioned. He translated Sophocles' *Elektra* (1739) and worked his way through Euripides. The revisions he made on his own Iphigenia drama illustrated his struggle to come to grips with the formal aspects of Greek tragedy. He recognized a vast difference between ancient Greek and regular French form but, unlike Postel and the Hamburg patriots, sought a compromise between the two.[3] Schlegel continued to respect the three unities and to use them as a critical standard when studying seventeenth-century German and English drama. His textual and structural comparison of Gryphius's

Leo Armenius and Shakespeare's *Julius Caesar*, which Borck's translation of the latter had inspired, appeared in 1741. Although Schlegel found Shakespeare guilty of more formal imperfections, he credited him with better character portrayal, and that Schlegel viewed as Shakespeare's greatest strength.[4]

Much less favorable than his evaluation of Gryphius was his 1741 critique of the seventeenth-century poet active in Nuremberg, Johann Klaj (1616-1656). While using the standard critical clichés in a humorously ironic manner, however, he made a passing remark about the relationship of Klaj's dramatic techniques to contemporary opera. He remarked about the spectators: "so müssen sie, wie wir in unsern Opern zuweilen gesehen haben, auch mit dem Helden zugleich träumen."[5] ("So they must, as we have sometimes seen in our operas, also dream along with the hero.") Schlegel thus recognized the operatic tendencies of the plays originating out of the Nuremberg circle associated with Harsdörffer. And, even more important in view of his and later writers' attempts to explain art's nonrational effect, he related the theater to the dream.

Schlegel claimed that pleasure was art's primary intention in "Von der Nachahmung," the three parts of which appeared in Gottschedian journals in 1742, 1743, and 1745.[6] To substantiate his claim, he distinguished two other kinds of imitation according to their intended effect: those intending to teach people a moral lesson belonged to history, while those seeking to make people take the imitation for the real thing were lies and belonged to the realm of deception. Schlegel did not wish to repudiate either Horace or Plato; he simply wished to establish pleasure as the source from which all of art's beneficial effects emanated. In "Abhandlung, dass die Nachahmung der Sache, der man nachahmet, zuweilen unähnlich werden müsse" (1745), Schlegel once again discounted the theory of artistic deception (*angenehmer Betrug*). This time he claimed that the work of art often had to be made purposely different from whatever it was imitating so that the audience would consciously recognize it as an illusion instead of actual reality. He provided theoretical support for an idea that Uffenbach had espoused earlier and that Bertolt Brecht (1898-1956) was to take up, develop, and make programmatic later. Schlegel maintained it was the artist's prerogative to create the artificial order by making his imitation as similar or dissimilar to nature as he alone deemed necessary: "Aber habe ich dadurch auch vielleicht der Unähnlichkeit zu einer zügellosen Herrschaft verholfen? Habe ich dadurch vielleicht ein Feld geöffnet, wo man ohne Regel herumirren, und seine Hirngespinste für Nachahmungen verkaufen wird? Nichts weniger, als dieses."[7] ("But have I through this perhaps assisted dissimilarity to unrestricted power? Have I through this perhaps opened an area where one will wander about without rule and sell his whims as imitations? Nothing less than this.") While considering it no crime to violate the boundaries of the naturally similar, he cautioned that it was much more difficult to integrate dissimilarities thoroughly and make them artistically convincing.

The arguments Schlegel advanced in his early essays implicitly supplied theoretical justification for opera. Mattheson had recognized the aptness of those arguments, had graciously given him credit for them, and had adopted them in his *Untersuchung*. Schlegel himself applied them to opera in 1745 in his preface to a complete German translation of the Destouches comedy Straube had tackled five years before. He used his standard analogy to the plastic arts to prove that no form of art could come any closer to simulating its natural model than its medium allowed. All media, he reiterated, were artificial, some more so than others. Consequently he considered it illogical to condemn opera because of the unnaturalness of its medium without condemning all the arts. His explanation of art's relationship to reality is worth quoting at length because it was a perceptive synthesis of ideas advanced by numerous critics in defenses and discussions of opera as well as of rhymed comedy and other literary forms:

Itzt glaube ich, wenn ein Grund die gereimte Comödie stürzen kann: So ist es nicht der, welcher mehr bewiese, als er soll, und alle Künste zugleich träfe, die der Natur nachahmen. Ich rede hier nämlich von dem, welchen man wider die Opern, vielleicht nicht glücklicher, als wider die gereimten Comödien, gebraucht hat. Hat man bey der Oper gesagt, es wäre unnatürlich, dass Helden ihre Thaten, ihren Zorn und ihr Mitleid sängen: So hat man wider die Comödie in Versen eingewandt; es wäre unnatürlich, dass Bürger ihre Entschlüsse und Einfälle reimten. Wenn es aber in der Dichtkunst unnatürlich ist, den Handlungen des bürgerlichen Lebens in Versen, und den Gemüthsbewegungen der Helden in Versen und Musik zugleich nachzuahmen: So ist es auch in der Bildhauerkunst unnatürlich, belebten Körpern durch unbelebte Körper, und z.E. schwarzen behaarten Pferde durch weisse Marmorsteine, die glatt und von keinen Haaren bedeckt sind, einer Pferdemähne, die aus einer unendlichen Anzahl kleiner Körperchen besteht, durch einen einzigen festen Körper, nämlich durch den Marmorstein nachzuahmen, welcher der äusserlichen Fläche einer Mähne ähnlich gehauen ist; so ist es auch in der Malerkunst unnatürlich, Körpern durch Flächen; so ist es auch in der Kupferstecherkunst unnatürlich, vielfarbigten Körpern durch einfarbigte Flächen nachzuahmen. Prosa und Verse sind noch nicht einmal so unterschieden als Körper und Flächen. Wenigstens ist der Unterschied zwischen den beiden ersten nicht grösser, als zwischen den beiden letzten. Verwirft man Reime und Sylbenmass in der Comödie, und gesungene Töne in der Oper darum; weil diese Eigenschaft der nachgeahmten Dinge ihre Eigenschaft widerspricht, die von der Sache, der man nachahmet, unzertrennlich ist, näm-

lich dieser, dass die Reden von den Menschen im bürgerlichen Leben niemahls abgezählt und gereimt, und dass
die Drohungen der Könige von ihnen niemahls gesungen
werden: So muss man auch alle diese angeführten Künste
verdammen.*[8]

In the eighteenth century opera continued to elicit many
speculations about artistic verisimilitude, for some people
insisted on comparing opera to reality and invariably concluded that it was more artificial than other theatrical
forms. Foregoing such comparisons, others argued along
with Schlegel that all dramatic genres were fundamentally
contrived and unreal precisely because they were art.[9]

A good indication of how readily Schlegel's critical ideas
were accepted is given by the defense of opera published

---

* Now I believe, if one argument can overthrow rhymed comedy, it
is not the one that would prove more than it is supposed to and at
the same time affect all the arts that imitate nature. I speak here of
course about the one used against operas, perhaps not more successfully than against rhymed comedies. Has one said about opera that
it would be unnatural for heroes to sing their deeds, their anger, and
their compassion, so one has protested against comedy in verse that it
would be unnatural for burghers to rhyme their decisions and notions. If it is unnatural in literature to imitate the actions of bourgeois life in verses and the emotions of heroes in verses and music together, so it is also unnatural in sculpture to imitate living bodies
through nonliving ones, and, for example, black-haired horses through
slabs of white marble, which are smooth and covered with no hairs, a
horse's mane consisting of an endless number of little particles through
one single solid body, to wit, the marble which is carved similar to the
external surface of a mane. So it is also unnatural in painting to imitate bodies through surfaces; so it is also unnatural in engraving to
imitate polychromatic bodies through monochromatic surfaces. Prose
and verse are not even as different as bodies and surfaces. At least the
difference between the first two is not greater than between the last
two. If one disallows rhyme and meter in comedy and the tones sung
in opera because the property of the imitation contradicts the property
inherent to the thing one is imitating—that is to say this, that the
conversations of people in bourgeois life are never measured and
rhymed and that the threats of kings are never sung by them—so then
one must also condemn all of these arts that have been cited.

in numbers 124 and 126 of *Die Staats- und Gelehrte Zeitung* of the *Hamburgischer Unpartheyischer Correspondent* (1745). It was presumably written by the editor Barthold Joachim Zinck (1718-1775), who resided in Hamburg as a scholar, journalist, and publisher after spending 1735 to 1741 in Ritzebüttel as tutor to the Brockes children. Zinck's role in contemporary literary life was not limited to Hamburg and the Brockes circle. Writers in other areas were well acquainted with him and his many publishing projects.[10]

Although *Die Staats- und Gelehrte Zeitung* had sometimes taken Gottsched's side in literary matters, under Zinck's editorship it expressed weary dissatisfaction with his authoritarian attitude and polemical fervor. The article defending opera was just one manifestation of this. It assumed an irreverent pose toward all literary authorities and purported to be in agreement with those citizens of Leipzig who were seditiously ignoring their home-town literary dictator. Zinck was obviously alluding to the Leipzig circle of poets that had already founded the *Bremer Beiträge* as a vehicle for their more liberal ideas. In any event, the motivation for Zinck's article apparently came from Gottsched's review of a recent edition of Voltaire's works for *Neuer Büchersaal der schönen Wissenschaften und freyen Künste* in July 1745. Zinck considered it absurd that Gottsched could admonish the eminent French writer for producing *Samson, Opéra* (1732) when he himself had prepared a libretto, *Die verliebte Diana*, around the same time.[11] Zinck tried to embarrass Gottsched further by discrediting his theories with arguments borrowed from one of Gottsched's prize students, Johann Elias Schlegel. Actually Zinck was defending opera with many of the arguments that had been cultivated in Hamburg since the late seventeenth century.

Like his predecessors, he was dubious about universally objective standards of artistic beauty and greatness. He questioned whether the ancients were to be considered authorities and whether it was necessary or even possible for opera to observe their dramatic rules. He refuted the Gottschedian criticism of Voltaire's disregard for the unities in *Samson* by making statements like the following: "Denn dass jede Veränderung des Ortes ein Fehler sey, ist durch nichts erwiesen, als durch ein gesagtes und eine sklavische Nachahmung der Alten."[12] ("Then that every change of place be an error is proven through nothing other than that which has been said and a slavish imitation of the ancients.") Zinck preferred to think that each dramatic work required only the limitations determined by its own particular subject and that those limitations were the only logical basis for judging it.

In addition to rejecting dogmatic judgments based on predetermined standards, Zinck saw absolutely no value in comparing a work with its model, whether nature or a literary source. He considered the artist free not only to select his source but also to alter it consciously for the particular needs of his work. Consequently he found Voltaire's adaptation of the facts perfectly justifiable: "Die Wunderwerke, die Simson thut, werden getadelt. Ich weiss aber nicht, wo das Gesetze geschrieben steht, dass ein dramatischer Dichter nichts zu seiner Fabel dichten dürfe? Ohne Zweifel hat Voltaire dieses eingeschaltet, theils die Augen der Zuhörer einzunehmen, theils auch die Frage des Königes durch eine Handlung zu beantworten, die sich auf dem Theater vorstellen liesse. Sollte Simson etwa auf dem Theater einen Löwen zerreissen?"[13] ("The wondrous things Samson does are censured. I do not know, however, where the law is written that a dramatic poet not be permitted to invent something for his plot. Undoubtedly Voltaire inserted this, in part to affect the eyes of the listeners, in part also to answer the king's question through an action that could be presented in the theater. Should Samson by any chance tear a lion to pieces on the stage?")

Zinck used such concrete examples throughout his discussion. The ones he chose indicate his ability to translate Schlegel's more abstract line of reasoning into terms that would be clear, three dimensional, and obvious to all of his newspaper's readers. He was not an original thinker, but he was an astute and persuasive popularizer who deflated Gottsched's objections by carrying them to their logical extreme. Operatic singing, he stated, was a medium for communication comparable to tragic verse. If one medium were condemned because of its improbability, he continued, then it logically followed that the other could also be condemned. When Zinck followed Schlegel further and compared the various arts, he found additional justification for continuous singing. He wrote that the artist's goal was not to copy nature slavishly but rather to approximate it as much as his chosen medium allowed. No artist, he added, could duplicate his model since all artistic media were totally different from nature.

He attacked Gottsched's methodological inconsistency by pointing out his failure to apply the same standards of judgment to other arts. If he had done so, Zinck claimed, then he would have discovered that all the arts made certain assumptions which the critic had to accept before even beginning his evaluation. Zinck wrote in Schlegelian fashion:

Eben so setzt der Operndichter zum Voraus, dass seine Arbeit soll gesungen werden. Ihn desswegen tadeln heisst, den Bildhauer tadeln, dass er aus Steinen menschliche Bilder macht, weil wir in der Natur keine steinerne Menschen finden. Die Unwahrscheinlichkeit des Singens ist ausser der Fabel, und wer den Aristoteles gelesen hat, wird wissen, dass die Fabel durch so eine Unwahrscheinlichkeit nicht verderbt wird. Es fordert niemand von einer Nachahmung, die ihn vergnügen soll, dass sie vollkommen die Natur ausdrücke. Man kann aus der Natur unserer Seele *a priori* sehen, dass dabey das Vergnügen wegfiele, und die Erfahrung bekräftigt diesen Satz.*[14]

* Quite certainly the librettist presupposes that his work is to be sung. To censure him on that account means censuring the sculptor for making human likenesses out of stones because we find no stony

To exemplify this idea about artistic pleasure, Zinck mentioned three-dimensional lifelike wax figures. They would not give the right kind of pleasure, he maintained, precisely "weil man sie so ähnlich machen könnte, dass sie von einem wirklichen Menschen gar nicht zu unterscheiden wären" ("because one could make them so similar that they would be not at all distinguishable from a real human being").[15] Therefore he considered it completely absurd of Gottsched to criticize Voltaire for failing to make his hero speak and act more like a real person: "Ein Operndichter will nicht den Simson in der Natur, sondern den Simson in einem Singespiele seinen Zuhörern darstellen. Es ist eben als wenn jemand den Simson auf Papier gezeichnet hätte, und ein Kunstrichter wollte kommen und sagen: muss denn eben Simson, dieser Held, dessen Muth und Arm die Philister mehr als einmal mit Graus und Schrecken erfahren haben, einen Papiermann abgeben?"[16] ("A librettist wants to present to his audience not Samson in nature but Samson in a musical play. It is just as if someone had sketched Samson on paper, and a critic wanted to come and say: must then Samson, this hero whose courage and arm the Philistines experienced with horror and terror more than once, must he be a paper man?") To emphasize the absurdity of Gottsched's demand for the exact imitation of nature, Zinck mockingly queried whether he really did believe his own contention that a drunken brawl at a peasants' dance in a spoken play would be preferable to a fine ballet by luxuriously costumed performers in an opera. He answered his own rhetorical question by stating that the brawl could indeed be truer to real life and thus more in agreement with the standards of naturalism outlined in the *Versuch einer Critischen Dichtkunst*.

---

people in nature. The improbability of singing has nothing to do with the plot, and whoever has read Aristotle, will know that the plot is not ruined by such an improbability. Nobody requires of an imitation, which is supposed to please, that it express nature perfectly. One can see a priori from the nature of our soul that there would then be no pleasure, and experience strengthens this proposition.

Surprisingly enough, Zinck's article was reprinted the following year in Bodmer's *Freymüthige Nachrichten Von Neuen Büchern und Andern zur Gelehrtheit gehörigen Sachen*.[17] The most likely reason was its attack against Gottsched's concept of imitation and not any desire on Bodmer's part to contribute to the defense of opera. Actually, the Swiss critic, though not as vehement, was quite similar to Gottsched in his disapproval. He agreed that opera hampered the development of good taste and led men astray by captivating their senses, but he believed, as he had written his Leipzig colleague on March 28, 1738, that it would die a natural death because of its inherent artistic weaknesses.[18] Bodmer considered contemporary opera a literary monstrosity that defied the time-honored dramatic rules and failed to teach a moral lesson as any respectable play should. He disliked Postel's librettos in particular because they were the most representative of what he termed operatic chaos. His strong aversion to the Hamburg librettist was clearly evident in a note to Johann Christian Rost's (1717-1765) *Das Vorspiel*. Bodmer endorsed Wernicke's antiopera position and quoted from his satire against Postel.[19] Bodmer hesitatingly admired Pietro Metastasio (1698-1782), prolific court poet in Vienna, however, because he thought his librettos presented no grave threat to the establishment of good taste. As he explained in a letter to Friedrich von Hagedorn on April 12, 1745: "Wären alle Opern so beschaffen, wie die des Metastasio, so hätten wir freilich für den guten Geschmack nichts zu fürchten. Wollte Gott, dass es unsre Landesleute in dem Drama so weit gebracht hätten, oder nur bringen könnten! Was ich am Metastasio aussetzen könnte, wäre vielleicht, dass er mir allzu süss singt."[20] ("If all operas were written like those of Metastasio, we would certainly have nothing to fear as regards good taste. Would God that our countrymen had succeeded in such a high degree with drama, or could only succeed! What I could fault in Metastasio would perhaps be that he sings much too sweetly for me.") Bodmer's colleague Breitinger also objected to contemporary opera on the grounds that it appealed exclusively to the senses. He believed it had a deleterious effect on the cultivation of regular drama because it was more successful in competing for the support of audiences. Despite their interest in imagination, sublimity, artistic reactions, the poetically wondrous, and other such critical topics, neither Swiss scholar attempted to discover just why opera was so much more successful.

BATTEUX'S NEW CODE

Neoclassicists had long considered opera illegitimate because it did not fit into their closed systems of pure genres. Scheibe struggled to legitimize it in 1739 by adopting the conventional formal criteria of spoken drama and by making it a separate subdivisible genre. Charles Batteux had less of a struggle, for he devised a new system which fully incorporated opera as a subspecies of drama. Both *Les Beaux-arts réduits à un même principe* (1746) and the expanded version of it, *Cours de belles lettres* (1750), were read, translated, and widely discussed in Germany. The French theorist wanted to eliminate the confusing and unnecessary superabundance of artistic rules by discovering that which they all shared. Through what he considered to be careful rational analysis, he found that the imitation of nature was this common denominator; it was the source of all the rules and therefore the decisive means for classifying and distinguishing genres as well as arts.

Instead of demanding an exact imitation of natural reality or real life like Gottsched, Batteux allowed for different types of nature and thus broadened the neoclassical interpretation of verisimilitude. A genre would be verisimilar, he contended, as long as it imitated that particular sphere of nature that its form, medium, and character permitted. If it tried to exceed these limitations, it would lose *vraisemblance*. According to Batteux's classification—which nonetheless resembled older conventional systems based on hierarchic social distinctions—tragedy was comparable to the epic insofar as both treated great and important actions. He subdivided the tragic like the epic genre into two "kinds" clearly distinguishable by the particular sphere of nature they imitated. The one that imitated heroic nature with human beings for characters he simply called tragedy. The one that treated the wondrous actions of the gods he called opera or the lyric play (*Spectacle Lyrique*). According to his newly devised code, both "kinds" had to respect the rules of the dramatic genre in addition to their own particular rules about themes, characters, and settings; they were to borrow neither topics nor techniques from each other because their basic assumptions were so completely different.

Since Batteux held that opera was a dramatic imitation of wondrous actions, he insisted that it had to follow laws of probability different from those of ordinary reality. Arguing that gods and demigods required an exalted language and the proper artifacts in order to seem probable to the human mind, he justified opera's continuous singing as well as its decorations, stage effects, machines, and other spectacular devices. He also justified the epic, fabulous, and novelizing tendencies that so many neoclassicists had condemned: "un Opera est donc, quant à la partie dramatique, la représentation d'une action merveilleuse. C'est le divin de l'Epopée mis en spectacle. Commes les acteurs sont des dieux, ou des héros demi-dieux; ils doivent s'annoncer aux mortels par des opérations, par un langage, par une inflexion de voix, qui surpasse les loix du vraisemblable ordinaire."[21] ("An opera, then, in its dramatic part, is the representation of a marvellous action. It is the divine part of the epic brought into exhibition. As the actors here are gods, or heroes, who are demigods, they must reveal themselves to men, by operations, speech, and an inflexion of voice, surpassing all the laws of common probability," *A Course of the Belles Lettres: or the Principles of Literature*, II,

261). By defining opera as a kind of tragedy with a purpose and rules of its own, Batteux made its place within his rationalistic literary system incontestable. He did not condemn opera unequivocably as a form of art, but the extrinsic standards he advocated were just as inflexible as those used by its earlier neoclassical opponents. While Batteux's code was warmly greeted by many German writers, its restrictions were stringent enough to motivate numerous others, among whom was Mattheson, to dispute the concept of opera as the genre of the wondrous and to continue scrutinizing the imitation of nature as an artistic principle.

Georg Friedrich Meier (1718-1777) was the student whose German adaptation and publication of Baumgarten's preparatory lectures for *Aesthetica* gave more widespread currency to that new field of philosophical investigation. Because of his training in aesthetics at the University of Halle, he became a relentless foe of those who upheld the imitation of nature as the essence of all art. Before turning his attention to Batteux he concentrated on Gottsched and systematically tore his theories to shreds. Meier believed Gottsched was so wrong about so very many artistic matters that he blamed him in *Untersuchung einiger Ursachen des verdorbenen Geschmacks der Deutschen in Absicht auf die schönen Wissenschaften* (1746) for insidiously ruining German tastes altogether.

A lengthier, more comprehensive critique came in *Beurtheilung der Gottschedischen Dichtkunst* (1747-1748). Meier pointed out the omissions and errors in *Versuch einer Critischen Dichtkunst* and devoted an entire section to an analysis of the chapter on opera. He reprehended Gottsched for his immoderate attitude, contending that only an incompetent critic would make such extreme and unfounded assertions. He then suggested that attending a few performances might give him reason to change his mind, for opera often captivated even its staunchest adversaries. Meier claimed he himself had heard that "einige Opernfeinde den Augenblick ihre Meinung geändert, so bald sie eine Oper gesehen" (p. 356; "some enemies of opera changed their opinion instantaneously as soon as they saw an opera").[22] Opera's warm reception among intelligent well-mannered people was another important factor he believed Gottsched had failed to recognize. Like opera's earliest proponents in Hamburg, Meier believed familiarity with actual works and their overall effect was essential to critical procedure.

While concurring that opera had imperfections, Meier disputed Gottsched's claim that it lacked the potential to be good. Many genres, he explained, were artistically poor in the beginning but improved with time. Consequently he saw no reason why opera could not do the same. Aristotle, he pointed out, had taken a flexible critical approach and, instead of condemning the underdeveloped genres of his era, allowed for continuing future progress. Gottsched's denial of such progress indicated to Meier that his familiarity with the ancient theorists' actual methodology and ideas was quite superficial despite the constant lip service he paid them.

Like some earlier writers, with whom he, however, forswore any acquaintance, Meier conceived of opera as a literary form created and controlled by the poet. He considered it great because it was theoretically a combination of ode and tragedy, the highest and most sublime forms in their respective genres. As he explained, when their "Vorzüge mit einander vereinigen, so bekomt man das allerschönste der Poesie" (p. 359; "merits combine with each other, one gets the most beautiful of poetry"). He disagreed with opera's opponents that such combinations were impossible and cited the emblem, the ode, and the cantata as examples of genres in which inherently different arts cooperated successfully.

Singing was, in Meier's opinion, the proper means of communication for opera because it enhanced and reinforced the emotional impact of the dramatic situation. Although he thought a defense of operatic singing should be unnecessary, he felt the Gottschedian objections to the medium warranted one: "Der Einwurf, dass es unnatürlich sey, wenn Personen singend einander einen guten Morgen bieten, sagt nicht viel. Denn der Operndichter muss lauter pathetische Gedancken vortragen, und in starcken Affecten hat man nicht so viele Ueberlegung, dass man die Wahrscheinlichkeit so scharf beurtheilen solte. Mitten in heftigen Affecten reden wir manchmal unmögliche Dinge. Folglich behaupte ich, dass die Wahrscheinlichkeit in einem heftigen Affecte anders sey, als sonst" (p. 359; "The objection that it is unnatural when people wish each other good morning singing does not say much. For the librettist must deliver many elevated ideas, and in strongly emotional states one does not have so much reflection that probability should be so sharply criticized. In intense emotional states we sometimes utter impossible things. Consequently I maintain that probability in an intense emotional state is different from usual"). Meier argued that operatic probability was different because opera portrayed a heroic action which was not supposed to be within the realm of ordinary reality: "Hier haben wir also den gantzen Begrif einer Oper, sie ist nemlich ein heroisches Drama, welches gesungen wird, oder überhaupt ein Drama, welches gesungen wird" (p. 359: "Here we have the whole idea of an opera: it is, to wit, a heroic drama that is sung, or any drama at all that is sung"). Meier did not, however, absolve opera from observing the traditional rules of the stage. Only by complying with those immutable standards did he think it would be able to realize its potentialities and obviate all grounds for criticism. It is one of the small ironies in the history of operatic defenses that Meier's operatic theory so closely resembled that of Batteux, whose assumptions, methodology, and theoretical speculations he was to repudiate in the following years.[23]

Batteux's reduction of all aesthetics to an imitation of nature was also repudiated by Johann Adolph Schlegel, younger brother of Johann Elias and father of the illustrious Romantics, Friedrich (1772-1829) and August Wilhelm (1767-1845). During his theological studies in Leipzig in the 1740s he, like his brother, joined Gottsched's circle only to discover a greater affinity for the ideas of Gellert and the Bremer Beiträger. Despite strong literary and critical inclinations, Johann Adolph persevered with theology and became a deacon in Pforta in 1751. Three years later he was appointed professor at the Gymnasium in Zerbst where he taught poetry as well as religion and conducted private sessions on literary theory. When he became pastor in Hannover in 1759, he continued holding such private sessions, and eventually his sons joined the other capable young men who participated.

While still a student in Leipzig, Johann Adolph Schlegel studied and translated the 1746 edition of Batteux. The translation, *Einschränkung der schönen Künste auf Einen einzigen Grundsatz*, was published anonymously in 1751, the very same year Denis Diderot (1713-1784) opposed Batteux in *Lettre sur les sourds et muets*. Schlegel appended seven essays on problems he thought the original had treated insufficiently or incorrectly. His essays dealt with the classification of the arts as well as poetry, the harmony of verse, the wondrous, and the pastoral. Footnotes, which he carefully labeled as the translator's, accompanied the text and commented further on dubious issues. Additional essays in subsequent editions indicate that he continued his questioning of Batteux, who in turn publicly criticized him.

What Schlegel opposed particularly was Batteux's approach to the arts. He failed to see any sense in setting up a closed system of rules for writers to follow. He saw even less sense in judging a work according to rules it did not intend to observe. Along with Gellert and the other Bremer Beiträger he interpreted the dramatic unities liberally: "Freylich muss der Dichter uns nicht ohne gegründete und wichtige Ursachen die Mühe machen, uns von einem Orte an den andern zu versetzen; die Regeln der Einheit des Ortes und der Zeit sind wirklich theatralische Regeln, aber nur zufällige, welche Ausnahmen leiden" (p. 192; "To be sure, without well-founded and important reasons the poet must not put us to the trouble of transferring ourselves from one place to another; the rules of the unity of place and time are really theatrical rules, but only incidental ones that sustain exceptions"). Schlegel considered them incidental because he thought they pertained only to the theatrical forms of the particular age that formulated them. If the ancients, he explained, limited the time and place of their dramatic plots, then they did so only in order to suit their own tastes and the needs of their own specific types of drama.

Schlegel believed artists should work according to their own tastes without blindly observing what essentially were historically irrelevant rules. As long as they gave pleasure by presenting the beautiful, the good, or both, their works were justified in his eyes. He wrote with words reminiscent of Baumgarten: "Die Poesie wird also die sinnlichste und angenehmste Vorstellung des Schönen, oder des Guten, oder des Schönen und Guten zugliech, durch die Sprache seyn. Diejenige, die beides vereinigt, wird die vollkommenste seyn; und beides ist so nahe mit einander verwandt, dass es sich fast nicht trennen lässt" (p. 291; "Through language poetry becomes the most sensuous and most pleasant representation of the beautiful, or the good, or the beautiful and the good together. That which combines both will be the most perfect, and both are so closely related to each other that they almost cannot be separated"). Without depreciating antiquity, Schlegel encouraged contemporary writers to find solutions to the more urgent artistic problems of their own age. Like Uffenbach, he suggested that one of the best ways to emulate the ancients might be to achieve independence from them: "Vielleicht würden wir in Erfindung derselben noch glücklicher seyn, wenn wir nicht zu schüchtern wären, von den Fusstapfen der Alten manchmal abzuweichen, da wir öfters nicht dazu gemacht sind, ihnen auf ihrer Bahn zu folgen, und durch neue Wege

vielleicht eher zu dem allgemeinen Ziele gelangen würden"
(p. 308; "Perhaps in the invention of these things we would
be even more successful if we were not too timid to depart
from the footsteps of the ancients, since we are often not
so made as to follow in their track. Through new paths we
would possibly arrive at the universal goal sooner"). Schlegel did not dispense with all regulatory devices, but he did
reevaluate their practical importance and show them in a
different perspective. Since he had granted the artist freedom to create his work as he saw fit, he cautioned critics
against approaching the resultant product with preconceived notions. And he urged them to experience the product to determine whether the artist completed it successfully according to his own basic assumptions.

Schlegel opposed closed artistic systems because he believed the arts themselves were not methodical. The fourth
of his essays, "Von der Eintheilung der Poesie," constituted
a refutation of Batteux's newly systematized code. Here
Schlegel likened the poetic arts to a burgeoning tree. And
he continued with the image of natural growth, which was
always to be expected but not predicted or controlled, to
explain that the arts could never be so conveniently circumscribed or limited to an exact number. He used geo-
graphical imagery when it came to the pastoral, opera,
cantata, and other art forms devised and developed since
the Renaissance. He related them, interestingly enough, to
the discovery of a new world on the American continent:
"Zum Erstaunen aller ist noch einer [Welttheil] erfunden
worden, der fast von einem eben so grossen Umfange ist,
als alle übrigen dreye zusammen. . . . Lasst uns eben diess
von der Poesie sagen! Nichts lässt sich bey ihr schwerer
bestimmen, als eine gewisse Anzahl von Gattungen, auf die
sie sich einzuschränken genöthigt seyn soll" (p. 307; "To
the astonishment of all, another has been discovered that is
almost of exactly as large a size as all three others together. . . . Let us say just this about poetry! Nothing is
more difficult to determine for it than a fixed number of

genres to which it should be obliged to restrict itself"). He further argued that art forms devised in future years would also have to be recognized and accepted just as America was after its existence had been empirically proven. No classification was valid to Schlegel unless it was flexible enough to incorporate the results of empirical discoveries. Rejecting something of excellent quality simply because it did not fit into any of the preestablished categories he considered the height of absurdity. He also considered absurd those who claimed that the discovery of more and more new art forms would precipitate poetic anarchy: "Und man wird nicht fürchten dürfen, dass man durch die Nachsicht gegen neuerfundene Gattungen einer zügellosen Einbildungskraft freye Gewalt geben werde, durch ihre seltsame Einfälle alles zu verwirren, und das Reich der Poesie zu einer Anarchie zu machen" (p. 327; "And one ought not to fear that tolerance toward newly invented genres will give an unrestrained imagination free authority to confuse everything through its peculiar whims and to transform the realm of poetry into anarchy"). He pointed to the various dramatic and lyric forms produced by the modern period as substantiation for his argument.

One of these forms, opera, had had an especially difficult time with the critics precisely because it defied classification: "Wie viel Stürme hat nicht die Oper auszuhalten gehabt, ehe sie ihren Platz behaupten können!" (p. 309; "How many storms has opera not had to weather before being able to retain its berth!"). Schlegel appreciated the fact that Batteux had ratified opera instead of condemning it, but he could not tolerate his stringent interpretation. He thought it resulted from the same kind of erroneous methodology that opera's earlier opponents had employed: "Eben so wie die ersten Bestreiter der Oper sich die Regeln des Trauerspiels von den Mustern der alten und neuern grossen tragischen Dichter abgezogen, und darum das lyrische Trauerspiel verwarfen, weil es kein Trauerspiel in der Form des Sophocles oder Corneille war: So bildet sich Herr Batteux seinen Begriff von der Oper bloss nach den Arbeiten des Quinault; und folgert daraus, dass die Personen, die uns die Oper vorstellt, Götter oder Halbgötter seyn müssen. Dieser Umstand war gleichwohl etwas zufälliges" (p. 311; "Just as the first opponents of opera abstracted the rules of tragedy from the examples of the great ancient and modern tragedians and therefore rejected lyrical tragedy because it was not tragedy in the form of Sophocles or Corneille, so Mr. Batteux forms his concept of opera solely from Quinault's works and infers from them that the persons opera presents must be gods or demigods. This circumstance, however, was something fortuitous"). He maintained that Batteux had prescribed the supernatural sphere for opera because he had had difficulties finding in it the sought after common denominator that was supposed to hold his preconceived system together. Since the operas he knew, Schlegel continued, did not imitate any conceivable aspect of ordinary nature, they would otherwise have stood out as blatant contradictions of the whole system. He believed Batteux demanded wondrous topics and marvelous figures in opera because that was the only way he could justify its continuous singing and accept it as probable.

Schlegel interpreted this stringent demand as a clear indication of Batteux's failure to understand very much about the relationship of artistic media, imitation, and probability. While Schlegel submitted that superhuman characters performing marvels would make the musical medium seem more probable, he insisted that operatic probability depended on internal structure or the relationship of individual parts. And he agreed with Gellert that achieving artistic unity was very difficult. Gellert explained in the preface to his *Das Orakel, ein Singspiel* (1747) that the reason he had not done more librettos was "nicht deswegen, weil ich diese Art der Gedichte für unnatürlich hielte; nein, sondern weil ich sie für sehr schwer halte, wenn sie schön seyn sollen" ("not at all because I consider this kind of poetry unnatural but because I consider it very difficult if it is to be beautiful").[24]

Most important for Schlegel's theory was that opera not be restricted to the realm of the wondrous just because its medium was a little more artificial than those of other genres and arts. Like his older brother as well as Zinck and Uffenbach, Johann Adolph Schlegel compared other genres and arts in order to prove that each was a make-believe fabrication, which relied on nature but which could never imitate it exactly:

> Die Oper entfernt sich von der wirklichen Natur noch um einen Grad weiter, als das Trauerspiel; aber wird darum das in der Oper aufhören, wahrscheinlich zu seyn, was nicht wunderbar ist? Den Nachahmungen der Bildhauerkunst fehlen die Farben der Natur, die den Nachahmungen der Malerey eigen sind. Würde man daraus wohl folgern können, dass die Bildhauerkunst nichts als höhere Wesen, nichts als Götter, vorstellen dürfe, weil dadurch gewissermaassen die Unähnlichkeit, die bey ihren Statuen, wenn sie gegen Menschen gehalten werden, sogleich ins Auge fällt, verdeckt oder glaublicher gemacht würde? Der müsste sehr billig seyn; der sich daran stossen wollte, dass die Musik in harmonischeren Tönen nachahmt, als die theatralische Declamation; und ihr die gewöhnliche Sprache zumuthen, hiesse, von der Poesie Prosa fordern.* (p. 313)

* Opera deviates from actual nature one degree further than tragedy does; but will that which is not wondrous in opera therefore stop being probable? The imitations of sculpture lack the colors of nature that are inherent to the imitations of painting. Would one therefore be able to conclude that sculpture must present nothing but higher beings, nothing but gods, because then the dissimilarity that immediately becomes evident in statues when contrasted with human beings would to some extent be hidden or made more credible? He would have to be very petty whoever took offense that music imitates in tones more harmonious than theatrical declamation. And expecting ordinary language of it would mean demanding prose of poetry.

To justify forms like opera, Schlegel questioned the authorities, revaluated traditional rules, and contended that historical and national conditions produced artistic multifariousness.[25] He tended to approach art pragmatically, differing from opera's earlier defenders only insofar as he refuted what he considered an inaccurate interpretation rather than an outright condemnation. He objected to the limitations imposed by strict artistic codes, whether Boileau's, Gottsched's, or Batteux's, and defended operatic singing as an artistic medium valid for treating any kind of subject. Schlegel argued that opera did not have to be unnatural for the same reason earlier defenders had argued that it did not have to be natural. Neoclassicists had striven for years to find an acceptably logical explanation for the operatic medium. And once they found that explanation by allowing for the supernatural sphere, critics like the Schlegels came along to prove that their explanations were not so logically consistent after all. As Johann Adolph Schlegel correctly surmised, the future demonstrated that opera, like spoken tragedy and the epic, could be used to treat bourgeois subjects as well as a whole range of others.

Several contemporary reviews indicate that Johann Adolph Schlegel's own age knew of his essays and acknowledged his perceptive observations. Lessing, whose warm review appeared in *Das neueste aus dem Reiche des Witzes* (1751), attributed the anonymous first edition to Gellert because its liberal critical attitude suggested him or one of the other Bremer Beiträger.[26] Moses Mendelssohn (1729-1786) reviewed it favorably in two of the *Briefe, die neueste Literatur betreffend* (1760). The eighty-fifth referred to Schlegel as a sensitive and discerning thinker although it criticized his ability to articulate complex theories clearly. In the eighty-seventh, Schlegel was credited with being the first to dispute successfully Batteux's artistic principles.[27] A more revealing appraisal came in 1771 in *Neue Bibliothek der schönen Wissenschaften und der freyen Künste*: "Unsre deutsche Kritik ist unserm Verfasser viel, sehr viel schuldig. Durch die Bestreitung des Batteuxischen Grundsatzes, hat er einen grossen Schritt zur Erfindung der bessern und richtigern Theorie gethan; und sein Unterschied zwischen Nachahmung und Ausdruck hat uns vielleicht zuerst auf die Bahn geholfen, die Unterschiede der verschiednen Künste und der verschiednen Unterarten einer Kunst, auf genaue Begriffe zu bringen." ("Our German criticism owes much, very much, to our author. By combatting Batteux's principle he made a great step toward the discovery of the better and truer theory; and his differentiation between imitation and expression helped us, perhaps first of all, onto the track for formulating exactly the differences of the various arts and the various subspecies of one art.") In evaluating the substantially enlarged third edition, the reviewer related Johann Adolph Schlegel's achievements to the general critical awakening in Germany: "Er hat die Revolutionen unsers Geschmacks und unsrer Schriftstellerey mit angesehen; hat selbst das seinige dazu beygetragen, sie zu Stande zu bringen."[28] ("He witnessed the revolutions of our taste and our writing and contributed his share toward bringing them about.") Johann Adolph Schlegel's other valuable legacies to the history of German criticism were his sons.

SIX

INTERACTION IN BERLIN
AT MID-CENTURY

THEATRICAL DIVERSITY

GERMAN theater witnessed the dawning of a new era during the 1750s and 1760s. The ideas that had evolved in the preceding decades began to converge in such a way as to stimulate reform, experimentation, and extraordinarily active debate. Italian grand opera, which had all but conquered the theatrical scene, remained exceedingly popular with audiences. The reaction against its complexities and highly stylized artificiality increased, however, as the effects of enlightened rationalism, Germanic patriotism, and a new bourgeois identity began to be more widely felt. Demands for simplicity, sobriety, and naturalness became louder and more frequent.

Composers and librettists strove to regain the nobility, clarity, and dramatic truth of Greek tragedy that had attracted generations of opera's exponents since the Renaissance. Grand opera would be more comprehensible and natural, these reformers contended, if both the text and the music were simplified and brought into a meaningfully unified relationship. And that meant eliminating extraneous elements or integrating them coherently into the totality of the work. With *Orfeo ed Euridice* in 1762, for example, Gluck and his librettist Ranieri da Calzabigi (1714-1795) began their operatic reform, which they continued, despite initial popular rejection, throughout the following decades.

Dissatisfaction with the formal and stilted Italian style manifested itself in other areas of theatrical endeavor, for there was a resurgence of smaller, less demanding musical plays produced in the German language. Spoken dialogue replaced the recitative, and the dominating musical feature became, as in the days of Reinhard Keiser, the simple melodies of the folksong. While some of these forms, like Klopstock's *Bardieten*, exploited Nordic mythology, others avoided mythological or historical characters and chose to present everyday happenings, mostly of a farcical nature. Italian and French forms like the intermezzo, *vaudeville*, and *opera buffa* were emulated, but it was the English comic opera that appealed most directly to German sensibilities. Borck, the Shakespeare translator, provided a German version of Charles Coffey's (d. 1745) *The Devil to Pay* in 1743. It attracted little attention when it was performed in Berlin that same year with the original English music; it became an overnight theatrical sensation, however, when Christian Felix Weisse adapted it for the Leipzig stage in 1752. The vehement Gottschedian attack that resulted involved most of the city, for the Leipzig burghers rose to Weisse's defense and subsequently circulated a number of small leaflets and advertisements vindicating their theater.[1]

The German operetta (*komische Oper* or *Singspiel*) took hold so quickly with the bourgeoisie for whom it was designed that practically every larger city wanted to boast of its own composer, poet, and ensemble. As its popularity increased so did experimentation with its theatrical possibilities. Similar works were created, and attempts were made to use its form for more serious plots, ones that treated some sentimental or deeply emotional subject. Musical theatrical plays in which the entire text was spoken, not sung, to an orchestral accompaniment were also tried around this time, and greater emphasis was placed on the lyrical quality of the drama. Such experiments eventually led to the *Melodrama* or lyrical monodrama in which one person, usually a female character, declaimed at length about her sad fate.

The spoken dramas Gottsched had been supplying, whether original pieces or translations from French, had indeed contributed to the general awakening of audience consciousness. His reform efforts had failed, however, because his dogmatic prescription of the French neoclassical code had not taken the theatrical realities of the German-speaking world into account. Gottsched's younger contemporaries were more successful because their awareness of such realities encouraged them to seek solutions congenial to the Germanic spirit and practicable for living theater. Although they often mentioned Gottsched, they were more inclined to concentrate their efforts on fighting what he represented: unfounded assertions, artistic prejudice, preconceived theoretical limitations, and pseudoclassicism. As their interest shifted from interpretations of the *Poetics* to the Aristotelian texts themselves, they scrutinized more closely the relationship between dramatic theory and theatrical practice. They studied Aristotle's treatment of music and spectacle as two of Greek tragedy's six essential components and became increasingly curious about contemporary musical theater. They sought reasons for its popularity, examined its artistic disposition, compared it to ancient drama, investigated its historical development, and discussed its potentialities as a fusion of the arts. Many of them even believed that opera provided a means through which the artistic spirit of classical antiquity could be understood if not possibly recaptured.

Such critical and aesthetic questions were rigorously debated in Berlin, where musical theater was a courtly affair rather than a commercial enterprise as in Hamburg or Leipzig. Opera's beginnings in Berlin coincided, more or less, with the founding of Prussia under Frederick III of Brandenburg, the son of the Great Elector, and its development remained closely connected to the rise of the kingdom. Frederick's consort, Sophia Charlotte, who arrived in 1684 from the musically active court of Hannover, was the one largely responsible for introducing opera to Berlin.[2] She had such great enthusiasm for Italian opera that she used every means available to foster it in her new surroundings. She urged her courtiers to participate with her in productions; she enlisted the aid of the court poet Johann von Besser; she sought experienced composers; and she herself provided librettos as well as music. When necessary, she fought to retain the professional musicians and artists she had been able to attract to Berlin. After her death in 1705, Prussian support of Italian operatic forms decreased, but interest in opera did not disappear entirely, for the court began looking to German poets, singers, and composers to supply suitable musical theatrical entertainments.[3]

With the accession of Frederick William I in 1713, opera suffered a severe setback. Since he considered the arts luxuries that could interfere with the development of his young nation, he forbade their cultivation and encouraged a Spartan way of life. Frederick William I demanded strict obedience from all his subjects, his own son being no exception. He expected his future successor to obey his will in all matters and did not hesitate to punish him for any infractions. By the time Frederick II himself became king in 1740, he was prepared to rule the state with the same ironclad discipline. Like his father, he was devoted to the development of Prussia but, unlike him, sought to improve the image of his court by fostering the arts. Grand opera in the Italian style received special attention, for it had long been his favorite. The performances he had attended while visiting Braunschweig and Dresden, two of the leading baroque operatic centers, had presumably left a lasting impression.[4] At these courts, opera had been a sign of power and prestige, and he lamented the fact that such important symbols were neglected in a great nation like Prussia.

As the ruling monarch of Prussia, Frederick had opportunity to change this. One of his first official acts was to order the construction of an opera house that would excel any other in Europe. When material difficulties prevented its completion on schedule, he had an interim theater built so that the already assembled singers and musicians could gratify his compelling desire for opera. Carl Heinrich Graun (1701-1759) served as composer, but the ensemble consisted predominantly of Italians, for Frederick despised what he incorrectly considered the vocal incompetence of his countrymen and the musical inferiority of the German language. The French were not much better in his opinion; their operas were musically boring even though their language, literature, and spoken dramas were worthy of emulation.

Frederick the Great set the tone for opera in Berlin, and everything, including the smallest details, had to meet his despotic specifications. In addition to demanding changes in the music and selecting, editing, or writing the librettos, he frequently attended rehearsals and coached the performers. Frederick saw to it that he got whomever or whatever he wanted for his opera and in more than one instance had singers forcibly abducted. Personal matters were not allowed to jeopardize the organization or quality of the ensemble; those who dared to disobey his royal decrees were usually imprisoned or otherwise punished. He even made attendance at performances compulsory for his army officers as well as his courtiers.

The beginning of the Seven Years' War in 1756 brought a quick halt to all productions and an exodus of performers, some of whom were grateful for the release. After the war ended in 1763, Frederick revived the theater in order to show the world that his nation was economically sound enough for such luxuries.[5] A new manager was appointed, and Johann Friedrich Agricola (1720-1774) became the chief composer. The monarch's interest in grand opera, however, began to wane so that he hardly visited his theater; the intermezzo had attracted his attention, and he turned to it for diversion.

This predilection for foreign works, whether Italian or French, precluded royal patronage of German-language theater in Berlin. The king's unequivocal rejection of indigenous efforts antagonized many people and made the defense of German art seem imperative. Essential disagreement over Germany's artistic potentialities created an intellectual climate in which experimentation and critical inquiry flourished. Newly founded journals enabled German writers to discuss the latest trends and achievements. Additional opportunity for discussion was provided by the so-called Montagsklub, a loosely formed organization of prominent burghers and literati that was founded in 1748 by Karl Wilhelm Ramler (1725-1798) and Johann Georg Schulthess (1724-1804).

Support for German Opera

Friedrich Wilhelm Marpurg (1718-1795) was among the most outspoken opponents of Italian opera in Berlin. He deplored Frederick the Great's linguistic preferences and operatic policies because he considered them major hindrances to the cultivation of genuinely German musical theater. His views on the subject were colored not only by his cultural patriotism and thorough training in music theory but also by his ardent devotion to the ancient classics and familiarity with current efforts to reform musical theater.

Marpurg founded *Der Critische Musicus an der Spree* in 1749 as a vehicle for those views. It was modeled after the journal Scheibe had published earlier in Hamburg and was equally polemical. When the first issue attacked the court composer Agricola for proclaiming the superiority of Italian opera, there began the heated dispute that the young Lessing tried to satirize in the *Tarantula* fragment. Marpurg fiercely rejected Italian opera's highly stylized artificiality and lack of dramatic excellence. He also took German composers to task because of their failure to recognize the beauties of their mother tongue. Although he agreed that the inherent musicality of the Italian language lent itself quite readily to opera, he disagreed that the German language was incapable of musical expression. In his opinion, it had untapped strengths and, furthermore, could be just as graceful, pleasant, and melodious as French or even Italian. The inferiority of indigenous musical works, he argued, stemmed from neglect rather than from the essence of the German language.[6]

Marpurg blamed such neglect on his own countrymen and what he considered their unwarranted predilection for things foreign. Like the generations of critics who preceded him, he claimed that Germany was a land "worinnen der Sohn vom Vater die Gewohnheit ererbet, Dinge, die nach der Fremde schmecken, ob sie gleich öfters von dem allerschlechtesten Wehrt sind, einheimischen Kostbarkeiten von ungleich grösserem Wehrt vorzuziehen" ("in which the son inherits from his father the habit of preferring things that smack of foreign parts, although they often are of the very least worth, over indigenous valuables of far greater worth").[7] And, he added, they learned that attitude from sovereigns like Frederick the Great whose contemptuous treatment of indigenous works had a demoralizing effect on native talent. German art only appeared to lack worthwhile characteristics, Marpurg explained, because it was unfairly compared with the more highly developed accomplishments of other lands. If fostered and given the proper models to emulate, it would not, he predicted, remain inferior for very long.

The lyrical dramas of Jean Philippe Rameau (1683-1764) were the models he recommended most highly. Marpurg, who had become acquainted with the French composer during a three-year sojourn in Paris in the late 1740s, agreed that opera's dramatic essence necessitated the subservience of music. He emphasized the importance of a simple, unornamented musico-dramatic style because he believed it most closely approximated what had been achieved in classical antiquity. While Winckelmann, the compatriot with whom he corresponded, devoted himself primarily to the ancients' plastic arts, Marpurg concentrated on their music and speculated about its relationship to drama. He too admired their consummate taste and their respect for naturally human proportions. In addition, he helped to perpetuate the phrase that had been used in operatic circles for decades. He advocated "eine edle Einfalt des Gesanges" ("a noble simplicity of song") in the preface to *Historisch-Kritische Beyträge zur Aufnahme der Musik*, the journal he founded in 1754, the year before the appearance of Winckelmann's *Gedancken über die Nachahmung der griechischen Wercke*.[8]

Marpurg's journal kept its readers informed about many of the day's burning issues. It reported frequently, though not altogether objectively, on the *guerre des bouffons*, the French operatic quarrel in which Diderot, Jean Jacques Rousseau (1712-1778), and Friedrich Melchior Grimm (1723-1807) extolled Giovanni Battista Pergolesi's (1710-1736) *La serva padrona* (1733) and attacked what they considered the overly cerebral music of Rameau. The journal presented a chronological catalogue of English operas, tracing England's operatic tradition from the Renaissance court masque, which was, Marpurg believed, "gewiss (wenn man die Sache nimt, wie man soll) eine Art von Oper" ("certainly [when one takes the matter as one should] a kind of opera").[9] Here and elsewhere he contended that the introduction of the totally unnatural and ornate Italian style had stifled indigenous developments. Marpurg repeatedly submitted the prevailing artistic theories and practices to critical examination. While appreciating the rationality of Batteux's system, for example, he remained skeptical about the common denominator, which relegated opera to the wondrous realm of gods and demigods. Metastasio's librettos had demonstrated to him that normal human beings and true events could be treated in a convincing and pleasing manner.[10]

Marpurg also used *Historisch-Kritische Beyträge* to provide information about the history of German opera. The bibliography he printed between 1757 and 1762 collated libretto titles from Gottsched's recently published *Nöthiger Vorrat* and Mattheson's *Musikalischer Patriot*. It was a direct descendant of the one Richey and the members of the

Teutschübende Gesellschaft had begun to prepare decades earlier. Marpurg's visit to Hamburg, acquaintance with Mattheson, and interest in Greek studies obviously made him aware of the society's scholarly achievements and patriotic aims. Presumably he even went on to discuss its activities with his close friend and associate, Lessing, who for years had relied on the philological works and anthologies of Johann Albert Fabricius. During his 1767-1770 sojourn in Hamburg, Lessing not only perused turn-of-the-century librettos but also came into contact with the family of Fabricius's son-in-law, Hermann Samuel Reimarus (1694-1768), whose revolutionary theological writings were to provoke the controversy that led to *Nathan der Weise, Ein Dramatisches Gedicht* (1779).

Christian Gottfried Krause (1719-1770), one of the contributors to Marpurg's *Historisch-Kritische Beyträge*, had similar concerns for the past, present, and future of opera. He gathered information assiduously and, after trying to assimilate it, produced an enormously long manuscript that received the careful if not very gentle criticism of many members of the Montagsklub. They believed its enthusiasm, conviction, and pertinence compensated for its eclecticism, difficult syntax, and rambling organization.[11] The result of their four years of copyediting and discussion was *Von der Musikalischen Poesie* (1752), a comprehensive treatise long hailed as the mainstay of Berlin operatic theory. It belonged to the tradition of works investigating the sources, relationships, and possible combinations of the sister arts.

Krause borrowed from many of those works but admired especially Jean Baptiste Dubos's (1670-1742) *Réflexions critiques sur la poésie et sur la peinture* (1719).[12] Dubos, who relied on ideas from English empirical philosophy, considered art to be the communication of certain feelings that were perceived through a sixth sense or instinct.[13] He opposed a priori rules and systems, arguing that critics should let their own emotional reactions rather than their reason guide them in making evaluations of particular works.[14]

His study of the development of the individual arts led to observations about the effects of climate and geography. They also led to observations about the differences in artistic media; he held that painting consisted of natural signs and poetry arbitrary ones.

Dubos, who frequented the Parisian opera regularly and even wrote about it, was also interested in the changes music had undergone since antiquity.[15] He believed many scholars had overlooked those changes and had therefore failed to differentiate the declamation of ancient tragedy from the singing of modern opera. He mentioned various differences throughout the first edition of his work but devoted a whole volume to them in subsequent revised and enlarged editions. Dubos had been known in the German lands at least since König mentioned him in 1727; most scholars today, however, believe he was generally ignored or rejected until Breitinger's *Critische Dichtkunst* (1740).[16] Since so many defenders of opera had similar ideas, it would be significant for the history of German aesthetics as well as applied criticism to determine whether they studied Dubos or whether they simply shared the same antecedents. One thing is certain, the members of the Montagsklub studied Dubos's work in one or another of the five editions printed before 1760, and they discussed its implications.

Krause's *Von der Musikalischen Poesie* is one example of Dubos's increasing importance in Berlin. Krause repeatedly referred readers to what Dubos had written about the ancient fusion of the arts and about attempts to revive it. His interest was presumably stimulated by the popular modern contention that intrinsic artistic differences precluded the possibility of perfect fusion. He rejected that contention, believing poetry could be fused with music so perfectly "dass von beyden zu gleicher Zeit einerley Gedanken, Empfindungen, und Leidenschaften ausgedrückt werden" (p. 2; "that the same thoughts, feelings, and passions could be expressed by both at the same time"). And he attributed the mediocrity of current attempts to poetry's loss of musicality and music's loss of simplicity. Both arts, he claimed, had been inseparable in the remote past. Poetry, he continued, had evolved out of singing when the invention of the written alphabet decreased the importance of oral recitation (p. 8). Krause also traced drama back to music. He wrote that it originated with the songs sung by Dionysian revelers and retained vestiges of its lyrical beginnings as it proceeded to develop into an exquisite theatrical form (pp. 10-11).

After discussing the origins of the lyric and dramatic genres, Krause turned to the history of their cooperation. He credited the Renaissance with recognizing their generic similarities and attempting to reestablish the long lost ancient style of theatrical declamation. But he blamed the competitive spirit of composers and poets for preventing the reestablishment of that style. Their failure to cooperate with each other, he explained, produced operas that were either bombastic and ponderous or dull and vapid. The Hamburg tradition supplied him with examples. He believed that even admirable poets like König had contributed to opera's downfall because of their refusal to recognize the need for naturalness and simplicity in texts to be set to music. Krause bemoaned the resultant critical attitude: "Man hat daher die ganze musikalische Poesie verachtet, und geglaubt, ein Gedichte könne nicht gut seyn, wenn es zur Musik bequem seyn solle" (p. 185; "One therefore despised all musical poetry and believed a poem could not be good if it were suitable for music"). He felt such an attitude was counterproductive because it led to condemnation rather than reform.

Like opera's earlier defenders, Krause developed this theory by seeking arguments to refute such condemnations. He had no less of a struggle than his predecessors when he attempted to articulate his conception of operatic fusion. His ideal opera was not an aggregation or even a combination of divergent arts, but one indivisible superart that was to be enacted with feeling, vivacity, and imagination. In it, he explained, music would enliven and animate the text. And the stage decorations, machines, and dances would be so organically integrated with the plot that they could not be separated from it. To sum up, he wrote: "helfen und dienen alle zu der Oper gehörige Stücke und Theile einander; sind sie ohne Unterlass darauf bedacht, wie sie reizen, blenden, und verführen mögen; sorgen sie alle zusammen für nichts als mit vereinigten Kräften zu rühren; so wird man sich eines bezaubernden Vergnügens versichert halten können" (pp. 446-447; "If all the pieces and parts belonging to the opera help and serve each other, if they are unceasingly intent upon how they may attract, dazzle, and entice, if they together all attend to nothing other than making an impression with united strength, then one will be assured of fascinating pleasure").

Krause viewed pleasure as opera's ultimate objective and sought to explain its whys and wherefores. His discussion shows indebtedness to Baumgarten's idea that the work of art was sensuously perfect (*sinnlich vollkommen*) and as such was enjoyed as well as perceived through man's non-rational faculties. Instead of coming right out and calling it aesthetic pleasure, Krause followed opera's other exponents and used words like "enchanting," "alluring," "dazzling," "fascinating," and "seductive" to describe it. He believed people attended performances not because they wanted to learn something but because they wanted to enjoy themselves (p. 380). And opera provided them with that enjoyment by touching their senses, moving their emotions, and appealing to their imagination.[17] Unlike art forms addressing reason or just one of the senses, he maintained, opera addressed what were essentially unexplained and unexpected aspects of the human being.

This concept of nonrational pleasure formed the basis of his discussion of critical methodology. Believing such pleasure depended totally on a theatrical experience, he insisted that critics attend performances before they made any evaluations. The text alone, he explained, would not, could not, please to the same degree because it was supposed to function only as an integral part of a greater whole. Those who failed to understand this, he continued, treated the text as a separate entity and condemned what they erroneously considered its lack of artistic independence, neglect of the rational faculties, or defiance of the conventional dramatic standards (pp. 372-373). To underscore the impossibility of transferring the rules of one art form to another, Krause pointed out that setting a spoken tragedy to music would not automatically make for a good opera. It seemed obvious to him that different forms required different rules.

In grappling with the problem of artistic rules, Krause turned to literary history. He claimed that many ancient writers, in addition to modern dramatists like Corneille, Racine, and Molière, had produced immortal works even though they had failed to observe rules prescribed by others (p. 364). The frequent arguments among the so-called literary authorities (*Kunstrichter*) supplied Krause with still more proof that such rules could not be absolutes. Like Lessing, with whom he became acquainted in Berlin, he attempted to distinguish between extrinsic and intrinsic rules (pp. 365-366).

The reaction of theatergoers was of particular interest to Krause. Their unabashed support of opera despite so many condemnations seemed to be the best indication of its inherent worth as an art form. He maintained that the literary authorities could learn much from those opera lovers who often attended performances and who knew what they liked without having to consult any rule books: "Man muss also in jeder Kunst den Liebhabern derselben etwas ablernen. Diese dringen auf das, was gefällt, und alles das kommt ihnen natürlich vor, gesezt, dass man auch noch keine Regeln darüber hätte" (p. 151; "In every art one must learn something from its devotees. They insist upon that which pleases, and it all seems natural to them, even supposing there were still no rules for it"). He even went so far as to attribute the derivation of artistic rules to the devotees of

171

art. Their innate ability to evaluate quality "hat den geist-
reichen Werken allemal den ersten Beyfall verschaffet; die
Regeln, nach welchen sie verfertiget werden, sind immer
erst nachher daraus hergeleitet worden" (p. 363; "always
secured ingenious works their earliest approval; the rules,
according to which they are constructed, have always been
derived therefrom only afterward").

Krause opposed constraints that conflicted with opera's
assumptions as a synthesis of divergent arts. He did not,
however, see any conflict arising from observance of the
unities (p. 425). He believed they contributed to the kind
of simplicity that was needed to produce a unified total
effect. His explanation resembled that of opera's earlier defenders who preferred "noble simplicity" to Italianate complexity: "Das Vornehmste, um welches der Operndichter
sich am meisten zu bekümmern hat, und wodurch sich ein
Singspiel hauptsächlich von einer Tragödie unterscheidet,
bestehet darinn, dass die Oper eine Handlung haben muss,
die ganz simpel, einfach, und ohne viel Verwirrung ist.
Dieses Simple der Fabel macht die gröste Vollkommenheit
des Singspiels aus, und es ist unumgänglich nöthig, die
Handlung, den Knoten und dessen Auflösung nicht zu
künstlich einzurichten" (pp. 435-436; "The principal
thing, with which the librettist has to concern himself most,
and which essentially distinguishes a musical play from a
tragedy, is that the opera must have a plain and simple
action without much complication. This simplicity of the
story determines the greatest perfection of the musical play,
and it is ineluctably necessary to construct the action, the
plot, and its denouement not too artificially").

Krause also attempted to consolidate many of the ideas
about artistic probability that had been circulating for
years. He stated that whatever seemed probable in opera
would not necessarily seem probable if transposed into
another context. Actual reality, he added, could not be the
determining factor, for if it were, there obviously would
be no sense to opera or, for that matter, any other form of

theater. With an argument strikingly similar to the one used earlier by Feind, he explained: "Man sollte aber mit diesem Worte nicht gleich alles, was sonderbar ist, belegen; sonst würde man auch sagen müssen, es sey ungereimt, in den Schauspielen alles bey Licht vorzustellen, was doch würklich am Tage vorgegangen ist" (pp. 411-412; "One should with this word, however, not immediately demonstrate everything that is peculiar, otherwise one would also have to say, it is absurd to present by candlelight everything that really happened during the day").

Krause's comparison of opera to the plastic arts indicates that he was familiar with the writings of the Schlegels, from whom he copied almost verbatim:

Eine Oper ist nicht die Handlung, nicht die That selbst; es ist nur eine Abschilderung derselben. Eine Nachahmung, die der Natur vollkommen ähnlich wäre, hiesse keine Nachahmung mehr, sondern wäre eine gleiche natürliche Handlung oder Sache. Der Begriff der Nachahmung bringt es mit sich, dass nicht alles eigentlich natürlich sey; sonst müste man weisse marmorne Bilder mit Fleischfarbe anstreichen, oder mit Fellen überziehen, damit sie Haare bekämen. Ahmt man nicht belebte Körper durch unbelebte, erhabene Körper durch Flächen, und vielfarbigte durch einfarbigte nach? Eine Nachahmung darf mit dem Urbilde nur so viel Aehnlichkeit haben, als zu dessen augenblicklicher Erkennung genug ist.* (pp. 371-372)

* An opera is not the action, not the deed itself; it is only a depiction of it. An imitation that would be totally similar to nature would no longer be called an imitation but would be an equivalent, natural action or matter. It is inherent in the concept of imitation that not everything would be strictly speaking natural, otherwise one would have to paint white marble figures with flesh color or cover them with fur so that they got hairs. Does one not imitate living bodies through nonliving ones, raised bodies through flat surfaces, and polychromatic through monochromatic ones? An imitation may have with the original only so much similarity as is sufficient for its instantaneous recognition.

Krause also made comparisons to purely literary genres and concluded that operatic singing was no less probable than any other medium through which reality was simulated. In this work, which appeared seven years before Lessing's essays on the fable, Krause recalled the observation made by earlier defenders of opera, and wrote: "Können die Thiere in der Fabel reden, so können die Menschen in der Oper singen" (p. 373; "If the animals in fables can speak, then people can sing in opera").

Krause scrutinized the whole question of operatic probability still further. He claimed a work would be probable as long as it was well enough organized and motivated to be convincing. By convincing he meant able to engross the spectators' imagination so completely that they never thought to notice its deviations from actual reality (p. 423). Because of its component arts, he contended, opera could do this better than any spoken dramatic form. Its machines, but especially its music, he continued, could be responsible for imbuing it with a different kind of life. And it was this different kind of life that spectators expected to experience when they attended a performance. Like Feind, with whom he shared more than one idea, Krause believed that spectators derived pleasure from voluntarily submitting themselves to the new order presented on the stage and using their imagination to pretend along with the performers. Krause's attempt to explain art's different kind of reality relies on the theory of willing deception but reinterprets it and updates it:

> In keinem Schauspiele glaubt der Verstand eine wahre Begebenheit zu sehen. Man kommt aber in den Affect, und täuscht sich mit Vergnügen in seiner Einbildung. Ohne diese vorgefasste Meynung und ohne diesen Betrug würden selbst die Unterredungen in der Epopee keine Glaubwürdigkeit haben. Das Herz und die Phantasie dessen, der ins Opernhaus gehet, ist schon vorbereitet, sich dem Betruge der Einbildungskraft, und den Ausbrüchen der Leidenschaften zu überlassen. Es wäre ihm damit nicht gedienet, und seine Hoffnung, sich zu belu-

stigen, würde nicht befriediget, wenn der Poet und der Musikus die Nachahmung vergässen, wenn sie die Poesie und die Musik aufgäben, und mit der Prosa, mit dem Sprechen, und mit einer wirklichen, und nicht zur Lust nachgeahmten Handlung vertauschten.* (p. 374)

Krause's suggestions for operatic topics reflect these views on probability and show that he, like so many of his contemporaries, disagreed with Batteux's theory of imitation. Opera, Krause contended, did not require marvelous topics in order to seem probable. While not excluding the marvelous entirely, he cautioned that it be employed carefully so as not to become exaggerated and ridiculous, characteristics he firmly opposed. Plots dealing with human beings were best, he maintained, since they allowed for the portrayal of actions and feelings that could easily move the emotions of the audience. He considered amorous subjects especially moving, for music and the other arts helped to reinforce the emotional impact and to express subtle changes in mood. On the other hand, he rejected tragic topics as generally unsuitable because he thought operatic form would make the effect too stark, perhaps even offensive. But, he added, they would be acceptable as long as the librettists were talented enough to use them appropriately. Krause transformed ideas that had persisted since the turn of the century to suit them to the increasingly popular interest in sentiment, mood, and imagination. His was not a particularly original work, but it was very influential.

* In no play does the intellect believe it is seeing a true event. One gets into the emotional state and deceives oneself with pleasure in one's imagination. Without this preconceived idea and without this deception even the conversations in the epic would have no credibility. The soul and fantasy of the one who goes to the opera house is [sic] prepared to surrender itself to the deception of the imagination and to the outbreaks of passion. It would be of no use to him, and his hope of enjoying himself would not be satisfied, if the poet and the composer were to forget the imitation, if they were to abandon the poetry and the music and substitute prose, speech, and action that was real instead of imitated for the sake of pleasure.

The Sphere of Influence

The warm reception Krause's work received in Berlin and other cities was indicative of the steadily growing interest in opera and its latent aesthetic possibilities. In Hamburg, where there was a long tradition of such interest, it was not only reviewed admiringly, it was also used to shed new light on what were essentially old ideas. Wilhelm Adolph Paulli (1719-1772), the city's poet laureate, frequently did so in the journals he published. The November 22, 1755 issue of *Poesie und Prosa zum Nutzen und Vergnügen* is perhaps the best example.[18] Paulli's purported intention was a comprehensive discussion of theater, but he soon focused on opera, explaining that he considered it the highest form of play yet devised by man. It was like a majestically clothed aristocrat in comparison to comedy, which he likened to a plainly dressed burgher. Comedy, he maintained, aimed to please a combination of the imagination and understanding, whereas opera concentrated on the imagination alone. Paulli found its effect so mystifying that he described it in verse with words very similar to Krause's:

> Die Dichtkunst und Music, Gesang und Tanz vereinet,
> Durch starke Zauberkraft oft neu zu schaffen scheinet,
> Oft Wunderwerke thut, und prächtig ausgeschmückt,
> So sehr das Auge rührt, als das Gehör entzückt.
> Wo Töne in das Herz der Kenner rührend dringen,
> Und unverstanden auch das Volk zum Beyfall zwingen:
> Kurz, die als Königinn in stolzer Majestät
> Von dem gemeinen Schmuck der Bühne sich erhöht,
> Und mit der Macht begabt, die Herzen umzukehren,
> Selbst ihren Tadler zwingt, sie lächelnd anzuhören.*

(p. 370)

* The union of poetry and music, song and dance often seems through strong magic power to create anew, often works miracles, and, sumptuously embellished, affects the eye as much as enchanting the ear. Where tones penetrate stirringly into the heart of the connoisseurs and force even ordinary people ununderstandably to applause:

After describing opera's seductive power, Paulli proceeded to outline its history and refute the objections of its opponents. His refutation followed what had become more or less the standard pattern in operatic defenses. He began by stating that it would not have found such widespread support among intelligent people of quality, including the monarchs in Berlin and Dresden, if it were as inferior as its opponents claimed. Then he mentioned opera's neglect of the conventional dramatic rules. Paulli minimized their importance in favor of other considerations, namely familiarity with music, painting, and dancing. According to him, artistic greatness always defied mathematical demonstration and prediction because it depended on something as changeable as taste. While he agreed that rules could be derived from the consensus of many people's taste, he disagreed that those rules were universal and immutable (p. 374).[19]

Probability was the question Paulli tackled next. He viewed continuous singing as an artistic medium of communication, compared it to those used in other arts, and concluded that all such media prevented the exact reproduction of nature. He blamed individual artists rather than their chosen media for creating what he termed artistic chaos (internal contradiction). Along with Krause, he suggested avoiding such chaos by never losing sight of nature's "noble simplicity," a concept he equated with natural order.[20] Paulli's comments about artistic fabrication were not as perceptive as those of many other writers, but he understood enough about it to reject the exact imitation of nature as an absolute requirement. The fact that he chose a concrete example was typical for a defender of opera in Hamburg: "Allein, da der Endzweck der Oper einzig und allein die Belustigung der Sinnen ist, so kömmt es hauptsächlich darauf an, ob dasjenige, was unsere Sinnen vergnügen soll, nothwendig natürlich seyn müsse? Ich glaube

in short, like a queen in proud majesty, it raises itself from the common decoration of the stage and, endowed with the power of converting souls, forces even its detractors to listen approvingly.

nicht, dass dieses nothwendig erfordert werde, und bin vielmehr der Meynung, dass es genug sey, wenn solche Vorstellungen nur nicht wiedersprechend sind. Wer findet zum Exempel an dem Anschauen eines wohlausgearbeiteten Feuerwerks nicht ein Vergnügen, ob er gleich, wenn er auch alle feuerspeiende Berge des Erdbodens besucht, nichts dergleichen in der Natur antreffen wird."[21] ("But, since the purpose of opera is purely and simply the amusement of the senses, the main point is whether that which is supposed to please our senses must necessarily be natural. I do not believe that this is necessarily required, and I am much more of the opinion that it suffices as long as such representations are just not contradictory. Who does not find pleasure, for example, in viewing well-composed fireworks, although he will encounter nothing of the sort in nature even if he visits all the erupting volcanoes on earth.") Paulli maintained that an obvious lack of rational probability would go unnoticed or would be purposely forgotten as long as the degree of enjoyment remained high. He agreed with Krause, from whom he quoted directly, that spectators attended operatic performances because they were willing, able, and ready to allow the imagination's deception (*Betrug der Einbildungs-kraft*).

Krause also found admirers and supporters in Leipzig, which was reputed to be the new center of musical theatrical developments and the home of the German *Singspiel*. One of its foremost composers, Johann Adam Hiller (1728-1804), recommended Krause's book without reservations because of its ideas on cooperative artistic collaboration.[22] Hiller's interest in such collaboration had evolved from his association with Leipzig writers like Gellert and from his study of composers like Johann Adolph Hasse (1699-1783), a major contributor to the Dresden opera and also to Frederick the Great's Berlin opera.[23] Hiller's abiding interest in collaboration manifested itself in various ways at various times throughout his life. In 1754 it came in the form of "Abhandlung von der Nachahmung der Natur in der

Musik," an essay Marpurg considered important enough to reprint in his journal the following year.[24] Batteux was the starting point from which Hiller quickly departed. His examination of the sources, products, and effects of imitation reviewed the ideas about art's essence, reality, and appeal that were under discussion in the early 1750s and developed them to their logical extremes. Hiller's essay represented yet another phase in the gradual shift from the theory of mimesis to one of expression.

Hiller considered the imitative instinct (*Trieb zur Nachahmung*) common to all human beings. He maintained that imitating a model was absolutely normal, but that the imitation or result had to be unnatural because it was not the model itself, not the real thing (p. 516). The arts, he continued, grew out of attempts to imitate nature's perfections and were therefore artificial. Like Krause, Gellert, and those directly involved with writing and performing musico-poetic works, he strove to explain how and why man was receptive to such artistic imitations. He eliminated the intellect (*der Verstand*), which communicated and perceived ideas through words, for it demanded logical exactitude and rational classification. The *je ne sais quoi* of the musical experience proved to him that there could be no exactitude or rationality in art's appeal: "Wir werden so unvermerkt, so sanft von ihr [music] gerührt, dass wir nicht wissen, was wir empfinden; oder besser, dass wir unsrer Empfindung keinen Namen geben können. Dieses Gefühl der Töne ist uns unbekannt, aber es erwecket uns Vergnügen, und das ist uns genug" (p. 523; "We are so suddenly and so gently affected by it [music] that we do not know what we are perceiving, or, better, that we can give no name to our perception. This feeling of the tones is unknown to us, but it arouses pleasure, and that is sufficient for us"). He then concluded that the spirit (*das Herz*), which communicated and perceived feelings through tones and other nonverbal means, must be the faculty that made man receptive to art. His explanation of that spirit's need to supplement nature suggests implicitly that he thought man had an innate desire to make or create like nature: "Unser Herz ist so unbeständig von Natur, dass ein beständiges Vergnügen für dasselbe kein Vergnügen ist. Das Neue, das Seltsame und Fremde schickt sich am besten zu seinem Unbestande. Da nun die Natur, ihm zu Gefallen, nichts neues hervor brachte; da auch ausser dem Gebiethe der Natur nichts zu finden war, sollte der Mensch es nicht gewaget haben, selbst etwas zu schaffen, welches das Mittel zwischen dem Natürlichen und Unnatürlichen wäre? Ich widerspreche mir nicht, wenn ich die Werke der Kunst also beschreibe" (p. 517; "Our soul is by nature so inconstant that a constant pleasure is no pleasure for it. The new, the peculiar, and the exotic are best fit for its inconstancy. Since nature brought forth nothing new to please it, since nothing was to be found even outside the realm of nature, should man not have dared to create something himself which would be the medium between the natural and the unnatural? I am not contradicting myself when I describe works of art thusly").

Hiller viewed feeling not only as the basis of art but also as the basis of art criticism. It was to opera that he turned to support his views. Following the standard pattern, he cited first its popularity among intelligent, well-bred people and then proceeded to discuss the approach of its opponents. His analysis of their failings reflects the suggestion made earlier by Dubos that the critic rely on his own feelings. It also seems to presage the suggestion made later by the Romantic Ludwig Tieck (1773-1853) that the critic become a child again. Hiller considered opera's opponents "zu fühllos, die süsse Gewalt der Töne zu empfinden, oder zu stolz es zu gestehen, dass man sie eben wie eine ungelehrte Seele empfinde" (p. 529; "too insensitive to perceive the charming power of music or too proud to admit that one perceives it just like an uneducated person"). They condemned opera, he contended, because Aristotle had known nothing about it and had given no rules for it (p.

531). In his opinion, their dependence on the neoclassical code was so great that it desensitized them and prevented them from doing what came naturally to most people, namely enjoying operatic performances. He maintained they did not and would not understand that "Man muss hier einzig und allein das Herz urtheilen lassen" (pp. 522-523; "Here one must purely and simply let the soul judge"). Furthermore he believed there was something about the operatic form, most likely its attempt to synthesize divergent arts, that made its practitioners avoid strict rules, disavow traditional codification, and constantly search for new ways of expression. When criticizing some negative aspects of contemporary musico-poetic experiments, he broke off in the middle of the paragraph, and wrote: "Doch ich suche hier etwas unter die Regeln zu bringen, das nie die Absicht und den Willen gehabt hat, sich den Regeln zu unterwerfen" (p. 533; "However, I am trying here to subject to the rules something that never had the intention or the will to submit to the rules").

Another of the crucial problems in criticism, according to him, was that many critics failed to distinguish art from nature (p. 541). Opera's opponents in particular, he explained, had made many procedural blunders precisely because of their failure to comprehend the basic differences. Unlike them, Hiller developed his interpretation of verisimilitude from what he claimed to know about the psychology of man's artistic reactions. He was puzzled by the fact that spectators enjoyed opera even though they knew it would be nonsensical in the real world. He was certain their pleasure did not derive from comparing opera with reality, but he could find no rational explanation for it. Consequently he resorted to a series of questions about the possible existence in human beings of certain mysterious inclinations:

Dinge, die durch einen ganz andern Sinn sollten begriffen werden, scheinen auf einmal ihre Natur geändert zu haben: wir glauben sie in den Tönen zu finden, und wir finden sie wirklich darinnen, so weit sie sonst davon unterschieden sind. Ist dieses nicht eine Art von Zauberey? Ich weis nicht was uns so gutwillig machet, dass wir uns hintergehen lassen, ohne es gewahr zu werden; oder wenn wir es merken, dass wir uns nicht wegen des Betruges schadlos zu halten suchen? Ist vielleicht eine geheime Neigung zum Sonderbaren und Fremden Schuld daran? oder haben wir zu wenig Herz, uns der Gewalt der Töne zu widersetzen? Es ist dieses ein Räthsel, das die Vernunft nicht leicht lösen wird, weil es ihr gleichsam nur im Traume vorgeleget wird.* (p. 534)

Hiller's interpretation is particularly significant because some of his younger contemporaries, among them Johann Gottfried Herder, began asking the same questions, answering them affirmatively, and making them programmatic in just a few more decades.

The wondrous was an important critical topic that Hiller considered generally misunderstood by opera's opponents. While agreeing with them that it posed one of the greatest dangers for all the arts, he insisted that it was one of the greatest sources of pleasure. The older operas of Leipzig and Hamburg had been bombastic and preposterous, he explained, because the wondrous had been flagrantly misused. Controlling it and using it tastefully as well as sensibly was, in his opinion, necessary but difficult. He maintained that only great artists, like Hasse, his favorite, were successfully able to do so. Their works seemed to rise "zu

---

* Things that should be comprehended through a completely different sense seem all at once to have changed their nature. We believe they are found in musical sounds, and we do really find them therein, though they are otherwise vastly different. Is this not a kind of magic? I do not know what makes us so obliging that we let ourselves be deceived without becoming aware of it; or when we notice it, that we do not seek to recoup on account of the deception. Is perhaps a hidden inclination toward the strange and the exotic to blame? Or do we have too little courage to resist the power of music? This is a puzzle that reason will not solve easily because it is put to it as though only in a dream.

einer fast göttlichen Würde, weil es uns unbegreiflich scheinet, dass es ein Mensch so hoch habe bringen können" (p.
542; "to an almost divine majesty because it appears incomprehensible to us that a human being could have succeeded so splendidly"). Hiller accepted imitation as an
underlying principle of human activity, but he, along with
many of his contemporaries, refused to join with Batteux
in restricting opera and making it the "genre of the wondrous."

Hiller's opportunity to implement some of his theories
came in 1764 when he wrote the music for some songs added to the newly revised version of Weisse's *Der Teufel ist
los*. The overwhelming success of his composition led to
further collaboration with Weisse and then also with
Daniel Schiebeler (1741-1771), a Hamburg writer who followed his operatic forebears in cultivating popular balladry, parody, local color, grotesqueries, and provincialisms.
The numerous *Singspiele* they produced made the aging
Gottsched rather unhappy, but they had the reverse effect
on the youthful Goethe, who became so fond of them during his student years in Leipzig (1765-1768) that he visited
Hiller to discuss common artistic concerns.[25] Hiller's fame
as a composer of German musical theatrical works spread
quite rapidly as more and more performances took place
not only in Leipzig but also in Hamburg, Berlin, and Weimar. They were especially popular with Weimar's musically inclined Duchess Anna Amalia (1739-1807), who in
the years to come was to compose scores herself and foster
the creation of librettos by far more talented poets.

Throughout his long life Hiller remained deeply concerned about the state of the performing arts in Germany.
When he recognized vocal talent in young students, he vol-
unteered to tutor them free of charge. One of his earliest
pupils was Corona Schröter (1751-1802), whose Leipzig performances left such a lasting impression on Goethe that he
later called her to Weimar and made her the leading lady
in various plays.[26] Hiller's tutorials led to the founding of

an academy, which he hoped would supply Germany with well-trained musicians and, above all, singer-actors. Like Ekhof and many of his other contemporaries, he strove to raise theatrical standards by working directly with performers and encouraging them to explore the practical techniques of the stage.

Hiller also thought the exchange of critical ideas was important, and from 1766 to 1769 he published *Wöchentliche Nachrichten und Anmerkungen die Musik betreffend.* Among other things it featured commentaries on repertoires and reviews of current productions. Many of those reviews reinforced ideas Hiller had articulated much earlier. The one having to do with the Viennese production of Gluck's *Alceste* developed his ideas on artistic freedom with the kind of vocabulary that was becoming more and more widely used: "in den Händen eines Mannes, der mit dem Geiste des Dichters setzet, und da, wo dem musikalischen Handwerker von den gemeinen Regeln Fessel angelegt sind, diese Fessel zerbricht, sich über die Regeln hinweg schwingt, und mit der Freyheit des Genies selbst Regel und Muster wird; in den Händen eines solchen Mannes muss die Musik Wunderwerke thun."[27] ("In the hands of a man who composes with the spirit of a poet, and where the musical craftsman is put into irons by the rules, smashes these irons, soars forth over the rules, and with the freedom of the genius, becomes himself rule and model; in the hands of such a man music has to work miracles.") Other reviews called for more collaboration among artists and less emulation of foreign models, whether ancient or modern. The lack of cultural patriotism, which had concerned opera's exponents since Harsdörffer's day, was singled out and blamed for the sorry state of German musical theater: "Wir Deutschen sind immer noch so unglücklich, dass wir keine Singspiele oder Opern in unserer Muttersprache haben. Woran liegt die Schuld? Gewiss weiter an nichts, als dass das Genie der Deutschen nicht genug geachtet, nicht genug hervorgezogen und aufgemuntert wird."[28] ("We Germans are still so unfortunate as to have no musical plays or operas in our mother tongue. What is to blame? Certainly nothing further than that the genius of the Germans is not given enough attention, preference, and encouragement.")

Hiller's Leipzig contemporary, Johann Wilhelm Hertel (1726-1789), was equally patriotic but much happier about the progress that had already been made. The preface to his *Sammlung Musikalischer Schriften* (1757-1758) boasted that Germany's new, more sophisticated musical practices had rendered study abroad totally unnecessary. Germans could now find everything they needed at home, including the writings of major theorists and critics (sig. 2^v). Hertel envisioned his collection as a serial supplementing what Mizler and Marpurg had already made available, but unforeseen circumstances prevented publication of more than the first volume, which consisted primarily of operatic essays translated from French with critical footnotes.

In his notes to Toussaint Rémond de Saint Mard's (1682-1757) "Réflexions sur l'Opéra" (1741), Hertel discussed the long history of operatic criticism and provided a bibliography of the major works on the subject. He considered such bibliographic research essential because he thought opera had provoked more disputes than any other form of art. After listing the foreign critics who had unequivocally condemned it, like Saint Evremond and Muratori, he mentioned those who objected merely to its superficial flaws, like Porée and Voltaire. He then turned to German writings and, in addition to noting those of the Gottsched school, carefully made known to his contemporaries the defenses of Hudemann, Uffenbach, Mattheson, Zinck, and, of course, Krause (pp. 36-38).

Hertel thought highly of Rémond de Saint Mard although he took issue with several of his points. One was the French writer's claim that opera had originated with the Greeks. Hertel considered opera a modern art form, which had been invented in Italy and which bore little resemblance to ancient tragedy.[29] Another point he questioned involved opera's purpose. In addition to deceiving the imagination of its spectators, he suggested that it edify their minds by illustrating vice punished and virtue rewarded. The reason for his suggestion was, however, purely pragmatic; he believed opera would not be so adversely criticized if it at least paid lip service to a noble purpose. Hertel, who was a performer and composer by profession, stressed objective rule while claiming at the same time that subjective feeling was perhaps the safest basis for critical evaluation.

His other notes are filled with similar unexplained contradictions. He had gleaned ideas from many theoretical writings and reiterated them without always fully comprehending their import. His reliance on Krause was great, for he repeatedly borrowed entire passages or sentences. This is particularly evident in his notes to the essay with which Élie Catherine Fréron (1718-1776), a confirmed supporter of Saint Evremond and opponent of Voltaire, had answered Rémond de Saint Mard. The key issue was continuous singing, and Hertel claimed it was difficult to defend because it was indeed far more unnatural than tragic verse. However, opera's intentions made him uncertain whether any such defense was even called for: "sie will nun durchaus als ein glänzendes Ungeheuer gefallen; und sie gefällt auch wahrhaftig der Critik und der Vernunft zum Trotz. Die Harmonie reitzt in der Oper mehr als die Vernunft" (p. 202; "It absolutely insists upon pleasing as a glittering monstrosity; and it does indeed truly please in defiance of criticism and reason. In opera harmony has a greater attraction than reason").

A word-for-word borrowing from Krause supplied justification for the improbabilities created by operatic decorations and machinery: "Wenn sie geschickt und nicht ohne Noth angebracht werden, so sind sie in der Oper mehr als in geredeten Trauerspielen zu dulten, weil die Musik das Herz so stark beschäftiget, dass die Einbildungskraft sich eher täuschen lässt, und der Verstand nicht Zeit hat daran

zu denken, dass dergleichen Dinge nach unsern aufgeklär-
ten Begriffen nichts sind" (p. 211; "If they are employed
aptly and relevantly, they are to be tolerated in opera more
than in spoken tragedies, because music engages the soul so
strongly that the imagination lets itself be deceived more
readily, and the intellect has no time to think that according to our enlightened ideas such things are nothing").
Krause's ideas on operatic synthesis helped Hertel explain
that a libretto was not a separate entity and that attendance
at performances was essential: "Sie wird auch nicht zum
Lesen, sondern zum Singen gemacht; man kann daher
nicht mit kaltem Blute von einer Oper urtheilen, sondern
man muss die ganze Vorstellung derselben sehen, hören
und fühlen" (p. 217; "It is not made for reading but for
singing; one therefore cannot judge an opera coldblood-
edly, one must rather see, hear, and feel the entire performance of it"). Those who reviewed this annotated collection
generally praised its intentions while pointing out its all too
obvious shortcomings. Hertel was not always right in his
notes, but he was very right in his patriotic optimism about
the upsurge in German musicological activities. His collection was an adequate, yet pedestrian predecessor for all
those musical anthologies, journals, histories, and diction-
aries that were to be published in Germany before the end
of the eighteenth century.

DUBOS VERSUS BATTEUX:
NICOLAI, RAMLER, AND MENDELSSOHN

Frederick the Great's patronage of theater reached its peak
in the years immediately preceding the Seven Years' War.
Without neglecting the French ensemble that performed
spoken dramas, he spent phenomenal sums of money on his
royal opera company. Its increasingly elaborate spectacles
of sight and sound served to stimulate interest for the resi-
dents of Berlin and to intensify discussion among the members of the Montagsklub, many of whom were avid opera-

goers. Older as well as newly founded periodicals were the vehicles through which they conveyed their operatic observations, suggestions, and analyses to a steadily growing reading public. There was a market for cultural news, especially about theater, and Berlin publishers sought out local talent to supply it. Christian Friedrich Voss (1722-1795) called on fellow members of the Montagsklub for contributions to his newspaper, and Marpurg did the same for his *Historisch-Kritische Beyträge*.

The journals published by Friedrich Nicolai (1733-1811) also contained articles, notes, and reviews by some of the most illustrious young men of the day. Nicolai was the son of a Berlin book dealer and was trained from early on to enter the family business. During the years of his apprenticeship, he found time to learn English, to read widely in philosophy as well as literature, and to keep informed about developments in the musico-poetic arts. The works he wrote in his early twenties reveal his ambition to be a critic and theorist; they also mark the beginning of his life-long devotion to Prussia and its cultural achievements. He refused to align himself with Leipzig's Gottsched or Zurich's Bodmer and Breitinger because he considered their systems artificial. He preferred the unsystematic approach and the independent attitude that seemed to him distinctive to Berlin criticism. This preference, which probably resulted as much from his business sense as from his critical acumen, brought him into contact with Lessing and Mendelssohn. He soon began corresponding with both of them on the nature of tragedy and collaborating on the *Briefe, die neueste Literatur betreffend*. Nicolai immersed himself in Dubos's *Réflexions critiques* and encouraged his new friends to ponder many of the ideas on aesthetics and tragedy that it presented. Their abiding interest in Dubos is attested to not only by their translations of various sections of his work but also by their frequent mention of him and his ideas.[30] Although Nicolai was eventually regarded as reactionary by a still younger generation whose brilliance he, like his king, failed to appreciate, his support of the avant-garde of the 1750s and 1760s helped bring Berlin to the forefront of intellectual activities in the German lands.

The anonymously published *Briefe über den itzigen Zustand der schönen Wissenschaften in Deutschland* (1755) was one of the early works in which Nicolai attempted to expound his theory of criticism. Like so many who preceded him, he did so by focusing on Gottsched and using him as an opponent. Nicolai disagreed with much of the commentary Gottsched had given in his recently published excerpts from Batteux (1754) and maintained that the best critic showed with a masterpiece rather than with spurious rules just what was needed for reform. Nicolai, a staunch defender of Milton and the English dramatists, opposed Gottsched's contention that the French alone were worthy of emulation. He stated that Gottsched had erred gravely in thinking Germans would prefer the French neoclassical code over what the ancient Greeks and Romans had actually written.[31] Nicolai bemoaned the fact that the premature death of Johann Elias Schlegel had deprived the German stage of its most promising playwright-critic. And he asserted that Lessing—whose bibliography already included numerous critical works and what turned out to be most of the dramas he was to write during his lifetime— was the only up-and-coming young man capable of taking over (p. 88).

Nicolai believed Gottsched's dictatorial stupidity, critical pedantry, and artistic insensitivity were even more apparent in his unequivocal condemnation of opera. In the third of these *Briefe*, he refuted that condemnation using ideas borrowed from Krause and articulated with the rhetorical passion of a devotee of Italian *opera seria*. Nicolai, who was never to accept Gluck's reform operas,[32] rejected Gottsched's subordination of music to poetry. He maintained that music was the most important of opera's component arts because it made the strongest impression on the audience. Those who attended performances, he argued, did not expect to follow the action through the words; they knew the music would somehow explain everything brilliantly (p. 16). Because of operatic music's expressiveness, he continued, people of good taste in Berlin, Dresden, and elsewhere were captivated, even transfixed by what they experienced in the theater: "Der Zuhörer steht erstaunt, er vergisst, dass er Vergnügens wegen gekommen ist, und theilet willig das schaudernde Erstaunen, das sich in dem Angesichte eines ieden Spielers zeiget—Wer rührte hier mehr, der Dichter oder der Musicus?" (p. 18; "The listener stands amazed, he forgets that he has come for pleasure and voluntarily shares the awesome astonishment visible in the face of each player. Who makes more of an impression here, the poet or the composer?")

In his opinion, Gottsched had committed one of the worst critical errors by neglecting to gain empirical familiarity with opera. If he had done his homework, Nicolai surmised, he would have had to observe one very significant fact. The fact was one Schiller pondered several decades later, namely that it was music that mitigated the failings or concealed the absurdities of mediocre librettos. This, Nicolai suggested, must have been true of the operas produced in early eighteenth-century Hamburg, for whoever read their texts had to agree with Wernicke's biting criticism of Postel.

Another of Nicolai's arguments defending music has to do with the psychology of man's artistic reaction and shows his attempt to digest the ideas of Leibniz and Baumgarten. He claimed that music appealed directly to the lower powers of the soul (die unteren Selenkräfte) where it gave rise to clear, but confused images that could influence the whole range of human emotions. Because of this he viewed instrumental music as an art sufficient in, of, and by itself. Nevertheless he believed it could easily be combined with certain other arts to produce even more splendid effects. While wise critics like Batteux and Krause refused to separate opera's arts, he added, an ignorant critic like Gottsched did so and, as a result, "wüthet in ihr Innerstes" (p. 24; "storms into its innermost part").

The journals Nicolai subsequently founded and edited show that his concept of musical theater hardly changed throughout the years. He remained indebted to Krause and never missed an opportunity to praise him. While considering Hertel's translations adequate and his bibliographic notes helpful, the review in the *Bibliothek der schönen Wissenschaften und der freyen Künste* (1758) found the collection disappointing in comparison to Krause's treatise.[33] Nicolai also remained severely critical of Gottsched. A review of *Nöthiger Vorrat* for the same journal (1758) called his operatic commentaries unfair and his admiration of Opitz, the acknowledged originator of German opera, logically inconsistent.[34] Furthermore, Nicolai remained loyal to the kind of Italianate grand opera fostered by Frederick the Great. A review for the *Allgemeine Deutsche Bibliothek* (1770) questioned the artistic quality of operettas about the lowest social classes and, in suggesting reforms, rejected the French musical style.[35]

Ramler, cofounder of the Montagsklub and one of its most productive members, was also concerned with defending opera but differed from Nicolai in most respects. He was a conservative poet whose approach was neither polemical nor empirical. It was firmly rooted in the tradition that had grown out of the writings of Horace, his model in poetry as well as criticism. Because he believed there were rational explanations for all aspects of art, he was less interested in studying the so-called new science of aesthetics than he was in investigating theories about the imitation of nature and their concomitant rules. His preference for the systematic philosophy of Wolff, Baumgarten's teacher, had developed during his years at the University of Halle and remained strong throughout his lifetime. He made it the subject of his lectures when he became *maître de la philosophie* at the royal military academy. And he discussed it with his ever widening circle of acquaintances in

Berlin. Among them was Johann Georg Sulzer (1720-1779), the Swiss mathematician and philosopher with whom he published a short-lived journal and with whom he resided for several months.[36] Like Frederick the Great, both men thought that the principles of Wolffian philosophy could be used to help improve the quality of artistic endeavors in Prussia. They sought to popularize them, each in his own way. Sulzer's contribution was *Theorie der schönen Künste* (1771-1774), the encyclopedia of the arts that grew out of his attempt to translate Jacques Lacombe's (1721-1811) *Dictionnaire des beaux arts* (1752).

While Sulzer studied Lacombe, Ramler turned to Batteux's systematization of the arts and, believing it merited attention, decided to make it more readily accessible to his countrymen. His translation of *Cours de belles lettres* appeared from 1756 to 1758 as *Einleitung in die Schönen Wissenschaften*. Contrary to what many scholars would have us believe, Ramler was not a totally unquestioning adherent of Batteux. He explained in his preface that he disagreed with two of Batteux's points but that he translated them without comment because he wanted to follow the French text faithfully, changing only the examples to suit German circumstances. One such point was bourgeois tragedy. Without mentioning that his friend Lessing had just completed one in Potsdam the year before, namely *Miss Sara Sampson* (1755), Ramler explained his disagreement with Batteux: "Auch habe ich zu seiner Abhandlung von der Tragödie, wo er die unheroischen Subjecte verwirft, nicht hinzusetzen dürfen: dass es sehr wohl möglich sey ein gutes bürgerliches Trauerspiel zu verfertigen, wenn man die Geschicklichkeit hat, alles das mit der grössesten Kunst zu verstecken, was uns bey niedrigen Personen anstössig ist. Ein solches Trauerspiel widerspricht seinen Regeln eigentlich nicht. Kan ich die Handlung auf diese Weise erhöhen, so gebe ich ihr den Werth der heroischen Handlung" (sig. b2r; "To his discussion of tragedy, where he disallows unheroic subjects, I was prohibited from adding that it would be very well possible to construct a good bourgeois tragedy if one has the skill to disguise with the greatest ingenuity everything that offends us in lowly persons. Such a tragedy does not actually contradict his rules. If I can elevate the action in this way, I give it the value of heroic action").

The second point with which he could not entirely agree was Batteux's classification of opera. Ramler refused to classify it as the kind of tragedy that dealt only with the wondrous actions of gods and demigods. This time he mentioned a specific author. He believed Metastasio's librettos had already proved successfully and, furthermore, tastefully that human beings could be portrayed in operatic form (sig. b^v). Allowing opera to portray human actions instead of divine ones and allowing tragedy to portray bourgeois actions instead of royal or noble ones was tantamount to negating Batteux's entire system as well as all other systems based on the imitation of nature. Unlike others in Berlin, Ramler saw no purpose in trying to reconcile abstract theory with empirical knowledge.

Ramler had become well acquainted with operatic practices as well as theories during his early years in Berlin. According to his correspondence with Wilhelm Ludwig Gleim (1719-1803), he thoroughly enjoyed performances of works by composers like Graun and Hasse and enthusiastically looked forward to the opening of each new season.[37] That correspondence also indicates that he was reading Krause's manuscript, discussing it with him, and suggesting revisions as early as 1748. Their common interest in the relationship of poetry and music subsequently led them to collaborate on *Oden mit Melodien* (1753, 1755). Ramler began his long career of writing dramatic and semidramatic texts to be set to music when Princess Amalia, the sister of Frederick the Great, commissioned him to write Graun a cantata. He complied with *Der Tod Jesu* (1754), which was for some time one of his better known works.

Ramler's main contribution to the operatic discussion in

Berlin came in 1756 when he produced two articles for Marpurg's *Historisch-Kritische Beyträge*. One was a translation of selections from Rémond de Saint Mard's "Réflexions sur l'Opéra" (1741). The other was his own "Vertheidigung der Opern." Ramler criticized opera's opponents for neglecting available evidence, but he himself really did not do much better. He simply cited full theaters as opera's most significant defense and hastily drew a comparison to the tragedies of Corneille and the English dramatists, which he considered similarly pleasing despite their many imperfections. Instead of analyzing actual practices of discussing current abuses, he borrowed from various theoretical writings in order to prove that opera was neither improbable nor unnatural. His arguments were rather eclectic and much more conservative than those of Marpurg and the others who wished to make poetry the dominant art. Ramler conceived of opera as a kind of drama in which music was a decorative accessory, slightly more important than dancing and stage sets. He claimed it was the poet's responsibility to control such accessories by observing as closely as possible the three unities and the rules of Horace. Violations were justifiable to him only if they helped make the operatic imitation of nature seem more probable.

Ramler tried to explain his concept of imitation further when he defended opera's continuous singing. His explanation lacked cohesiveness because he relied on ideas from diverse sources without always realizing that they were incompatible. He began with the animal fable—the form his colleague and friend Lessing was to analyze a few years later. If the fable, Ramler argued along with Krause, could imitate nature with animals that purportedly spoke the language of man, then opera should be allowed to use a musical means of communication. He agreed with the Schlegels about the artificiality of those means, and he even reiterated the Schlegels' analogy to the plastic arts: "Allein, kann man die wohlgetroffene Nachahmung in einem Kupferstiche schön finden und des Menschen Farbe bey einem schönen

Marmorbilde vergessen, so wird man auch die Unähnlichkeit vergessen können, wenn die menschlichen Handlungen in singenden Tönen nachgeahmet werden, zu denen die Instrumente nur noch gleichsam einen Nachklang hinzu thun" (p. 85; "But if one can consider the successful imitation in an engraving beautiful and forget human coloration in a beautiful marble statue, one will also be able to forget the dissimilarity when human actions are imitated in vocal music to which the instruments add only as it were resonance"). However, he followed Batteux in attempting to find a rational explanation for the kind of nature opera's musical means could imitate. Ramler believed he found it in the Wolffian formulation that had been contemplated in a different context by Sulzer's compatriots, Bodmer and Breitinger: "Kann man sich nicht vorstellen, man sey in einer andern Welt, wo die Menschen langsamer reden und handeln?" (p. 85; "Can one not imagine one is in another world where the people speak and act more slowly?").

Ramler had problems explaining the differences between natural and artistic truth. He also had problems explaining why people attended opera when they knew full well that what took place on stage would be completely improbable in the real world. His explanation was one that had often been given in earlier operatic defenses, but by 1756 it had become rather old-fashioned. Ramler wrote that human reason suspended all comparisons to reality and allowed itself to be deceived for the sake of pleasure, and then he queried: "Ist es eine grössere Kunst, sein Herz eine kleine Zeit zu betrügen, oder ist es wichtiger, diese grosse Wahrheit bald zu entdecken, dass alles Betrug sey?" (p. 88; "Is it a greater trick to deceive the soul for a short time, or is it more important to soon discover the great truth that everything is deception?").

Moses Mendelssohn, the erudite scholar and philosopher of the Montagsklub, was drawn into the operatic discussion because of his dissatisfaction with such explanations. He shared Ramler's admiration for Wolff and Leibniz and agreed that the arts should be described systematically. He disagreed, however, about the common denominator for that system. He considered Batteux's "imitation of nature" insufficient because it failed to account for the effect of the artistic product on its audience. That effect was the common denominator Mendelssohn preferred. Although he appreciated the contributions to aesthetics made by Baumgarten and Meier, he criticized their narrow perspectives, claiming they had derived their theories from poetry and rhetoric alone. He insisted that no theory would be valid unless all the arts, especially music, were given careful consideration.[38] His own attempt to do so led to stricter observation at the Berlin opera and closer scrutiny of Dubos's *Réflexions critiques* with its differentiation of artistic signs or means of expression. He discussed his ideas at length with Nicolai and Lessing, both of whom had already worked on Dubos, and requested their suggestions on the essay he was drafting. He published it in 1757 under the title "Betrachtungen über die Quellen und die Verbindungen der schönen Künste und Wissenschaften."[39]

Mendelssohn called art the sensuous expression of perfection. In describing that perfection as something harmonious in and of itself, he tried to show how the imitation of nature figured in the creative process.[40] Nature, he explained, was so diverse that its overall unity and order could not possibly be perceived, much less imitated. Because human limitations, he continued, prevented the imitation of nature's infinite variety, the artist could do no more than select the most beautiful aspects of the parts he was able to perceive and then bring them together into a meaningful new relationship. Mendelssohn wrote: "Was sie [nature] in verschiedenen Gegenständen zerstreuet hat, versammelt er in einem einzigen Gesichtspunkt, bildet sich ein Ganzes daraus, und bemühet sich, es so vorzustellen, wie es die Natur vorgestellt haben würde, wenn die Schönheit dieses Vorwurfs ihre einzige Absicht gewesen wäre" (pp. 240-241; "What she [nature] dispersed in various objects, he assembles in one single viewpoint, forms a totality out of them, and strives to present it as nature would have if the beauty of this subject had been her only intention"). Since the resultant work of art was the sum of the most beautiful aspects of several parts of nature, he thought it came closer to ideal beauty than any single part by itself. He contended that such works of art provided pleasure because they presented beauty in a way that was comprehensible enough for human beings to experience. According to him, it was the inherently human desire to experience beauty that allowed art to gain control over the soul and to arouse and quiet the passions. Studying the aesthetic experience would, he suggested, reveal much not only about art but also about the soul itself.

Mendelssohn's ideas on combinations of the arts derived from this theory. He stated that the artist had to recognize the intention of his chosen art and organize his work accordingly in order to present humanly comprehensible and therefore pleasurable beauty. He believed that individual arts could never be synthesized so that they still remained equals within the synthesis because of their varying, often conflicting intentions. They could only, he explained, be brought together if one art were singled out as the principal one to which all others must be subordinated. The principal art's intention, he added, should always dominate, unless an insolvable conflict arose, that is, something that threatened the unity of the work.

Before proceeding to the possible kinds of combinations, Mendelssohn examined the intentions of the individual arts in order to discover their differences. He maintained that they differed from each other because their signs or means of expression required them to observe different laws. Music, sculpture, painting, and the dance, he explained, were comprised of natural signs, or those that were based in the actual characteristics of the object. Such signs, he continued, appealed to the sense of sight or the sense of hearing and were therefore limited in what they could present. On the other hand, he explained, poetry and rhetoric appealed to the mind and were capable of expressing everything it could conceptualize because they consisted of arbitrary signs, or those that in themselves had nothing in common with the object. He further distinguished arbitrary and natural signs by whether they were successive in time or simultaneous in space.

Mendelssohn argued that these fundamental differences determined the kinds of combinations that could be accomplished successfully. Arbitrary signs, he maintained, combined relatively easily with natural ones as long as they were all successive in time. He believed the ancients had produced such combinations by subordinating music to poetry in their choruses and hymns as well as in their declamation. He cited modern opera as the opposite possibility; in it poetry and painting served to clarify, enhance, or focus the emotional effect of music: "Der Ausdruck der Empfindung in der Musik ist stark, lebhaft und rührend, aber unbestimmt. Man spürt sich von einer gewissen Empfindung durchdrungen; aber unsere Empfindung ist dunkel, allgemein, und auf keinen einzelnen Vorwurf eingeschränkt. Diesem Mangel kann durch die Hinzuthuung deutlicher und willkührlicher Zeichen abgeholfen werden. Sie können den Vorwurf von allen Seiten bestimmen, und die Empfindung zu einer individuellen Empfindung machen, welche leichter zum Ausbruche kömmt. Geschieht nun diese nähere Bestimmung der Empfindungen in der Musik, vermittelst der Dichtkunst und der Malerey oder Verzierungen der Bühne; so entsteht die Oper der Neuren" (p. 261; "The expression of feeling in music is strong, lively, and moving but indeterminate. One is conscious of being filled with a certain feeling, but our feeling is obscure, general, and limited to no one single theme. This lack can be obviated through the addition of distinct and arbitrary signs. They can determine the theme from all sides and make the feeling into an individual one which bursts forth more easily. If this closer determination of the feelings in music happens by means of poetry and painting or stage decorations, there results the opera of the moderns"). Since he considered music the major operatic art, he claimed its rules always had to be given precedence. And he asserted that the poetic or dramatic rules had to be readjusted, altered, or, perhaps, even disregarded if they conflicted with those of music: "Die Musik, oder der sinnliche Ausdruck durch die natürlichen Zeichen der Töne, ist bey dieser Art von Verbindung der Künste der Hauptendzweck; daher müssen alle Ausnahmen von Seiten der Dichtkunst geschehen. Sie kann von ihren besondern Regeln, als der Einheit des Ortes, der Zeit und der Handlung, füglich abweichen, wenn es zum Besten der Musik geschieht. Ja der Dichter muss sich in allen seinen Ausdrückungen nach den Bedürfnissen des Tonkünstlers richten. Er darf seinem Genie nicht den völligen Lauf lassen, sondern er muss jederzeit auf die Hauptkunst zurück sehen, auf deren Endzweck alles abzielen soll" (pp. 261-262; "Music, or the sensuous expression through the natural signs of tones, is the principal final purpose in this kind of combination of arts; therefore all the exceptions must happen on the part of poetry. It can properly deviate from its specific rules, like the unity of time, place, and action, if music benefits. In all his phrases the poet must indeed be governed by the needs of the composer. He is not permitted to indulge his genius but rather must always consider the principal art, at whose final purpose everything should aim"). Adding a third successive art, namely dancing, he thought feasible, though a little more problematic. He claimed the ancients had done it, and he cited among his modern examples *Montezuma* (1755), the opera Frederick the Great had worked on with Graun.

After discussing some other possibilities, Mendelssohn went on to speculate about combining several successive arts with several simultaneous ones. He stated that perfect fusions of such divergent kinds of beauty could only be found in nature: "Dieses Geheimniss hat sich die Natur fast allein vorbehalten. Sie verbindet in ihrem unermesslichen

199

Plan, die Schönheiten der Töne, Farben, Bewegungen und Figuren durch unendliche Zeiten und gränzenlose Räume in der vollkommensten Harmonie" (p. 267; "This secret nature has reserved almost solely for herself. In her infinite design she combines in the most perfect harmony the beauties of tones, colors, motions, and figures through immeasurable times and boundless spaces"). He thought human limitations precluded the successful imitation of that grand unity in diversity. Opera represented to him the attempt to do so, but it could only be considered a fusion in the figurative sense (p. 267).

Mendelssohn continued to explore opera's implications for aesthetics in the coming years. In "Betrachtungen über das Erhabene und das Naive in den schönen Wissenschaften" (1758), he described the sublime as the sensuous expression of perfection that arouses admiration, and he cited opera as an example.[41] Nicolai, who shared his operatic interests, if not all of his views, apparently tried to encourage still further discussion. He suggested that they correspond with Lessing and compile the letters into a book after each of them had written an essay on the subject.[42] Lessing was the one who defaulted, but the publication of his *Laokoon* in 1766 indicates that he did not forget.

SEVEN

LESSING'S CONSOLIDATION

FRENCH, ITALIAN, AND ENGLISH

GOTTHOLD Ephraim Lessing's first sojourn in Berlin began in 1748. He left Leipzig, where he held a scholarship to study theology, because he was financially unable to pay the notes he had underwritten for several actors. His association with them derived from his great fascination for drama and the performing arts. That fascination originated during his school years, when he studied the ancient dramatists and practiced writing his own texts. It increased rapidly after his introduction to actual stage performances in Leipzig. The Neuber troupe, which at the time was more concerned with its own survival than with Gottschedian reforms, had expanded its repertoire to include works by promising German playwrights, popular plays, and translations of modern French dramas. The free pass Lessing secured through his stageworthy translations from the French enabled him to become even more familiar with the practical aspects of living theater. The regularity of his attendance made him a known figure among the members of the troupe. And his incipient dramatic talent was quickly recognized, for the Neuber troupe produced *Der junge Gelehrte* in January 1748.

That same year it also received a piece entitled *Der Kuss, oder Das ganz neu musikalische Schäfer-Spiel, So in einer Comödie aufgeführt* from his freethinking cousin, Christlob Mylius (1722-1754). Mylius had become acquainted with the troupe through Gottsched, whom he at first admired but later learned to despise. His early articles in support of Gottschedian principles marked the beginning of what was to be his active yet short-lived career in the field of journalism. He went to Berlin in 1748 because he thought its developing publishing business would provide better opportunities for a freelance writer to earn a living. Lessing followed when his impecuniousness—which was to influence many decisions throughout his life—prevented him from matriculating at another university for the next semester. They quickly became known in Berlin intellectual circles, participated in local activities, and worked together on various publications.

Their first joint venture was *Beyträge zur Historie und Aufnahme des Theaters* (1750). They ambitiously planned to provide reports about current conditions, surveys of historical issues, and translations of works from various periods and lands. The report about Berlin, which was written in 1749, began with words of praise for Frederick the Great's cultivation of the arts and then turned to the two ensembles he supported, describing in each case the theater building, the auditorium, the stage, the audience, the repertoire, and the performers. The descriptive comments gave an inkling of the inductive approach, constructive attitude, and sharply witty style that was soon to become characteristic of Lessing's literary journalism. The Italian ensemble was taken up after the French. Although the editors believed Berlin's Italianate opera belonged more to the musical than the theatrical sphere, they thought it was such a major attraction in the city that it merited detailed treatment. And they treated it without condemning it as an aberrant form of theater. Graun's scores were considered splendid enough to justify his world renown while Leopoldo di Villati's (fl. 1748-1770) librettos were severely criticized: "Er stoppelt seine Opern alle aus Tragödien zusammen; und was er verändert, das verschlimmert er."[1] ("He patches all his operas together out of tragedies, and whatever he changes, he makes worse.") Some of the singers fared no better when the weaknesses in their voices, appearances, and acting abilities were discussed.

Such topics were especially important to Lessing, for he

was becoming more and more concerned about the performing arts and their effect on the quality of theater in the German lands. His concern stimulated him to further investigation, contemplation, and comparison. After translating Francesco Riccoboni's (1707-1772) *L'Art du Théâtre* for the *Beyträge*, he worked on Rémond de Sainte Albine's (1699-1778) *Le Comédien* and began his own essay on acting, which was to remain unfinished.[2] He also studied material on ancient pantomimes, dances, masks, and choruses, hoping to find clues that would lead to constructive suggestions for the improvement of German theater. Much of his effort was directed toward discovering how and why ancient techniques of stage presentation differed from modern ones.[3] Opera figured importantly in the juxtaposition of those differences, not only because of the acknowledged aims of its Renaissance originators but also because of the discussion it continued to foment in Berlin and elsewhere.

Lessing's "Kritik über die 'Gefangenen' des Plautus," which appeared in the *Beyträge* in 1750, brings together some of the arguments from that discussion. The fictitious correspondent, whose letter formed the basis for Lessing's critical treatment, reviewed the problems of theatrical declamation and singled out the ones connected with opera's continuous singing. In order to show how such problems could be solved, the correspondent described his and other reactions toward an opera Frederick the Great allegedly had performed:

Mein damaliger Aufenthalt an einem Orte, wo ein gekrönter Weltweise das prächtigste der Schauspiele oder, wie andre sagen, das ungereimteste Werk, so der menschliche Verstand jemals erfunden, die Oper, einem Volke zeigte, so bisher dergleichen kaum dem Namen nach kannte, gab mir noch mehr Gelegenheit, hierauf zu denken. Ein jeder sagte seine Meinung von Arien und Rezitativen, als von den allergemeinsten Sachen, so dass die Oper der Vorwurf aller Unterredungen ward. Ich befand mich bei einer derselben, wo, nachdem verschiedenes von dem Natürlichen und dem Wahrscheinlichen der Oper war geredt worden, einer von der Gesellschaft in die Worte eines Dichters unserer Zeit ausbrach: "Die Vernunft muss man zu Hause lassen, wenn man in die Oper geht"; mithin, setzte er hinzu, müsse man nicht viel Vernunft da suchen wo keine anzutreffen sei, sondern sich an der Wollust begnügen, die man durch das Gehör und das Gesicht empfände. Denn allerdings sei nichts widersinnischer, als zwei Helden vor sich zu sehen, welche von den allerwichtigsten und oft sehr heftig bewegenden Sachen sich singend besprechen. Ich sagte hierauf, dass man diesem Unnatürlichen abhelfen könne, wenn man nur die Arien singen liesse und das Rezitativ deklamieret würde. Dieses könne der Oper, anstatt ihr etwas von ihrer Pracht zu benehmen, einen neuen Zierat verschaffen, indem dieses liebenswürdige Schauspiel dadurch dem Natürlichen näher kommen würde. Meine Gedanken fanden damals Beifall, wenigstens wurde ihnen nicht widersprochen. * (XIII, 114-115)

In summarizing prevalent attitudes toward opera, he obliquely made fun of Saint Evremond, Gottsched, and

* My sojourn of that time gave me even more opportunity to reflect upon this. It was a place where a philosopher-king exhibited the most magnificent of plays, or as others say, the most absurd work the human mind ever invented, the opera, for people who hitherto hardly knew of it by name. Everybody was uttering an opinion about arias and recitatives as about the most common matters, so that opera became the subject of all conversations. I found myself in one of them, where after various things had been said about the natural and the probable of opera, one of the group broke into the words of a poet of our time: "One must leave reason at home when one goes to the opera." Therefore, he added, rather than seeking much reason where there is none, one must content oneself with the sensual pleasure experienced through the ear and the eye. For certainly nothing is more nonsensical than to witness two heroes discussing in song the most important and often intensely moving matters. I responded that one could obviate this unnaturalness if only the arias were sung and the recitatives declaimed. Instead of detracting from its magnificence this could supply a new ornament in that this charming play would thusly

those literal-minded people who gave credence to their a priori pronouncements.

Lessing considered such pronouncements not only erroneous but pernicious. He explained why in "Über die Regeln der Wissenschaften zum Vergnügen; besonders der Poesie und Tonkunst," the verse epistle he wrote in 1749 for Marpurg's *Der Critische Musicus an der Spree*. Lessing, who was already quite friendly with Marpurg, had assimilated much from the operatic discussion in Berlin. His verse epistle deserves particular attention because it portended the future; it contained so many of the ideas he was to refine in the coming years that it can almost be viewed as the manifesto for his life's work. The opening lines state that music is universal, that it is perceived through the feelings of the soul, and that the pleasure it gives is inexplicable. After asking whether music can be evaluated strictly according to predetermined rules, Lessing mounts his attack against the all-pervasiveness of carping criticism. He sees its source in the misuse of reason. Reason, he explains, should provide illumination and happiness for mankind instead of being like a dictator whose insatiable desire for conquest of the entire universe brings nothing but unhappiness. To outline the workings of this will to power, Lessing addresses himself to false reason:

> So kömst du, statt ins Herz, in einen Criticus,
> Der, was die Sinne reizt, methodisch mustern muss,
> Und treibst durch Regeln, Grund, Kunstwörter,
>   Lehrgebäude,
> Aus Lust die Quintessenz, rectificirst die Freude,
> Und schaffst, wo dein Geschwätz am schärfsten
>   überführt,
> Dass viel nur halb ergötzt, und vieles gar nicht
>   rührt.* (I, 182, 33-38)

---

come closer to the natural. My thoughts found approbation at that time, at least they were not contradicted.

* Instead of coming into the soul, you come into a critic, who has to examine methodically whatever charms the senses, and with rules,

Man's innate ability to feel emotion and to experience pleasure, he contends, is inhibited and therefore spoiled by devotion to the prescriptions of false reason. Lessing supports his contention with several examples. One is the peasant's reaction:

> Was einen Bauer reitzt macht keine Regel schlecht;
> Denn in ihm wirkt ihr Trieb noch unverfälschlich ächt;
> Und wenn die kühne Kunst zum höchsten Gipfel flieget,
> So schwebt sie viel zu hoch, dass ihn ihr Reitz vergnüget.†
>
> (I, 183, 53-56)

Another example is Orpheus, whose art he claims was so genuinely beautiful that it tamed wild people and aroused humanity in them. Yet another of Lessing's examples is opera. He compares Hasse and Graun to Orpheus and states that they improve the human condition by teaching what cannot otherwise be taught.

In explaining how false reason prevents true artistic appreciation, Lessing reveals his concern about ridding German audiences of their allegiance to spurious authorities. He also reveals his concern about developing critical principles that do justice to the work as a totality. The rule books, he states, have allowed spectators to think themselves critics. They become so involved dissecting the work and comparing its parts to the rules that they are incapable of recognizing any intrinsic quality:

---

first principles, technical terms, and systems, you force the quintessence out of fancy, rectify joy, and see to it, where your idle talk runs over most sharply, that much only half delights and much has no effect at all.

† Whatever charms a peasant discredits no rule, for in him its driving force still operates truly genuinely. And when audacious art flies to the highest pinnacle, it soars much too high for its charm to please him.

Erst drengt er durch die Wach, sich toll ins
    Opernhaus,
Urtheilt erbärmlich dann, und strömt in Tadel aus.
Die Wendung war zu alt, die kam zu oftmals wieder;
Hier stieg er allzuhoch, hier fiel er plötzlich nieder;
Der Einfall war dem Ohr zu unerwartet da,
Und jener taugte nichts, weil man zuvor ihn sah;
Bald wird das Traurige zum Heulen wüster Töne,
Bald ist die Sprach des Leids zu ausgekünstelt
    schöne;
Dem ist das Fröhliche zu scheckernd possenhaft,
Und jenem eben das ein Grablied ohne Kraft;
Das ist zu schwer gesetzt, und das für alle Kehlen;
Und, manchem scheint es gar ein Fehler, nie zu
    fehlen;
Das Wort heisst zu gedehnt, und das nicht gnug
    geschleift;
Die Loge weint gerührt, wo jene zischt und pfeift.
Wo kömmt die Frechheit her, so unbestimmt zu
    richten?
Wer lehrt den gröbsten Geist die Fehler sehn und
    dichten?
Ist nicht, uneins mit sich, ein Thor des andern
    Feind?
Und fühlt der Künstler nur sie all auf sich vereint?
Ist nicht der Grund, weil sie erschlichne Regeln
    wissen,
Und, auf gut Glück, darnach vom Stock zum Winkel
    schliessen?
Er ists. Nun tadle mich, dass ich die Regeln schmäh,
Und mehr auf das Gefühl, als ihr Geschwätze seh.*
(I, 184, 89-110)

---

* First he frantically forces his way through the watch into the opera
house, then judges miserably, and streams forth in censure. This
phrase was too old, that one recurred too often. Here he rose all too
sharp, and here he suddenly fell flat. This idea surprised the ear too
much, and that one was worthless because it had been seen before.

Since philosophers began meddling in artistic matters, Lessing adds, there have been innumerable critiques but few masterpieces. The blame, he asserts, lies with the deductions and abstractions they contrived in order to mask their own insufficiencies. His reference to Bodmer in the following lines is indicative of his desire to maintain a critical position independent of the academicians:

> Kunstwörter müssen dann der Dummheit
>   Blösse decken,
> Und ein gelehrt Zitat macht Zierden selbst zu
>   Flecken.
> Ach arme Poesie! anstatt Begeisterung,
> Und Göttern in der Brust, sind Regeln jetzt
>   genung.
> Noch einen Bodmer nur, so werden schöne
>   Grillen
> Der jungen Dichter Hirn, statt Geist und Feuer
>   füllen.*
> (I, 185, 127-132)

Sometimes the mournful becomes the howling of wild tones, sometimes the language of sorrow is too elaborately beautiful. For one person the merry is too jestingly farcical, and for the other even the one dirge without efficacy. This is set too difficultly, and that is for all voices. And to some it even seems to be an error never to err. That word is too drawled and that not slurred enough. This box weeps agitatedly when that one hisses and boos. Where does this insolence come from to judge so indeterminately? Who teaches the coarsest mind to see and devise errors? Disagreeing with themselves, is one fool not the enemy of the other? And does only the artist sense them all concentrated on him? Is not the reason because they know surreptitious rules and according to them argue at random from the general to the specific? That it is. Now censure me for reviling the rules and for paying more attention to emotion than to their babble.

* Technical terms then must cover up stupidity's nakedness, and an erudite quotation makes even ornaments into flaws. O, poor poetry, instead of enthusiasm and gods in your breast, rules are now enough! Just one more Bodmer and beautiful vagaries, instead of spirit and fire, will fill the brains of young poets.

What Lessing writes about the poet anticipates his later comments on genius and its self-regulating ability:

> Ein Geist, den die Natur zum Mustergeist beschloss,
> Ist, was er ist, durch sich; wird ohne Regeln gross.
> Er geht, so kühn er geht, auch ohne Weiser sicher.
> Er schöpfet aus sich selbst. Er ist sich Schul' und Bücher.
> Was ihn bewegt, bewegt; was ihn gefällt, gefällt.
> Sein glücklicher Geschmack ist der Geschmack der Welt.
> Wer fasset seinen Werth? Er selbst nur kann ihn fassen.†
>
> (I, 185-186, 165-171)

The last few lines of Lessing's epistle affirm the worth of popular musical traditions, like the songs of primitive shepherds and rustic villagers, by questioning the snobbish opinion that only an opera by Graun can provide pleasure.

Lessing became even more involved with the critical problems suggested by the Berlin opera when two of his close friends began a rather heated dispute over musical styles. The crux of their dispute was whether opera in the German language was at all possible. Agricola, the court composer, was a dedicated proponent of Italian operatic music and had published two letters giving what he considered proof of its superiority. They were quickly answered by Marpurg who supported the French style of Rameau because he believed it offered the best solution to Germany's musical problems. Mylius sided with Marpurg, but Lessing attempted to remain nonaligned. The fragmentary *Tarantula, Eine Possenoper,* which he began in 1749 during the dis-

† A spirit whom nature determined an exemplary spirit is what he is through himself and becomes great without rules. He proceeds, so boldly he may proceed, safely without instruction. He draws out of himself. He is his own school and books. Whatever moves him, is moving. Whatever pleases him, is pleasing. His auspicious taste is the taste of the world. Who fathoms his worth? Only he himself can fathom it.

pute, was intended to illustrate the shortcomings of both positions. Its title, prefaces, and three completed scenes satirize not only the artistic insufficiencies of the Berlin opera but also the complaints of contemporary would-be reformers.[4] Lessing deftly describes the quality of the text by claiming it had Villati's imprimatur. And he alludes to Frederick the Great's editing and writing of texts with a comment about wanting to seek his advice.

The three scenes of this satirical fragment deal with a physician tying to arrange the marriage of his daughter to a musician who is unaware of her faithful love for another man. The first scene opens with a chorus of patients singing about the healing arts and proceeds to outline the advantages of the sickness motif for opera. This motif, Lessing points out, is artistically probable because it requires operatic machines and stage requisites in order to seem true to life. His amusing notes for the stage directions explain: "Unter den Kranken kann man allerhand beliebige wunderbare Figuren aufführen; Leute mit Buckeln, mit Stelzen, ohne Hände und Füsse, womöglich auch ohne Kopf. Will man was recht Besondres machen, so kann man einige in Betten auf den Schauplatz tragen oder sie durch den Himmel mit Stricken hernieder lassen, weil doch wahrscheinlich ist, dass es um das Haus eines grossen Arztes sehr gedränge sein müssen. Bei dieser Gelegenheit wäre also das Flugwerk auf eine sehr natürliche Weise anzubringen" (X, 51; "One can present among the sick people all kinds of optional, wondrous figures: people with humpbacks, with wooden legs, without hands and feet, possibly even without heads. If one wants to do something right special, one can have some of them carried onto the stage in beds or have them descend through the loft with ropes, because it is indeed probable to have a big crowd around the house of a great physician. On this occasion the flies would thus be put into operation in a very natural way"). Mediocre singing, Lessing writes, would insure verisimilitude since people who are really sick could not possibly be in good voice. His directions remind the producers that "die Kranken hin und wieder in dem Singen Fehler machen müssen, damit die Wahrscheinlichkeit, wider welche man bisher in den Opern so vielfältig verstossen hat, desto besser beobachter werde" (X, 51; "The sick people have to make mistakes in singing now and then so that probability, against which one has hitherto so abundantly transgressed in operas, is all the better observed").

The beginning of the second scene finds the doctor and the musician quarreling over their arias. This quarrel then leads to a discussion about the validity and probability of operatic singing. The physician, who believes that one must do only those things in opera that are done in real life, explains that he retains probability by singing all the time, even while tending his patients: "Drum habe ich auch in meinem Haus ganz weislich verordnet, dass fein alles gesungen wird. Es klingt noch einmal so gut. Ich singe auch meistenteils bei den Kranken, wenn ich Arzneien verordne. Es haben mich zwar einige ausgelacht, aber die Narren wissen nicht, dass ich es nur deswegen tu', damit man doch einen wahrscheinlichen Grund angeben könne, warum in dieser Oper alles gesungen wird. Den Grund pflegen die Herren Opernschreiber sonst immer zu vergessen" (X, 53-54; "Therefore in my house I very prudently decreed that everything will be nicely sung. It sounds twice as good. I also mostly sing among the patients when prescribing medicines. Some did indeed laugh at me, but the fools don't know that I only do it so that a probable reason can be given for singing everything in this opera. That reason the gentlemen librettists are in the habit of always forgetting").

The third scene is dominated by the daughter and her true lover whose lamentations are designed to give the composer opportunity to express a variety of passions. The scene ends as they notice the musician approaching, but the confrontation does not take place because this is where Lessing ended his sketch. Only the stage directions for the fourth scene were completed, and their references to changing the scenery suggest that he more than likely intended to take up the unities.

Lessing must have considered the question of artistic verisimilitude too abstract or too academic to warrant further investigation. He concentrated on more concrete matters in the reviews he wrote in the early 1750s. In one on Schlegel's translation of Batteux, he praised the appended essays but was less interested in analyzing them than in discussing the faithfulness of the German rendition (VIII, 48-49). He expressed his admiration for Aristotle and questioned Gottsched's knowledge of Greek when reviewing Michael Conrad Curtius's (1724-1802) translation of the *Poetics* (IX, 272). Two other reviews cast even graver doubts not only on Gottsched's competence but also on his integrity. One of them had to do with the defense of Milton by Nicolai, whom Lessing was soon to meet and befriend (IX, 296).

The other concerned one of the polemical leaflets that appeared during the controversy over Weisse's 1752 adaptation of Coffey's operetta *The Devil to Pay*. This review appeared on July 21, 1753 in *Die Berlinische Privilegirte Staats- und gelehrte Zeitung*. In it Lessing refuted Gottschedian claims about musical theatrical works and urged critics to realize "dass überhaupt keine englische Stücke eine ernstliche Beurteilung nach den strengen Regeln der theatralischen Dichtkunst auszuhalten fähig sind; dass es eine falsche Kritik sei, wenn man verlangt, dass jedes komische Stück eine allgemeine Moral enthalten müsse" (IX, 263; "that absolutely no English plays are able to stand serious judgment according to the strict rules of theatrical poetry; that it would be false criticism to demand that every comic piece contain a universal moral lesson"). In addition to challenging the assumptions of Gottsched's methodology, Lessing questioned the advisability of emulating French dramas and implied that much could be learned from English plays like the one in question. According to him, it was important to keep in mind "dass es vielleicht nicht allzu wohl getan sei, wenn wir unsre Bühne, die noch in der Bildung ist, auf das Einfache des französischen Geschmacks einschränken wollen; dass das angeführte englische Stück bei allen seinen Fehlern noch immer von einem grossen komischen Genie zeige, welchem es gefallen hat, die Natur aus dem Gesichtspunkte eines holländischen Malers nachzuahmen" (IX, 263; "that it would, perhaps, not do all too well if we wanted to limit our still developing stage to the simplicity of French taste; that the above-mentioned English play for all its faults still shows evidence of a great comic genius who liked to imitate nature from the point of view of a Dutch painter"). This review clearly anticipates the famous seventeenth "Literaturbrief" of February 16, 1759, which defended the comic potential of Hanswurst, upheld Shakespeare as a far greater tragic poet than Corneille, and provided a fragment of a supposedly old German Faust drama. In both cases, Lessing unequivocally rejected the French neoclassical code as foreign to the German spirit.

Laokoon and the Essence of Ancient Theater

Lessing appreciated French neoclassicism less and less as his knowledge about the history of European theater increased. While never failing to admire its achievements, he viewed it within its own historical context and attributed its origins to a peculiarly French interpretation of antiquity. The evolution of that interpretation became clearer to him as he studied the ancient texts and the commentaries produced by generations of writers since the Renaissance. His interest in Greek and Roman dramas was not just philological or antiquarian. It was also practical. He sought to extract the secrets of their success because he wanted to bring new dignity to contemporary theater and thereby improve the quality of life in the German lands.

Lessing founded the *Theatralische Bibliothek* in 1754 as part of his campaign to free German theater from the constricting domination of the French neoclassical code. The essays he wrote and the works he chose to translate investigated the more liberal tendencies in France itself, reevaluated the dramas of ancient playwrights, or emphasized the rich theatrical heritage of Italy, Spain, and England. Seneca was one ancient playwright whose tragic greatness he believed had been sadly misunderstood by the French and their German followers. His essay, "Von den lateinischen Trauerspielen, welche unter dem Namen des Seneca bekannt sind" (1754), examined the texts in order to correct the misunderstanding. Unlike others who had compared Seneca's *Hercules Furens* with Euripides' drama on the same subject, Lessing considered the different cultural conditions under which they were written and asked his own rhetorical question: "Allein, ist es billig, einen Dichter anders als nach den Umständen seiner Zeit zu beurteilen?" (XIII, 181; "But is it fair to criticize a poet other than according to the conditions of his time?"). Lessing, who was attuned to his own times, believed Seneca's *Hercules Furens* would lend itself easily to operatic treatment and, in making suggestions for modern poets, wrote: "So viel ist augenscheinlich, dass aus dem Stücke des Seneca mit kleinen Veränderungen, eine vollkommene Oper zu machen sei" (XIII, 186; "So much is apparent; with small modifications a complete opera could be made out of Seneca's play"). He thought it would require substantial changes if it were to be presented to contemporary audiences as a spoken drama. Opera alone, he contended, had all the mechanical and scenic means for staging such wondrous events and would even allow for some borrowing from Euripides. Operatic music would help avoid monotonous portrayal of its wide range of passions, and he went on to add: "Auch die Erfindung des Ballettmeisters würde sich hier nicht auf dem Trockenen befinden, auf welchen man in einem Schauspiele, das so vorzüglich zum Vergnügen des Gesichts und des Gehörs bestimmt ist, billig auch mit sehen muss" (XIII, 187; "Even the invention of the ballet master, which one

214

must rightly watch in a play that is above all intended for the pleasure of the eye and the ear, would not be left high and dry here").

Lessing continued contemplating the relationship of opera to ancient drama in the hope of deriving some practical lessons. Although opera was never one of his major concerns, he had become more and more intrigued by references to it in some of the post-Renaissance theatrical writings and treatises he studied. Most important among them was Dubos's *Réflexions critiques*. It treated the question of *ut pictura poesis* and distinguished arbitrary from natural signs, but Lessing was more interested in the part that dealt with the organic interdependence of the arts in Greek tragedy. Dubos contended that such interdependence had determined ancient staging and acting techniques. He explained that the Greek dramatists had used musical notation in order to force performers not only to interpret their lines correctly but also to gesture properly with their hands and bodies. While insisting that historical changes in music made opera radically different, Dubos acknowledged a similarity in its musical intention: "Enfin une Tragedie dont la declamation seroit écrite en notes, auroit le même mérite qu'un Opera. Des Acteurs mediocres pourroient l'executer passablement. Ils ne pourroient plus faire la dixième partie des fautes qu'ils font, soit en manquant les tons, & par consequent l'action propre aux vers qu'ils recitent, soit en mettant du pathetique dans plusieurs endroits qui n'en sont pas susceptibles."[5] ("In fine, were a tragedy to have its declamation written in notes, it would have the same merit as an opera; that is, very indifferent actors might execute it tolerably. They could not commit the tenth part of the faults they are liable to, either in mistaking the tones, and consequently the action suitable to the verses they recite, or in affecting the pathetic in several parts that will not admit of it," *Critical Reflections on Poetry, Painting and Music*, III, 235). Lessing translated this part of Dubos's work and published it as "Ausschweifung von den theatralischen Vorstellungen der Alten" in the *Theatralische Bibliothek* in 1755.[6] It was the same year he tried to incorporate some of his ideas about acting into a dramatic text. Many of the lines in *Miss Sara Sampson* were written in such a way as to prevent actors from misinterpreting the kinds of gestures he envisioned for them.[7]

Lessing found many similar ideas in the writings of Diderot, who was to see to a French translation of *Miss Sara Sampson* in 1761. Diderot also opposed the stifling effect of neoclassical rules, rejected the outworn conventions of French drama, criticized the state of the performing arts, and encouraged the study of English as well as Italian theater. He advocated cultivating bourgeois drama because he thought it had more truth, naturalness, and relevance for contemporary audiences. His desire to enliven theatrical portrayal led to suggestions for reforming the art of acting that put as much burden on the dramatist as on the actor. Unlike Voltaire, who had during his years in Berlin been Lessing's eating companion, Diderot did not believe that opera destroyed Greek tragedy in some respects while reviving it in others. He considered opera a worthy successor and admired especially the way its music could intensify the emotional impact of the text. These views provided such strong confirmation for Lessing's own that he made them available in the translation, *Das Theater des Herrn Diderot* (1760). Its preface put Diderot in the same class as Aristotle and struck another blow at Gottsched's adulation of the neoclassical code (XI, 31).

Lessing studied and translated so many essays, articles, and books about theater that we might almost consider him a clearing house for critical ideas. He read what the Greeks and Romans had written, familiarized himself with what French and Italian critics said and, as he became more and more aware of the different kinds of drama popular in England, increased his concern for English theoretical writings. Never accepting anything on the basis of authority alone, he always weighed the advantages and disadvantages

of ideas espoused by other critics and came to his own con-
clusions. His attempt to translate faithfully forced him to
find suitable German expressions and thus helped to develop
the prose style that has secured him a place among the
world's finest critics. Also important for Lessing's development as a critic was his association with Nicolai and Mendelssohn. Although they often disagreed with one another,
they all had the same enthusiastic interest in discussing
theater and other artistic matters. Lessing's departure for
Leipzig in 1755 necessitated continuing the discussion in
letters. Their own writings were the basis for many of
them. Nicolai's treatise on tragedy led to reconsideration of
Dubos as well as Aristotle (XII, 486 and 510). Lessing's
Miss Sara Sampson stimulated an exchange of ideas about
the playwright's responsibilities to those who would perform his work (XII, 514-515). Mendelssohn's essay about
the sources and combinations of the arts provoked Nicolai's
painstaking criticism and helped sustain Lessing's interest
in developing his own ideas on the subject.

Lessing's ability to assimilate, synthesize, and put to use
what he learned from others produced a number of works
that are milestones in German literary history. One of
them, *Laokoon oder über die Grenzen der Malerei und
Poesie* (1766), took up ideas that had been circulating for
years and brought them together in a new, more meaningful relationship.[8] Lessing originally intended a three-part
work that would treat systematically the essential differences between the individual arts. The *Laokoon*, which dif-
ferentiated poetry from the plastic arts, was the first of those
parts. Lessing continued to draft his ideas on music and
the dance and to discuss them with his associates, but he
never put them into finished form. The inherent limitations of artistic media interested him for several reasons,
the most important being their implications for theater.[9]
He considered the recognition of such limitations to be the
prerequisite for synthesizing arts that appealed simultaneously to different senses. His hope was to provide informa-

tion that would help modern artists achieve something comparable to Greek tragedy.

Lessing's notes for the unfinished parts of this comprehensive study discussed the practical as well as theoretical possibilities of synthesizing the arts. He analyzed two of these arts, music and poetry, in a way familiar to us from the published *Laokoon*. They were similar, he maintained, in that they both appealed directly to the sense of hearing and progressed through time. He attributed their differences to the different measures of time required by their signs. Music, he explained, employed tones, or natural signs which had meaning only when occurring in succession; that is, a single tone would be absolutely meaningless if it occurred without being related to other tones. Poetry, he continued, communicated through words, or arbitrary signs, which were so pregnant with meaning that one of them could express as much as a whole succession of tones. And this, he claimed, caused the major problems in any attempt to combine the two arts. His observation of modern practices indicated to him that one art was always singled out as the dominating one, and all others were made subservient to it. The examples he cited were from opera: the Italian style focused on music as its principal art while the French tended to emphasize poetry. Neither, he added, integrated them into the kind of unity possible in antiquity because they overlooked the need for complete artistic cooperation.

Such cooperation, Lessing contended, presupposed awareness of music's unavoidable retarding effect on the one hand and poetry's unavoidable accelerating effect on the other. Since he thought music required much more time in order to convey the same thing as one single word, he urged the avoidance of laconic expression in poetry. He believed such terseness would require from music an impossible amount of concentration. If these divergent arts, he speculated, could come together and compromise without relinquishing their artistic integrity, the resultant synthesis would be a supreme form of art. Lessing's concern for the differences in artistic media led to a brilliant solution of a theoretical problem that had perplexed numerous writers on opera, and it is worth quoting at length:

Die Vereinigung willkürlicher, aufeinanderfolgender hörbarer Zeichen, mit natürlichen, aufeinanderfolgenden hörbaren Zeichen ist unstreitig unter allen möglichen die vollkommenste, besonders wenn noch dieses hinzukömmt, dass beiderlei Zeichen nicht allein für einerlei Sinn sind, sondern auch von eben demselben Organo zu gleicher Zeit gefasst und hervorgebracht werden können.

Von dieser Art ist die Verbindung der Poesie und Musik, so dass die Natur selbst sie nicht sowohl zur Verbindung, als vielmehr zu einer und eben derselben Kunst bestimmt zu haben scheinet.

Es hat auch wirklich eine Zeit gegeben, wo sie beide zusammen nur eine Kunst ausmachten. Ich will indes nicht leugnen, dass die Trennung nicht natürlich erfolgt sei, noch weniger will ich die Ausübung der einen ohne die andere tadeln, aber ich darf doch bedauern, dass durch diese Trennung man an die Verbindung fast gar nicht mehr denkt, oder wenn man ja noch daran denkt, man die eine Kunst nur zu einer Hilfskunst der andern macht, und von einer gemeinschaftlichen Wirkung, welche beide zu gleichen Teilen hervorbringen, gar nichts mehr weiss. Hernach ist noch auch dieses zu erinnern, dass man nur eine Verbindung ausübet, in welcher die Dichtkunst die helfende Kunst ist, nämlich in der Oper, die Verbindung aber, wo die Musik die helfende Kunst wäre, noch unbearbeitet gelassen hat. Oder sollte ich sagen, dass man in der Oper auf beider Verbindung gedacht habe; nämlich auf die Verbindung, wo die Poesie die helfende Kunst ist, in der Arie; und auf die Verbindung, wo die Musik die helfende Kunst ist, im Rezitative? Es scheinet so. Nur dürfte die Frage dabei sein, ob diese vermischte Verbindung, wo um die Reihe die eine Kunst der andern subservieret, in einem und eben demselben Ganzen natürlich sei, und ob die wollüstigere, welches ohnstreitig die ist, wo die Poesie der Musik subservieret, nicht der andern schadet, und unser Ohr zu sehr vergnüget, als dass es das wenigere Vergnügen bei der andern nicht zu matt und schläfrig finden sollte.

Dieses Subservieren unter den beiden Künsten, bestehet darin, dass die eine vor der andern zum Hauptwerke gemacht wird, nicht aber darin, dass sich die eine bloss nach der andern richtet, und wenn ihre verschiedne Regeln in Kollision kommen, dass die eine der andern so viel nachgibt als möglich. Denn dieses ist auch in der alten Verbindung geschehen.* (IV, 504-505)

---

* The combination of arbitrary, successive, audible signs with natural, successive, audible signs is of all the possible ones incontestably the most perfect, especially when we add the fact that both kinds of signs are not only for a single sense but can also be apprehended and elicited by the very same organ at the same time.

Of this kind the combination of poetry and music is such that nature itself seems to have intended them not merely for combining but rather for one and the same art.

There actually was a time when together they both constituted only one art. I do not, however, want to deny that the separation did not ensue naturally, even less do I want to criticize the practice of the one without the other. But I may at least regret that owing to this separation almost nobody thinks of union any longer, or if somebody does think about it, he makes the one art only into an auxiliary of the other and knows nothing at all about a joint effect produced by both in equal parts. After this, also to be mentioned is that there is only one combination in which poetry is the auxiliary art, namely in opera. The combination, however, where music would be the auxiliary art has remained untreated. Or should I say, that in opera the combination of both has been considered, namely the combination where poetry is the auxiliary, in the aria, and the combination where music is the auxiliary art, in the recitative? It seems so. Only the question might remain, whether this mixed combination, where one art is in turn subservient to the other, would be natural in one and the same totality, and whether the more voluptuous one, which is indisputably

Lessing realized that more emphasis was placed on drama in contemporary French opera, but he still viewed it as a primarily musical form. The results of his continuing deliberations about the means for making music the auxiliary art found expression during his association with the Hamburg theater; they will be discussed later.

After treating music and poetry in his *Laokoon* notes, Lessing went on to mention the inclusion of other arts. He considered pantomime and dancing particularly important, for he believed they had been integral elements of the grand synthesis in antiquity. Here again he strove to make careful distinctions. Pantomime and dancing, he maintained, differed from poetry and music insofar as they appealed to the sense of sight. Although they occurred in space, he explained, they progressed through time because they involved movement. He claimed that this dependence on time was precisely what they had in common with music and poetry. Visual arts, he then concluded, could be combined successfully with auditory arts as long as all were progressive in time. Imperfect combinations would only result, he explained, if one art existed in space while the other progressed in time. The example he gave of this is a familiar one, the combination of painting and poetry. Lessing scrutinized the differences and similarities of these arts because he thought they would reveal something about the essence of theatrical portrayal. They figured as an important yet small part in a much broader artistic scheme which, however, he never finished outlining. His abiding interest in pantomime's mute communication and danc-

---

when poetry subserves music, does not harm the other and please our ear too much for it not to consider the lesser pleasure from the other too dull and slow.

This subservience among both arts consists of making the one art the principal work over the other and not of guiding the one according to the other and having the one yield as much as possible to the other when their diverse rules collide. For this took place also in the ancient union.

ing's living pictures stimulated him to begin translating Jean Georges Noverre's (1727-1810) *Lettres sur la danse et sur les ballets* (1760), the book that was instrumental for the development of dramatic ballet, or what has been called danced drama. Lessing left its completion to Johann Joachim Christoph Bode (1730-1793), his friend and business associate in Hamburg. It appeared in 1769.[10]

Music in the Hamburg Theater

Lessing went to Hamburg in 1767 to become the resident critic of the Hamburg National Theater. The man who was largely responsible for his appointment, Johann Friedrich Löwen (1729-1771), had long believed that the German lands could not realize their theatrical potential because they lacked a center comparable to Paris and London. His aim was to make Hamburg such a center by establishing a standing theater company that would not depend on the whims of wandering troupes or the vicissitudes of the box office. Although writers like Gellert and Johann Elias Schlegel had suggested similar reforms, Löwen took the initiative and actively campaigned for their institution. He appealed to the patriotic sympathies of some prominent Hamburg citizens and talked them into taking over the management of the theater and providing full financial support for it. Playwrights were to receive prizes for outstanding work, and an academy was to be founded for the exchange of ideas.

Löwen, who had published a manual on acting in 1755, was particularly concerned with the actors of the company.[11] He knew their performances would improve considerably if their skills were better, but he believed there was much more to it than technical training. His feeling for practical matters indicated that actors not only deserved but also needed the stability that came with the promise of steady salaries and future pensions, so he worked toward making it possible. He wanted to change their personal attitudes by teaching them to think of themselves as artists rather than as craftsmen. He also wanted to instill in them a patriotic pride in their language and its achievements. His *Geschichte des deutschen Theaters* (1766) was part of his attempt to increase their understanding of the German theatrical tradition that had originated in the remote past. Löwen explained that German theater had failed to progress very far beyond its beginnings because the managers of wandering troupes were ignorant, greedy, or careless. According to him, they knew so little about acting that they could neither recognize inherent talent nor give their performers meaningful direction. The major exception was Caroline Neuber, whom he credited with ushering in a new era. Löwen acknowledged Gottsched's efforts to dignify the German stage but believed they involved only "verschiedene Kleinigkeiten, die mehr die Policey des Theaters, als seine magische Kunst betreffen" ("various small matters that have more to do with the policy of the theater than with its magic art").[12] What Löwen wanted for the Hamburg National Theater and what he found in Lessing was a dramaturgist whose vision put the magic of theater into its proper perspective. Löwen's 1767 address to the consortium of citizens who were about to become theatrical entrepreneurs indicated quite clearly his familiarity with Lessing's recently published *Laokoon* and his feelings of affinity for it: "Mahlerey und Poesie haben ihre Grenzen: jene noch weit engre als diese. Aber das Theater hat sehr wenige; beynahe gar keine. Hier kann man alles wagen, wenn nur in der Art nicht verfehlt wird, womit as geschicht."[13] ("Painting and poetry have their bounds; the former far narrower than the latter. But theater has very few; almost none at all. Here one can dare everything if the way it happens does not fail.")

Lessing accepted the appointment to the Hamburg National Theater because he hoped it would enable him to apply the theories he had been working on and to appraise them in the light of actual practices. The announcement for the *Hamburgische Dramaturgie,* which he wrote on April 22, 1767, stated his intentions quite explicitly. He wanted to record critically the artistic development of the actors as well as the dramatists. He hoped his comments on the plays, many of which he realized would not be master-pieces, would help to influence public taste and eventually improve the repertoire. The first seven issues dealt with the opening night of the theater. After discussing the text, Lessing turned to the actors and analyzed their perform-ances. His analysis in the issue of May 15, 1767 is indicative of his continuing attempt to explain acting as an art that was both simultaneous in space and progressive in time: "Die Kunst des Schauspielers stehet hier zwischen den bil-denden Künsten und der Poesie mitten inne. Als sichtbare Malerei muss zwar die Schönheit ihr höchstes Gesetz sein; doch als transitorische Malerei braucht sie ihren Stellungen jene Ruhe nicht immer zu geben, welche die alten Kunst-werke so imponierend macht" (V, 45; "The art of the actor stands right in the middle between the plastic arts and poetry. As visible painting beauty must indeed be its high-est law; however, as transitory painting it does not always need to give its positions that repose which makes the an-cient works of art so impressive"). As a temporal art, he explained with ideas from the *Laokoon,* acting could por-tray the violent, the exaggerated, and the audacious, but as a spatial art it had to avoid dwelling on such characteristics too long so as to prevent their effect from becoming over-whelmingly severe. Lessing, who attributed Shakespeare's success to his firsthand knowledge of the stage, considered Hamlet's advice to the players the golden rule of acting. It urged them to moderate their gestures and to avoid flailing their arms wildly through the air. Lessing believed the proper use of hands and arms was essential and, in addi-tion to studying ancient chironomy, took special note of Hamburg performers who he thought instinctively compre-hended the art. Ekhof was one, and Sophie Friederike Hensel (1738-1790) was another. On June 12, 1767 he lauded her portrayal of Sara Sampson's death. He wrote that she controlled her fingers poignantly as well as naturally and placed herself "in der malerischsten Stellung" (V, 76; "in the most pictorial position").

Other nonverbal means of communication also concerned Lessing.[14] Instrumental music was of particular significance because he believed the modern theater orchestra could substitute to some extent for the Greek chorus. His attempt to learn from ancient drama led once again to consideration of the possible ways of combining music and poetry. While he viewed contemporary opera's emphasis on music as one possibility, he thought other possibilities had not yet been fully explored. Several issues of the *Hamburgische Dramaturgie* were devoted to such exploration. In them he discussed ideas about using music as an auxiliary art to enhance the action of spoken drama. They were the kind of ideas that helped prepare the way for the incidental music Beethoven wrote for Goethe's *Egmont*.

Performances of Voltaire's *Sémiramis* (1748) occasioned Lessing's comments. On June 2, 1767 he stated his disapproval of Voltaire's attitude toward the achievements of French theater. He considered him arrogant for thinking "dass die tragischen Dichter seiner Nation die alten Griechen in vielen Stücken weit überträfen" (V, 63-64; "that the tragic poets of his nation far surpass the ancient Greeks in many respects"). He implied that Voltaire had written his tragedy merely to show that the ancients were poor benighted primitives who lacked the ability to create spectacular stage sets. Lessing believed *Sémiramis* failed to produce a genuinely tragic effect because of its dependence on such externalities: "Es macht so viel Lärmen auf der Bühne, es erfordert so viel Pomp und Verwandlung, als man nur immer in einer Oper gewohnt ist" (V, 64; "There is so much bluster on the stage, there is so much pomp and transformation required as one is only accustomed to in an opera"). He maintained in the June 5, 1767 issue that the internal structure of a text should produce the tragic effect by giving the actors something to enact. In his opinion, Shakespeare knew how to do it very well, but Voltaire not at all. Lessing thought it was Voltaire's ignorance of pantomime and scenic matters that allowed him to have a ghost emerge from its tomb in broad daylight before a large assembly. Such a scene, Lessing explained, was very difficult to stage because it required different reactions from each member of the assembly in order to avoid "die frostige Symmetrie eines Balletts" (V, 68; "the frosty symmetry of a ballet").

A repeat performance of *Sémiramis* prompted Lessing to point out how instrumental music could mitigate the failings of such a text and make for a more enjoyable theatrical experience. He began by reviewing theoretical speculations about this idea in the July 28, 1767 issue. He credited Johann Adolph Scheibe with the pioneering discovery that each drama required its own rather than some arbitrarily chosen musical accompaniment.[15] Lessing agreed that such accompaniment had to relate directly to the dramatic action in order to supplement the intended effect. He chose to present Scheibe's ideas because he thought they acknowledged and helped to clarify music's inherent limitations. Lessing appreciated these ideas but recognized their shortcomings: "Zwar die Regeln selbst waren leicht zu machen; sie lehren nur, was geschehen soll, ohne zu sagen, wie es geschehen kann. Der Ausdruck der Leidenschaften, auf welchen alles dabei ankömmt, ist noch einzig das Werk des Genies" (V, 124; "The rules themselves were indeed easy to make; they only teach what is supposed to happen without saying how it can happen. The expression of the passions, upon which everything depends, is still uniquely the work of the genius"). He claimed there were so few examples of such dramatic music that no general principles or rules could be derived from them. The two examples he briefly mentioned in the concluding sentence of this issue, one by Hertel and the other by Agricola, indicated that he was nevertheless interested in making an attempt.

On July 31, 1767 Lessing turned his attention to Agricola's incidental music for *Sémiramis*. Although he did not say so, his contemporaries knew that it was written at his suggestion. Herder even remarked on it in 1774 when writing of the continuity of "acts" and the function of the chorus in Greek tragedy. Herder's words are worth quoting, for they serve to illuminate Lessing's intentions and ultimate objectives: "Eigentliche Aufzüge wie wir, hat die Griechische Bühne nicht gehabt, weil der Chor alles band, und ursprünglich Alles war. Die Aufzüge nach Zweck des Stücks musikalisch zu binden, hat z.E. beim Trauerspiel Semiramis der Berlinische Tonsetzer Agricola auf Lessings Veranlassung glücklich versucht."[16] ("Proper acts like we have the Greek stage did not have, because the chorus united everything and originally was everything. At Lessing's instigation, the Berlin composer Agricola successfully tried, for example, with the tragedy Sémiramis to unite the acts musically according to the purpose of the play.")

Lessing stated that Agricola's introductory orchestral composition presented the tone of the drama and suggested its plot in such a way as to prepare the spectators for the performance. The entr'acte music, he continued, sustained the all-important dramatic suspense by summing up the past action rather than foreshadowing what was to follow. He believed Agricola had used the suggestive artistic character of music especially well in dealing with sudden changes in emotional intensity and mood. Lessing's explantation of music's possible relationship to a text of spoken drama derived from Mendelssohn's ideas but took them a few steps further. Music, he wrote, "lässt uns in Ungewissheit und Verwirrung; wir empfinden, ohne eine richtige Folge unserer Empfindungen wahrzunehmen; wir empfinden wie im Traume; und alle diese unordentliche Empfindungen sind mehr abmattend als ergötzend. Die Poesie hingegen lässt uns den Faden unserer Empfindungen nie verlieren; hier wissen wir nicht allein, was wir empfinden sollen, sondern auch, warum wir es empfinden sollen; und nur dieses Warum macht die plötzlichsten Übergänge nicht allein erträglich, sondern auch angenehm. In der Tat ist diese Motivierung der plötzlichen Übergänge einer der grössten Vorteile, den die Musik aus der Vereinigung mit der Poesie ziehet; ja vielleicht der allergrösste" (V, 127; "leaves us in uncertainty and confusion; we feel without noticing a proper sequence of our feelings; we feel as if in a dream; and all these confused feelings are more fatiguing than pleasing. Poetry, on the other hand, never lets us lose the thread of our feelings. Here we know not only what we are supposed to feel but also why we are supposed to feel it. And it is just this why that makes the sudden transitions not only bearable but also pleasant. In fact this motivation of sudden transitions, is one of the greatest advantages that music draws from the union with poetry, perhaps even the greatest of all"). Agricola's successful treatment of the ghost scene indicated to Lessing that the musical medium could be used quite effectively to compensate for a text's lack of probable motivation.

The repertoire of the Hamburg National Theater included so many different kinds of musical and quasi-musical plays that some discussion of them in the *Hamburgische Dramaturgie* was inevitable. Löwen's *Das Rätsel oder Was den Damen am meisten gefällt* was taken up in the August 7, 1767 issue. Lessing agreed with Löwen in calling it a theatrical "pleasantry" that could be enjoyable if performed well, and he deferentially tried to avoid critical analysis: "Mache aus einem Hexenmärchen etwas Wahrscheinlichers, wer da kann!" (V, 134; "Make out of a fairy tale something more probable, whoever can!"). Instead he wrote about some of the sources of the plot. He thought Löwen had not used Voltaire's story or Charles Simon Favart's (1710-1792) musical play, *La fée Urgèle ou ce qui plaît aux Dames* (1765). Lessing mentioned nothing, however, about the possibility that Löwen might have used one of the early versions of Schiebeler's *Lisuart und Dariolette*. Schiebeler, the native of Hamburg whose fame derived from his collaboration with Hiller, had written a dramatic epilogue on the same subject in 1763 and, after Favart's play became known, expanded it into a comic opera text that was printed in the *Hamburgische Unterhaltungen* in 1766. It relied on fantastic happenings for its content and ballads for its form, so Schiebeler called it a "romantic opera."[17] The word "romantic" was employed more and more frequently in reference to operettas as librettists increased their experimentation with popular ballads (*Bänkelgesänge*) and poetic romances (*Romanzen*). Lessing understood the word "romantic" to mean unnatural, complicated, contrived, or like a chivalric romance, and he employed it at least three times in the *Hamburgische Dramaturgie* but not once in reference to any of the musical plays he discussed (V, 344, 354, 357).

Lessing depended on more precise words to evaluate Favart's comic operas and verse plays interpolated with songs. Without going so far as to call them great theater, he lauded their comic wit and character depiction. Of particular interest to him was their dramatization of fairy tales, religious legends, and moralizing stories. He devoted several issues to Favart's *Soliman Second* (1761) and discussed at length its adaptation of the story by Jean François Marmontel (1723-1799), who himself was a rather prolific librettist and a staunch defender of the Italian comic tradition in the subsequent Parisian feud against Gluck. On August 21, 1767 Lessing stated his general approval: "Ich rate allen, die unter uns das Theater aus ähnlichen Erzählungen bereichern wollen, die Favartsche Ausführung mit dem Marmontelschen Urstoffe zusammenzuhalten" (V, 150; "I advise all among us who want to enrich theater with similar stories to maintain Favart's execution together with Marmontel's original subject matter"). His objections, which came on August 25, 1767, had to do primarily with the improbability of Marmontel's characters. Lessing explained by combining his concept of genius with the concept of artistic probability that had been evolving for years.

His explanation shows how he assimilated ideas from the past and transformed them to suit the present:

> wenn ich nur gefunden hätte, dass, ob sie [the characters] schon nicht aus dieser wirklichen Welt sind, sie dennoch zu einer andern Welt gehören könnten; zu einer Welt, deren Zufälligkeiten in einer andern Ordnung verbunden, aber doch ebenso genau verbunden sind als in dieser; zu einer Welt, in welcher Ursachen und Wirkungen zwar in einer andern Reihe folgen, aber doch zu eben der allgemeinen Wirkung des Guten abzwecken; kurz, zu der Welt eines Genies, das— (es sei mir erlaubt, den Schöpfer ohne Namen durch sein edelstes Geschöpf zu bezeichnen!) das, sage ich, um das höchste Genie im Kleinen nachzuahmen, die Teile der gegenwärtigen Welt versetzet, vertauscht, verringert, vermehret, um sich ein eigenes Ganze daraus zu machen, mit dem es seine eigene Absichten verbindet.* (V, 153)

Lessing rejected the French neoclassical code with its three unities, pure genres, and numerous other prescriptions because he believed it did not and could not apply to the true genius who, in creating his artistic microcosmos, followed internal laws that were as inscrutable as those of God. It was to those laws that he gave most of his attention. He strove to derive them from the works themselves, whether they combined arts, mixed genres, or explored other previously untapped possibilities. His defense of Euripides,

---

* If I had only found that, although they are not from this real world, they could nevertheless belong to another world, to a world whose contingencies were united in a different order, but still just as closely united as in this, to a world in which causes and effects do indeed follow in a different sequence but at least aim for the universal effect of the good; in short, to the world of a genius, which— (permit me to signify the nameless creator through his most noble creature!)— which, I say, in order to imitate the supreme genius on a small scale, transfers, interchanges, reduces, increases the parts of the present world to make out of them his own totality, one with which he combines his own intentions.

whom he considered the most tragic of tragic poets, contained a clear statement about the kind of critical principles he advocated:

> Was will man endlich mit der Vermischung der Gattungen überhaupt? In den Lehrbüchern sondre man sie so genau voneinander ab, als möglich; aber wenn ein Genie, höherer Absichten wegen, mehrere derselben in einem und eben demselben Werke zusammenfliessen lässt, so vergesse man das Lehrbuch und untersuche bloss, ob es diese höhere Absichten erreicht hat. Was geht mich es an, ob so ein Stück des Euripides weder ganz Erzählung, noch ganz Drama ist? Nennt es immerhin einen Zwitter; genug, dass mich dieser Zwitter mehr vergnügt, mehr erbauet, als die gesetzmässigen Geburten eurer korrekten Racinen, oder wie sie sonst heissen. Weil der Maulesel weder Pferd noch Esel ist, ist er darum weniger eines von den nutzbarsten lasttragenden Tieren?* (V, 210-211)

Lessing's association with the Hamburg National Theater was almost from the very start beset with aggravating problems. The actors rebelled against public criticism. Audiences demanded what they wanted. And there was trouble with Löwen, whose administrative ability apparently did not match his ego. The last issues of the *Hamburgische Dramaturgie* appeared in the spring of 1769, two years after the initial announcement. It was a bitter disappointment to Lessing that the Hamburg National Theater had failed to

---

* What after all is really intended with the mixture of genres? In the textbooks they are separated from each other as precisely as possible. But, when a genius, for the sake of higher intentions, lets several of them fuse in one and the same work, one should forget the textbook and simply investigate whether he achieved these higher intentions. What does it matter to me whether such a play of Euripides is neither completely narrative nor completely drama? Go ahead and call it a bastard. It is enough that this bastard pleases and edifies me more than the legitimate offspring of your irreproachable Racines, or however they may be called. Because the mule is neither horse nor donkey, is it therefore any less one of the most useful beasts of burden?

effect what he considered substantive reforms. He left in 1770 believing Hamburg was the city least likely to become a national theatrical center. Nevertheless his stay there was profitable in more ways than one. He met his wife, found a business associate, became better acquainted with Ekhof, and absorbed much from the liberal intellectual tradition that had persisted in Hamburg for decades.

The Reimarus library supplied him with many materials. In it he found the proceedings of the Teutschübende Gesellschaft, and he read more about Fabricius, Brockes, Weichmann, and their patriotic colleagues (XIX, 107; 223-226). Hamburg's long history of theatrical disputes aroused his curiosity and, since opera was a major part of that history, he studied available librettos. Among them were texts by Postel, Hunold, Feind, Hotter, and Praetorius. In addition to recording his reactions to them, he wrote a very brief historical sketch of German musical theater. He believed Ayrer's *singets spiele* exemplified early indigenous efforts that had not been corrupted by the intrusion of Italian opera and other forms foreign to the Germanic spirit. Lessing's notes were collected and published posthumously in 1790 by Johann Joachim Eschenburg (1743-1820), a latter-day Hamburg patriot, opera enthusiast, and Shakespeare scholar. The *Kollektaneen zur Literatur*, as they were entitled, represent yet another link in the chain of critical writings that connected the seventeenth century with the age of Goethe.

EIGHT

ASSERTION OF CULTURAL IDENTITY

JUSTUS MÖSER ON THE ACHIEVEMENTS OF THE GERMANIC SPIRIT

PRUSSIA emerged from the Seven Years' War as a dominant power among the numerous states comprising the Holy Roman Empire of the German Nation. In the postwar years Frederick the Great devoted himself to consolidating his state and making his army strong enough to check Austrian expansion in central Europe. Many contemporary writers in Berlin and elsewhere admired the accomplishments of his foreign as well as domestic policies and wanted to view him as a sovereign of old Germanic stock. Some of them tried in vain to convince him of the worth of indigenous artistic efforts. His abiding and very outspoken support of French culture, while not at all unusual among aristocrats or even burghers of the period, seemed so contradictory to them that they often singled him out and blamed him for inhibiting the development of native talent. He never let them cherish any hope of gaining his support for a national theater that would affirm their own heritage and use it to instill feelings of German consciousness, pride, and solidarity in their contemporaries.

After the failure of the Hamburg National Theater, some German writers looked to Vienna, hoping for the patronage of Joseph II (1741-1790), a sovereign who had great ideals but little sense of the political realities in his widespread realm. While they largely ignored Joseph's attempt to revive the moribund empire, they were attracted by his concern for cultivating things German and by his willingness to nationalize the well-known Burgtheater. Their protest against foreign cultural domination continued throughout the late 1760s and, steadily gaining momentum, burst forth in the 1770s with unprecedented energy. By 1782, when Schiller's (1759-1805) *Die Räuber* was produced with overwhelming success at the so-called national theater in Mannheim, many of the minor as well as major German territories already had resident acting companies willing and able to perform works by the generation that had grown up amid the protests and assiduously learned from its elders. The Austro-Prussian struggle for supremacy, which was to continue during the last decades of the eighteenth century and prove politically disastrous during the Napoleonic era, helped sustain the kind of territorial particularism that had for centuries prevented any one city from becoming the cultural center of gravity in the German-speaking world.

Justus Möser (1720-1794) was one of the elders from whom the younger generation learned a great deal.[1] His background, experience, and interest in jurisprudence influenced much of his thought. He advocated English, that is, Germanic law, which, he often explained, grew naturally out of decisions about particular events. Whatever the object of his investigation, he worked empirically, gathering the available concrete evidence and submitting it to careful rational analysis. He also worked comparatively, for he wanted to discover the interrelationships of man's varied activities and achievements. He strove to account for all the factors that gave a specific culture its distinctive character and coherence. His ultimate aim was to teach his fellow Germans to recognize their own identity, affirm it, and cultivate it. Whether opposing Gottsched and his followers in *Harlekin oder Vertheidigung des Groteske-Komischen* (1761) or Frederick the Great in *Über die deutsche Sprache und Literatur* (1781), he articulated his views in a simple, down-to-earth style that left an indelible impression on the minds of his contemporaries.

Möser publicized the Germanic past whenever he could. He often wrote that the Romans had not only feared but also revered the ancient Germans because they represented a well-unified society in which freedom reigned supreme and all activity contributed to the commonweal. He proudly agreed with Montesquieu (1689-1755) that the Saxons had invented everything really important about liberty, justice, and participatory government. And he claimed that the other tribes had made equally significant contributions. One example of his attempt to extol ancient Germanic culture was his tragedy about Arminius, the Cheruscan prince who defeated the Roman legions of Varus in the Teutoburg Forest during the first century. Arminius, or Hermann, as many preferred to call him, had been a subject of literary interest since the sixteenth century, when reformers, like Ulrich von Hutten (1488-1523), viewed him as the embodiment of their ancient forebears' virtue, purity, and strength; he received steadily increasing operatic as well as dramatic treatment in the 1730s and 1740s, for he had come to symbolize the fight for liberation from foreign domination. In the preface to his *Arminius* (1749), Möser stated that Tacitus's *Germania* must have given an honest account since much of it still held true for certain segments of the rural population.[2] He took issue with those who denounced the ancient Germans as crude, insensitive barbarians, maintaining that Tacitus omitted mention of their fine sensibilities and feelings because he had intended to describe only how they differed from the Romans. Möser urged German writers to investigate their own past further and to awaken their countrymen to its richness by portraying it in their works.

He also encouraged investigation of the folk and the unique forms of entertainment it enjoyed. Like so many earlier patriotic writers, he rejected the neoclassical code and disputed the fashion that considered French artistic achievements the touchstone of all taste. His *Harlekin* defended the popular comic tradition with arguments that were to exert far greater influence on the subsequent development of German criticism and aesthetics than those of Lessing's seventeenth "Literaturbrief" (1759). Möser con-

centrated on the grotesque, which he claimed was first perfected by Cervantes in *Don Quixote*, and explained it as an
intentional deviation from all the norms of beauty, real or
ideal. In so doing, he not only repudiated the dogma of
mimesis and the idea of one universal taste, but he also
strengthened the foundation for the concept of genius and
the theory of original creation. The form and style of his
essay, which was reprinted in 1777 at the height of the
Sturm und Drang, contributed greatly to the effectiveness
of his argumentation. Möser created a Harlequin figure and
let it present its own witty, sometimes ironic, always humor-
ous defense.

Harlequin assumes the guise of the nonintellectual who
has gained whatever wisdom he has through common sense
and experience. While purporting to admire the erudition
of his critics, he relies on his extensive firsthand knowledge
of living theater to point out their methodological errors
and inconsistencies. He good-naturedly pokes fun at them
for asserting that he cannot possibly provide pleasure when
they have not even attended his performances or considered
his age-old popularity. Harlequin, who remains rather
suspicious of his critics' vocabulary, happily eschews the
term "comedy" for his plays. The word "harlequinade" is
more to his liking, for he believes it allows him to retain
his individual integrity rather than be, like the lion who is
called a cat, subsumed under a major generic heading and
then required to perform accordingly. His plays, he states,
are similar to opera's numerous variants in that they are
"keinesweges blosse Spielarten ihrer Gattung, sondern eigne
fruchtbare Geschlechter" (IX, 70; "by no means mere
varieties of their species, but individual, fertile genera").
He prefers the word "harlequinade" for two other reasons:
it not only immortalizes him but also connotes considerable
progress over the puerile plays of his predecessor Hanswurst.
And progress, or natural growth, is something he stresses
when speaking of the new and different art forms that
human beings constantly devise to satisfy their inherent

need for pleasure: "Die Sphäre des menschlichen Vergnügens lässt sich noch immer erweitern" (IX, 68; "The sphere of human pleasure can be yet still further expanded").

Many of Möser's artistic views derived from his conception of nature as a dynamic, continually evolving organism comprised of infinite varieties and latent possibilities that could not be philosophically delimited, mathematically regimented, or scientifically predicted. Although nature might seem wild and arbitrary, he was confident that it unified its overwhelming diversity and governed itself according to its own laws. Möser revered the intrinsic laws operating within nature, but he unequivocally rejected the extrinsic rules invented and codified by the schoolmen. He believed they hampered the kind of lawful self-regulation that would evolve if nature—especially human nature —were left to its own devices.

And Möser's Harlequin wants to be left alone. He claims he is tired of being condemned for his neglect of the schoolmen's rules. The harlequinade, he explains, has its own intrinsic laws, which are just as valid for it, as those of other art forms are for them. If there is any common denominator to be found among them, he continues, then it is that each has its own inimitable kind of unity. The unities of time, place, and action have nothing to do with it, as far as he can see, and furthermore, "wenn die Absicht eines Verfassers ist, alle Regeln zu verletzen, und er thut es auf eine glückliche Art, so ist sein Werk einig und vollkommen" (IX, 92; "if the intention of an author is to offend all the rules, and he does so successfully, his work is unified and complete"). He speaks of unity in the singular rather than the plural, for he means the organically necessary interrelationship of all parts. As nature regulates itself by bringing together and synthesizing many divergent elements, so, Harlequin contends, does each great work of art, whether a painting, a poem, a comedy, a tragedy, an opera, a harlequinade, or a musical piece.

Opera serves as Harlequin's main example when he discusses the schoolmen's criticism of his failure to imitate nature. He claims the operatic form has continued to evolve uninterruptedly according to its own assumptions despite similar criticism. The argument often advanced by its loyal defenders, he maintains, is just as applicable to his harlequinade and, for that matter, even to Shakespearean drama: instead of imitating nature, they all create their own artificial but equally true nature. Operatic defenders had usually challenged the interpretation of mimesis that was current in their time and in so doing, had gradually made opera into a symbol for the artificiality of all art. It was with Möser's essay that opera began being considered a symbol for nonmimetic artistic expression. The explanation he has his Harlequin give shows that critical emphasis had definitely shifted from the work to its creator and his imagination:

Die Oper ist eine Vorstellung aus einer möglichen Welt, welche der Dichter nach seinen Absichten erschaffen kann, wenn er nur im Stande ist, selbige dem Zuschauer glaublich zu machen. Die einzige Natur, welche wir in unsrer wirklichen Welt haben, ist zu enge für die Einbildung des Dichters, und Alles, was der Opernschöpfer von dieser ohne Noth entlehnt, zeugt von seiner Schwäche. Es würde lächerlich seyn, wenn die Operngötter gleich Adams Kindern sprächen, indem daraus eine Mischung verschiedner Naturen entstehen würde. Die Opernbühne ist das Reich der Chimären; sie eröffnet einen gezauberten Himmel; und da die Engel in ihrem seligen Aufenthalt beständig singen sollen, so müsste die Einbildungskraft desjenigen Operndichters sehr matt seyn, welcher seinen Göttern diese Art des höhern Ausdrucks und die Harmonie der theatralischen Sphären entziehen wollte. Es kann also der grösste Lobspruch, den man einer Oper, oder einem Heldengedicht, welches seine eigne Welt hat, geben kann, eben darin bestehen, dass beide in Vergleichung unsrer Welt völlig unnatürlich sind. Und in dieser

Absicht sagt Pope von Shakespeare, dass man letztern beschimpfe, wenn man ihn einen Maler der Natur nenne, da er vielmehr ein Schöpfer neuer Urbilder gewesen.* (IX, 72)

Möser believed opera, the harlequinade, and all such theatrical forms provided audiences with pleasure by appealing to their imagination and letting them experience on a small scale the wonder of creation. He upheld the imagination as the strongest and most characteristic of all human faculties because he thought it allowed intuitive comprehension of universal truths that reason was too limited not only to grasp but even to recognize. And this, he argued in his defense of revealed religion, "Schreiben an den Herrn Vicar in Savoyen" (1762), was why images, symbols, and allegories always had greater impact than rational argument. In attempting to show the limitations of rational cognition, he referred to what several others of his generation, especially musicians, like Hiller, considered man's innate inclination toward the unusual, the abnormal, the strange, and the dreamlike (V, 247).

Möser shared many other ideas with his contemporaries.

---

* Opera is a representation of a possible world, which the poet can create according to his own intentions as long as he is capable of making it credible for the spectator. The only nature we have in our real world is too confined for the imagination of the poet, and everything the creator of opera unnecessarily borrows from it is evidence of his weakness. It would be ridiculous if opera's gods spoke exactly like Adam's children because a mixture of different natures would result therefrom. The operatic stage is the realm of the chimeras; it reveals a conjured up heaven; and since the angels are supposed to sing continually in their blessed abode, the imagination of the librettist would have to be very dull to want to deprive his gods of this kind of higher expression and the harmony of the theatrical spheres. It can therefore be the greatest eulogy one can give an opera or a heroic poem which has its own world to say that in comparison with our world both are completely unnatural. And with this intention Pope says of Shakespeare that one would be insulting him if one called him a painter of nature since he was much more a creator of new archetypes.

Lessing recommended *Harlekin* as an example of genuine criticism, and Möser in turn applauded Lessing's analysis of the fable for its emphasis on the significance of intuitive perception.[3] Both agreed that undue adulation of the French prevented the cultivation of imagery that could restore the long lost common foundation of German culture. Nicolai, with whom Möser became quite good friends, considered *Harlekin* a gold mine for those working to restore that foundation.[4] He could not, however, condone Möser's interest in relating the popular ballad to the development of the operetta. Nor could he, despite his love for England and its theater, understand Möser's excitement about having seen a revival of *The Beggar's Opera* during an eight-month sojourn in London (1763-1764). Their interpretation of genius was quite similar although Nicolai protested much more vehemently when he thought the younger generation confused natural self-regulation with lawlessness. Möser accepted Nicolai's *Freuden des jungen Werthers* (1775) as an amusing parody of Goethe's novel (IX, 156), but he refused to join with him in condemning the young author who seemed to have so much potential for future growth. The good humor, wit, and objectivity with which Möser stated his views won him the allegiance as well as the respect of his younger contemporaries. Goethe and Herder, who included his preface to *Osnabrückische Geschichte* in their *Von deutscher Art und Kunst* (1773), appreciated his historiography and applied its principles as well as its findings in their own works.

They also appreciated the way he rose to their defense when their efforts were censured by Frederick the Great in *De la littérature allemande* (1780). Möser's *Über die deutsche Sprache und Literatur* (1781) contended that the French reacted to nature, and consequently conceived of unity, so differently from the Germans that their works of art could not possibly serve as models for emulation. Because the French required an easily perceptible unity, he explained, they sacrificed everything to a rational ideal, re-

jecting whatever failed to conform. Their geometrical gar-
dens, their regular tragedies, their government, their entire
way of life proved this to him. His examination of English
gardening, theater, and government revealed no such simplicity or predictability. It revealed that the English, whose
Anglo-Saxon origins he never failed to mention, retained
the essentially Germanic predilection for nature's infinite
varieties, novelties, and surprises. That predilection was no
longer visible in Germany itself, he concluded, because it
had been stifled by scholars and aristocrats who insisted
upon slavishly imitating the Romans and their descendants.
Though suspecting that artistic wildness might result,
Möser encouraged his contemporaries to begin acknowledging their Germanic spirit and attempting to unify great
diversity. Homer and Shakespeare, he claimed, could provide enough inspiration and guidance, for neither had produced works that snobbishly excluded certain aspects of life.
Goethe's *Götz von Berlichingen* might have signified the
barbarity of German dramatic taste to Frederick the Great,
but it signified the dawn of a new era to Möser. He thought
there should be more works about Germany before the introduction of Roman law and—with words that unfortunately appealed to baser elements in the twentieth century
—maintained: "Der beste Gesang für unsre Nation ist unstreitig ein Bardit, der sie zur Vertheidigung ihres Vaterlandes in die Schlacht singt; der beste Tanz, der sie auf die
Batterie führt, und das beste Schauspiel, was ihnen hohen
Muth giebt" (IX, 141; "The best song for our nation is
incontestably a bardic song, which it sings to battle in defense of the fatherland; the best dance, the one which leads
it to the battery, and the best play, the one which gives it
great courage").

HERMANN AND THE BARDIC MODE

Friedrich Gottlieb Klopstock's attempts to provide patriotic
works began during the 1750s and continued for the rest

241

of his life. While still composing *Der Messias* (1748-1773), the religious epic that brought him acclaim as the regenerator of German verse and diction, he studied the Germanic past, contemplated its poetic possibilities, and wrote poems like "Hermann und Thusnelda" (1752). His interest in that past was awakened by his associates in Copenhagen, where Nordic antiquities had long been investigated and cherished. It increased considerably in the 1760s after James Macpherson (1736-1796) published the forgeries that he, for a while at least, successfully passed off as third-century Gaelic epics by Ossian. Klopstock and his countrymen in Copenhagen were less concerned with Ossian's authenticity than they were with reviving the poetic style of their own ancestors and using it to help release the German spirit from foreign bondage. They cultivated the Celtic word "bard" because of the connotations that had accrued since the seventeenth century, when scholars applied it to all ancient North European poets—Scandinavian, Germanic, and Anglo-Saxon as well as Celtic—in order to distinguish them from the Greeks and Romans.

As Klopstock's patriotic inclinations increased, he revised some of his earlier poems, giving them a decidedly Germanic tone. The mythology, landscape, and atmosphere of the north began to supplement, then supplant, that of the south in his works. He also turned more and more from the classical metrical patterns, which he knew how to use masterfully, to the freer rhythms of the bards. His "Der Hügel und der Hain" (1767), in which the singers are a bard, a classical poet, and a contemporary, inspired the young writers in Göttingen so much that they joined together to practice what it preached. The members of what has since been called the Göttinger Hainbund asserted their Germanic identity by rejecting the Greek Parnassus in favor of the local grove and by assuming what they considered typically bardic names.

The greatest source of inspiration for them was Klopstock's *Hermanns Schlacht, Ein Bardiet für die Schaubühne* (1769). He chose to call it a *Bardiet* in order to clarify his intentions. In the first of the many footnotes accompanying the text, he cited Tacitus's use of the word *barditus*, which referred to the battle cry, as proving that the ancient Germans, like the Celts, had had bards to record in song the heroic deeds of their nation.[5] He intended to revive such bardic songs and make them the basis for a theatrical form that would be totally different from the kind of conventional spoken drama associated with the Greco-Latin tradition. Klopstock, who appreciated Scheibe's efforts to develop German music and musical drama, paid much attention to his work's stageworthiness. In addition to using the songs to accentuate events or moods described in the prose dialogue, he gave explicit directions about gestures, dances, instrumental music, and other nonverbal techniques, especially gradations of sound and lapses into silence. Lessing, with whom he discussed his intentions during occasional visits to Hamburg in 1767, welcomed the first draft enthusiastically and predicted in letters to Nicolai and other Berlin friends that the finished work would be just as epoch making as *Der Messias*.[6] Lessing also recommended it to his friend Bode, who was to gain repute as the dynamic organizer of Hamburg theater enthusiasts and the willing printer of other such patriotic works, including Herder's *Von deutscher Art und Kunst.*

The edition of *Hermanns Schlacht* that appeared in 1769 was dedicated to Emperor Joseph II. Klopstock prepared it hoping for an imperial appointment in Vienna. Joseph sympathized with his ideas about spiritual unity and rewarded him for the dedication but made no appointment. Klopstock was somewhat more successful in his attempt to win Gluck, the imperial composer, as an associate. Gluck was so impressed with *Hermanns Schlacht* that he promised to set its bardic songs to music. His enduring favorite, which, contemporaries reported, brought tears to his eyes when he sang it, was the one that concluded the play:

> Wodan! unbeleidigt von uns,
>> Fielen sie bey deinen Altären uns an!
>> Wodan! unbeleidigt von uns,
>>> Erhoben sie ihr Beil gegen dein freyes Volk!*[7]

Gluck, who did not think in terms of an operatic version, worked slowly, apologizing for his lack of progress whenever he wrote or visited Klopstock. He claimed he wanted to take pains with the composition because it was the only one specifically for his own countrymen rather than for foreigners.[8] Actually he had become embroiled in the Parisian operatic dispute that resulted in the commission to do *Iphigénie en Tauride* (1779). Although his settings for seven of Klopstock's odes appeared in 1785, his work on *Hermanns Schlacht* remained incomplete. Steadily deteriorating health prevented him from keeping in contact with Klopstock and from acknowledging the later bardic plays, *Hermann und die Fürsten* (1784) and *Hermanns Tod* (1787).

Gluck never considered Klopstock a potential librettist, but others of his generation did. The patriotism of the bardic play appealed to writers of varying theoretical persuasions. Among the more conservative was Johann Georg Sulzer, who upheld the neoclassical code because it suited his Wolffian principles. Like his friend Ramler, he looked to poets to reform opera and make it imitate nature in a dramatic form that was merely supplemented with music. In the article on opera in his *Allgemeine Theorie der Schönen Künste* (1773-1775), he discussed the long-range utilitarian purpose of such reform. He claimed contemporary Germans lacked the kind of cultural unity that had enabled the Greeks to perfect their tragedy, which he considered "im Grunde eine würkliche Oper" ("fundamentally

---

* Woden, without being wronged by us, they attacked us at your altars. Woden, without being wronged by us, they raised their ax against your free people.

an actual opera").[9] Since no sovereign seemed willing, he hoped poets would take the initiative and work to reunify the German-speaking world. He therefore urged them to study their own heritage, read Ossian, and emulate the form Klopstock had invented for *Hermanns Schlacht*. Sulzer thought the *Bardiet* was completely new, yet closer to the Greek ideal than any other type of modern drama because it allowed for music's inclusion in a way that was not only effective but also rationally comprehensible.

Heinrich Wilhelm von Gerstenberg, who was equally enthusiastic about *Hermanns Schlacht*, represented a much more progressive critical position. He opposed all rationalistic systems that reduced the arts to imitations of nature because he believed they failed to account for the creative imagination of genius. The artistic theories he espoused as well as the dramatic forms he cultivated were influenced to a great extent by his love for music. While emphasizing music's importance for lyric poetry and for drama, he refused to consider it the servant of any other art. Like Nicolai, with whom he corresponded, he considered instrumental music an independent art that was in itself fully capable of expressing the whole range of human emotions. Gerstenberg shared many interests with Nicolai and the others in Berlin. He sudied Dubos, admired English Renaissance drama, emphasized the importance of genius, and attempted to explain the essence of opera as well as tragedy. He supported Marpurg's historical investigations, and he agreed with Mendelssohn's contention that music had to be included in any general theory of aesthetics.

Gerstenberg himself was an amateur musician who enjoyed organizing musical evenings in his Copenhagen home. The circle of German intellectuals, especially his close friends Scheibe and Klopstock, often convened there for informal concerts and discussions.[10] Opera was a particularly important topic of discussion because it allowed them to combine their musical interests and their patriotic concerns. They all opposed Italianate grand opera. And they all worked, each in his own way, to develop musical theatrical forms that would do justice to the Germanic spirit. Gerstenberg contributed actual texts, theoretical statements, and reviews of current experimentation. The cantata received much of his attention, for he believed its very conciseness increased the emotional poignancy of the plot and sustained the all-important mood without tiring the audience. He welcomed Ramler's *Pygmalion*, which was written in 1768, five years after Rousseau's, claiming it provided worthy competition for the Italians, who, he thought, should not consider musical theater their exclusive domain.[11] Although Gerstenberg presumably wrote several cantatas for his soirees, the only one I know to have been published was *Ariadne auf Naxos* (1767).[12] It was the text that the actor and rather successful playwright Johann Christian Brandes (1735-1799) took up in 1774, altered, and made into a full-fledged melodrama consisting of spoken dialogue with musical accompaniment. Brandes's work, when performed the following year in Greek costume and with music by Georg Benda (1722-1795), aroused so much excitement that a unique vogue began. Many writers, including Goethe as well as Gerstenberg, experimented further with what was believed to be a brand new theatrical form.[13]

Gerstenberg's experiments resulted in *Minona, oder Die Angelsachsen, Ein tragisches Melodrama* (1785). He had studied the Nordic past since his youth, had often published on the subject, and had long wanted to recapture the melancholy, mysterious atmosphere found in the poetry of the ancient bards and skalds.[14] He considered the melodrama especially suitable for doing so. His thorough familiarity with the poetic works of classical as well as Nordic antiquity had enabled him as early as 1766 to detect certain Homeric traces that made Ossian's authenticity seem quite dubious.[15] Nevertheless, he appreciated what he called the Ossianic spirits, depicted them in *Minona*, and in 1812, when attempting to incorporate Schiller's suggestions into a modernization of the text, refused to delete them. Without them, he claimed, "mein Drama von den Angelsachsen würde nicht zugleich meine Oper von Minona und der Zukunft sein" ("my drama about the Anglo-Saxons would not at the same time be my opera about Minona and the future").[16]

While Gerstenberg explored the expressive possibilities of the cantata and the melodrama, his friend Klopstock continued working with the *Bardiet*. The first one, *Hermanns Schlacht*, received Gerstenberg's glowing words of praise in a review for the *Hamburgische Neue Zeitung* (1769). In addition to examining its patriotic sentiments and historical accuracy, he discussed its dramatic structure in detail. Most significant is his discussion of the bardic songs. He thought Klopstock demonstrated more successfully than any of his contemporaries how the chorus of Greek tragedy could be adapted and made meaningful for modern theater. The others were so unsuccessful, Gerstenberg wrote, because they, unlike Klopstock, failed to understand the ancient conception of mimesis. Instead of attempting to produce an illusion of nature that could be taken for the real thing, he explained, the ancients had used choruses, dances, instrumental music, and other nonnaturalistic elements in order to create "eine zweite dichtrische Natur" ("a second poetic nature").[17] In his opinion, Klopstock understood that full well, for the bardic songs together with the free dithyrambic metrical system and the elevated poetic language removed *Hermanns Schlacht* from the world of ordinary reality to a higher idealized artistic realm. Gerstenberg cited its delineation of character and its portrayal of manners as further reasons for considering it an immortal masterpiece comparable only to the dramas of Sophocles and Shakespeare.

Comparing *Hermanns Schlacht*, which did not even pass the test of its own time, with Sophoclean and Shakespearean drama may seem at first to be simply the kind of compliment one eighteenth-century friend would pay another. Gerstenberg's interpretation of Shakespeare's works and genius in five of the *Briefe über Merkwürdigkeiten der Litteratur* (1766) indicates that it was more than just that. He saw what he thought were similarities between Klopstock and Shakespeare. Gerstenberg's letters on Shakespeare had apparently been prompted by the appearance of Wieland's prose translation,[18] which Gerstenberg rejected without equivocation. He maintained that Wieland had totally distorted the texts in an attempt to bring them into line with the French neoclassical code. Gerstenberg, who, like Möser, believed the Anglo-Saxons were among the most original of all peoples, preferred to consider Shakespeare's dramas "living pictures of moral nature" rather than species or subspecies of certain predetermined genres. The only genre designations that would not be irrelevant, he claimed, were the ones Polonius spoke of in *Hamlet*. And even they, he quickly added, did not do full justice to the *Tempest* and *Midsummer Night's Dream*, "da sie sich fast ganz der Natur der Oper nähern" ("since they almost wholly approach the nature of opera").[19] Gerstenberg admired the great versatility of Shakespeare's genius and, in giving the description of it that was to become very influential, referred once again to opera: "Er hat Alles—den bilderreichen Geist der Natur in Ruhe und der Natur in Bewegung, den lyrischen Geist der Oper, den Geist der komischen Situation, sogar den Geist der Groteske—und das Sonderbarste ist, dass Niemand sagen kann, diesen hat er mehr, und jenen hat er weniger."[20] ("He has everything—the richly metaphoric spirit of nature at rest and in motion, the lyrical spirit of the opera, the spirit of the comic situation, even the spirit of the grotesque—and the strangest thing is that no one can say he has this more and that less.") Here and elsewhere in his critical writings, he chose to use the word "opera" because it connoted not only the lyric spirit but also the unlimited possibilities of the artistic imagination.

Gerstenberg summed up his operatic theory in "Schlechte Einrichtung des Italienischen Singgedichts: Warum ahmen Deutsche sie nach?" (1770). He opposed the Italianate style because he thought its declamatory arias and its elaborately accompanied recitatives were contradictions in terms. The aria, like any song, he maintained, should transform the spoken words that signified ideas into "tonal pictures of feelings." On the other hand, he pointed out, the very essence of declamation precluded any such transformation; declamation could not be considered song as long as the words continued to signify ideas rather than paint feelings. Since the recitative originated in declamation, he explained, it should heighten, yet follow closely, the normal accentuation of the spoken words in order to convey the ideas they signified. Reciting, he insisted, was as different from singing as one language from another. In his opinion, everyone, except the Italians and their imitators, knew that no two languages could be spoken in the same breath.

Gerstenberg had many other objections to Italian opera. Most of them had to do with those features of musical virtuosity, like the coloratura aria, that set it so far apart from Greek tragedy. He believed the Greeks' strong sense for human proportions had enabled them to invent and perfect a recitative style that respected natural speech while still elevating it. Along with Dubos, Marpurg, and other theorists, he attributed the loss of that style to modern musical progress, especially the invention of new instruments. Gerstenberg's concern was for the future. He hoped continuing experimentation would produce an operatic form "wo, wie in den Trauerspielen der Alten, nicht der Gesang, sondern die Recitation den Ton des Werks bestimmt" ("where, as in the tragedies of the ancients, the recitation rather than the song determines the tone of the work").[21] In concluding his essay, he stressed the necessity of freeing German opera from foreign domination so that it could create and cultivate its own world, the rich world of the artistic imagination: "Welch ein Werk könnte die Oper seyn! welch ein Werk, wenn man sich gleich Anfangs um die Franzosen und Italiener, und ihre alten Madrigale, und ihre gothischen Begriffe unbekümmert, gelassen hätte! welch ein Werk. wenn man noch itzt die eigenthümliche Welt der Oper, (ich meyne hier weder Götter, noch Feen, noch Sylphen, noch Zaubrer, ich meyne die Welt einer edlen und der Gottheit würdigen Imagination), so zu nutzen versuchte, als schon das blosse Ideal derselben die brüderlichen Genien der Dichtkunst und der Tonkunst dazu einladet."[22] ("What a work opera could be! What a work, if at the very beginning one had been unconcerned about the French and Italians and their old madrigals, and their Gothic conceptions! What a work, if one tried right now to use the proper world of opera [I mean here neither gods, nor fairies, nor sylphs, nor sorcerers, I mean the world of an imagination that is noble and worthy of the deity], as the mere ideal of it already summons the brotherly geniuses of poetry and music to it.")

Although Gerstenberg inclined toward the melancholy, the brooding, and the tragic, he was also interested in the ridiculous, the grotesque, and the comic, at least in theory. He greatly admired Gay's ballad operas, sometimes citing titles like *What d'ye call it* or referring to the "tragicomipastoralfarce" in discussions of genre. He believed the German language lacked the vocabulary and the syntactical patterns to express a similar variety of comic nuances. And he agreed with Möser that the overriding French influence was to blame. Lessing's *Minna von Barnhelm* (1767) must have made quite an impression, for Gerstenberg publicly encouraged him in 1768 to try his hand at comic operettas, wishfully thinking that a German Pergolesi might come forth to set them to music.[23] In Gerstenberg's opinion, Schiebeler revealed excellent comic talents in his operettas, and they would have to suffice in the absence of anything better.[24]

EUROPEAN CONTEXTS:
THE "ROMANTIC" OPERATIC WORLD

Opposition to the proliferation of bardic poetry was not long in coming. Some writers considered its style unnecessarily primitive and wholly unpoetic. Others thought its historical basis rather dubious because of the paucity of available original works. Still other writers believed its assumptions threatened the humanistic tradition that had evolved since classical antiquity. Although they were all equally patriotic about fostering their own German culture, they preferred to emphasize the greater European context within which it existed. They continued to investigate the Greco-Roman classics but gave increasing attention to the medieval and Renaissance texts that were becoming more readily accessible. Their studies of Spanish and Italian as well as French and English literature led to speculations about the kinds of traits certain works seemed to share. They compared the adventures, loves, and enchantments depicted by Homer with those they read about in Ariosto, Spenser, and Cervantes. European and oriental fairy tales —which were to be collected and published in the German language in the 1780s—were sometimes included in such comparisons. These writers not only gained a greater sense of literary history but also found a rich reservoir of topics to experiment with.

Musical theater, which remained the most popular public entertainment in the 1760s and 1770s, served as the proving ground for much of that experimentation. Although no tradition of grand opera in a distinctively German style resulted, the abundance of musical and quasi-musical theatrical forms that were cultivated set important precedents for what was to follow in subsequent decades. Grand opera seemed most suitable for dramatizing the fairy tale and the poetic romance with their wondrous happenings. Lyric drama, melodrama, monodrama, duodrama, and dance drama were thought appropriate for the portrayal of human emotions and internalized or psychological action. Comic opera, operetta, and musical comedy were considered well suited for parodies, satires, and even travesties of chivalric love, knight errantry, and other such topics.

Daniel Schiebeler was one writer who chose to experiment with the last. He came from a well-to-do merchant family in Hamburg, and had he been born a half-century earlier, probably would have been equally comfortable among the city's intellectuals. As it was, he became very close with Michael Richey, the Gymnasium teacher who awakened his interest in classical as well as modern literature and encouraged him to develop his poetic talents.[25] Those talents lay primarily with popular balladry, parody, and comic romance. Schiebeler recognized the potential of such forms for musical theater and, while a student in Leipzig, tried incorporating them into the librettos he wrote or adapted. The success of *Lisuart und Dariolette, oder die Frage und die Antwort* (1766), his first collaboration with Hiller, catapulted him to fame and made him one of Weisse's acknowledged competitors.

Schiebeler gave his views on libretto writing in "Anmerkung zu Lisuart und Dariolette," which appeared in Hiller's *Wöchentliche Nachrichten* on November 2, 1767. In order to defend his text, which was based on Chaucer's "Tale of the Wife of Bath," he discussed the epic tradition and the wealth of subjects it offered for theatrical experimentation. Making operas out of epics, novels, and even parts of the Bible had been an established practice in Europe in the last quarter of the seventeenth century. The Hamburg librettists staunchly defended that practice when Pietistic clergymen denounced its deleterious effects on the Christian soul and when neoclassical critics condemned it for contradicting the concept of pure genres. While continuing to uphold artistic freedom, early eighteenth-century librettists became increasingly interested in the relationship of form and content. Some wished to contain opera's epic tendencies by simplifying plots and making them more dramatic. They represented a classical point of view, for they either adapted to the French neoclassical code or tried looking beyond it to Greek tragedy itself. Others, however, continued to cultivate opera as a totally modern theatrical possibility. They thought its musical medium, together with its machines and stage sets, made it suitable for dramatizing epics and novels and for inventing still other theatrical forms. Schiebeler subscribed to that point of view, and he used a form of the word "romantic" to describe it.

The words *romanhaft, romanisch,* and *romantisch* were being used with greater frequency in the 1760s to affirm the particular kind of poetic reality created in medieval epics and Renaissance romances. Gerstenberg defended Spenser's *Faerie Queene* as an "anthology of romantic adventures" in 1766, and the following year Herder explained that the romantic taste of the Spaniards and Italians was a "branch of oriental superstition" that had combined with the "Gothic taste for chivalric adventures" and the "Roman Catholic propensity for crusades and other holy adventures."[26] Schiebeler was much less gifted a theorist who adopted such ideas without fully comprehending their implications. His "Anmerkung zu Lisuart und Dariolette" exemplifies not only how the jargon of current research was popularized but also how it was made to apply to musical theater.

Schiebeler began with a brief historical sketch of what he considered the romantic epic. He wrote that it originated in Provence when poets recounted in prose the loves and the adventurous exploits of King Arthur, Lancelot, Tristan, and other knights of the Round Table. Their tales, he continued, were exported to Italy where they were so enthusiastically received that poets versified them to make them still more effective. He named Boccaccio, Boiardo, Ariosto, and Tasso as the Italian poets who helped to bring the newly invented form to perfection. Spenser was the English example he cited and Voltaire the French. He agreed with Gerstenberg that Homer told of the knights of his day in a way that was basically no less "romantic." Ovid's *Metamorphoses*, Schiebeler added, shared some of those very same romantic characteristics. As far as the Germans were concerned, he thought they had not yet produced any "romantic" works in their own language other than the poems of the *Minnesänger* that Bodmer had made known. His hope for the future lay not with Klopstock, who, he thought, was much too heroic, but rather with Wieland (p. 136), who had already published *Komische Erzählungen* (1762) and *Don Sylvio von Rosalva* (1764).

Schiebeler cited such background in order to show how different kinds of theatrical forms evolved from different kinds of epics. Speculation about drama's evolution from other genres, whether lyric, epic, or both, was increasing in the last half of the eighteenth century. While some writers sought the origins of Greek tragedy in the dithyramb, others preferred to concentrate on the madrigal and opera, or the ballad and the ballad opera. Schiebeler, who was more interested in content than form, tried to systematize the relationships between kinds of epics and kinds of theatrical works. In so doing, he expanded some of the ideas he had absorbed, whether consciously or not, from Batteux and his German commentators. The serious epic, Schiebeler wrote, produced the usual heroic tragedy or the heroic opera, which Metastasio, his favorite, had perfected. Ovid's *Metamorphoses*, he continued, had led to operas about divine beings, like many of those by Quinault.

After mentioning that comedy and comic opera derived from the comic epic, he turned to the romantic epic. He considered it so important because he believed along with Hiller that there was an innate human predilection for the kinds of subjects and styles it presented. In Schiebeler's opinion "Der Hauptcharacter der romanischen Epopee ist das Abendtheuerliche. Der Haupt-Inhalt sind die Begebenheiten irrender Ritter. Es ist eine Vermischung des Ernsthaften mit dem Komischen in derselben; man lese nur den Ariost, und man wird alles dieses darinne finden" (p. 137;

"The main characteristic of the romantic epic is the adventurous. The main contents are the experiences of
knights errant. It is a mixture of the serious with the comic;
one need only read Ariosto, and one will find all this
there"). He maintained that its serious side was the source
of romantic tragedies like Voltaire's *Tancred* and romantic-
tragic operas like Quinault's *Roland*. He thought its playful side (*scherzhaft*) resulted in romantic comedy and romantic-comic opera, although he complained of difficulties
in finding examples based on something other than the
magical occurrences in the world of fairies. In an attempt
to preserve the integrity of his rather shaky system, he
wrote: "Diese Comödien aber sind mehr als Töchter des
Feyenmährchens anzusehen, welches in der That einige Art
der Aehnlichkeit mit der romanischen Epopee hat, aber
doch nicht eins und dasselbige mit ihm ist" (pp. 137-138;
"These comedies are to be viewed more as daughters of the
fairy tale, which in fact has a kind of similarity with the
romantic epic but is however not one and the same with
it").

He offered his own *Lisuart und Dariolette* as an example
of the romantic-comic opera, apologizing for originally giving it the subtitle "comic opera" when it was intended to be
so much more. His advice to fellow librettists was to explore similar possibilities: "Die alten Geschichten der
Amadisse, des Esplandians, des Tirants, des Palmerins, des
Sonnenritters, des Orlando, können tausend Süjets an die
Hand geben" (p. 138; "The old stories of the Amadises,
Esplandian, Tirante the White, Palmerin, the Knight of the
Sun, Roland can offer a thousand subjects"). Those who
followed that advice usually gave their texts the subtitle
Schiebeler recommended, namely romantic-comic opera or
operetta. Critics of such texts took up the word "romantic"
in one or another of its forms and began adding to its connotative value. The reviewer of *Lisuart und Dariolette* for
the *Allgemeine Deutsche Bibliothek* (1769), for example,
lauded the efforts of both Hiller and Schiebeler. He

255

thought the choice of a "romantic" subject had "wenig-stens eine neue Art von schiklicher Gelegenheit verschaffet, sich bisweilen aus der niedrigen und manchmal possier-lichen Schreibart, in welche die blos komischen Rollen sie einzwängen, der erhabnern mit guter Art zu nähern" ("at least created a new kind of clever opportunity now and then to get out of the low and sometimes farcical style of writing, into which the merely comic roles forced them, and to approach the more sublime with good style").[27] It was left for still later theorists to make the sublime a ma-jor characteristic of the romantic, and when they did so, opera was often mentioned in one way or another.[28]

NINE

CULMINATION AND CONTINUATION: WIELAND

Alceste

CHRISTOPH Martin Wieland's contribution to the history of German musical theater was even greater than Schiebeler had hoped or anticipated. In addition to the heroic epic, *Oberon* (1780), which Schiller contemplated dramatizing[1] and which Carl Maria von Weber (1786-1826) made the basis for a romantic opera (1826), Wieland provided his own operatic works and theories. Like so many of his older as well as younger contemporaries in the 1770s, he patriotically supported the idea of German lyric drama in a German rather than Italian musical style. He did not believe that cultivation of the *Bardiet* could bring that idea to fruition, so he strongly rejected it, thereby intensifying his longstanding feud with the Göttinger Hainbund.[2] The *Singspiel* form developed by Hiller, Weisse, and Schiebeler seemed to offer far better possibilities. Wieland considered it agreeable and even quite pleasing, although he wrote: "ich kann nur noch eine andere Art davon denken, welche ein schöneres Ideal hätte."[3] ("I can think of yet another kind which would have a more beautiful ideal.")

Closer consideration of such ideals began after his arrival in Weimar in 1772. Duchess Anna Amalia, whose son he was appointed to tutor, actively fostered musical theater in its various forms and sought texts for court performances. Wieland prepared *Idris und Zenide* (1772), a mock heroic ballet based on a poem he had written earlier about a knight errant searching for the statue that would free his beloved from enchantment. A ballet was also included in *Aurora, ein Singspiel in einem Aufzug* (1772), the cantata-like text he produced for the duchess's birthday celebration. He later discounted it as a "Missgeschöpf" ("miscreation") that should be forgotten.[4]

Wieland's pride in the other text he had worked on that year was much much greater. His interest in the Alceste theme, which Gluck's opera (1767) presumably had stimulated, led to *Alceste, ein Singspiel in fünf Aufzügen* (1773). Wieland believed it clearly demonstrated how an ancient drama like Euripides' *Alceste* could be altered to produce a brand new operatic form compatible with the German spirit. He wrote "Briefe an einen Freund über das deutsche Singspiel, Alceste" for his journal *Der Teutsche Merkur* (1773) in order to justify his alterations. After several paragraphs defending the musicality of the German language, he explained that he had reduced the number of characters, shortened the long monologues, omitted the choruses, and transformed the heroine's role. Like Postel and other earlier librettists who had radically altered ancient Greek tragedies, he maintained that he had had to do so because the modern operatic stage demanded simplified plots, short cantabile dialogue, convincing character portrayal, and, above all, diversity and change.[5] Wieland thought he had surpassed both Euripides and Metastasio, his two favorite dramatists, in giving his text "einen Grad von innerlicher Wahrheit, der den Zuhörer nie bis zu dem Gedanken, dass sie nur ein Mährchen ist, erkalten lässt" (IX, 388; "a degree of internal truth, which never lets the listener come to the thought that it is only a fairy tale [make-believe]").

Other comments emphasized his work's stageworthiness. He claimed he had made its verse lyrical and poetic rather than rhetorical and philosophical in order to suit the operatic medium. He considered the arts of nonverbal communication just as important, if not more so: "Ich glaube, dass, zumal in einem lyrischen Schauspiel, die Kunst wenig Worte zu machen, ungleich grösser ist. Wie unendlich ist die Sprache der Empfindung von der Sprache der Rednerschulen verschieden! Was für unaussprechliche Dinge kan

sie mit Einem Blick, Einer Gebehrde, Einem Tone sagen!"
(IX, 406; "I think that particularly in a lyric play the art of
making few words is far greater. How infinitely different is
the language of feeling from the language of oratorical
schools! What ineffable things it can say with a glance, a
gesture, a tone!"). The emotional impact was intensified
still further by the score, he explained, because the composer Anton Schweitzer (1735-1787), who happened to be
good friends with Hiller, had known how to supplement
the poetic art when transitions were needed and also how
to compensate for it when its outer limits were reached.
Wieland asserted admiringly, yet perhaps all too hastily
considering their later arguments, that Schweitzer understood full well that the composer's role in an operatic collaboration had to be a totally subservient one.

When performed in Weimar and Mannheim, *Alceste* met
with such great success that Wieland was acclaimed the regenerator of German-language opera. Those reviewers who
missed the performances generally concentrated on the libretto and praised its high quality. One claimed he had
read it "nur als vortrefliche Poesie" ("only as excellent
poetry"), while another wrote that it was "ein Schauspiel,
welches, auch getrennt von der Musik, noch wesentliche
Vorzüge besitzt" ("a play which still possesses substantial
merits even when separated from the music").[6] The young
Goethe, however, did not concur. He considered its treatment of classical antiquity so painfully inaccurate and Wieland's attitude in the "Briefe" so presumptuously self-serv-
ing that he sketched the bitingly satirical farce, *Götter,
Helden und Wieland* (1773). Although he had intended it
only for his circle of friends, he agreed to have it printed
when prompted to do so by Jakob Michael Reinhold Lenz
(1751-1792), a resolute *Sturm und Drang* opponent of Wieland and everything he stood for.[7] Wieland's response to
the printed version was more gracious than either friend
could have anticipated. He thought it showed that Goethe
was a latter-day Aristophanes, just as *Götz* had proven him

to be a latter-day Shakespeare.[8] Wieland's supporters responded much less graciously toward the young, irreverent Goethe. A good example is Johann Jacob Hottinger's (1750-1819) *Menschen, Tiere und Goethe, Eine Farce* (1775).

Wieland also published "Über einige ältere deutsche Singspiele, die den Nahmen Alceste führen" in *Der Teutsche Merkur* in 1773. His critical analysis of the three texts, while never losing historical perspective, served to illuminate the importance of his own. He criticized the first one, a translation from the Italian, for bearing more resemblance to the *Amadis* and chivalric romances than to Euripides' drama. Other than the names, he thought it had "nicht den mindesten Geschmack von dem Lande und der Zeit, woraus die Begebenheit genommen ist" (XIV, 3; "not the least flavor of the land and time from which the event is taken"). He considered the inclusion of Hanswurst in the second one, which had been adapted from the French, particularly "baroque" (XIV, 18). The more sonorous language of the third one, König's *Alceste* (1719), did not, he claimed, mitigate the absurdities of its plot. Such texts made Saint Evremond's condemnation of opera seem justifiable to him. Wieland, however, refused to condemn them, contending they were produced when artistic tastes had not yet developed very far. At that time, he added, nonaesthetic considerations were so influential that many German librettists felt compelled to defend not only their own artistic practices but also the very idea of opera. Wieland gave a few excerpts from the libretto prefaces and mentioned Elmenhorst, Neumeister, and Mattheson, but he did not discuss the pros and cons of opera any further. He intended to reserve that for a future essay.

IDEAS ON REGENERATING GERMAN OPERA

When "Versuch über das deutsche Singspiel und einige dahin einschlagende Gegenstände" appeared in 1775, it contained much more than a discussion of opera controversies. Wieland's careful study of the critical writings associated with those controversies had helped refine his own ideas about regenerating German opera. He bemoaned the fact that there was no indigenous operatic tradition and claimed to be as astonished about it as the Englishman Dr. Charles Burney (1726-1814) had been in his recently published observations of the German musical scene. He agreed with Burney that it could not be attributed to Germany's native language, which, for all its guttural sounds, was indeed much more musical than French. Wieland also agreed with him that it could not be attributed to a lack of musical ability, inclination, or genius. The Germans, he explained, loved music as much as other peoples, studied it in their public as well as private schools, and could boast of composers like Keiser, Telemann, Händel, Hasse, Graun, Bach, Gluck, Naumann, and Haydn, who could compete easily with their best Italian contemporaries.[9]

Wieland attributed Germany's operatic deficiency to the widely held notion of *opera seria* as "ein Werk der Feerey" (XIV, 76; "a work of fairyhood"). He claimed it originated with the Italians, who produced expensive spectacles that only appealed to effeminate spectators seeking momentary diversion. The Italians retained their control, he explained, because German sovereigns neither supported indigenous talent nor recognized art's great significance for the "Beförderung der Humanität" (XIV, 75; "promotion of culture").

To break that control, Wieland suggested the Germans create their own new and more interesting form of musical play and distinguish it from all others by calling it the *Singspiel*. He envisioned it as a combination of poetry, music, and action that would quickly gain favor throughout the land, even in smaller cities, because it would be no more expensive to produce than spoken tragedy. Its beneficial influence on public conduct, he continued, would be recognized by ruling sovereigns who would then agree to

support local theaters and found schools for training performers. Such flourishing institutions, he predicted, would
spread good taste in the German lands and thereby raise
the general cultural level.

In the second section of the essay, Wieland tried to show
how and why the complaints against Italianate opera would
not apply to the new German *Singspiel*. The *Saggio sopra
l'Opera* (1755) of Francesco Algarotti (1712-1764), who
had resided at Frederick the Great's court in the 1740s, presented what Wieland considered the most sophisticated
summary of the main complaints, so he quoted it and used
it as the starting point for his discussion.[10] Wieland's arguments and the very vocabulary with which he advanced
them indicate his close familiarity with the writings of German opera's exponents in Berlin, Copenhagen, Hamburg,
and Leipzig. Instead of bewitching the senses of its spectators with elaborate costumes, complicated scenery, intricate
choreography, and musical virtuosity, he claimed, the *Singspiel* would affect their emotions through the simplicity of
its plot, the poignancy of its action, and the poetry of its
language. With the same words as Krause, he wrote of its
deceiving the imagination (*Täuschung der Fantasie*) in order to touch the heart (*Rührung des Herzens*).

The new German genre, Wieland contended—more like
Marpurg—would resemble ancient, specifically Euripidean
tragedy more closely than any other because of its vocal
and instrumental music. Wieland's defense of the musical
medium was essentially the same one Feind suggested, Mattheson pursued, Uffenbach expanded, the Schlegels refined,
and Krause affirmed. It included the standard comment
about experiencing live performances, the often-repeated
comparison to rhyme, painting, and engraving, and the
usual conclusion that a condemnation of any one artistic
medium was tantamount to condemning them all. His
other comments about operatic verisimilitude show that he
had assimilated many ideas from his predecessors and that
he applied them to suit his own purposes. He wrote that

each dramatic form presupposed a certain hypothetical contract between the spectator, who agreed to suspend his disbelief, and the poet and the actor, who promised as effective a deception (*Täuschung*) as possible. By deception Wieland meant that which seemed real even though the human intellect easily recognized it as unreal. Addressing fictitious spectators, he explained that the poet, composer, and singer "verlangen nicht von euch, dass ihr poetische, musikalische und dramatische Nachahmung, und ein dadurch entstehendes Ideal für die Natur selbst halten sollt" (XIV, 81; "do not demand of you that you take poetic, musical, and dramatic imitation and an ideal arising therefrom for nature itself"). He maintained that the *Singspiel* deserved a position among the accepted dramatic forms "in so fern als es den grossen Zweck der Täuschung und innigen Theilnehmung auf Seiten der Zuschauer wirklich zu erreichen fähig ist" (XIV, 82; "insofar as it is capable of really attaining the great goal of deception and earnest participation on the part of the spectators"). Unlike Hiller, Möser, and Gerstenberg, Wieland was less interested in scrutinizing the aesthetic experience, the artistic imagination, and the creative process than he was in modifying contemporary mimetic theory.

The kinds of subjects suitable for musical dramatic imitation were taken up in the third section of the essay. Algarotti again served as the catalyst. Wieland agreed that opera was similar to Greek tragedy, but he warned against exaggerating the similarity or otherwise misinterpreting it. To him, as to so many of his predecessors, awareness of historical and cultural differences seemed to be the best safeguard. He claimed government, national character, religion, customs, and conditions had changed so much since antiquity that it would be totally senseless to attempt to make the *Singspiel* use exactly the same subjects as ancient tragedy. He further claimed that the more highly developed music of the modern world would render any such attempt impossible.

Wieland preferred to view the *Singspiel* as a modern kind of melodrama in which the lyrical was far more important than the dramatic. His indebtedness to Krause, Lessing, and Mendelssohn is evident in his treatment of the musical component. Wieland stressed the importance of understanding the essence of music because he believed that it was precisely what necessitated the careful selection of subject matter for lyric drama. He stated that music had certain inherent limitations, but he hesitated to commit himself and explain them, insisting that no one could foresee what a great composer might successfully produce. To strengthen his point, he mentioned artists who had stretched the limitations of their art to the outermost: Michelangelo had made paintings move with life, and Homer had captured Helena's immortal beauty by describing its effects on others. Wieland was less hesitant about explaining the purpose of music. He contended it was to please the emotions by beautifying everything it imitated. In his opinion, music could not imitate violent passions, shocking actions, tragic events, or ugly things, for it would either have to alter them completely or become unbearable cacophony and thus contradict its own purpose.

The subjects Wieland considered best for *Singspiel* plots were those that would let music reveal psychological states and internalized actions in such a way as to intensify their effect on the emotions of audiences. Consequently he rejected anything requiring logical proofs, heavy-handed rhetoric, long dialogues, complicated intrigues, dances, *divertissements*, or fairy-tale wonders. Mood, feeling, and sentiment were foremost considerations in his ranking of potential subject matter. Like so many of baroque opera's exponents, he ranked the pastoral highest. He believed the beautiful simplicity of the shepherds' life style would quickly captivate contemporaries weary of the complexities of modern society. Then came mythology and its numerous divine beings. He thought the heroic world of the ancient Greeks could provide equally attractive but slightly less accessible plots, so he placed it next. It was closely followed by the era of knight errantry, which he, along with Gerstenberg, Schiebeler, and others, thought comparable "in allen wesentlichen Stücken mit der heroischen Heldenzeit der Griechen" (XIV, 89; "in all important respects to the valiant heroic age of the Greeks"). History ranked last. Although Wieland considered plots dealing with historical figures and events the least appropriate for lyric drama, he refused to join with Algarotti in rejecting them outright. He thought talented collaborators might just come forth in the future and treat them effectively.

The fourth and concluding section of the essay discussed the need for artistic cooperation. Wieland sought to explain how the composers of Italian opera usurped so much power and, in the name of music, robbed poetry of its dignity and rightful place. He reviewed Algarotti's claims about the degeneracy of modern music but discounted them as typical of the kind that scholars had uttered since Plato's day. He paid closer attention to Algarotti's allegation that the Italians' inborn susceptibility to fashion crazes influenced their musical tastes. Wieland surmised that the Italians heard and sang the latest operatic arias so often that they quickly became bored from overexposure and demanded still newer ones. Such demands, he continued, had enabled the *prima donna* and the *primo uomo* to tyrannize the composer as well as the poet. And as a result, there developed the concept of opera as a theatrical spectacle that provided sensuous pleasure for the eye and ear without any lasting artistic merit.

Wieland blamed contemporary audiences for supporting that concept and for preventing wider acceptance of much needed reforms. He lauded Metastasio's attempt to produce texts of literary worth but bemoaned the fact that Metastasio had been the exception rather than the rule. He welcomed Gluck's reform operas, contending they marked the beginning of an epoch in which the original dignity of opera's poetic component would be restored. They exemplified to him most clearly just how the operatic stage could be liberated from its bondage to Italian musical conventions. If Gluck occasionally catered to audience preferences by reverting to those conventions, Wieland explained, it was because he himself realized that the time was not yet ready for consistent, thoroughgoing reform.[11] Wieland ended his essay by reiterating the prerequisites for a successful reformation of the German lyric stage: not only would a series of composers as enlightened as Gluck be necessary, but also a generous patron who would foster the *Singspiel* as Pericles had fostered the tragedies of Sophocles and Euripides.

Wieland hoped Joseph II would become that patron and make Vienna into the Athens of the German-speaking world. Actually he had long wanted an imperial appointment and was as disappointed as Klopstock and Lessing about not receiving one. The prospects in Mannheim seemed somewhat better, for the Elector Palatinate, Karl Theodor (1724-1799), had already demonstrated his interest in cultivating things German, especially theater. He had dismissed his French actors and was seeking native talent for the German theatrical company he planned to found. Because of his search, German artists representing various generations, philosophies, and stylistic preferences were drawn to Mannheim in the late 1770s. The year 1777 stands out as one of the most eventful. The younger generation heralded Karl Theodor's efforts and interpreted them as a sign that things were indeed beginning to improve. Friedrich (Maler) Müller (1749-1825), one of the many *Sturm und Drang* writers who warmly supported German musical theater and also prepared texts, was delighted that Lessing visited Mannhein in 1777 to consider becoming the dramaturgist of the new company.[12] Their discussion about the dramatic possibilities of Faust's salvation might have helped Müller in his work, but it did not convince Lessing to accept the position. His experience with the Hamburg National Theater coupled with his observations of the Mannheim situation made him dubious about the whole business.

Wieland became equally dubious about it during his visit to Mannheim in the winter of 1777. He was there for the rehearsals of *Rosemunde, Ein Singspiel*, a collaboration with Schweitzer that had caused nothing but problems from the very outset. The sad story of the British King Henry II's (1133-1189) mistress, which was treated in history, balladry, and also Addison's libretto, had attracted Wieland because he thought he could use it to prove his theory about the suitability of historical subjects for the lyric stage (XIV, 181-182; XII, 162). The task was obviously harder than he originally anticipated, for he often complained of being dissatisfied with his work. Disagreement with Schweitzer about the composer's contribution compounded the problems. Although other colleagues, including Goethe, tried to be helpful, Wieland failed to deliver the text by the deadline.[13] When the auditions were finally held, another visitor in Mannheim that winter, Wolfgang Amadeus Mozart (1756-1791), participated.[14] Mozart also attended a performance of *Alceste*, which had been added to the repertoire two years earlier, but he liked it less than the other German opera he saw. That was *Günther von Schwarzburg*, which Karl Theodor had recently requested of Ignaz Jakob Holzbauer (1711-1783), the composer, and Anton Klein (1748-1810), the Mannheim professor of poetry and philosophy.[15]

Mozart missed the premiere of *Rosemunde*. It was originally scheduled for January 1778 but had had to be canceled because Karl Theodor suddenly fell heir to Bavaria and decided to move his entire court to Munich. Wieland was not the only one upset by his decision. The elector's Palatine subjects became angry that he deprived them of all theatrical entertainments by taking his ensembles along to Munich. To placate them, he signed a decree in September 1778 that called a national theater into being under the supervision of Heribert von Dalberg (1750-1806), the man who would in a very short while not only assemble some of the finest German performers but also obtain Schiller's early dramas for Mannheim. With that company safely in Dalberg's hands, Karl Theodor turned his attention to the Munich theatrical scene, which he strove to upgrade with works by German poets like Wieland and composers like Mozart. Despite Karl Theodor's continuing support, it was with the ideas of Dalberg and also with those of local audiences that Wieland had to contend when *Rosemunde* finally had its premiere in Mannheim in 1780.[16] Their cool reception of the text was yet another indication to him that theatrical tastes were very poor in the German lands.

EURIPIDES, OPERA, AND THE ABDERITES

Wieland's dramatic experiments were as well intentioned as his theoretical writings and translations, but all of them missed the mark. They had little effect on the tastes of the average Germans whom he so desperately wanted to reach and educate. When he used the novel, the literary form at which he was a consummate master, he was more successful in provoking them into an awareness of their own foibles. One of his greatest successes was *Die Abderiten*, which he began publishing in installments in *Der Teutsche Merkur* in 1774. It told of the notoriously foolish people who lived in the Thracian republic of Abdera during the Periclean age, and it did so in such an obviously satirical way that no one could fail to understand that the Germans were meant.

Wieland's Mannheim experiences sparked his satirical wit and stimulated his creative fancy so much that in 1778 he reworked those parts of *Die Abderiten* that had already appeared in order to include "Euripides unter den Abderiten."[17] This episode, which became the third book when the novel was printed as a separate volume in 1781, represents the grand synthesis of all his theatrical experiences, observations, readings, and theories. It is particularly important because it is a milestone in the continuing discussion about opera's relationship to Greek tragedy. With the charm, humor, and imagination that won him such wide acclaim, Wieland created a work of fiction that perpetuated the major issues of that discussion and made them come alive for all his readers.

The inclusion of an operatic episode in a novel was not unusual. Some older German writers, like Hans Jakob Christoffel von Grimmelshausen (ca. 1622-1676), did so in order to show the strengths and weaknesses of their heroes in the face of voluptuous deception. At the same time that librettists were plundering novels and epics for adaptation into operatic form, more and more novelists were mentioning opera in their fiction or incorporating something about it. The historical interrelationships of these art forms certainly warrant more investigation than I have been able to give them.[18] The results might not be as interesting as what we have learned about the early twentieth-century filmmakers who transformed popular novels into motion pictures and the novelists, who subsequently attempted to adapt cinematic techniques for their novels. But then again they might be. Whatever the results, the importance of Wieland's specific contribution would most likely not diminish. There were too many who took up precisely where he left off. Younger contemporaries, like Johann Jakob Wilhelm Heinse (1746-1803), and still later writers, like E.T.A. Hoffmann (1776-1822), continued portraying the operatic debate in their fiction and gave it added, still newer dimensions.[19]

In the first two chapters of "Euripides unter den Abderiten" Wieland telescopes German theatrical history and satirizes the conditions caused by what he considered the misguided patriotism of his countrymen. Here and elsewhere he courts the reader's attention by insisting that there are no intentional innuendoes about any particular contemporary city.[20] He begins with the origins and present state of theatrical interest in Abdera. Its citizens, who twenty years earlier demanded nothing more than occasional poetry, became smitten with theater after they learned it was fashionable among the Athenians, with whom they naturally wished to compete. When the Abderites decided to found their own theater, it of course had to be a national one. In addition to Athenian plays, there were those from the factory they established to adapt their own "rohe Nazionalprodukte" ("raw national products")— an oblique allusion not only to the Mannheim school but also to the Göttinger Hainbund and the other bardic poets (X, 123).[21]

Eventually it became a matter of honor to have someone in the family who had manufactured a comedy, tragedy, or "Singspielchen" (X, 125). The all-important musical accompaniment for those plays was overseen by Nomofylax, the general manager of the national theater who considered himself "ein grosser Musikverständiger und der erste Komponist seiner Zeit" (X, 127; "a great musical expert and the foremost composer of his time"). The description given of him typifies contemporary criticism of German operatic composers. Nomofylax took great pride in the speed with which he could transfer and adapt his eminently singable melodies to any text. He thought he was far too good to set indigenous plays to music, so he left them for his pupils and concentrated on the Athenian imports. The Abderites reacted to them in the same way Wieland thought German audiences reacted to musical theater; they were so ignorant about genuine quality that they warmly applauded whatever he produced for their stage. Instead of seeking an explanation for the effectiveness of any given performance, they preferred to comment on the costumes, scenery, and other incidentals. Their insatiable desire for theatrical diversion led "zu einer so hohen unbeschränkten dramatischen Apathie oder vielmehr Hedypathie" ("to such great, boundless dramatic apathy or rather hedypathy [sweet indifference]") that even unquestionably poor plays caused them no pain (X, 122).

The satire becomes more pointed in the third chapter where Wieland discusses the most prominent Abderite playwrights. Hyperbolus represents the original geniuses of the *Sturm und Drang* and the arrogant nationalists. In addition to working on a national heroic epic in forty-eight cantos, Hyperbolus "machte Tragödien und eine Art Stücke, die man jetzt komische Opern nennt" (X, 129; "made tragedies and a kind of play that is now called comic opera"). They were pasted together from Aeschylus, Sophocles, and Euripides, whose combined talents he thought he could not match his. Hyperbolus was particularly critical of Sophocles, claiming he lacked "die Riesenstärke, der Adlersflug, der Löwengrimm, der Sturm und Drang, der den wahren tragischen Dichter macht" (X, 131; "the colossal strength, the aquiline flight, the leonine fury, the storm and stress that makes the genuine tragic poet"). The Abderites accepted his criticism as law, for they thought a man who had produced one hundred and twenty plays and who had had so much firsthand experience must certainly know what he was talking about.

Hyperbolus's only serious rival was Paraspasmus, whose recent play about Niobe consisted of lots of action, pantomime, wild gesticulation, and incoherent gurglings. The readers of *Die Abderiten* interpreted the reference to Niobe to mean Maler Müller's lyrical drama (1778), but Wieland vigorously denied any connection, claiming it was all purely coincidental. It was no small coincidence in view of the fact that he had discussed *Niobe* with Müller during his sojourn in Mannheim and disputed his conception of opera as well as his interpretation of classical antiquity. The other Abderite playwrights cannot be as easily identified with contemporary German authors. They are cleverly constructed caricatures of current theatrical trends.[22] Antifilus, the friend with whom Paraspasmus invented two new tragic genres, "die griesgrammische und die pantomimische" (X, 132; "the morose and the pantomimic"), typifies those whose desire for originality resulted in texts requiring exaggerated acting styles. Thlaps stands for those who espoused naturalism on the stage and who therefore wrote sentimental bourgeois dramas dealing with everyday affairs. Wieland's fourth chapter explains how the Abderites obtained funds to remunerate such native talent and to make their national theater the most famous in the world. First they negotiated with the sovereign of Macedonia who—like Karl Theodor —paid for the building costs in exchange for certain political concessions. Then they held a plebiscite and voted to change their own laws.

The fifth chapter describes a performance the Aberdites had been eagerly awaiting. It was Euripides' *Andromeda* (a work that exists only in fragments). Here Wieland very ingeniously satirizes what he considered the gravest misconceptions about ancient tragedy, opera, and their relationships. Opera had long been viewed in terms of Greek tragedy, whether as a revival of it or an improvement upon it. Wieland portrays his ancient Abderites, who exemplify modern foolishness, as doing the reverse. He makes them conceive of Euripidean drama in terms of Italianate grand opera. He heightens the satirical effect of this chapter by describing the performance and its reception according to the pattern that was often followed by reviewers. The librettist's minimal importance is evident from the few sentences devoted to him and his text. The Abderites had looked forward to the premiere of the new Athenian play, for they held Euripides in high esteem: "Verschiedene seiner Tragödien oder Singspiele (wie wir sie eigentlich nennen sollten) waren schon öfters aufgeführt, und allemahl sehr schön gefunden worden" (X, 136; "Various of his tragedies or musical plays [as we should properly call them] had been performed often and had always been considered very beautiful").

The greater attention given the composer's contribution,

which is taken up next, indicates how much more important it is considered. Nomofylax, whose score was loud and noisy as well as sublime and moving, "hatte sich selbst komponiert; unbekümmert, ob seine Musik den Text, oder der Text seine Musik zu Unsinn mache" (X, 136-137; "had composed himself [according to his own ideas], unconcerned whether his music made nonsense of the text or whether the text made nonsense of his music"). He later admitted, "dass er selbst mit keinem seiner Spielwerke (wie er seine Opern mit vieler Bescheidenheit zu nennen beliebte) so zufrieden sey wie mit dieser Andromeda" (X, 138; "that he himself was satisfied with none of his play-works [as he with much modesty liked to call his operas] as much as with this *Andromeda*"). After explaining that the orchestra did justice to his music, in spite of the fact that it had some genuinely gifted musicians, Wieland spends most of the rest of the chapter on the singers. The highly amusing description of them reflects the tradition of eighteenth-century operatic satire and also the views he himself put forth earlier. The singers sang so well that the performance was often disrupted by applause and shouts for encores of the best arias. A few times the illusion was completely destroyed because the singers lost their place and were unable to resume without much ado. The corpulent diva, who epitomized Abderite sex appeal, enraptured the men in the audience both with her revealing costume and her vocal virtuosity. Some thought it was as if Euripides had written the play just for her. The ladies in the audience were less enthusiastic. They criticized her costume and her stage presence, although they praised the demonstrations of coloratura skill that she inserted whenever she could. In discussing the other members of the cast, Wieland mentions that some danced adequately while others could not dance, sing, or act. The chorus, which was comprised of elaborately costumed schoolboys, dutifully tried to fulfill its function despite mishaps that provoked general, uncontrollable laughter. Wieland concludes with a brief mention of the stage setting. It was not considered successful because the machinery either did not work properly or was otherwise too noticeable.

The sixth chapter deals with Euripides' unexpected attendance at the Abderite performance of his play. Wieland adapted an old satirical technique in order to work this chapter into the general framework he had created when he began the novel.[23] Writers had long speculated about how famous people of the past would react to new and different conditions were they to return to earth. Depictions of such reactions obviously derived from the point of view of the particular writer. Those who believed in the superiority of the modern world depicted their ancients as being deeply and favorably impressed by the products of progress. On the other hand, the writers who were dissatisfied with their own times or who simply viewed antiquity as superior depicted their ancients as being severely critical of modern institutions, customs, and art forms. Both points of view were represented throughout the early history of operatic criticism. Since Harsdörffer's period, opera's defenders often claimed that the ancient dramatists would have much to learn from their modern counterparts. The opponents of opera, and later, the critics of Italianate grand opera, insisted that they would be appalled.

Wieland's treatment of time adds an amusing twist to all this. Unlike Goethe, who has Euripides exist in the realm of the immortals in *Götter, Helden und Wieland*, Wieland portrays his Euripides as living and breathing in antiquity. His ancient Abderites represent the modern world in that fictitious antiquity, so he has Euripides visit them in order to experience what will become of his dramas in subsequent ages. Euripides, whose identity is unknown to the Abderites, attempts to remain diplomatically noncommittal when asked his opinion about the *Andromeda* performance. They become so persistent that he weakens and gives an evaluation of its music: "im Ganzen ist der Sinn und Ton des Dichters verfehlt. Der Karakter der Personen, die Wahrheit der Leidenschaften und Empfindungen, das eigene Schickliche der Situazionen—das, was die Musik seyn kann und seyn muss, um Sprache der Natur, Sprache der Leidenschaft zu seyn—was sie seyn muss, damit der Dichter auf ihr wie in seinem Elemente schwimme, und empor getragen, nicht ersäuft werde—das alles ist durchaus verfehlt—kurz, das Ganze taugt nichts!" (X, 143; "on the whole the poet's purport and style have been missed. The character of the persons, the truth of the passions and feelings, the particular appropriateness of the situations—that which music can be and must be in order to be the language of nature, the language of passion—what it must be so that the poet floats on it as in his element and is carried upward, not drowned—all that is completely missing—in short, the whole thing is worthless").

The Abderites, who have never exercised any critical judgment, find such devastating remarks totally incomprehensible. They remain as dense as Nomofylax, who continues to argue that his music is perfectly suitable for the text. When he offers to solicit the opinion of Euripides, the stranger promptly identifies himself as one and the same. After their initial astonishment subsides, the Abderites begin to doubt Euripides' identity and demand the kind of proof that shows they cannot distinguish art from nature. Eventually someone comes forth with acceptable proof. The sentence Wieland has the extremely exasperated Euripides utter as he vainly attempts to leave Abdera condemns what operatic composers had done to ancient tragedies: "und der Nomofylax soll mich—komponieren, wenn ich in meinem Leben wieder komm!" (X, 147; "and Nomofylax can—compose me, when I come again in my life!").

Wieland begins the seventh chapter with a paragraph explaining that no mortal being will ever be able to understand the mysteries of coincidence. On one level he is referring to the similarities to the Mannheim theatrical scene, while on another he means the events that happened to bring Euripides to Abdera on the very day his *Andromeda* was performed.[24] Wieland then relates those events in order to poke fun at German sovereigns like Karl Theodor who he thought supported the arts only as long as there were political advantages. The ambitious Macedonian sovereign, who had earlier helped the Abderites establish their national theater, was bored with other diversions and now wanted to have his very own court theater. Consequently he offered Euripides the well-paying job of manager and gave him a free hand in assembling the best in the business.[25] Although the route through Abdera was not the shortest, Euripides chose it because he had heard so much about its citizens and wanted some firsthand experience with their society.

In the eighth and ninth chapters Wieland lets Euripides learn still more of the peculiar customs and ways of the Abderites. They give him a tour of their city, open their homes to him, and invite him to stage his own rendition of *Andromeda*. The senate's official permission, which he himself never requested or wanted, comes in the tenth chapter. Nomofylax seems acquiescent, exclaiming, as so many composers of *opera seria* might have, "ohne Zweifel hat der Poet den Text und die Musik selbst gemacht, und da muss es wohl ein ganzes Wunderding seyn" (X, 164; "without doubt the poet himself manufactured the text and the music, and therefore it must indeed be a complete phenomenon"). Actually he does everything in his power to discourage Euripides and to sabotage the preparations.

The eleventh chapter is devoted to the performance by Euripides' handpicked company. This performance, unlike the earlier one, is in complete accord with Wieland's concept of the ideal *Singspiel*. He describes it as quintessential theater. The pattern he follows is very different from the one used in chapter five. Here Wieland includes discussion of related aesthetic, anthropological, and cultural matters. He has become not only more speculative but also downright fond of the Abderites, whom he likens to noble primitives.[26] The Abderites, Wieland begins, were so desirous of theatrical novelty that they were disappointed about seeing the same play they had already seen a few days earlier. When the performance began, the actors' natural gestures, actions, and tone seemed strange to them, for they—like Wieland's interpretation of German audiences—were "gewohnt ihre Helden und Heldinnen wie Besessene herum fahren zu sehen, und schreyen zu hören wie der verwundete Mars in der Iliade" (X, 165; "accustomed to seeing their heroes and heroines darting about like the possessed and to hearing them scream like wounded Mars in the *Iliad*"). The natural stage setting was also something they had never experienced before. All the components of the play were so well integrated in this rendition that before the Abderites knew it they were spellbound. Wieland's explanation is worth quoting, for it is an abbreviated version of his *Singspiel* theory:

> Da nun überdiess die Musik vollkommen nach dem Sinne des Dichters, und also das alles war, was die Musik des Nomofylax Gryllus—nicht war; da sie immer gerad aufs Herz wirkte, und ungeachtet der grössten Einfalt und Singbarkeit doch immer neu und überraschend war: so brachte alles diess, mit der Lebhaftigkeit und Wahrheit der Deklamazion und Pantomime und mit der Schönheit der Stimmen und des Vortrags vereinigt, einen Grad von Täuschung bey den guten Abderiten hervor, wie sie noch in keinem Schauspiel erfahren hatten. Sie vergassen gänzlich, dass sie in ihrem Nazionaltheater sassen, glaubten unvermerkt mitten in der wirklichen Scene der Handlung zu seyn, nahmen Antheil an dem Glück und Unglück der handelnden Personen, als ob es ihre nächsten Blutsfreunde gewesen wären.* (X, 166)

* Since moreover the music was now in perfect conformity with the poet's purport and thus was everything the music of Nomofylax Gryllus was not; since it always directly affected the heart and was always new and surprising in spite of the greatest simplicity and singability: so all this, united with the vivacity and truth of the declamation and pantomime and with the beauty of the voices and the de-

In the following paragraphs Wieland presents his ideas about man's reaction to art. His didactic intent could not be any more explicit, for he speaks directly to his own contemporaries, calling them "die empfindsamen Frauenzimmerchen und Jünkerchen unsrer vor lauter Empfindsamkeit höchst unempfindsamen Zeit" (X, 166; "the sensitive little ladies and gents of our time, a time that has become highly insensitive from so much sensitiveness"). He chides them for becoming so sophisticated that they have deadened their innate ability to experience and enjoy art. Instead of allowing the work to captivate their imagination and manipulate their emotions, they prefer to dissect it, philosophize about it, and compare it to endless others. He claims they can learn much from the Abderites whose very human kind of foolishness allows for a natural, spontaneous, and uninhibited reaction to genuine art. Like Krause and Hiller before him and Tieck after him, Wieland suggests to his contemporaries that they become children again in order to experience the magic of art.[27] His twelfth chapter, which concludes the Euripides episode, warns them about what might result if they forgot to return to the reality of the adult world. The Abderites, Wieland explains, contracted a bad case of "Schauspielfieber, womit wir bis auf diesen Tag manche Städte unsers werthen Deutschen Vaterlandes behaftet sehen" (X, 173; "stage fever, with which we still to this day see many cities of our worthy German fatherland afflicted").

The uproar that *Die Abderiten* caused in German intellectual circles prompted Wieland to publish explanations of his artistic intentions, methods, and style. One of them is directed toward his readers in Mannheim, who considered

---

livery, produced a degree of deception among the good Abderites, such as they had never before experienced in a play. They forgot entirely that they were sitting in their national theater, believed themselves to be unobserved in the midst of the real scene of action, sympathized with the fortune and misfortune of the characters as if they had been their very closest friends.

themselves cruelly victimized by the Euripides episode. In it, Wieland complained that most of his other novels had been similarly confused with *Schlüsselromane (romans à clef)* because there was so little acknowledgment of the creative process through which they were produced. He therefore reminded his readers that he, like any other poet, assimilated certain things from the real world and transformed them completely in order to give them universal meaning and validity. His novel about the Abderites was to be considered a work of poetry rather than a mirror of reality. If it seemed so applicable to current conditions in the real world, he argued tongue in cheek, then the universal truths it contained were to blame. Still maintaining the pretense, he insisted that no one German city alone inspired the book about Abderite theater. He claimed it was a composite picture drawn from the preceding thirty years of German theatrical history. In so doing, he revealed what he considered the fallacious reasoning behind the argument that the German lands could have a national theater: "Wiewohl ich, meines Orts, mit Niemand einen Krieg anfangen werde, der bey dieser Gelegenheit auch über diejenigen lachen—oder weinen will, die unter einer Nation, die keine gemeinsame Hauptstadt hat, und so lange sie ihre itzige gesetzmäsige Verfassung behält, keine haben kann, von Nationaltheatern reden, oder das teutsche Theater ihres Hofes, ihrer Stadt, eigenmächtig zum Nationaltheater erheben wollen.—Doch dies nur im Vorbeygehen, in Kraft der lieben teutschen Freyheit, vermöge deren, (wie man uns versichert) jedem ehrlichen Teutschen und Deutschen erlaubt seyn soll, über National-Angelegenheiten seine unmassgebliche Meynung zu sagen."[28] ("I though for my part will begin a war with no one, who on this occasion wants to laugh—or cry about those who speak of national theaters among a nation that has no common capital and cannot have one, so long as it retains its present legal system of government, or about those who arbitrarily want to elevate the German theater of their court, their city to the rank of national theater. However, this only in passing, on the strength of esteemed Germanic freedom, by virtue of which [as one assures us], each honorable Germanic person and German person should be allowed to speak his humble opinion about national affairs.")

Wieland was as patriotic as most of his fellow writers. He too believed theater provided one of the best opportunities for educating public tastes and thereby raising the general level of culture in the German lands. But he understood that merely giving something a name did not automatically make it so. Consequently he encouraged his countrymen again and again to observe the concrete realities very carefully and to use their common sense. His own observations of the German theatrical scene had led to his attempt to invent and cultivate a more idealized version of the *Singspiel*. He believed it was precisely the form that would reach audiences already so overwhelmingly receptive to musical theater. Wieland's *Singspiel* theory represents a high point in the tradition that had been evolving in German operatic writings since the seventeenth century. Its ideas were sometimes old-fashioned and often derivative, but the form in which he presented them sparkled with the kind of newness and relevance that younger contemporaries, even hostile ones, were to appreciate.

EPILOGUE

THE critical thought of the Goethean age represents the culmination of tendencies, attitudes, and habits that had been evolving uninterruptedly since the Renaissance. Opera figured importantly in that evolution. As both a theatrical reality and an artistic potentiality, opera continued to stimulate so much interest and so much debate that it became one of the shibboleths of German criticism. Succeeding generations of German critics took up ideas from the past and, modifying them for application to opera, transformed them for the future. Their operatic writings reflected shifts in artistic values, philosophical points of view, and critical methodologies. More significant was that they very often anticipated such shifts and sometimes even helped to induce, retard, or accelerate them.

Among the major shifts anticipated in operatic writings were those having to do with the way classical antiquity and its artistic achievements were viewed. Although opera had lost its resemblance to the Greek dramatic forms it was intended to restore, those who wrote about it repeatedly compared it to them or otherwise associated it with them. In so doing, they scrutinized the conceptions of antiquity that prevailed during their period. While many Germans accepted the prevailing conception with few or no questions, there were others who challenged it when it contradicted their own views, interests, practices, and observations. The increasing number of disputes that ensued is indicative of the continuing interaction between those who subscribed to pseudoclassical notions and those who advocated certain loosely defined indigenous ones. The modifications, reforms, and changes produced by this interaction contributed to the gradual formation of a distinctively German version of the classical ideal.

The early seventeenth-century conception of antiquity

had been formed by Renaissance scholars who, despite their good intentions, continued to view ancient Greece through Roman eyes. Their attempts to reconcile Aristotelian and Platonic theories with the Horatian rhetorical tradition resulted in rules purporting to illuminate universal artistic secrets. Some patriotic German writers, like Opitz, adopted those rules in order to improve the cultural level of the German lands. Others became so suspicious of the so-called ancient authorities that they rejected their rules, oftentimes in favor of more compatible ones. Harsdörffer, for example, did not conceive of antiquity as an ideal toward which he and his colleagues should aspire. His cultivation of indigenous artistic possibilities and also his concern for the musicality of the German language supported the patriotic tendency that had continued to develop since the days of Hutten and that was to increase in strength after France arrogated the leadership in interpreting the ancient classics. Harsdörffer and those like him could be said to represent the moderns in the German version of the quarrel with the ancients.

As the French conception of classical antiquity emerged toward the end of the seventeenth century, it began to receive greater critical attention in the German lands. Some writers, like Wernicke, accepted its codification of the classical ideal as a means for dignifying German theater and thereby educating public tastes. They objected to opera as an aberration of that rationally comprehensible ideal. Others, like the Hamburg librettists, refused to succumb to the new foreign ideology that restricted artistic invention to the tangible and held up as the only basis for critical judgment a rule book of standardized styles, genres, and goals. They preferred the freedom associated with their own cultural heritage, and they repeatedly praised earlier seventeenth-century writers, like Lohenstein, for fostering study of the Germanic past. Their writings illuminate the slow but steady movement toward an empirical critical approach with emphasis on particulars rather than universals. Postel, who experimented with Germanic topics at some length, considered himself as competent as the French to interpret classical antiquity. His attempt to make Homer and Greek drama readily accessible to the citizens of Hamburg did not exhibit an understanding more profound than that of anyone else at the time. It did, however, help to reawaken and stimulate interest in seeking similarities between the Germans and the ancient Greeks.

That interest grew in the early decades of the eighteenth century as Postel's successors disputed the universality of French neoclassicism. Most of them thought there were no such eternally valid standards for artistic beauty. Their affirmation of cultural differences sustained the concern about studying the effects on art of social conditions, historical events, geography, and climate. For the members of the patriotic Hamburg societies, understanding the spirit of classical antiquity, rather than any Frenchified versions of it, was just as important as cultivating the Germanic past and present. They viewed the formalism of French drama as one extreme, the other being the complexity of the Italian grand opera that was supplanting the German. Their firm belief in the musicality of their native tongue encouraged continuing experimentation with the aria and other forms of lyrical expression. Their research led to further inquiries not only about original Greek texts but also about German traditions, especially musical theater.[1] They provided an alternative when others were trying to make the French conception of antiquity the only ideal worthy of discussion and emulation. Their liberal critical attitude brought them into many conflicts, first with Bodmer and Breitinger and then with Gottsched. The notable scholars of Zurich and Leipzig became so annoyed when confronted with such strong resistance that they tried to give Hamburg the reputation of being the home of bad taste and ignorance about the ancients. Because of such rhetoric, historians of German literature all too often omit mention of the Hamburg patriots' contributions to the evolution of critical thought.

Gottsched's version of the French neoclassical code served as a kind of productive irritant in the second quarter of the eighteenth century. Members of the older generation joined with their younger colleagues to point out its methodological inconsistencies, historical inaccuracies, and critical fallacies. Opera remained one of the focal points in their discussions because Gottsched had made it into a symbol for everything he thought was wrong with German theatrical tastes. Many of opera's defenders, beginning with Hudemann and Uffenbach, stressed the spurious origins of the rules with which he condemned it. They interpreted his reliance on such rules as a sign of his complete ignorance of the genuine essence of ancient theater. Some believed Meier was correct in claiming that Gottsched had such superficial familiarity with Aristotle's *Poetics* that he confused it with the numerous commentaries written about it. Others agreed with Zinck that imitating the ancients as Gottsched conceived of them would be not only demeaning but counterproductive. Along with other contemporaries in Hamburg and elsewhere, Zinck firmly opposed foreign artistic and critical domination.

The rationalists of the Enlightenment were not as unmusical or unlyrical as some historians of German literature would have us believe. Even those who subscribed to the Gottschedian code frequently disputed his operatic ideas and the assumptions from which they derived. Disciples, like Scheibe, might have thought that contemporary opera was a far cry from Greek tragedy, but they would not accept his complete denial of its artistic potential. The reforms they suggested were designed to realize that potential and to regenerate German-language opera. Their opposition to the concept of generic purity supported the tendency to reexamine and reconsider the role of music and spectacle in ancient theater.

That tendency became stronger in the 1750s as more and more Germans sought to understand classical antiquity on its own terms. Their search was not purely antiquarian. They wanted to discover meaningful ways to reform indigenous theater and to stimulate feelings of cultural unity among their countrymen. This seemed especially urgent to writers in Berlin where royal patronage supported French neoclassical drama and Italianate grand opera. The austerity of the one seemed as bad to them as the complexity of the other, so they strove to find a middle course that would be compatible with the German spirit. Their desire to understand that spirit resulted in reevaluations of the middle ages and the sixteenth century as well as of classical antiquity. They developed a strong affinity for Shakespeare and, in studying his plays, found that his ability to unify great diversity was more in keeping with the essence of ancient tragedy than anything suggested by the Franco-Roman neoclassical code. They believed the Greek tragedians had created supreme works of art because they had known how to coalesce and blend into an indivisible unity arts that appealed simultaneously to different senses. They analyzed the limitations of poetry, painting, dancing, and music in their search for the means whereby those arts could be brought together once more. Their hope was to institute changes in German theater by providing practical suggestions for performers. They devoted as much effort to the performing arts of antiquity as Winckelmann did to the plastic arts. And opera, both in practice and in theory, became one of their more important considerations. Marpurg, who was very interested in reviving "the noble simplicity of song," attempted to study the music of the ancients. Krause concentrated on the relationship of their music to their poetry. Mendelssohn contemplated the implications of their artistic syntheses. Lessing investigated, among other things, their declamation, pantomime, chironomy, saltation, and other nonverbal means of communication. Lessing and his Berlin colleagues may have disagreed with many of Winckelmann's ideas, but they seconded his emphasis on the need for finding direct access to antiquity.

Contemporaries who attempted to fulfill that need in the 1760s became increasingly antagonistic toward the Romans and the French. They opposed their policy of cultural domination and absorption because they believed it not only distorted Greek antiquity but had also stifled native talent. They pitted the French against the English, who had long since come to exemplify an indomitable Germanic people, and the Romans against the Greeks. The more they studied, the more they compared the territorial particularism of the German lands with the city-states of ancient Greece. Winckelmann's interpretation encouraged them to believe that ancient Greek culture was essentially so unified that it superceded specific local political differences. They idealized that unique kind of cultural unity and hoped to realize it in their own world by cultivating theater by, of, and for the Germans.

Some concentrated on spoken drama, but others continued to experiment with musical theatrical forms. While Gluck—who had met Winckelmann in Rome—was striving to reform the conventions of Italianate grand opera, his friends from Copenhagen were attempting to regenerate the German lyric stage. Scheibe worked with program music for spoken drama, Klopstock with the *Bardiet*, and Gerstenberg with the cantata and the melodrama. In their opinion, Nordic antiquity merited as much scholarly research as Greek antiquity. The ultimate aim was to derive as much artistic profit as possible from both. They repeatedly wrote about deriving inspiration from Greek tragedy and about adapting its components to suit the needs of contemporary German theater. The chorus presented as many problems for them as it had for their long line of predecessors. Some writers thought Klopstock had successfully resolved those problems with his bardic songs. Others pursued Lessing's suggestion about substituting the modern orchestra.

Among them was Herder, who tried his own hand at quasi-operatic, melodramatic texts in the early 1770s, around the same time that Brandes was transforming Gerstenberg's *Ariadne auf Naxos* into a melodrama (1774) and Gluck was working on *Iphigénie en Aulide* (1774). Herder's advice to his countrymen was a newer version of what older generations had preached, namely, that they should recognize their own cultural identity and rely on their own creative genius instead of imitating foreign models.[2] Because of such advice, many *Sturm und Drang* writers became as interested in regenerating German musical drama as they were in revolutionizing German spoken drama. Their interest benefited both. It led to the creation of theatrical works that purposely dissolved the boundaries between the two. Elements of the *Melodrama, Monodrama, Duodrama, Singspiel,* and *Lyrisches Drama* became all-pervasive in German theater. Historians of German literature have sometimes noticed the musical structure, lyrical quality, or operatic aspect of a specific drama, but they have not often compared it to others performed around the same time. Nor have they fully explored the implications of the musical and visual components that many German dramatists were consciously attempting to incorporate into their texts. All too often has the importance of the plastic arts been stressed and the importance of music been ignored in discussions of *die deutsche Klassik*.[3]

As so often in the history of Western thought, the younger generation built its programs out of the *aperçus*, ideas, and suggestions of its elders. Some younger men in the 1770s learned from their elders by at first reacting negatively or impatiently toward them. Goethe and Maler Müller collided with Wieland because of differences of opinion about the spirit of Greek antiquity and its resuscitation on the German lyric stage. Others reacted more favorably toward the older generation. Wieland's ideas about antiquity made greater sense to Heinse, who also admired Gluck. He thought Gluck had learned from Klopstock's odes how to combine Greek rhythm with German melody.[4] Goethe, Maler Müller, and Heinse all admired Lessing's contributions and viewed his *Laokoon* as their starting point.

Understanding the origin, function, and essence of the ancient choral convention remained acutely important to them and their contemporaries. They questioned why it had ceased to flourish and why it had never been successfully revived. As they debated such questions, they gave even greater attention to opera. Herder and Schiller stand out, for they succinctly synthesized age-old ideas and imbued them with new philosophical meaning.[5] The writers of the Enlightenment had nurtured the seminal ideas of the past, but those who followed brought them to full maturity so that they could provide nourishment for the immediate present and energy for the future. The younger men of the late eighteenth century developed their own conception of Greek antiquity, and in so doing, they stimulated advances in classical philology and archaeology, for which Germany has since been so famous. Their enthusiasm also transformed the Hellenizing tendency into a full-fledged Grecomania.

German operatic writings anticipated many other ideas that were made programmatic in the closing decades of the eighteenth century. The discussion engendered by opera since its very inception in the German lands had contributed to the formation of modern critical habits and the affirmation of Romantic premises of taste. The seeds of the new are always latent in the old, yet the new cannot be classified as such until it becomes the dominant force of the age and determines the general trend of thought. The poets, critics, and philosophers of the late eighteenth century harvested what the past had sown. They appeared at the right historical moment, had the necessary breadth of view, and made known their insights in such a way that their own age recognized their validity and adopted them. German Classicism and Romanticism were not antipodal tendencies. They both became manifest during the same decades because they evolved simultaneously out of the interaction between those who espoused the Franco-Roman neoclassical code and those who upheld the ancient Germanic idea of establishing law by precedent.

The doctrine of mimesis, which remained the foundation of that code, received the greatest attention from German defenders of opera.[6] They repeatedly disputed the prevailing interpretations of it. The earliest Hamburg librettists did so by contending that opera was a man-made poetic fabrication, no less real than other forms of art and consequently no more harmful or deceptive. They supported the ancient idea about the suspension of disbelief for the sake of pleasurable recreation. Barthold Feind illuminated the fallacies in Saint Evremond's interpretation of mimesis by using common sense to point out the differences between art and reality. According to him, all the arts had to be make-believe because they used media that were artificial to begin with. He submitted that some media were certainly more naturalistic than others and thus allowed for closer simulation of nature. But he insisted that variation in the degree of simulation did not change the fact that all art is essentially artificial. Considering opera nothing more than a shadow play or phantasm (*Schattenspiel*) formed out of poetic fictions, he argued that the order it presented had to be based on an artificial or at least different kind of logic.

Those who followed in the 1720s explored the implications of Feind's ideas. They scrutinized the imitation of nature as a basic artistic principle and the related questions of verisimilitude and probability. They became increasingly concerned with the artistic significance of spontaneity, novelty, irregularity, parody, popular balladry, and the wondrous. Their writings contributed to the continuing development of an inductive approach that relied on common sense. Praetorius emphasized the importance of capturing a certain poetical quality that would appeal to the imagination of the audience. Some of his colleagues claimed that opera employed the unnatural, the varied, the poetic, and the allegorical in order to absorb the attention of audiences so totally that they felt transported into some other world, which could be likened only to the land of Ovid's *Metamorphoses*. Mattheson preferred to call it "eine kleine Kunst-Welt" ("a little art world"). He tried to explain that operatic reality was something created by artists who, without aiming to duplicate nature, selected certain essential features from nature and, using a particular artificial medium, presented them in a meaningfully different order. He believed that questioning any one medium was the same as questioning them all. Writers like Mattheson refused to relinquish the idea of mimesis, but as their concept of nature began to change, so too did their theories of its imitation.

As Gottsched was condemning opera for its lack of verisimilitude in the 1730s, more and more writers compared it to certain literary forms and attempted to distinguish them all from reality. They explored the artificiality of art still further and, in so doing, nullified his particular interpretation of the mimetic doctrine. Hudemann claimed that opera depended on the exact same kinds of fictions used throughout the ages in poetic works. He maintained that opera as an art form could not in itself be considered improbable, but that particular works that were either unconvincing or poorly performed could be. Uffenbach, who included a defense of rhyme, believed ancient tragedy as well as opera presented a "hypothetical" reality. Handbook writers, like Fabricius, combined such ideas with current philosophical speculations in order to explain that opera was comparable to the fable in that it presented "events out of another possible world." In the course of these debates, opera began to emerge as a symbol for the essential artificiality of all art.

The mimetic doctrine came under still stronger attack in the 1740s. Observations about artistic truth, probability, and verisimilitude together with Baumgarten's ideas on aesthetics invalidated its universality and suggested other avenues of investigation. Johann Elias Schlegel used an analogy to the plastic arts to show that neither opera nor any other art form could come closer to simulating its natural model than its medium permitted. He attributed the degree of similarity to the individual artist's intentions. And he suggested that the work had to be made consciously different from its model so that it could be recognized as illusion. His writings provided theoretical foundation for the baroque idea about highly stylized artistic illusion. They were greatly appreciated by older writers, like Mattheson, who had been struggling to find such a foundation for some time. They were also appreciated by Zinck, Krause, and many others who often quoted from them in order to defend opera.

During the 1750s many of opera's German defenders repudiated Batteux's liberalized, yet prescriptive doctrine of mimesis. They objected to having opera restricted to imitating the wondrous nature of gods and demigods just because of its musical medium. They believed artistic verisimilitude was achieved through internal structure or the relationship of individual parts. Johann Adolph Schlegel argued that opera did not have to be unnatural for the very same reasons his predecessors had argued that it did not have to be natural. He insisted that all artistic media were merely conventions used for communication rather than factors determining the choice of subject. Like opera's earlier defenders, mid-eighteenth-century writers observed and studied what they considered its overwhelming power to please. They tried to explain why the socially elite as well as less distinguished audiences found its make-believe so attractive. The spectator, they generally began, knows that opera is senseless and absurd if compared with reality; however, he enjoys it when he experiences it in a theater. Since his pleasure obviously does not come from any such comparisons, they continued, he must enjoy opera by submitting to the artificial order it presents on the stage and by using his imagination to pretend along with the performers. Their careful consideration of pleasure and make-believe served to increase interest in explaining imagination, intuition, and other aspects of human psychology.

While some mid-century proponents of opera relied on the Schlegels for explanations about man's artistic reaction, others turned directly to Dubos or Baumgarten and his exegetes. Still others looked elsewhere. Hiller included ideas that had been circulating for years within the milieu of performing artists and living theater. His attempt to tackle the complex question of man's imitative instinct included mention of an inborn need to bridge the gap between the natural and the unnatural with works of art. He explained that opera captivated audiences because it appealed to certain mysterious human inclinations toward the unknown and the ineffable. It was, according to him, a puzzle that reason could not possibly solve because it was posed magically, as if in a dream. Hiller agreed with his predecessors that opera's opponents were unable to derive pleasure from a performance because they insisted on reacting in a conscious, studied, or analytical way. He suggested that the unlearned man's reaction was preferable because it was spontaneous and uninhibited and thus much more genuine. His suggestion pointed the way to the future when writers like Möser, Herder, and then Tieck rejected courtly and scholarly taste as the touchstone for all taste and encouraged close study of the folk, the rustic, the primitive, and the child.

Lessing, who had already speculated about the incorruptibly genuine artistic reaction of peasants and savages, was among those contemplating the dreamlike quality of the musical experience. He appreciated it but thought it could prove very tiresome unless poetry provided a thread giving direction to the manipulated emotions. Herder, on the other hand, affirmed what he considered music's avoidance of the laws of logical causality and clarity. He thought opera gave unsurpassed pleasure because it instantaneously transported its spectators from the world of conceptual thought into the magical and beautiful world of the dream. In the fourth part of *Adrastea* (1801), he wrote: "Unnöthiger Weise hat man sich über dies Wunderbare der Oper gequält, wie Menschen an dergleichen Träumen der Un- oder Uebernatur Geschmack finden können. Sind wir im wirklichen Traum nicht eben sowohl in einer Zauberwelt? und wie wahr sind uns die Träume! Darfs also keine Kunst geben, die uns mit den schönsten Träumen aufs schönste auch wachend vergnüge? Einmal in eine Welt gesetzt, in der Alles singt, Alles tanzet, entspreche auch die Welt ringsum dieser Gemühtsart; sie bezaubre."[7] ("One agonized needlessly over this operatic wondrousness and how human beings can relish such dreams of unnaturalness or supernaturalness. Are we in an actual dream not just as much in a magic world? And how real our dreams are to us! May there be no art which pleases us most beautifully with the most beautiful dreams while we are awake? Once placed into a world in which everyone sings, everyone dances, the world all around also conforms to this turn of mind; it enchants.")

The critical vocabulary with which Herder and his contemporaries described operatic reality had developed out of the interaction between writers of opposing artistic predilections. Opera's detractors criticized it for its immoral deceptions, magical enchantments, novelistic adventures, Gothic complexities, baroque monstrosities, and chivalric inanities. Its defenders often countered with terms like *poetische Fiktion, Spiel der Sinnen, Wunderwerk, Bezauberung der Bühne, eine andere Welt,* or *ein Traum* (poetic fiction, sensuous play, miracle, enchantment of the stage, another world, a dream). Sometimes they expressed their own ideas by modifying their opponents' negative terms with adjectives or adverbs that defused them. At other times opera's defenders imbued those terms with brand new meaning by simply affirming their formerly negative connotations. This is generally true in the evolution of German critical vocabulary; it becomes most striking, however, in the 1760s when Romantic premises of taste were being ever more heartily endorsed.

Even the words *romanhaft, romanisch,* and *romantisch* gained new connotative value during that decade. They had long been associated with opera because of the novels and epics so many early librettists had attempted to adapt to operatic form. Opera's opponents had repeatedly condemned the practice of bringing to the stage the daydreams, reveries, ravings, and visions of fantastic Arabian and Spanish novels. Adaptations of Cervantes's *Don Quixote* had been considered especially contemptible. As later critics began reevaluating such chivralric novels, as well as medieval and Renaissance romances, they referred to them with some form of the word "romantic," and they meant it in a positive sense. In the 1760s writers like Schiebeler consciously took up one or another of those forms and applied it to the operatic texts they adapted from Ariosto, Tasso, or Cervantes. They included it in their subtitles as well as in their stage directions. The reviewers of such works used it in their articles and added still more to its meaning. It became a standard term in operatic criticism for describing, first, a fanciful, poetic style, then, the past ages in which such styles were cultivated, and, eventually, opera itself. By 1797 Friedrich Schlegel was warmly affirming opera's similarities with the "fantastic" novel.[8] He further wrote in his notebooks: "Die Oper muss romantisch sein, da Musik und Mahlerei es sind; die moderne Tanzkunst vielleicht eine Mischung romantischer Fantasie und classischer Plastik. Man müsste die Alten darin übertreffen können."[9] ("The opera must be romantic since music and painting are; modern dance perhaps a mixture of romantic fantasy and classical form. One should be able to surpass the ancients therein.") When Tieck reviewed late eighteenth-century German theatrical developments in 1825, he described the melodramas, monodramas, and duodramas as artistically sterile, and he praised what he called the romantic operas and operettas that were so widely popular. He also believed: "Wenige von den neuern Komponisten, auch den besten, haben so rein und vollständig die wahre romantische Oper aufgefasst, als Mozart."[10] ("Few of the modern composers, even the best, understood genuine, romantic opera so absolutely and completely as Mozart.")

Justus Möser attempted to give the word chimerical positive connotations when he used it in the 1760s to describe opera's "own possible world." He chose it for the same reason earlier defenders of opera had chosen the word "hypothetical." He too wanted to clarify the difference between logical and aesthetic probability. He believed chimerical aptly described how opera brought to life in the real world something the librettist and his collaborators had imagined and, through their artistry, had made seem probable. When they borrowed from the prosaic world of facts and figures, or when they imitated it in some other naturalistic way, he thought they merely revealed the limitations of their own imaginations. Nothing great, beautiful, original, or awe inspiring could, in his opinion, ever result from imitation of any kind. Shakespeare exemplified to him the supreme artist whose new and different reality pleased so much precisely because it satisfied man's urgent need to participate in the wonders of creation.

Gerstenberg's attention focused on many of the same issues in the 1760s. He emphasized the importance of man's imaginative faculty because it could intuit universal truths that reason was too limited to perceive. And he believed the poet had to be completely free from all predetermined restrictions so that he could cultivate his own rich imagination and create another world, or "a second poetic nature." Gerstenberg, together with Möser and other like-minded critics, helped to bring the long battle against the doctrine of mimesis to a successful conclusion. They formulated more precisely and more convincingly than any of their predecessors the theory of nonmimetic expression. Opera had long symbolized the artificiality of all art, but they made it into a symbol for artistic creativity and freedom.

Late eighteenth- and early nineteenth-century German poets, critics, and philosophers often referred to opera when distinguishing art from nature, clarifying artistic truth, explaining the aesthetic experience, or discrediting naturalistic tendencies in the performing arts as well as in the plastic arts. They recapitulated the arguments and used the vocabulary that had become standard in operatic writings. Goethe provided one of the most articulate and convincing recapitulations in "Über Wahrheit und Wahrscheinlichkeit der Kunstwerke," the dialogue that appeared in 1798 in the first volume of *Die Propyläen*. By constructing a dialogue that allowed divergent points of view to be seen in full, Goethe was able to lead his readers through a maze of aesthetic ideas and force them to come to the simple, common sense conclusion that all art is essentially make-believe. He used opera to exemplify the work of art as a carefully circumscribed, artificial little world (*eine kleine Kunstwelt*) and to explain the aesthetic experience as participation in that world. According to his theory, the creator of opera, like any other artist, strove to integrate his chosen components into such an indivisible unity that the audience would quickly become enraptured and have no chance to analyze, reflect, or think of deception. Every artist purposely eschewed natural truth for the sake of "eine innere Wahrheit, die aus der Konsequenz eines Kunstwerks entspringt" ("an intrinsic truth that arises from the consistency of a work of art").[11] Goethe contended that the audience derived its pleasure from being elevated to the artist's lofty level and from being allowed for a short while at least to share in the process of creation.

Schiller had long questioned how art could be make-believe and at the very same time in complete accord with nature. The letter he wrote Goethe on December 29, 1797 shows that he too was reexamining opera in his search for an answer. He complained about what he considered the vulgarly naturalistic tendencies in contemporary theater. To combat them he suggested introducing nonnaturalistic elements and eliminating everything "was nicht zu der wahren Kunstwelt des Poeten gehört" ("that does not belong to the true art world of the poet").[12] There seemed to be much that could be learned from the operatic stage. He claimed he had always been confident that a new, more ideal tragic form could develop out of opera just as Greek tragedy had developed out of the Dionysian chorus. Among the possibilities he thought worth considering was the mysterious way its music and its technical marvels had of obviating even blatant dramatic deficiencies. Another was its ability to unify divergent elements and thereby transcend its own limitations. Yet another was the theatrical probability it could create without servilely imitating nature.

Despite his purported confidence in opera's potentialities, Schiller did not comply with his contemporaries' many requests for an original German libretto. He preferred to do what so many dramatists, librettists, and composers before him had done, that is, attempt to capture the essence of the ancient Greek chorus and adapt it in a meaningful way for the contemporary stage. The chorus seemed to him to be the best means for achieving independence from the servile imitation of ordinary reality. He considered that reality too narrow and too oppressive to permit the experiencing of genuine artistic pleasure, which he interpreted as the spiritual freedom that came from active participation in the universal moral order.

Schiller's answer to the question of how art could be simultaneously real and ideal came in "Über den Gebrauch des Chors in der Tragödie," which was printed with *Die Braut von Messina* in 1803.[13] It was a grand synthesis of post-Renaissance arguments distinguishing art from nature. Schiller conceived of nature as a universal idea that could not be perceived with the senses because it existed far beyond the world of appearances. He thought it could only be grasped and given form in this world by the art of the ideal. The conclusion, he wrote, "ergibt sich daraus von selbst, dass der Künstler kein einziges Element aus der Wirklichkeit brauchen kann, wie er es findet, dass sein Werk in *allen* seinen Teilen ideell sein muss, wenn es als ein Ganzes Realität haben und mit der Natur übereinstimmen soll" ("results automatically that the artist can use no single element of reality as he finds it, that his work must be hypothetical in all its parts if it is to have reality in its entirety and be in accordance with nature").[14]

Schiller insisted that traditional doctrines of mimesis destroyed the genuinely poetic and artistic by requiring what was essentially a deceptive illusion of nature rather than truth itself. His observations and investigations indicated that such requirements had been far more harmful for theater than for any other form of art. The explanation he gave bears striking resemblance to the one advanced, refined, and perpetuated by the steady line of opera's defenders, whose philosophical orientation, it goes without saying, was decidedly less sophisticated:

alles ist nur ein Symbol des Wirklichen. Der Tag selbst auf dem Theater ist nur ein künstlicher, die Architektur ist nur eine symbolische, die metrische Sprache selbst ist ideal, aber die Handlung soll nun einmal real sein und der Teil das Ganze zerstören. So haben die Franzosen, die den Geist der Alten zuerst ganz missverstanden, eine Einheit des Orts und der Zeit nach dem gemeinsten empirischen Sinn auf der Schaubühne eingeführt, als ob hier ein anderer Ort wäre als der bloss ideale Raum, und eine andere Zeit als bloss die stetige Folge der Handlung.

Durch Einführung einer metrischen Sprache ist man indes der poetischen Tragödie schon um einen grossen Schritt näher gekommen. Es sind einige lyrische Versuche auf der Schaubühne glücklich durchgegangen, und die Poesie hat sich durch ihre eigene lebendige Kraft, im einzelnen, manchen Sieg über das herrschende Vorurteil errungen. Aber mit den einzelnen ist wenig gewonnen, wenn nicht der Irrtum im Ganzen fällt, und es ist nicht genug, dass man das nur als eine poetische Freiheit duldet, was doch das Wesen aller Poesie ist. Die Einführung des Chors wäre der letzte, der entscheidende Schritt—und wenn derselbe auch nur dazu diente, dem Naturalism in der Kunst offen und ehrlich den Krieg zu erklären, so sollte er uns eine lebendige Mauer sein, die die Tragödie um sich herumzieht, um sich von der wirklichen Welt rein abzuschliessen und sich ihren idealen Boden, ihre poetische Freiheit zu bewahren.*[15]

Schiller, whose own dramatic corpus became such a bountiful source for later nineteenth-century operatic texts, aimed to write and did indeed succeed in writing plays of high literary quality that were effective on the stage.[16] He firmly believed "das tragische Dichtwerk wird erst durch die theatralische Vorstellung zu einem Ganzen; nur die Worte gibt der Dichter, Musik und Tanz müssen hinzukommen, sie zu beleben" ("the tragic work of poetry becomes

---

* Everything is only a symbol of the real. The day itself on the stage is only an artificial one, the architecture is only a symbolic one, the metrical language itself is ideal, but the action should then as matters stand be real, and the part should destroy the whole. So the French, who were first to misunderstand the ancients completely, introduced to the stage a unity of place and time in the most ordinary empirical sense, as if here were a place other than merely ideal space and a time other than merely the steady succession of the action. By introducing a metrical language one has in the meantime already come a big step closer to poetic tragedy. Several lyrical attempts have been successfully performed on the stage, and poetry through its own kinetic energy has with difficulty obtained in particulars many a victory over the reigning prejudice. But with particulars little is won when the error in its entirety does not fall, and it is not enough that one tolerates only as a poetic liberty that which is surely the essence of all poetry. The introduction of the chorus would be the last, the decisive step—and even if it only served to declare war openly and honestly against naturalism in art, it would be a living wall, which tragedy pulls around itself in order to seclude itself chastely from the real world and to preserve its ideal ground, its poetic freedom.

a totality only through theatrical performance; the poet gives merely the words; music and dance must be added in order to enliven it").[17] The particular style of acting and the particular techniques of production that he and Goethe introduced at the Weimar theater were logical extensions of their nonmimetic theory. They represent the triumph of conscious artistry over naturalism. That triumph was one for which German defenders of opera had helped lay the foundation. It is a pity that the musical and operatic aspects of Schiller's and Goethe's late dramatic works are not more widely acknowledged. If they were, we might be able to experience stage productions of *Jungfrau von Orleans, Wilhelm Tell*, and both parts of *Faust* that would give due recognition to the full creative genius of each author.

NOTES

1. Hugo Goldschmidt deals first with the development of music aesthetics and then treats European operatic theory in *Die Musikästhetik des 18. Jahrhunderts und ihre Beziehungen zu seinem Kunstschaffen*. His is one of the earliest works to delimit the field for musicology and to comment on early German operatic ideas. It remains helpful, yet, like all such pioneering efforts, becomes less valuable when we notice how inaccurate and sadly incomplete it is. Goldschmidt's own biases prevented him from seeing and appreciating more than one tradition. In reviewing the book, Arnold Schering disputes those biases and emphasizes that eighteenth-century music aesthetics developed inductively out of observations of concrete examples and actual practices, rather than deductively from academic speculations, *Zeitschrift für Musikwissenschaft*. He suggests that the theory and practice of imitating nature be treated within a historical framework. Walter Serauky followed that suggestion but continued to uphold the contention that music aesthetics developed deductively, *Die musikalische Nachahmungsästhetik im Zeitraum von 1700 bis 1850*. His primary intention was to relate European music theory to the dominant philosophical schools of thought.

Wilhelm Bernhard Schwan pays more attention to the views of literary men in *Die opernästhetischen Theorien der deutschen klassischen Dichter*. However, he presents the ideas of Wieland, Goethe, and Schiller as if they had existed in a vacuum. Willi Flemming, on the other hand, suspects there might have been a tradition beginning with Hamburg operatic writings, but he does not pursue the matter further, "Einführung," *Die Oper*, pp. 18-34. Harold Jantz agrees with Flemming that there was an undercurrent of protest against conventional critical ideas in Hamburg and goes a step further in suggesting that a new approach developed from opera because it required defense against anachronistic and foreign rules, "German Baroque Literature," pp. 362-365.

It was not within Herbert M. Schueller's intended scope to study opera's role in the evolution of critical thought in "Corre-

spondences between Music and the Sister Arts according to 18th
Century Aesthetic Theory." However, the questions his findings
lead him to ask as he concludes his article are the kind that I
have asked and have found answers for in operatic writings:
"Was it really true, as literary histories say, that 18th century
writing was dominated by a simple theory of imitation? Or was
the theory one of expression? And also, was 18th century (or
'neoclassical,' or 'pre-Romantic') writing really dominated by
form, or was form secondary to something else? Probably some of
the conventional notions about 18th century aesthetic thought
need to undergo reexamination," p. 359.

2. III, 147.

3. *A History of Modern Criticism: 1750-1950*, I, 144.

4. "The Modern System of the Arts: A Study in the History of
Aesthetics," pp. 44-45.

ONE: ANCIENT OR MODERN

1. Flemming, "Einführung," *Die Oper*, p. 65.

2. *Weltliche Poemata*, I, 104. Page references to primary sources
will be given in the text wherever possible.

3. Leo Spitzer contends that the cosmic feeling of the baroque
age was clearly reflected in opera, which he views as a characteristic expression of world harmony, *Classical and Christian
Ideas of World Harmony*, p. 120. According to his interpretation,
"all the other arts, subordinated to the triumphant music of love,
came to be fused, to give us the baroque *Gesamtkunstwerk*. The
glorification of music by music became a glorification of music
by all the arts," p. 122. Spitzer maintains further that the idea of
"the *Gesamtkunstwerk* harks back, not to the mechanistic nineteenth century, but to the quite unmechanistic, the world-har-
mony-seeking fourth century of Ambrose," p. 163, n. 44.

4. Marvin T. Herrick, *Tragicomedy: Its Origins and Development in Italy, France, and England*, pp. 24-27 and 41.

5. For a descriptive account of the early German libretto, see
Ludwig Schiedermair, *Die Deutsche Oper: Grundzüge ihres Werdens und Wesens*, pp. 38-44.

6. Later on, however, operas were presented by wandering
companies like those of Mingotti, Locatelli, and Nicolini. See

Irmtraud Schreiber, *Dichtung und Musik der deutschen Opernarien, 1680-1700*, p. 7, and Karl Borinski, *Die Poetik der Renaissance und die Anfänge der literarischen Kritik in Deutschland*, pp. 213 and 363. In describing the situation in mid-seventeenth-century Italy, Nino Pirrotta contends that it was precisely wandering companies that saw to the diffusion of opera, "*Commedia dell' arte* and Opera," p. 317. His treatment of the rivalry between Italian companies of operatic performers and *comici dell' arte* is fascinating enough to stimulate curiosity about the possibility of something similar in the German lands, pp. 317-318.

7. See Ernst Hövel, *Der Kampf der Geistlichkeit gegen das Theater in Deutschland im 17. Jahrhundert*, pp. 40-43 and 97, n. 3.

8. Among the best studies is Hellmuth Christian Wolff's *Die Barockoper in Hamburg (1678-1738)*. See specifically, I, 10-11.

9. Friedrich Chrysander, "Die zweite Periode der Hamburger Oper von 1682 bis 1694, oder vom Theaterstreit bis zur Direction Kusser's," cols. 289, 305, et passim.

10. *Sämtliche Schriften und Briefe*, III, no. 444, p. 513. For discussion of his experiences at the musically active Hannoverian court, see Rudolf Haase, *Leibniz und die Musik*, pp. 19-21.

11. Quoted by Ludwig Meinardus, *Rückblicke auf die Anfänge der deutschen Oper in Hamburg*, p. 56. See also Alphons Peucer, "Die Hamburger Oper von 1678 bis 1728."

12. For general background on the development of terminology, see K. A. Schild, "Die Bezeichnungen der deutschen Dramen von den Anfängen bis 1740," and Robert Haas, "Geschichtliche Opernbezeichnungen: Ein Überlick."

13. Heinz Degen, *Friedrich Christian Bressand*, p. 6.

14. Gustav Friedrich Schmidt, *Die frühdeutsche Oper und die musikdramatische Kunst Georg Caspar Schürmanns*, I, 19.

15. Ibid., pp. 56 and 81-82.

16. Rudolf Pechel, *Christian Wernickes Epigramme*, pp. 30ff; Hermann Vogel, *Christian Friedrich Hunold (Menantes)*, pp. 20-22; Solveig Olsen, *Christian Heinrich Postels Beitrag zur deutschen Literatur*, pp. 17-18.

17. His *Iphigenia* (1699), for example, was produced again in 1710 and was selected as the one complete opera text to be included in Christian Friedrich Weichmann's anthology, *Poesie der*

Nieder-Sachsen, I, 326-382. Georg Philipp Telemann reworked the score for the 1722 revision of *Gensericus* (1693), which was still being performed as late as 1734.

18. *Kollektaneen*, ed. Eduard Stemplinger, *Lessings Werke*, ed. Petersen and Olshausen, XIX, 225, no. 326.

19. *German Baroque Literature: A Catalogue of the Collection in the Yale University Library*, I, 348.

20. *Die Verstöhrung Jerusalem*, sig. A4^r.

21. Sig. a5^v and p. 256. Postel's great admiration for Milton was already evident in the preface to *Adonis* (1697), (sig.)( )(^{v}). In his section on *Die Listige Juno*, Olsen does not take up the implications for the evolution of German critical thought of either Hamburg interest in Homer, as contrasted to that of the French neoclassicists, or Postel's evaluation of Milton and its subsequent repercussions in German criticism, *Christian Heinrich Postel*, pp. 213 and 223-225.

22. Christlob Mylius and Johann Andreas Cramer, eds. *Bemühungen zur Beförderung der Critik und des guten Geschmacks*, I, 512-513.

TWO: RULE BY PRECEDENT OR BY CODE

1. Spitzer contends that the rejection of opera by the rationalists of the Enlightenment derived from their inability "to hear the 'world concert,' " *Classical and Christian Ideas of World Harmony*, p. 123.

2. My references are to *Oeuvres en Prose*, ed. René Ternois, III, 151. For additional information, see Irving Lowens, "St. Evremond, Dryden, and the Theory of Opera," and Quentin M. Hope, *Saint Evremond: The Honnête-Homme as Critic*.

3. René Guiet, *L'Évolution d'un genre: Le livret d'opéra en France de Gluck à la Révolution (1774-1793)*, pp. 1-6.

4. Wolff, *Die Barockoper*, I, 42; Friedrich Chrysander, ed., "Mattheson's Verzeichniss Hamburgischer Opern von 1678 bis 1728," 12, 14 (14 April 1877), col. 218, nos. 88-89; Hans Schröder, *Lexikon der hamburgischen Schriftsteller bis zur Gegenwart*, 3, 382-383, no. 1,716.

5. Sig. A3^v. Masen's work was so well known in both Protestant and Roman Catholic circles during the late seventeenth century that Willi Flemming has called it "die eigentliche Poetik des Barock" ("the true poetics of the baroque"), "Einführung," *Das*

Ordensdrama, p. 18. For general background and information about editions, see N. Scheid, *Der Jesuit Jakob Masen*. For historical relationships, especially comparisons to Lessing, see Nikolaus Nessler, *Dramaturgie der Jesuiten Pontanus, Donatus und Masenius*, pp. 32 and 40.

6. Johann Jakob Brucker, for example, wrote to Gottsched on 29 November 1752 that he had seen *"Mazenii palaestra* überall" ("everywhere"), Theodor Wilhelm Danzel, *Gottsched und seine Zeit*, p. 364.

7. Hunold satirized Wernicke with the names Narweck and Wecknarr when deriding his literary stance in the comedy, *Der thörichte Pritschmeister* (1704). Betsy Aikin-Sneath correctly points out that "Hunold's satire must have become well-known, for in *Jöcher's Gelehrten-Lexikon* (p. 818) the article on Wernicke is given under the heading Narweck," *Comedy in Germany in the First Half of the Eighteenth Century*, p. 65.

8. Philipp Spitta, "Ueber die Beziehungen Sebastian Bachs zu Christian Friedrich Hunold und Mariane von Ziegler," pp. 5-7 and 11-12.

9. Hunold's own manual, *Academische Neben-Stunden, allerhand neuer Gedichte/ Nebst Einer Anleitung zur vernünftigen Poesie*, was published uncompleted in 1713, seven years after his departure from Hamburg. The part that appeared deals mainly with rhetorical figures, style, techniques of poetry, and words. In it, Hunold lamented his former way of life and some of his earlier works—"ich wünschte/ dass viele meiner Schrifften in ihrer ersten Gebuhrt erstickt wären" ("I wish that many of my writings had suffocated at first birth"), sig. A3^r. However, he did not recant his comments on opera, nor did he attempt to define it or give rules for it. Joachim Dyck points out that Hunold's manual was one of the first to treat the novel but did so according to the conventional rhetorical principle of decorum, *Ticht-Kunst: Deutsche Barockpoetik und rhetorische Tradition*, p. 15.

The frequent republication of many of Hunold's writings indicates that there was continuing interest in them. A purported letter writer to Johann Andreas Cramer's *Der Schutz-Geist*, 9 (7 July 1746), 78, for example, reported: "Ich habe des Menantes allerneueste Poesie in meiner Jugend auswendig gelernt, und ich bin nachher von den grössten Dichtern Deutschlandes nach dem Hunold unterrichtet worden." ("I memorized Menantes' "Very

Newest Poesy" in my youth and was later instructed by Germany's greatest poets after Hunold.") Hermann Vogel mentions several other mid-century references, *Hunold*, pp. 118-119. See Hans Kuhnert Kettler's excellent *Baroque Tradition in the Literature of the German Enlightenment, 1700-1750*, p. 27. The persistence of grand opera in the baroque fashion and the writings in its defense are outside of Kettler's intended scope.

10. C. Grant Loomis points out that Neumeister's *Specimen Dissertationis Historico-Criticae De Poëtis Germanicis* (1695) was based on original sources from the Leipzig University library, "Erdmann Neumeister's Contribution to Seventeenth Century Bibliography," pp. 222-223.

11. Renate Brockpähler mentions only two in *Handbuch zur Geschichte der Barockoper in Deutschland*, pp. 373-374; see also Gustav Friedrich Schmidt, "Zur Geschichte, Dramaturgie und Statistik der frühdeutschen Oper (1627-1750)," 6, 142.

12. Those scholars who have taken note of Feind remain sharply divided about his contributions to the evolution of German critical thought. While some view him as a proponent of incipient German neoclassicism, others view him as its opponent. Hans Heinrich Borcherdt claims Feind believed that "die Handlung die drei Einheiten zu berücksichtigen habe. Der Wunsch nach einer rationalistischen Umformung der Oper ist hier schon unverkennbar" ("the action had to heed the three unities. The wish for a rationalistic transformation of opera is here already unmistakable"), "Geschichte des deutschen Theaters," col. 1,164. Bruno Markwardt contends that Feind's defense of opera did not really mean he opposed the neoclassical code: "Sein Sonderthema nötigt ihn zu dieser Sehart" ("His particular topic forced him to this way of seeing things"), I, 282.

My own findings support the *aperçus* of Karl Borinski, to whom I am indebted for several other such leads. Borinski wrote in his pioneering work, *Die Poetik der Renaissance und die Anfänge der literarischen Kritik in Deutschland*, that Feind "ist ein begeisterter Anhänger des 'Landes der Musik' und steht in entschiedenem und bewusstem Gegensatz gegen die neuen classischen Theorien, welche die Oper für ein unnatürliches Missverständniss erklärten und das Ideal des antiken Dramas in Racines tragédie fanden" ("is an enthusiastic partisan of the 'land of music' and stands in resolute and conscious opposition to the new classical theories that pronounced opera an unnatural misunderstanding and found the ideal of ancient drama in Racine's tragedy"), pp. 364-365. Feind's writings illuminate the critical activity of the period so well that I believe they deserve a monograph making them more widely known.

13. *Deutsche Gedichte*, pp. 61-62. Subsequent page references to this essay as well as to the other one the volume contained, "Gedancken von der Opera," will be given in the text.

14. *Select Translations from Scaliger's Poetics*, pp. 73-81. The implications of the debate about the superiority of Virgil over Homer have been treated often and in depth. One study that sums them up very succinctly for eighteenth-century German literature is Friedrich Braitmaier's *Geschichte der Poetischen Theorie und Kritik von den Diskursen der Maler bis auf Lessing*, I, 24. Georg Finsler discusses the broader, European picture in *Homer in der Neuzeit von Dante bis Goethe: Italien, Frankreich, England, Deutschland*, pp. 135-137 and 153-169.

15. The so-called "bards" fascinated the intellectuals of this period so much that they attempted not only to explain the various etymologies of the word but also to outline the history of the concept. See, for example, Daniel Georg Morhof, *Unterricht von der Teutschen Sprache und Poesie*, pp. 140-152. Also, Johann Heinrich Zedler, *Grosses vollständiges Universal Lexicon Aller Wissenschafften und Künste*, 3, col. 447. Frank L. Borchardt discusses the antecedents of this interest in *German Antiquity in Renaissance Myth*, pp. 168-171, 179, and 218. I shall discuss its continuation in the later eighteenth century in chapter eight in "Hermann and the Bardic Mode."

16. Sir William Temple, "Of Poetry" (1690), J. E. Spingarn, ed., *Critical Essays of the Seventeenth Century* (1957), III, 79.

17. John George Robertson maintains that Bodmer learned of "Sasper" from the Italian Antonio Conti, *Studies in the Genesis of Romantic Theory in the Eighteenth Century*, pp. 102 and 281.

18. Robert Haas points out that Feind's text served as the model for Rademin's *Römische Lucretia, Musica bernesca* (1731), which was performed by wandering troupes as late as 1751, "Wiener deutsche Parodieopern um 1730," pp. 205 and 218.

THREE: CONTINUITY IN CHANGE

1. Garold N. Davis, *German Thought and Culture in England, 1700-1770*, pp. 42-43, 64-70, and 76-80.

2. Sig.)(3ʳ. See also G. F. Schmidt, *Schürmann*, II, 91.

3. Wolfgang Stammler treats the history of the first part of this phrase in his enlightening article, " 'Edle Einfalt,' Zur Geschichte eines kunsttheoretischen Topos." His conclusion is: "Die ganze behandelte Formel war nicht neu, als Winckelmann sie aufgriff. Er kann nicht als ihr Erfinder gelten. Aber den Begriff 'edle Einfalt' idealisierte er in vorher nicht erfasster Vertiefung; und diese erhöhende Bedeutung erhielt durch ihn das ganze griechische Volk," p. 382. ("The whole treated formula was not new when Winckelmann took it up. He cannot count as its inventor. But he idealized the concept 'noble simplicity' in hitherto unrealized depth; and the entire Greek race received through him this exalting significance.") To show that "noble simplicity" was well known in the early eighteenth century, Stammler points out that the phrase had been used in *Der Patriot* on 13 June 1726 in reference to taste and then on 28 December 1726 in regard to language. He also mentions that Johann Christoph Gottsched referred to "edle Einfalt" in *Ausführliche Redekunst* in 1736, and that Johann Mattheson spoke of it pertaining to music in *Kern musikalischer Wissenschaft* in 1737, p. 360. As far as the plastic arts were concerned, Stammler explains that Oeser had been taught to value "Einfalt und Stille" by Raphael Donner (1693-1741), under whom he studied sculpture. According to Stammler, pp. 370-371, Oeser, a dedicated enemy of baroque art, instilled his dislike in Winckelmann and, perhaps, was even the first to combine simplicity and grandeur in the same phrase.

The backgrounds of German conceptions of classical antiquity would be further illuminated, I believe, if someone undertook a study to see how "edle Einfalt" was employed in regard to opera. Winckelmann, who corresponded with Friedrich Wilhelm Marpurg, the eminent Berlin music theorist, was himself interested in musical drama; see, for example, Winckelmann's *Briefe*, II, 274-277, no. 527. For Winckelmann's knowledge and support of contemporary operatic endeavors, see Hermann Joseph Abert, *Niccolo Jommelli als Opernkomponist*, p. 46, n. 3. Jommelli (1714-1774), sometimes called the "Italian Gluck," attempted to reform opera along the lines of Greek tragedy, and Winckelmann presumably was deeply impressed with the results. They first met in Rome, where efforts to simplify opera and rid it of extravagant excesses had been made since the founding of the Arcadian

Academy in 1692. The librettos of Silvio Stampiglia (1664-1725), one of the reformers, had often been translated into German or performed on German stages in Italian. Another of the Arcadian Academy's members, Gian Vincenzo Gravina (1664-1718) became the patron of Pietro Metastasio, prolific librettist in Vienna. For information on the operatic activities of the Arcadian Academy, see Patrick J. Smith, *The Tenth Muse: A Historical Study of the Opera Libretto*, pp. 65-67. For productions in the German lands of Stampiglia's texts, see Brockpähler, *Handbuch*, pp. 63, 92, 95, 101, 136, 210, and 258. J. G. Robertson discusses the literary activities, *Genesis of Romantic Theory*, pp. 16ff. Those German exponents of opera who referred to "noble simplicity" in their writings will be discussed in the text.

4. This is listed as No. 188 in Mattheson's "Verzeichniss," which identifies its author as a man named Schwemschu and its composer as Johann Paul Kuntz, *Allgemeine Musikalische Zeitung* (18 April 1877), col. 249. For discussion of the text, see Wolff, *Die Barockoper in Hamburg*, I, 101-102.

5. Christian Petersen, "Die Teutschübende Gesellschaft in Hamburg," p. 534.

6. I have seen only the revised and enlarged editions of 1720 and 1742, which are word for word the same on theatrical poetry, pars. 69-81, pp. 136-138. See p. 137 for his definitions of operatic forms.

7. Max Rosenmüller, *Johann Ulrich König*, p. 81. The only record of this review is in number 38 of the society's proceedings, which were not available to me.

8. Published together with *Des Freyherrn von Caniz Gedichte*, ed. J. U. König, p. 259. Unlike later German operatic writers, who will be discussed subsequently in the text, König rejected Jean Baptiste Dubos's idea that artistic taste was like a sixth sense, p. 252. Alberto Martino agrees with other scholars that König's essay introduced Dubos's *Réflexions critiques sur la poésie et sur la peinture* (1719) to Germany, *Geschichte der dramatischen Theorie in Deutschland im 18. Jahrhundert*, I, 55-56. Martino does not consider the possibility that many of opera's defenders might have shared Dubos's critical theory or might have had the same intellectual antecedents, pp. 56 and 70-71.

9. The letter is quoted in Rosenmüller, *König*, pp. 64-65.

10. Bodmer did, however, later publish his own critique of

Hamburg critical tendencies in *Anklagung Des verderbten Geschmackes Oder Critische Anmerkungen über Den Hamburgischen Patrioten, Und die Hallischen Tadlerinnen.*

11. Rosenmüller, *König*, pp. 89 and 109.

12. *Der Patriot*, I, 243. See Siegmund A. E. Betz, "The Operatic Criticism of the *Tatler* and *Spectator*." Schröder, *Lexikon der hamburgischen Schriftsteller* 6, p. 267, attributes the *Patriot* article to Richey. Wolfgang Martens does not consider the long history of such operatic views and mistakenly interprets it as a maneuver to avoid offending Hamburg burghers, *Die Botschaft der Tugend: Die Aufklärung im Spiegel der deutschen Moralischen Wochenschriften*, pp. 490-492.

13. Beekman Cox Cannon, *Johann Mattheson, Spectator in Music*, pp. 32-35.

14. Schröder, *Lexikon der hamburgischen Schriftsteller* 4, no. 2,200, pp. 395-396. Helpful information on the diplomatic corps in early eighteenth-century Hamburg can also be found in the anonymously published "Listen der in Hamburg residirenden, wie der dasselbe vertretenden Diplomaten und Consuln," p. 442.

15. Eventually Benedikt von Ahlefeldt, the Danish-Norwegian ambassador with whom Mattheson was friends, managed the theater alone and vainly continued the revitalizing efforts, Feodor Wehl, *Hamburgs Literaturleben im achtzehnten Jahrhundert*, pp. 45-46.

16. Pp. 96-100. Davis, *German Thought and Culture in England*, pp. 89-91.

17. It was printed in book form in Hamburg in 1721. Karl Jacoby points out that Shakespeare was quite well known in Hamburg in the opening decades of the eighteenth century, *Die ersten moralischen Wochenschriften Hamburgs am Anfange des achtzehnten Jahrhunderts*, pp. 11-13.

18. P. 160. Subsequent writers used the same or very similar vocabulary to describe opera. A good example is to be found in *Kurzgefasstes Musicalisches Lexicon* whose authors are assumed by Robert Eitner to be Johann Christoph Stössel and Johann David Stössel, *Biographisch-Bibliographisches Quellen-Lexikon*, 10 vols. (Leipzig, 1898), s.v. Lexicon and Barnickel, who presumably was the anonymous editor of the 1749 version. They write: "Opern, behalten unter den weltlichen musicalischen Sachen, ohnstreitig den Vorzug, weil man in selbigen gleichsam einen

Confluxum aller musicalischen Schönhieiten antreffen kan. Da hat ein Componist rechte Gelegenhieit seinen *inventionibus* den Zügel schissen zu lassen," p. 267. ("Among secular musical matters, operas are indisputably superior because one can therein find as it were a confluence of all musical beauties. There the composer has suitable opportunity to give free reign to his inventiveness.") Scholars have raised some questions about this handbook's dependence on Johann Gottfried Walther's *Musikalisches Lexicon oder Musikalische Bibliothec*. Its definition of opera simply as "ein musicalisches Schauspiel," p. 451 ("a musical play"), indicates that at least in this instance the authors of the later work did more than merely transcribe their predecessor.

19. I, 3 (1722), 87-88. Alfred Loewenberg considers this "the first opera review in the first German musical periodical," *Annals of Opera: 1597-1940*, 1, col. 93.

20. Hans Peter Herrmann disputes those modern scholars who have claimed that Bodmer and Breitinger applied Leibniz's idea of "possible worlds" to aesthetics; he presents convincing evidence that they appropriated it directly from Wolff, *Naturnachahmung und Einbildungskraft: Zur Entwicklung der deutschen Poetik von 1670 bis 1740*, pp. 252-255 and 260. He makes no mention of their feud with the writers in Hamburg, where such ideas had been in the air since the early years of the eighteenth century.

Wolfgang Preisendanz mentions that Gottsched contradicted himself by condemning opera with the same arguments that supported the animal fable, but he does not pursue the matter further. He turns to Gottsched's debate with Bodmer and Breitinger and claims "in dieser Auseinandersetzung scheinen die beiden Schweizer manchmal einen Punkt zu erreichen, den dann erst wieder die Dichtungstheorie um 1800 eingeholt hat" ("in this discussion, the two Swiss sometimes seem to reach a point which poetic theory then only caught up with again around 1800"), "Mimesis und Poiesis in der deutschen Dichtungstheorie des 18. Jahrhunderts," p. 543. Preisendanz compares their ideas about "another artistic world" to those of the German Romantics without mentioning opera or those writers who perpetuated such ideas throughout the eighteenth century.

Of great benefit to our understanding of German critical developments would be an investigation of the reception of Plato's aesthetics from the Renaissance up to and beyond the influential period of Anthony Ashley Cooper, Earl of Shaftesbury (1671-1713).

FOUR: COLLISION AND CONCESSION

1. Eugen Reichel, "Gottsched und Johann Adolph Scheibe," p. 663.

2. See, for example, the letter to Johann Arnold Ebert (1723-1795), dated 27 May 1744, *Friedrichs von Hagedorn Poetische Werke*, V, 136.

3. Brockpähler, *Handbuch*, p. 252. See also Gustav Friedrich Schmidt, "Die älteste deutsche Oper in Leipzig am Ende des 17. und Anfang des 18. Jahrhunderts."

4. Hermann Kretzschmar, "Das erste Jahrhundert der deutschen Oper," p. 289. Helpful information is also to be found in Fritz Reuter's "Die Entwicklung der Leipziger, insbesondere italienischen Oper bis zum siebenjährigen Krieg," pp. 3 and 8.

5. *Gesammelte Schriften*, III, 219.

6. Ibid., pp. 224-225.

7. *Beyträge zur Critischen Historie der deutschen Sprache, Poesie und Beredsamkeit*, III, 12 (1735), 614.

8. *Die Opern, ein Lustspiel*, in *Die Deutsche Schaubühne*, II, 2d rev. ed., 77-162. In the preface to this volume, Gottsched explained, "ich habe durch die Güte eines werthen Freundes, nicht nur ein völliges Verzeichniss aller daselbst jemals aufgeführten Singspiele, sondern auch eine sehr grosse Sammlung derselben, zu dem Ende, geschenkt bekommen, dass ich mich ihrer in dieser Absicht bedienen könnte," sig. a8ᵛ ("through the kindness of a dear friend I received as a present not only a complete catalogue of all the musical plays ever performed there but also a very large collection of them for the purpose of being able to make use of them to this end"). That collection presumably served him well when he prepared *Nöthiger Vorrath zur Geschichte der deutschen Dramatischen Dichtkunst, oder Verzeichniss aller Deutschen Trauer-, Lust- und Sing-Spiele, die im Druck erschienen, von 1450 bis zur Hälfte des jetzigen Jahrhunderts*. It seems ironic that many later eighteenth-century defenders of opera relied on it, in one way or another, for information to support their cause.

9. *Der Deutschen Gesellschaft in Leipzig Eigene Schriften und Uebersetzungen in gebundener und ungebundener Schreibart*, II (Leipzig, 1742), 552-565.

10. *Beyträge zur Critischen Historie*, III, 10 (1734), 312. I believe Alfred R. Neumann overestimates Gottsched's suggestions for reform as signifying a change of heart about opera, "Gottsched versus the Opera," pp. 303-305.

11. *Beyträge zur Critischen Historie*, II, 8 (1734), 651. Ludwig's essay was reprinted in *Neu-Eröffnete Musikalische Bibliothek*, ed. Lorenz Christoph Mizler von Kolof, II, 1 (1740), 1-27.

12. Reprinted Hamburg, 1937, pp. 14-15.

13. Kettler, *Baroque Tradition*, discusses the enthusiastic reception of Ziegler's novel, p. 100, the sequels, continuations, and adaptations written by others, including Hamann, pp. 102-104, and the dramatizations, especially operatic versions, pp. 114-117. He does not mention that the young Friedrich (Maler) Müller attempted to make an opera out of Ziegler's *Asiatische Banise*, Friedrich Adolf Schmidt, "Maler Müllers Stellung in der Entwicklung des musikalischen Dramas," p. 179.

14. Editions of Hamann's handbook appeared in 1725, 1728, 1737, 1751, and 1765. Though supposedly revised in 1737, Kettler found no differences when he compared the editions, *Baroque Tradition*, p. 92.

15. Goedeke reports that it appeared under the pseudonym Philaretus in Hamann's *Die Matrone*, I (November 1728), no. 48.

16. Danzel, *Gottsched*, p. 129.

17. *Hamburgische Auszüge*, 12 (1728), 832-837.

18. *Proben einiger Gedichte und Poetische Übersetzungen*, pp. 147-172. References in the text are to this edition. Mizler later published the essay in *Neu-Eröffnete Musikalische Bibliothek*, II, 3 (1742), 120-151.

19. Several reviews attest to the warm reception Hudemann's operatic defense was given in Hamburg: *Hamburgische Berichte* (16 February 1732), 117-118; *Niedersächsische Nachrichten* (10 January 1732), 17-18, and (11 February 1732), 104-105. The last one praised his attempt "die Verdienste hiesiger Hochberühmten Männer, als Brockes, Richey, Mattheson, Telemann, &c nach seiner Art zu erheben. Nur wäre zu wünschen, dass man in der Vorrede nicht allzukünstlich, noch in der Widerlegung der Critischen Dicht-Kunst allzuleise verfahren hätte" ("to promote in his way the contributions of local, highly famous men like Brockes, Richey, Mattheson, Telemann et al. It would have been desir-

able not to have proceeded all too artificially in the preface, nor all too gently in the refutation of the 'Critical Art of Poetry' ") .

20. Danzel, *Gottsched*, p. 117, referred to Hudemann's letter but did not print it.

21. P. 727. Gottsched's review of Hudemann's *Proben* appeared in *Beyträge zur Critischen Historie*, III, 10 (1734), 268-316. A note in *Hamburgische Berichte* (20 July 1736), 525, reports that Hudemann had already been accepted for membership in the Gottschedian Deutsche Gesellschaft.

22. It formed the preface to *Gesammelte Neben-Arbeit in gebundenen Reden* sig. a2r-sig. c8v. Mizler later published it in *Neu-Eröffnete Musikalische Bibliothek*, III, 3 (1747), 377-408.

23. See Eberhard Preussner's interesting, although not altogether objective *Die musikalischen Reisen des Herrn von Uffenbach*, pp. 11 and 167-168.

24. According to a review in *Niedersächsische Nachrichten* (14 January 1731), 29, Uffenbach was already quite well known for sharing ideas with the defenders of opera in Hamburg. See Willibald Nagel, "Deutsche Musiker des 18. Jahrhunderts im Verkehr mit J. Fr. A. von Uffenbach," pp. 70-71 and 90-91.

25. Claus Schuppenhauer's *Der Kampf um den Reim in der deutschen Literatur des 18. Jahrhunderts* provides invaluable information about the history of rhyme in Italy, France, and England as well as in Germany. He devotes a section (pp. 261-282) to spoken drama, but it was not his intention to relate the discussion about rhyme to the discussion about artistic media and theatrical verisimilitude.

26. Jean Pierre de Crousaz (1663-1750) had distinguished between absolute and hypothetical propositions in *Traité du beau*, p. 148. Markwardt, *Geschichte der deutschen Poetik*, II, 58 and 487-488, suggests that Gottsched relied on that distinction when writing on the fable, thus implying he gave greater currency to it. Herrmann, *Naturnachahmung*, p. 128, n. 148, is, as far as I have been able to determine, correct in writing the following about the term "hypothetical": "Es handelt sich also auch hier, wie bei so vielen Formeln in dieser Zeit, um 'freies Gedankengut,' nicht um Begriffe, die an einen bestimmten Autor gebunden sind." ("As with so many formulas in this period, it is a question here of 'free intellectual property' and not of concepts that are bound to one specific author.")

27. I quote from the rev. and enl. ed. (Leipzig, 1745), which retained the original issue dates, p. 21.

28. Heinz Kindermann, *Theatergeschichte Europas*, IV: *Von der Aufklärung zur Romantik*, pt. 1, p. 491.

29. See Georg Popp's still useful summary *Über den Begriff des Dramas in den deutschen Poetiken des 17. Jahrhunderts*; Reichel, "Gottsched und Johann Adolph Scheibe," p. 667; Torben Krogh, *Zur Geschichte des dänischen Singspiels im 18. Jahrhundert*, p. 110.

30. See specifically *Der Critische Musikus*, 67 (8 December 1739), 611-618.

31. Krogh, *Zur Geschichte des dänischen Singspiels*, pp. 7-8. For much of the information presented here and in the next paragraph, I am indebted to John Wallace Eaton's *The German Influence in Danish Literature in the Eighteenth Century: The German Circle in Copenhagen, 1750-1770*, especially pp. 9-11 and 170-179.

32. Franz Wöhlke, *Lorenz Christoph Mizler: Ein Beitrag zur musikalischen Gelehrtengeschichte des 18. Jahrhunderts*, pp. 8-9, 19, 95, and 123.

33. I,5 (1738), 2.

34. II,1 (1740), 18, n. 20.

35. II,3 (1742), 27, n. 19.

36. II,2 (1742), 162, n. 2.

37. II,2 (1742), 186-187, n. 25.

FIVE: TRADITION, TRANSFORMATION, AND TRANSITION

1. Straube's essay was published in *Beyträge zur Critischen Historie*, VI, 23 (1740), 466-485. Schlegel's essay appeared in VI, 24 (1740), 624-651; see *J. E. Schlegels Aesthetische und Dramaturgische Schriften*.

2. According to Elizabeth M. Wilkinson, Schlegel was a pioneer in aesthetics first, because he realized that art's very forms require it to differ from life and second, because he insisted on art's right to nonnaturalistic expression, *Johann Elias Schlegel: A German Pioneer in Aesthetics*, 2d ed., pp. 2 and 4. Although she viewed Schlegel as a solitary figure in the history of German criticism, she points out that he had one antecedent in the eccentric librettist Barthold Feind, pp. 12-14. That Wilkinson treated their

theories as inexplicably isolated instances is in many ways understandable, for there was little or no information available about
the role of opera in the evolution of German critical thought.
Otherwise she would surely have noted the steady line of critics
leading from Feind and his Hamburg colleagues to Schlegel. My
own findings force me to question at least part of Wilkinson's
otherwise very perceptive evaluation of Feind: "His position,
notwithstanding occasional lapses into a less aesthetic kind of
reasoning, is far in advance of Gottsched's. Yet, despite their
greater validity, his views carry no authority. His voice is completely drowned in the clamour of Gottsched's campaign against
opera," p. 14. It was, as I have found, precisely the clamor of
Gottsched's campaign that inspired so many of opera's defenders
to clarify the aesthetic issues involved. In their search for explanations, they seem to have heard at least echoes of Feind's
voice.

3. Hermann Bünemann, *Elias Schlegel und Wieland als Bearbeiter antiker Tragödien: Studie zur Rezeption der Antike im 18.
Jahrhundert*, pp. 23, 40, and 86.

4. *Aesthetische und Dramaturgische Schrifften*, pp. 71-95, especially 92-93.

5. Ibid., p. 42. See also the editor's comment, p. lviii.

6. Ibid., pp. 106-160.

7. Ibid., p. 104.

8. "Vorrede des Uebersetzers zu Der Ruhmredige, Ein Lustspiel
in Versen, in fünf Aufzügen," *Aesthetische und Dramaturgische
Schrifften*, pp. 163-164. Comparing the media of poetry, painting,
engraving, and sculpture had become such a frequent practice
among critical theorists that it would be difficult to trace ac-
curately the exact sources of Schlegel's argument. He assimilated
many ideas from his wide reading in German as well as French
and made them his own by adapting them in various combinations in order to explicate particular problems. Antoniewicz mentions the French writers important in shaping his views, p. xxxvii,
but maintains that those views could just as well have been
shaped by post-Renaissance critical traditions, p. xliii. Aikin-
Sneath, *Comedy in Germany*, claims Schlegel felt a particular
affinity with the members of the French academy, p. 30, and
names as the source for his comparison of artistic media Claude
François Fraguier (1666-1728), p. 32. What is most important, in

my opinion, is that Schlegel articulated and applied that comparison in a more sophisticated way than Bostel, Feind, Mattheson, or any of his other German predecessors.

9. Wilkinson underestimated the widespread acceptance of Schlegel's views when she wrote that they "remained without direct results" and exerted no influence on contemporary thought, *Johann Elias Schlegel*, p. 97. As I shall point out subsequently, there were many writers in the 1740s and 1750s who preferred Schlegel to Batteux, ibid., p. 54, and who either reiterated the Schlegelian arguments or developed them further in order to defend opera. Their defenses support Wilkinson's evaluation of Schlegel, but at the same time they indicate that it is actually not "amazing how Schlegel's views point forward beyond those of his contemporaries and immediate successors and anticipate the attitude to art at the end of the century," ibid., p. 133. They also indicate that there was indeed a direct line of succession from Schlegel to Moses Mendelssohn and Goethe, ibid., pp. 138-139.

10. Schröder, *Lexikon der hamburgischen Schriftsteller* 8, 246, no. 4,562, reports that Zinck saw several parts of Brockes's *Irdisches Vergnügen in Gott* through the press. For Zinck's other literary connections, see, for example, *Briefwechsel zwischen Gleim und Ramler*, 242, 6, no. 3, and Justus Möser, *Sämmtliche Werke*, X: *Briefwechsel*, 138, no. 1.

11. *Staats- und Gelehrte Zeitung*, 124 (4 August 1745), col. 6. Gottsched had been so embarrassed about his libretto that he tried to explain publicly how he got himself into such a predicament. His explanation appeared in *Der Deutschen Gesellschaft in Leipzig eigene Schriften und Uebersetzungen* (1735), and it is so rarely mentioned in scholarly works that I believe several sentences are worth quoting. I quote from the 2d enl. ed. Leipzig, 1742: "Vor einem Jahr und drüber, wurde auf Befehl eines Durchl. Hauptes ein Singespiel von mir gefordert, welches bey der Feyer eines Hochfürstlichen Geburtsfestes musicalisch aufgeführet werden sollte. Das war nun eine harte Versuchung vor mein poetisches Gewissen! Ich war eben in solchen Umständen, dass mir an der Gnade dieses Durchl. Herzoges sehr viel gelegen war; die ich aber gewiss durch eine abschlägige Antwort verscherzet haben würde. Was war also zu thun?" p. [4]. ("More than a year ago a libretto, which was to be performed musically at the celebration of a princely birthday party, was requested of me by order of an au-

gust highness. Now that was a difficult temptation for my poetic conscience! I was in just such circumstances that the favor of this illustrious duke was of great concern to me, and I would certainly have forfeited it by refusing. What therefore was to be done?"). After giving some details about how he came upon the subject for his libretto, he wrote, "Es ist vielleicht eben so schlecht als alle übrige Gedichte dieser Gattung: Wiewohl ich doch unzählige Fehler vermieden zu haben glaube, die anderwärts sehr gemein sind. Allein, was kann das machen, wo die Sache an sich selbst nicht taugt? Auch die allerbeste, und von allen Fehlern gesauberte Oper, wird dennoch eine Oper bleiben. Das ist genug gesagt, um zu zeigen, dass das innere Wesen und der ganze Grund solcher Vorstellungen aus lauter widersinnischen Dingen bestehet," p. [5]. ("It is perhaps just as inferior as all the other poems of this genre, although I believe I avoided countless errors that are very common elsewhere. But, what can that do where the matter itself is worthless? Even the very best opera, one purged of all errors, will nevertheless remain an opera. That is enough said in order to show that the essence and whole basis of such presentations consist of nothing but absurdities.") It is interesting that Gottsched did not think to compare himself with the French dramatists, especially Corneille and Racine, who wrote librettos despite their grave reservations about opera. Hans Michael Schletterer, *Das deutsche Singspiel von seinen ersten Anfängen bis auf die neueste Zeit*, pp. 223-224, n. 71, claims that Gottsched not only wrote *Diana* but also prepared an operetta in 1733 at the request of Duke Christian of Saxony-Weissenfels. Danzel, *Gottsched*, p. 121, implies that Gottsched strove to have the products of such activities suppressed.

12. *Staats- und Gelehrte Zeitung*, 126 (7 August 1745), cols. 7-8.

13. Ibid., col. 8.

14. Ibid., 124 (4 August 1745) , col. 8.

15. Ibid. The comparison to wax figures was apparently discussed earlier by an editor of Boileau's *Art Poetique*, but I have thus far not discovered which one or where. Adam Smith used it later in the *Theory of Moral Sentiments* (1759); see Walter Jackson Bate, "Introduction, Part II, The Development of Modern Criticism: Romanticism and After," *Criticism: The Major Texts*, p. 274.

16. *Staats- und Gelehrte Zeitung*, 126 (7 August 1745), col. 7.

Zinck's next few sentences also point to the questions posed by future critics. He wrote: "Man muss sich einbilden, Simson wird der Delila seine Liebe im Ton: Im Schatten grüner Bäume etc. klagen. Aber dieses heisst, von den Kräften der Musik urtheilen, ohne dass man ihre Gränze kennt." ("One must imagine Samson bemoaning his love to Delilah in tune, in the shade of green trees, etc. But this means judging the powers of music without knowing its limits.")

17. III, 5 (1746), 35-38.

18. Danzel, *Gottsched*, p. 191.

19. *Critische Betrachtungen und freye Untersuchungen zum Aufnehmen und zur Verbesserung der deutschen Schau-Bühne*, p. 52. See also "Versuch einer Critik über die Deutschen Dichter," lines 415-442, *Vier kritische Gedichte*, p. 60.

20. *Auszüge des von Hagedornischen Briefwechsels, Poetische Werke*, p. 184.

21. *Cours de belles lettres ou Principes de la littérature*, II, 245.

22. Michael Conrad Curtius later used opera as an example when attempting to explain that the music and spectacle of Greek tragedy had had overwhelming appeal for audiences, *Aristoteles Dichtkunst*, p. 119, n. 80.

23. See *Betrachtungen über den ersten Grundsatz aller schönen Künste und Wissenschaften*. Manfred Schenker discusses Meier's opposition in *Charles Batteux und seine Nachahmungstheorie in Deutschland*, pp. 65 and 126-127.

24. "Vorrede" (1747), *Sämtliche Schriften*, III, vii-viii. Like Gottsched, he was complying with a request. Gellert's text, which was based on a French prose epilogue, was later published separately (Braunschweig, 1771) and was set to music by Friedrich Gottlob Fleischer (1722-1806).

25. Joyce S. Rutledge presents an overall view of Schlegel's contributions to German aesthetics and critical thought in *Johann Adolph Schlegel*, pp. 219-221.

26. *Lessing's Werke*, ed. Petersen and Olshausen, VIII, pp. 48-49.

27. Lessing et al., *Briefe, die neueste Literatur betreffend*, V, 85 (21 February 1760), 115, and V, 87 (28 February 1760), 137. For discussion see Joyce Rutledge, *Johann Adolph Schlegel*, pp. 204-206 and 226, n. 56.

28. XI, 2 (1771), 255-256. Joyce Rutledge, *Johann Adolph Schle-*

gel, p. 206, identifies the reviewer as a Professor Garve, presumably Christian Garve (1742-1798), Gellert's successor in Leipzig.

SIX: INTERACTION IN BERLIN AT MID-CENTURY

1. Jakob Minor, *Christian Felix Weisse und seine Beziehungen zur deutschen Literatur des achtzehnten Jahrhunderts,* pp. 147-151.

2. Brockpähler, *Handbuch,* p. 69; Curt Sachs, *Musik und Oper am kurbrandenburgischen Hof,* p. 77.

3. Sachs, *Musik und Opera,* pp. 122 and 126.

4. Hugo Fetting, *Die Geschichte der Deutschen Staatsoper,* p. 15.

5. Ibid., pp. 40-41.

6. *Der Critische Musicus an der Spree,* I, 1 (4 March 1749), 3-4.

7. Ibid., 43 (23 December 1749), 348-349.

8. *Historisch-Kritische Beyträge,* I, 1 (1754), iii.

9. Ibid., IV, 1 (1758), 27.

10. Ibid., V, 1 (1760), 3.

11. See, for example, *Briefwechsel zwischen Gleim und Ramler,* 242, no. 57 (3 February 1748), p. 97.

12. Paul F. Marks contends in a very enlightening musicological study that "Krause put into words what was accepted practice by 1752," "The Rhetorical Element in Musical *Sturm und Drang*: Christian Gottfried Krause's *Von der musikalischen Poesie,*" p. 101. Marks does not, however, mention Krause's admiration for Dubos, other than briefly remarking that he accepted Dubos's "idea on the imitations of inflexions, accents and movements," p. 102.

13. Eugen Teuber, "Die Kunstphilosophie des Abbé Dubos," pp. 370-371.

14. *Réflexions,* 4th rev. and enl. ed., II, 360-361 and 363. The more frequent use of the word *rühren* in mid-century German critical works seems to indicate that many writers were not only contemplating ideas like Dubos's but also attempting to apply them.

15. Alfred Lombard, *L'Abbé Du Bos: Un initiateur de la pensée moderne (1670-1742),* pp. 280-281.

16. Martino, *Geschichte der dramatischen Theorie,* pp. 70-71. Lombard points out, however, that Frederick the Great had read

Dubos's work in 1738 and that it had already become "un ouvrage classique" in Germany by the 1740s, *L'Abbé Du Bos*, p. 361.

17. Krause's emphasis on *Rührung* is also evident in two writings subsequently published in Marpurg's *Historisch-Kritische Beyträge*: a review of Scheibe's *Thusnelde*, I, 2 (1754), 137, and "Vermischte Gedanken," III, 6 (1758), 527.

18. Marks, "The Rhetorical Element," p. 101, prefers to stress that interest in Krause's work persisted into the 1770s and 1780s. Another of the earlier examples worth mentioning appeared in the *Hamburgische Beyträge*, II, 3 (1755), 694-706.

19. Also, "Vorrede," *Poetische Gedanken von Politischen und Gelehrten Neuigkeiten*, V (1753), sig.) (5ᵛ.

20. *Poesie und Prosa*, II, 23 (5 June 1756), 177-178.

21. Ibid., I, 47 (22 November 1755), 372.

22. *Wöchentliche Nachrichten und Anmerkungen die Musik betreffend*, I, 33 (10 February 1767), 254.

23. Karl Peiser, *Johann Adam Hiller: Ein Beitrag zur Musikgeschichte des 18. Jahrhunderts*, pp. 7-8 and 9-10.

24. It originally appeared in *Neue Erweiterungen der Erkenntnis und des Vergnügens*, III, 14 (1754), 140-168. The page numbers in my text refer to the reprint in Marpurg's *Historisch-Kritische Beyträge*, I, 6 (1755), 515-543.

25. See Goethe's review of "Für Freunde der Tonkunst" (1824), *Gedenkausgabe* XIV, 337-338, and *Dichtung und Wahrheit*, bk. 8, *Gedenkausgabe* X, 360.

26. Romain Rolland, *Goethe and Beethoven*, pp. 102-103. Gertrud Schmehling (la Mara) (1749-1833) was another of Hiller's famous pupils; see Francis Rogers's delightful article, "Some Prima Donnas of the Latter Eighteenth Century," pp. 155-157.

27. III, 17 (24 October 1768), 127.

28. I, 33 (10 February 1767), 253.

29. In a note to Voltaire's essay on Greek tragedy, Hertel recommended Lessing's 1755 translation of Dubos for those interested in distinguishing the two theatrical forms, p. 29. Marpurg, incidentally, also published "Du Bos, von den theatralischen Vorstellungen der Alten, nach der Uebersetzung des Hrn. M. Lessing," *Historisch-Kritische Beyträge*, II (1756), 448-464, 521-541; III (1757), 80-94, 268-276; IV (1758), 151-186, 498-558; V, 1 (1760), 45-94; V, 4 (1762), 327-340.

30. For example, "Des Abts du Bos Anmerkungen von der

Beschaffenheit des Genies einiger Dichter und Mahler," *Biblio-thek der schönen Wissenschaften und der freyen Künste*, III, 1 (1758), 1-29; III, 2 (1758), 215-227; IV, 1 (1758), 411-438, and "Von der Kritik der Empfindungen über eine Stelle des Herrn Du Bos," VIII, 1 (1762), 1-20. Lombard, *L'Abbé Du Bos*, p. 368, maintains that the aim of their whole theoretical effort was to reconcile the writings of Dubos and Aristotle. Martino, *Geschichte der dramatischen Theorien*, pp. 75-76, mentions the German translations and references in order to support his thesis about the development of "die emotionale Kunsttheorie" ("the emotional theory of art").

31. *Briefe über den itzigen Zustand der schönen Wissenschaften in Deutschland*, p. 11. Page numbers given in the text refer to this edition.

32. *Beschreibung einer Reise durch Deutschland und die Schweiz im Jahre 1781*, IV, 527-530.

33. III, 1, 188-189.

34. Ibid., p. 93.

35. XI, 2, 2-5.

36. Leopold Friedrich Günther von Göckingk (1748-1828), "Ramlers Leben," in Ramler's *Poëtische Werke*, pt. 2, pp. 308-310.

37. See *Briefwechsel zwischen Gleim und Ramler*, 242, nos. 19, 31, 34, 97, 124, 151, 172, and 244, nos. 208, 246, 263, 275.

38. "Georg Friedrich Meier's *Auszug aus den Anfangsgründen aller schönen Künste und Wissenschaften*" (review), *Bibliothek der schönen Wissenschaften und der freyen Künste*, III, 1 (1758), 130-138. Kristeller claims that Lessing's notes for the continuation of the *Laokoon* are his attempt to meet Mendelssohn's criticism about failing to include all of the arts, "The Modern System of the Arts," vol. 13, p. 37. I shall take up the matter in "*Laokoon* and the Essence of Ancient Theater," chapter 7.

39. *Bibliothek der schönen Wissenschaften und der freyen Künste*, I, 2 (1757), 231-268; page references in the text refer to this edition. It was later entitled "Über die Hauptgrundsätze der Schönen Künste und Wissenschaften" and published in Moses Mendelssohn's *Philosophische Schriften*, II, 95-152.

40. Wilkinson, *Johann Elias Schlegel*, pp. 111-112, explains Mendelssohn's ideas by writing that they represented a combination of the two leading contemporary currents in aesthetic theory:

art based on intuition and art as imitation of nature. See Frederic Will, Jr., "Cognition through Beauty in Moses Mendelssohn's Early Aesthetics," pp. 97-98.

41. *Bibliothek der schönen Wissenschaften und der freyen Künste*, II, 2 (1758), 243, and for Mendelssohn's explanation of "edle Einfalt," 261. In evaluating Mendelssohn's contribution to the evolution of German aesthetic thought, Armand Nivelle wrote that his ideas "deuten auf die kühnsten Ausführungen des Irrationalismus und der Romantik voraus" ("anticipate the boldest accomplishments of irrationalism and romanticism"), *Kunst-und Dichtungstheorien zwischen Aufklärung und Klassik*, p. 59.

42. Moses Mendelssohn, *Gesammelte Schriften*, no. 33 (1 July 1757), p. 110, and no. 51 (2 April 1758), pp. 219-220.

SEVEN: LESSING'S CONSOLIDATION

1. *Lessings Werke*, ed. Petersen and Olshausen, XII, 66. Volume and page numbers henceforth given in the text refer to this edition.

2. *L'Art du Théatre* (Paris, 1750), *Lessings Werke*, XII, 76-114, and *Le Comédien* (Paris, 1747), *Lessings Werke*, XII, 221-250.

3. Hans Oberländer represents a particular scholarly point of view when he contends, "Ihre Fähigkeit [the ancients'] zu theoretischer Behandlung und das Verhältnis der darstellenden Kunst zu den anderen Künsten ist alles, was Lessing an Erkenntnis aus der Antike schöpfte" ("Their ability for theoretical treatment and the relationship of the performing art to the other arts is all the knowledge that Lessing drew from antiquity"), *Die geistige Entwicklung der deutschen Schauspielkunst im 18. Jahrhundert*, p. 97.

4. I discuss the status of scholarship in my article, "Lessing and Opera: A Re-Evaluation," pp. 98-99, and also 95.

5. (Paris, 1719), pp. 576-577. It is interesting to note that the title page of this, the first edition shows a representation of Laocoön beneath "*ut pictura poesis.*" Lombard, *L'Abbé Du Bos*, p. 289, discusses quite perceptively Dubos's influence on the development of eighteenth-century French theories of acting. To my knowledge there has been no comprehensive investigation of the effect of acting and acting theories on dramatic productivity in Germany. It would be not only very interesting but also very

valuable to determine how the changing interpretations of the doctrine of mimesis and the developing theory of nonmimetic expression related to acting styles and techniques of stage production.

6. Lessing translated part three of the fifth edition (1746); XIII, 232-394, specifically, 387.

7. Theodore Ziolkowski contends that Lessing attempted to deal in practice with the theories of Riccoboni and Sainte Albine and to mediate between the two schools of thought that were developing, "Language and Mimetic Action in Lessing's *Miss Sara Sampson*," pp. 265-269.

8. Konrad Leysaht viewed Dubos as Lessing's most important precursor in discerning the limitations of poetry, *Dubos et Lessing*, pp. 7-9.

9. For Lessing's ultimate intention with the *Laokoon*, see the letters written to Nicolai on 13 April 1769 and 26 May 1769, *Sämtliche Schriften*, ed. Lachmann, 3rd rev. and enl. ed., see Muncker, XVII, 286-291. The thirty-eighth of the *Briefe antiquarischen Inhalts* is also of importance, *Werke*, ed. Petersen and Olshausen, XVII, 185.

10. *Sämtliche Schriften*, ed. Lachmann, 3rd rev. and enl. ed., Muncker, X, 439, n. 1.

11. The manual was *Kurzgefasste Grundsätze über die Beredsamkeit des Leibes* (Hamburg, 1755). See Heinrich Stümke's commentary in his edition of Löwen's *Geschichte des deutschen Theaters (1766) und Flugschriften über das Hamburger National-theater (1766 und 1767)*, pp. xv and xxv.

12. *Schriften*, IV, 41.

13. "Anrede an die sämtlichen Mitglieder des Hamburgischen Theaters bey der Uebernehmung des Directorii," *Geschichte des deutschen Theaters*, p. 95.

14. Not to be forgotten is Lessing's interest in Hanswurst and other stock figures that had evolved initially through reliance on costume and gesture, V, 92. As more and more of his contemporaries concerned themselves with acting and the arts of nonverbal communication, increasing attention was given not only to opera but also to the theatrical practices of England, Spain, and Italy. The commedia dell' arte as well as the plays of Carlo Goldoni (1707-1793) and Carlo Gozzi (1720-1806) became important subjects of critical discussion.

15. See chapter 4, n. 30.

16. *Herders Sämmtliche Werke*, ed. Suphan, V, 394.

17. Schiebeler's operatic views will be discussed in "European Contexts: The 'Romantic' Operatic World," chapter 8.

EIGHT: ASSERTION OF CULTURAL IDENTITY

1. For a more comprehensive discussion of Möser's writings and contributions to German critical thought, see my article, "Justus Möser: Pre-Romantic Literary Historian, Critic, and Theorist."

2. *Sämmtliche Werke*, ed. B. R. Abeken, IX, 201. Volume and page references given in the text are to this edition. Richard Kuehnemund's *Arminius or the Rise of a National Symbol in Literature (From Hutten to Grabbe)*, is a biased, yet nevertheless useful study. He mentions Möser in passing, p. 60, and gives some information about the operatic treatment of Arminius, pp. 52-53.

3. *Hamburgische Dramaturgie*, no. 18 (30 June 1767), *Werke*, ed. Petersen and Olshausen, V, 93.

4. *Bibliothek der schönen Wissenschaften und der freyen Künste*, VII, 2 (1762), 335. See also Ludwig Bäte, *Justus Möser, Advocatus patriae*, p. 206.

5. *Klopstocks Werke*, p. 53.

6. Ibid., pp. 6 and 21.

7. Ibid., p. 146.

8. See Gluck's letters in *Briefe von und an Klopstock* (1867), no. 136 (14 August 1773), pp. 252-253 and no. 166 (10 May 1780), pp. 293-295; and Alfred Einstein, *Gluck*, tr. Eric Blom, pp. 124-128 and 182.

9. *Allgemeine Theorie der Schönen Künste*, II, 351. The patriotic intent is clear in the opening sentences of that paragraph: "Der festeste Grund, um die Oper als ein prächtiges und herrliches Gebäude darauf zu setzen, wäre ihre genaue Verbindung mit dem Nationalinteresse eines ganzen Volkes. Aber daran ist in unsern Zeiten nicht zu denken." ("The firmest foundation upon which to set opera as a magnificent and splendid building would be its close connection with the national interest of an entire people. But in our times that is not to be contemplated.")

The authorship of this article on opera has never been satisfactorily clarified. Scholars have often subsumed it in the category of "music-related" ones and attributed it to Johann Abraham Peter Schulz (1747-1800), whom Sulzer mentions in the preface to the first edition. What they overlook, however, is that Schulz is credited only with the articles on music after the letter S, sig. 2ᵛ. Sulzer, whose musical knowledge was considered wanting by colleagues in Berlin, most likely discussed opera with them and sought their assistance but put the article into finished form himself. Johannes Leo maintains that Sulzer drafted each article himself and reworked each of the contributions of his collaborators, *Zur Entstehungsgeschichte der "Allgemeinen Theorie der Schönen Künste" J. G. Sulzers*, pp. 36-37 and 54, n. 16. The rationalistic concept of opera that the article presents and the reference to the author's other articles seem to be sufficient evidence that Sulzer did indeed write it himself.

10. O. Fischer, "Zum musikalischen Standpunkte des Nordischen Dichterkreises," pp. 245 and 251. Paul F. Marks makes the interesting point that one of their favorite diversions was experimenting with "text parody," which at the time "was considered to be a legitimate means of perfecting vocal music," "Aesthetics of Music in the Philosophy of *Sturm und Drang*: Gerstenberg, Hamann and Herder," p. 248.

11. H.W.v. Gerstenberg, *Rezensionen in der Hamburgischen Neuen Zeitung, 1767-1771*, Deutsche Literaturdenkmale, 128, 79.

12. Klaus Gerth refers to *Die Amerikanerin, ein lyrisches Gemählde, In Musik gesetzt von J.C.F. Bach* (Riga, 1776) in his *Studien zu Gerstenbergs Poetik*, p. 224. I have not been able to verify the statement.

13. Albert Köster maintains that the Germans developed their own traditions rather than merely imitating Rousseau's *Pygmalion*, "Das lyrische Drama im 18. Jahrhundert," *Preussische Jahrbücher*, pp. 190 and 194. He points out that Ramler, who had long been interested in dramatic recitation, tutored the star of *Ariadne*, Charlotte Brandes, in speech, p. 191. Even more interesting is Köster's discussion of the influences of the musical melodrama on the dramatic works of Goethe, Herder, and Schiller, pp. 199-200. For Goethe's evaluation of the 1815 revival of his *Proserpina* (1778), see *Jubiläums-Ausgabe* XXXVII, 69-77 and 305-306.

14. Eaton, *German Influence*, p. 108.

15. *Briefe über Merkwürdigkeiten der Litteratur*, Deutsche Literaturdenkmale, 29, 56-57.

16. *Vermischte Schriften*, I, 25. Goethe's letter of 10 December 1789 to Johann Friedrich Reichardt (1752-1814) is indicative of his interest in exploring Ossianic possibilities for the lyric stage, *Gedenkausgabe* XIX, 154, no. 104.

17. *Rezensionen*, Deutsche Literaturdenkmale, 128, 280. It is not only interesting but also significant that Schiller briefly considered preparing *Hermanns Schlacht* for the Weimar stage in 1803, around the same time he was working out his ideas about poiesis versus mimesis for the essay on the tragic chorus that was to appear with *Die Braut von Messina*. See, Goethe, *Gedenkausgabe* XX, no. 908 (20 May 1803), p. 931, and no. 910 (24 May 1803), pp. 933-934.

18. *Shakespeares Theatralische Werke*.

19. *Briefe über Merkwürdigkeiten des Litteratur*, Deutsche Literaturdenkmale, 29, 140.

20. Ibid., p. 125.

21. *Briefe über Merkwürdigkeiten der Litteratur*, Deutsche Literaturdenkmale, 30, 342.

22. Ibid., p. 344.

23. *Rezensionen*, Deutsche Literaturdenkmale, 128, 42.

24. Ibid., pp. 318-319.

25. Karl Heinrich Jördens, *Lexikon deutscher Dichter und Prosaisten*, 4, 435. For Schiebeler's relationship to Bode, Eschenburg, and Telemann, see pp. 439-441.

26. *Briefe über Merkwürdigkeiten der Litteratur*, Deutsche Literaturdenkmale, 29, 17ff. and Herder's *Sämmtliche Werke*, ed. Suphan, I, 266. See also Richard Ullmann and Helene Gotthard, *Geschichte des Begriffes "Romantisch" in Deutschland*, pp. 81-85. They maintain that the word was used "auf der Strasse, es war in jeder Gasse zu Hause, ehe es an die Geister kam, die ihm einen noch über die Mode gesteigerten Einfluss gaben," p. 26 ("on the street, it was at home in every alley before reaching the intellectuals who gave it influence that was heightened even beyond the fashion"). See also Raymond Immerwahr, *Romantisch: Genese und Tradition einer Denkform*, p. 88.

27. X, 2 (1769), 180. The use of the word "romantic" by Schiebeler and his reviewers seems to indicate that one of Immerwahr's otherwise very sound comments merits further investigation: "Die Musik gehörte jedoch nicht zu den populären Künsten, die sich von Anfang an mit dem Wort *romantisch* ver-

banden," *Romantisch*, p. 181. ("Music did not, however, belong to the popular arts that were connected with the word 'romantic' from the very beginning.")

28. Immerwahr, *Romantisch*, p. 101.

NINE: CULMINATION AND CONTINUATION: WIELAND

1. In a letter to Christian Gottfried Körner on 19 December 1787, Schiller wrote: "Weil du mir neulich von der Oper Medea schriebst, so muss ich Dir sagen, dass ich Wieland habe versprechen müssen, den Oberon doch noch zu bearbeiten, und ich halte es wirklich für ein treffliches Sujet zur Musik," *Briefe*, I, 445, no. 234. ("Because you recently wrote me about the opera Medea, I must tell you that I have had to promise Wieland to work up Oberon after all, and I really do consider it an excellent subject for music.")

2. *Der Teutsche Merkur*, II, 2 (1773), 160-161. Wieland's own youthful interest in the remote Germanic past had been of very short duration. The epic about Hermann with which he had hoped to impress Bodmer in the early 1750s remained unfinished, Friedrich Sengle, *Wieland*, pp. 36-37 and 45.

3. *Ausgewählte Briefe*, II, no. 173 (22 February 1770), p. 351.

4. *Gesammelte Schriften*, ed. Deutsche Kommission der Königlich Preussischen Akademie der Wissenschaften, Erste Abteilung: *Werke*, XI, 57. Volume and page numbers henceforth given in the text refer to this edition.

5. In summarizing the content of the *Alceste* letters and the other operatic essays, Albert Fuchs does not treat the earlier German writers mentioned by Wieland himself, "Wieland et l'esthétique de l'opéra." L. John Parker, who gives a short historical account of German musical theater, provides information about selected librettos but does not mention the antecedents of Wieland's theory, *Christoph Martin Wielands dramatische Tätigkeit*, pp. 29-54. Ruth Zinar, who mentions Hans Sachs's *Alkestis* (1555), but writes nothing of König, or even Postel, believes Wieland exemplifies eighteenth-century attitudes about limiting the selection of Greek tragic subjects to those dealing with self-sacrifice and nobility, "The Use of Greek Tragedy in the History of Opera," p. 85.

6. *Allgemeine Deutsche Bibliothek*, XXI, 1 (1774), 189, and

Christian Heinrich Schmid, *Chronologie des deutschen Theaters* (1775), reprinted in Schriften der Gesellschaft für Theatergeschichte, I, 212.

7. See John Rutledge, *The Dialogue of the Dead in Eighteenth-Century Germany*, pp. 107-109 on Goethe and pp. 86-95 on Wieland.

8. Compare L. John Parker, "Wieland's Musical Play 'Die Wahl des Herkules' and Goethe," p. 176.

9. *Dr. Burney's Musical Tours in Europe*, II: *An 18th-Century Musical Tour in Central Europe and the Netherlands*, p. 31. For Burney's evaluation of Wieland, see pp. 241-242. Also pertinent is Burney's *A General History of Music from the Earliest Ages to the Present Period*, p. 947.

10. It is important to remember that Algarotti was in Berlin when the so-called Montagsklub was actively engaging in its discussion of opera, and that he published his views several years after Krause, but around the same time as Marburg, Lessing, Nicolai, Ramler, and Mendelssohn. Wieland's association with Sulzer in the mid-1750s should also not be forgotten. Rudolf Erich Raspe (1737-1794) claimed to have used the Livorno 1764 edition for his *Versuche über die Architectur, Mahlerey und musicalische Opera, aus dem Italiänischen des Grafen Algarotti*, "Versuch über die musikalische Opera," pp. 219-300. Fuchs overestimates Wieland's "loyalty" to and dependence on Algarotti's views; along with most other commentators, he does not mention the interest in opera in Berlin, question which edition of Algarotti Wieland used, or consider that the Raspe translation might have altered the critical vocabulary of the original, "Wieland et l'esthétique de l'opéra," p. 630. Fritz Martini, interestingly enough, believed it was precisely the influence of Algarotti and Gluck that helped Wieland become "das Bindeglied zwischen der Oper und dem neuen Drama" ("the connecting link between opera and modern drama"), "C. M. Wieland und das 18. Jahrhundert," p. 251.

11. Modern scholars have long questioned the sincerity and originality of Gluck's intentions to reform opera. Aubrey S. Garlington, Jr. uses Gluck as his main example and shows that four of the major "reform" operas contain significant traces of the marvelous, "*Le Merveilleux* and Operatic Reform in 18th-Century French Opera," especially pp. 493-494.

12. Friedrich Adolf Schmidt, "Maler Müllers Stellung in der Entwicklung des musikalischen Dramas," p. 180.

13. Emilie Marx, *Wieland und das Drama*, pp. 104-107, especially p. 106, and Bernhard Seuffert, *Wielands Abderiten*, pp. 19-20.

14. For Mozart's relationship to Karl Theodor and the Mannheim stage, see Daniel Heartz, "The Genesis of Mozart's *Idomeneo*," pp. 1-3 and 17-18.

15. Schiedermair, *Die deutsche Oper*, interprets the choice of subject as a decisive turning point, and he quotes from the preface to show the nationalistic intentions of the libretto: " 'Ist nur die Asche Roms und Athens allein verehrungswürdig und kostbar? Sind dies auch noch Griechen und Römer, die auf unseren Schaubühnen erscheinen oder hören wir nur ihre Namen nennen? Wir werfen unsere Augen auf fremde Tugendmuster, die vielleicht niemals gewesen sind, und sehen nicht, was in unserem Schosse ist,' " p. 128. ("Are only the ashes of Rome and Athens alone venerable and precious? Are these even Greeks and Romans appearing on our stages, or do we just hear their names being called? We cast our glances at foreign paragons of virtue that perhaps never existed, and we do not see what is in our own lap.")

16. *Gesammelte Schriften*, XII, ed. Wilhelm Kurrelmeyer, pp. A57-A58.

17. Seuffert presents letters and other helpful biographical information in order to explain that Wieland's experiences in Mannheim spurred him to resume his work on the novel, *Wielands Abderiten*, pp. 15-25, especially p. 25. Ludwig Edelstein points out some ancient sources for the Euripides episode, claims that much of Wieland's criticism also pertained to Greek theater, and concludes that one of the novel's main objectives was to censure the contemporary grecomania, "Wielands 'Abderiten' und der Deutsche Humanismus," pp. 443-444, 448, and 453.

18. It is well known that the German Romantics advocated and attempted to make programmatic the fusion of genres and art forms. August Wilhelm Schlegel, for example, hoped for "eine Erzählung mit Gesang (eine Gattung, von der sich eben so wohl eine mannichfaltige Bearbeitung denken lässt, als von dem Schauspiele mit Gesang)" ("a story with song [a genre for which just as multifarious a treatment can be imagined as for the play with

song]"), *Athenaeum, Eine Zeitschrift*, I, 1 (1798), Neudrucke Romantischer Seltenheiten, I, 172. And his brother Friedrich wrote: "Ja, ich kann mir einen Roman kaum anders denken, als gemischt aus Erzählung, Gesang und andern Formen" ("Yes, I can hardly imagine a novel other than one mixed out of narrative, song, and other forms"), "Brief über den Roman," *Gespräch über die Poesie, Kritische Friedrich-Schlegel-Ausgabe*, II: *Charakteristiken und Kritiken I (1796-1801)*, p. 336.

Alfred Robert Neumann presents a convincing analysis of Novalis's *Heinrich von Ofterdingen* (1802) and shows how and where it employs operatic devices, "The Evolution of the Concept *Gesamtkunstwerk* in German Romanticism," pp. 177-183. It is unfortunate that no one has followed his lead. It is also unfortunate that so little is known about the historical interrelationships of the novel and opera during the early decades of the eighteenth century when the foundations of the German Romantic movement were being laid.

19. *Hildegard von Hohenthal*, Heinse's *Sämmtliche Werke*, V and VI, and "Der Dichter und der Komponist," *Die Serapionsbrüder*, Hoffmann's *Sämtliche Werke*, VI, 76-98.

20. As usual, Wieland attempts to present multiple points of view and in so doing changes his narrative stance from chapter to chapter. If I occasionally seem to equate Wieland with his narrator (s) in my discussion, I do so only for the sake of clarity. My main objective is to show that Wieland did indeed translate the German operatic debate into fiction, rather than to analyze the structure of the novel. For information on Wieland's narrative techniques, see Wolfram Mauser, "Wielands 'Geschichte der Abderiten,'" pp. 167-171; Steven R. Miller, *Die Figur des Erzählers in Wielands Romanen*; Lieselotte E. Kurth-Voigt, *Perspectives and Points of View*.

21. Seuffert discusses only the "naturalistic" works produced in Mannheim, *Wielands Abderiten*, pp. 36-38.

22. Seuffert's identifications of those playwrights are not only interesting and helpful, but they also seem probable from a purely biographical point of view, ibid., pp. 38-41. During the creative process, however, Wieland obviously transformed those models into caricatures that would have more universal and lasting significance, and, as a result, he created something quite different.

23. In his fascinating discussion of Dionysian allusions in Wie-

land's novel, John Whitton observes that Euripides appears in Abdera shortly before writing the *Bacchae*. He also discusses Aristophanes' *Frogs* as a "classical precedent for using Euripides as a character in a satirical work" and lists parallels between it and the novel, "Sacrifice and Society in Wielands *Abderiten*," pp. 216-217.

24. Whitton finds support for his thesis in Wieland's very choice of *Andromeda*, where there is a double motif of social salvation. He does not, however, compare the two performances or relate them to Wieland's theory of musical theater, ibid., p. 222.

25. Seuffert argues that Wieland's Euripides can be none other than Lessing, *Wielands Abderiten*, p. 41.

26. W. E. Yuill contends that Wieland becomes markedly more urbane and tolerant from the Euripides episode on, and to support his contention he explains that the Abderites no longer merely have the innocence of young children but have become "perfect fools," "Abderitis and Abderitism: Some Reflections on a Novel by Wieland," pp. 76 and 84-85.

27. Yuill notes that Wieland praised the Abderites' artistic reaction, but he does not mention that the only time Wieland did so was when they were reacting specifically to the performance staged by Euripides himself, ibid., p. 85.

28. "Auszug aus einem Schreiben an einen Freund in D*** über die Abderiten im 7ten St. des Teutschen Merkurs d.J." (1778), X, 11. Wieland's earlier remarks on the subject provide an interesting comparison; see, for example, "Zusätze des Herausgebers zu dem vorstehenden Artikel," specifically IV: "Der Eifer, unsrer Dichtkunst einen Nationalen-Charakter zu geben, etc.," *Der Teutsche Merkur*, II, 2 (1773), 174-183.

EPILOGUE

1. Richard Engländer's contribution would have been much more valuable if he had recognized the fact that many Germans had been supporting the cultivation of indigenous opera long before 1800, "The Struggle between German and Italian Opera at the Time of Weber."

2. *Ueber die neuere Deutsche Litteratur: Zwote Sammlung von Fragmenten* (1767), *Sämmtliche Werke*, ed. Suphan, I, 306.

3. The result is that there has been little desire among students

of German literature to undertake studies like Brewster Roger-son's *"Ut musica poesis*: The Parallel of Music and Poetry in Eighteenth Century Criticism,"* which concentrates on English literature.

4. See, for example, *Hildegard von Hohenthal, Sämmtliche Werke*, V, 303, 314, 329, and 365-366. Also see *Aphorismen, Sämmtliche Werke*, VIII, ii, ed. Albert Leitzmann (Leipzig, 1925), 508 and 512. Compare also Herder's interpretation of the relationship between Gluck and Klopstock, *Briefe zu Beförderung der Humanität*, VIII (1796), 102, *Sämmtliche Werke*, ed. Suphan, XVIII, 119.

5. See Wolfgang Nufer, *Herders Ideen zur Verbindung von Poesie, Musik und Tanz*, p. 83, and Konrad Burdach, "Schillers Chordrama und die Geburt des tragischen Stils aus der Musik," 143, 93.

6. It has also received a great deal of attention from modern literary scholars, who, however, seldom take operatic writings into consideration. They perpetuate the contention of Sigmund Lem-picki that the earliest stirrings of a change came in the writings of Bodmer, Breitinger, and the elder Schlegels, who "alle suchen sich von dem Joche der mimetischen Theorie frei zu machen" ("all seek to free themselves from the yoke of mimetic theory"), *Geschichte der deutschen Literaturwissenschaft bis zum Ende des 18. Jahrhunderts*, p. 301. Others, like Herbert M. Schueller, have noticed that the "imitation of nature" lost importance and meaning in theories involving all the arts, "Correspondences between Music and the Sister Arts," p. 345.

7. *Sämmtliche Werke*, ed. Suphan, XXIII, 333-334. Romantics like Tieck who were interested in Spanish drama, especially Calderon, were to probe the artistic significance of the dream still more fully; see Tieck's *Dramaturgische Blätter*, I, 298. Of related interest is Jackson I. Cope's *The Theater and the Dream: From Metaphor to Form in Renaissance Drama*.

8. *Literary Notebooks 1797-1801*, p. 83, no. 701.

9. Ibid., p. 55, no. 400.

10. *Dramaturgische Blätter*, I, 325-326.

11. *Jubiläums-Ausgabe* XXXIII, 88.

12. Goethe, *Gedenkausgabe* XX, 480. R. M. Longyear points out in "Schiller and Opera" that "virtually all of his dramas require music, some of it quite elaborate; musical metaphors and char-

acterizations abound in his dramatic, poetic, and even philosophical writings; and music plays a subordinate but important
role in his esthetic theories," p. 171. Longyear explains that
Schiller's attitude toward opera changed in the 1790s under
Goethe's influence, pp. 176-177, and he also discusses Schiller's
high opinion of Gluck, pp. 179-180. He does not, however, investigate the relationship between Schiller's concept of opera and
views on mimesis.

13. Unlike his predecessors in the field who considered the play
Schiller's *Gesamtkunstwerk*, Robert T. Clark, Jr. views it as an
attempt to put theory into practice so that. poetry teaches the
ideal while music prepares the soul, "The Union of the Arts in
Die Braut von Messina," p. 1,141. Walter Silz, who views the
preface as an unsuccessful attempt to use theory for the justification of practice, believes any critical reader would realize that the
chorus in *Die Braut von Messina* does not measure up to Schiller's
own theoretical standards and that "any drama that did so would
be virtually opera," "Chorus and Choral Function in Schiller,"
p. 150. Silz concentrates on Schiller's " 'choral urge,' " p. 161, and
to show how it manifested itself, he examines *Wallenstein*, pp.
158-164, *Maria Stuart*, pp. 164-165, *Die Jungfrau von Orleans*,
pp. 165-166, *Wilhelm Tell*, pp. 166-167, and the lyric poetry, pp.
167-170.

14. Schiller, *Sämmtliche Schriften*, ed. Goedeke, XIV, 6.

15. Ibid., p. 7.

16. Paul Weigand writes that "there is scarcely a play by Schiller
that has not at some time or other been employed as the basis for
an opera text," "Schiller's Dramas as Opera Texts," p. 249.

17. Schiller, *Sämmtliche Schriften*, ed. Goedeke, XIV, 3.

BIBLIOGRAPHY

PRIMARY SOURCES

Aubignac, François Hédelin d'. *La Pratique du Théâtre*. Paris, 1657.

———. *The Whole Art of the Stage*. Tr. anon. London, 1684.

Batteux, Charles. *Les Beaux-arts réduits à un même principe*. Paris, 1746.

———. *Cours de belles lettres ou Principes de la littérature*. 2d ed., 4 vols. Paris, 1753.

———. *A Course of the Belles Lettres: or the Principles of Literature*. Tr. Mr. Miller. 4 vols. London, 1761.

Baumgarten, Alexander Gottlieb. *Meditationes philosophicae de nonnullis ad poema pertinentibus*. Tr., with original text, introduction, and notes, Karl Aschenbrenner and William B. Holther. Berkeley and Los Angeles, 1954.

Beccau, Joachim. *Theatralische Gedichte/ und Übersetzungen*. Hamburg, 1720.

Bertuch, Georg. *Disputatio juridica de eo quod justum est, circa ludos scenicos operasque modernas, dictas vulgò "Operen."* Kiel, 1693.

Birken, Sigmund von. *Singspiel/ betitelt Sophia*. Bayreuth, 1662.

———. *Teutsche Rede- bind- und Dicht-Kunst/ oder Kurze Anweisung zur Teutschen Poesy*. Nuremberg, 1679.

Bodmer, Johann Jakob. *Anklagung Des verderbten Geschmackes Oder Critische Anmerkungen über Den Hamburgischen Patrioten, Und die Hallischen Tadlerinnen*. Frankfurt and Leipzig [Zurich], 1728.

———. *Critische Betrachtungen und freye Untersuchungen zum Aufnehmen und zur Verbesserung der deutschen Schau-Bühne, Mit einer Zuschrift an die Frau Neuberin*. Bern, 1743.

———, ed. *Freymüthige Nachrichten Von Neuen Büchern und Andern zur Gelehrtheit gehörigen Sachen*. 20 vols. Zurich, 1744-1763.

———. *Vier kritische Gedichte*. Ed. Jakob Baechtold. Deutsche Litteraturdenkmale des 18. und 19. Jahrhunderts in Neudrucken, 12. Heilbronn, 1883.

Bodmer, Johann Jakob and Johann Jakob Breitinger, *Die Discourse der Mahlern.* 4 pts. Zurich, 1721-1723.

Bostel, Lucas von. *Atis, Oder Der stumme Verliebte/ In einer Opera.* Wolfenbüttel, 1717.

————. *Der Glückliche Gross-Vezier Cara Mustapha, Erster Theil/ Nebenst der grausamen Belagerung/ und Bestürmung der Käyserlichen Residentz-Stadt Wien.* (Hamburg, 1686), 3rd printing, n.p., n.d.

————. *Das Unmöglichste Ding In einem Sing-Spiel.* Hamburg, 1684.

Bressand, Friedrich Christian. *Arcadia, oder Die Königliche Schäferey/ in einem Singe-Spiel.* Braunschweig, 1699.

————. *Hercules Unter denen Amazonen/ In einer Opera.* 2 pts. Hamburg, 1694.

————. *Die Plejades Oder das Sieben-Gestirne/ in einem Sing Spiele.* Braunschweig, 1693.

Burney, Charles. *Dr. Burney's Musical Tours in Europe.* Ed. Percy A. Scholes. 2 vols. London, New York, Toronto, 1959.

————. *A General History of Music from the Earliest Ages to the Present Period (1789).* Ed. Frank Mercer. 2 vols. New York, 1935; rpt. New York, 1957.

Camerer, J. J. "Von Opern und Comödien." *Braunschweigische Anzeigen,* I, 46 (9 June 1745), 745-750.

Critique Des Hamburgischen Schau-Platzes/ In einem schertzhafften Prologo. Hamburg, 1725.

Crousaz, Jean Pierre de. *Traité du beau.* Amsterdam, 1715.

Curtius, Michael Conrad. *Aristoteles Dichtkunst ins Deutsche übersetzet, Mit Anmerkungen und besondern Abhandlungen versehen.* Hannover, 1753. Rpt. in Documenta Semiotica. Ed. Walter A. Koch. Hildesheim and New York, 1973.

Dubos, Jean Baptiste. *Critical Reflections on Poetry, Painting, and Music, With an Inquiry into the Rise and Progress of the Theatrical Entertainments of the Ancients.* Tr. Thomas Nugent. 3 vols. London, 1748.

————. *Réflexions critiques sur la poésie et sur la peinture.* Paris, 1719. 4th rev. and enl. ed. 3 pts. Paris, 1740.

Ebeling, H. "Kurze Geschichte der deutschen Dichtkunst." *Hannoverisches Magazin,* V (1767), 81-92; 97-112; 113-128.

Elmenhorst, Heinrich. *Charitine, oder Göttlich-Geliebte.* Hamburg, 1681.

―――. *Dramatologia Antiqvo-Hodierna, Das ist: Bericht von denen Oper-Spielen.* Hamburg, 1688.

―――. *Der Im Christenthum Biss in den Todt Beständige Märterer Polyeuct Vorgestellet In Einem Singe-Spiel.* Hamburg, 1689.

―――. *Die Macchabaeische Mütter Mit Ihren Sieben Söhnen, In einem Singe-Spiel.* Hamburg, 1679.

―――. *Orontes, Der verlohrne und wieder gefundene Königliche Prinz aus Candia/ In einem Singe-Spiel.* Hamburg, 1678.

―――. *Die Wol und beständig-liebende Michal Oder Der Siegende und fliehende David, In einem Sing-Spiel.* Hamburg, 1679.

Fabricius, Johann Andreas. *Versuche in der Teutschen Rede-Dicht- und Sprachkunst.* Blankenhain and Weimar, 1737.

Feind, Barthold. *L'amore ammalato: Die kranckende Liebe, Oder: Antiochus Und Stratonica, Musicalisches Schau-Spiel.* Hamburg, 1708.

―――. *Bellerophon, oder: Das in die Preussische Krone verwandelte Wagen-Gestirn/ . . . In einer Operetta.* Hamburg, 1708.

―――. *La Costanza Sforzata: Die Gezwungene Beständigkeit/ Oder Die listige Rache Des Sueno . . . In einem Sing-Spiel.* Hamburg, 1706.

―――. *Desiderius, König der Langobarden/ Musikalisches Schauspiel.* Hamburg, 1709.

―――. *Deutsche Gedichte.* Stade, 1708.

―――. *Der durch den Fall des Grossen Pompejus Erhöhete Julius Caesar, In Einem Sing-Spiel.* Hamburg, 1710.

―――. *Der Fall Des grossen Richters in Israel/ Simson, Oder: Die abgekühlte Liebes-Rache der Debora, Musicalisches Trauer-Spiel.* Hamburg, 1709.

―――. *Die Kleinmüthige Selbst-Mörderin Lucretia, Oder: Die Staats-Thorheit des Brutus, Musicalisches Trauer-Spiel.* Hamburg, 1705.

―――. *Masagniello furioso, Drama Musicale, . . . Die Neapolitanische Fischer-Empörung, Musicalisches Schau-Spiel.* Hamburg, 1706.

Feind, Barthold. *Das Römische April-Fest, Musicalisches Lust-und Tantz-Spiel.* Hamburg, 1716.

————. *Die Römische Unruhe, Oder: Die Edelmüthige Octavia, In einem Sing-Spiel.* Hamburg, 1705.

Fiedler, Gottlieb. *Der Grossmüthige Roland In einem Singe-Spiel.* Hamburg, 1695.

————. *Der Grossmüthige Scipio Africanus, In einem Singe-Spiel.* Hamburg, 1694.

————. *Der Hochmüthige Alexander, . . . In einem singenden Schau-Spiel.* Hamburg, 1695.

Forkel, Johann Nicolaus. *Allgemeine Litteratur der Musik, oder Anleitung zur Kenntniss musikalischer Bücher.* Leipzig, 1792.

Frederick the Great. *De la littérature allemande, Ergänzt durch: Justus Möser, Über die deutsche Sprache und Literatur, Christian Thomasius, Von Nachahmung der Franzosen.* Hamburg and Darmstadt, 1969.

Gellert, Christian Fürchtegott. *Sämmtliche Schriften.* 10 pts. Leipzig, 1769-1774.

Gerber, Ernst Ludwig. *Historisch-Biographisches Lexicon der Tonkünstler.* 2 vols. Leipzig, 1790-1792.

Gerstenberg, Heinrich Wilhelm von. *Briefe über Merkwürdigkeiten der Litteratur.* Ed. Alexander von Weilen. Deutsche Literaturdenkmale des 18. und 19. Jahrhunderts, 29 and 30. Heilbronn, 1886.

————. *Rezensionen der Hamburgischen Neuen Zeitung, 1767-1771.* Ed. O. Fischer. Deutsche Literaturdenkmale des 18. und 19. Jahrhunderts, 128. Berlin, 1904.

————. *Vermischte Schriften.* 3 vols. Altona, 1815-1816.

Gleim, Johann Wilhelm Ludwig and Karl Wilhelm Ramler. *Briefwechsel zwischen Gleim und Ramler.* Ed. Carl Schüddekopf. Bibliothek des Litterarischen Vereins in Stuttgart, 242 and 244. Tübingen, 1906-1907.

Goethe, Johann Wolfgang von. *Gedenkausgabe der Werke, Briefe und Gespräche.* Ed. Ernst Beutler. 24 vols. Zurich, 1949-1954. 2 suppl. vols. Zurich, 1960-1964.

————. *Sämtliche Werke, Jubiläums-Ausgabe.* Ed. Eduard von der Hellen. 40 vols. Stuttgart and Berlin, 1902-1907; index vol. 1912.

Gottsched, Johann Christoph, ed. *Beyträge zur Critischen Historie der deutschen Sprache, Poesie und Beredsamkeit.* 8 vols. Leipzig, 1732-1744.

————. *Der Biedermann* (1727-1729). *Gesammelte Schriften.* Ed. Eugen Reichel, III. Berlin, 1903.

————. *Die Deutsche Schaubühne nach den Regeln und Exempeln der Alten.* 6 vols. Leipzig, 1740-1745; 2d rev. ed. Leipzig, 1746-1750.

————. *Nöthiger Vorrath zur Geschichte der deutschen Dramatischen Dichtkunst, oder Verzeichniss aller Deutschen Trauer-Lust- und Sing-Spiele, die im Druck erschienen, von 1450 bis zur Hälfte des jetzigen Jahrhunderts.* 2 vols. Leipzig, 1757-1765; rpt. Hildesheim and New York, 1970.

————. *Versuch einer Critischen Dichtkunst.* Leipzig, 1730.

Gruber, Johann Sigmund. *Beyträge zur Litteratur der Musik.* Nuremberg, 1785.

————. *Litteratur der Musik, oder Anleitung zur Kentnis der vorzüglichen musikalischen Bücher.* Nuremberg, 1783.

Hagedorn, Friedrich von. *Poetische Werke.* Ed. Johann Joachim Eschenburg. Pt. 5: *Auszüge des von Hagedornischen Briefwechsels.* Hamburg, 1800.

Hamann, Johann Georg, ed. *Hamburgische Auszüge aus neuen Büchern und Nachrichten von Allerhand zur Gelahrtheit gehörigen Sachen.* Hamburg, 1728-1729.

————. *Margaretha, Königin in Castilien, In einer Opera.* Hamburg, 1730.

————. *Die Matrone.* 3 pts. Hamburg, 1728-1730.

————. *Poetisches Lexicon.* Rev. ed. Leipzig, 1751.

Hamburgische Berichte von den neuesten gelehrten Sachen. Ed. Johann Peter Kohl. Hamburg, 1732-1758.

Hamburgische Beyträge zu den Werken des Witzes und der Sittenlehre. Ed. J. D. Leyding, J. C. Unzer, and J. F. Löwen. 2 vols. Hamburg, 1753-1755.

Harsdörffer, Georg Philipp. *Frauenzimmer Gesprächspiele.* 8 pts. Nuremberg, 1644-1649. Ed. Irmgard Böttcher. Deutsche Neudrucke: Barock. Ed. Erich Trunz, 18. Tübingen, 1968-1969.

Heinse, Johann Jakob Wilhelm. *Sämmtliche Werke.* Ed. Carl Schüddekopf. 10 vols. Leipzig, 1903-1925.

Herder, Johann Gottfried. *Sämmtliche Werke.* Ed. Bernhard Suphan. 33 vols. Berlin, 1877-1913.

Hertel, Johann Wilhelm, ed. *Sammlung Musikalischer Schriften, grösstentheils aus den Werken der Italiäner und Franzosen übersetzt, und mit Anmerkungen versehen.* 2 pts. Leipzig, 1757-1758.

Hiller, Johann Adam. "Abhandlung von der Nachahmung der Natur in der Musik." *Neue Erweiterungen der Erkenntnis und des Vergnügens,* III, 14 (1754), 140-168. Rpt. in *Historisch-Kritische Beyträge zur Aufnahme der Musik.* Ed. F. W. Marpurg, I, 6 (1755), 515-543.

——. *Lebensbeschreibung berühmter Musikgelehrten und Tonkünstler neuerer Zeit.* Leipzig, 1784.

——, ed. *Wöchentliche Nachrichten und Anmerkungen die Musik betreffend.* 3 vols. Leipzig, 1766-1769; rpt. Hildesheim and New York, 1970.

Hinsch, Hinrich. *Claudius, Römischer Käyser / In einem Sing-Spiele.* Hamburg, 1726.

——. *Der irrende Ritter D. Quixotte de la Mancia, Lust-Spiel.* Hamburg, 1690.

——. *Die verdammte Staat-Sucht / Oder Der verführte Claudius, In einem Sing-Spiel.* Hamburg. 1703.

Höveln, Konrad von (pseud. Candorin). *Eren- Danz- Singe Schauspiel-Entwurf,* n.p., 1663.

Hoffmann, Ernst Theodor Wilhelm (Amadeus). *Die Serapionsbrüder, Gesammelte Erzählungen und Märchen. Sämtliche Werke.* Ed. Eduard Grisebach, VI. Leipzig, n.d.

Hotter. *Störtebecker und Jödge Michaels . . . In einem Singe-Spiel.* 2 pts. Hamburg, 1701.

Hottinger, Johann Jacob. *Menschen, Tiere und Goethe, Eine Farce.* Altona, 1775.

Hudemann, Ludwig Friedrich. *Diocletianus der Christenverfolger und Phädra, Zwey Trauerspiele.* Wismar and Leipzig, 1751.

——. "Gedanken von den Vorzügen der Oper vor Tragedien und Comedien." *Neu-Eröffnete Musikalische Bibliothek.* Ed. L. C. Mizler von Kolof, II, 3 (1742), 120-151.

——. *Proben einiger Gedichte und Poetischen Übersetzungen, Denen ein Bericht beygefügt worden, welcher von den Vorzügen der Oper vor den Tragischen und Comischen Spielen handelt.* Hamburg, 1732.

Hübner, Johann. *Neu-vermehrtes Poetisches Hand-Buch, Das ist, eine kurtzgefaste Anleitung zur Deutschen Poesie.* New rev. ed. Leipzig, 1720; 2d new rev. ed. Leipzig, 1742.

Huet, Pierre Daniel. *Traité de l'origine des romans.* Facsimile rpt. of 1st ed. of 1670 and Eberhard Werner Happel's translation of 1682. Stuttgart, 1966.

Hunold, Christian Friedrich (pseud. Menantes). *Academische Neben-Stunden allerhand neuer Gedichte/ Nebst Einer Anleitung zur vernünftigen Poesie.* Halle and Leipzig. 1713.

————. *Theatralische/ Galante und Geistliche Gedichte.* Hamburg, 1706.

Klopstock, Friedrich Gottlieb. *Briefe von und an Klopstock: Ein Beitrag zur Literaturgeschichte seiner Zeit.* Ed. J. M. Lappenberg. Braunschweig, 1867.

————. *Werke.* Ed. R. Hamel. Deutsche National-Litteratur, Historisch-kritische Ausgabe, 48. Berlin and Stuttgart, n.d.

König, Johann Ulrich. *Die getreue Alceste In einer Opera.* Hamburg, 1719.

————. *Sancio, Oder die Siegende Grossmuth, In einem Sing-Spiele.* Hamburg, 1727.

————. *Theatralische, geistliche/ vermischte und galante Gedichte.* Hamburg and Leipzig, 1713.

————. "Von dem guten Geschmack in der Dicht- und Rede-Kunst." *Des Freyherrn von Caniz Gedichte.* Ed. J. U. König. Leipzig and Berlin, 1727.

Krause, Christian Gottfried. *Von der Musikalischen Poesie.* Berlin, 1752. Mit einem Register vermehrt, Berlin, 1753; rpt. Leipzig, 1973.

Lamprecht, Jacob Friedrich. *Schreiben eines Schwaben an einen deutschen Freund in Petersburg von dem gegenwärtigen Zustande der Opera in Hamburg.* Hamburg, 1736; rpt. Hamburg, 1937.

Lediard, Thomas. *Eine Collection Curieuser Vorstellungen, In Illuminationen Und Feuer-Wercken.* Hamburg, 1730.

————. *The German Spy.* London, 1738.

————. *Julius Caesar in Aegypten, In einem Sing-Spiele.* Hamburg, 1725.

Leibniz, Gottfried Wilhelm. *Sämtliche Schriften und Briefe.* Ed. Preussische Akademie der Wissenschaften. Vol. 3: *Allgemeiner Politischer und Historischer Briefwechsel.* Leipzig, 1938.

Lessing, Gotthold Ephraim. *Sämtliche Schriften.* Ed. Karl Lachmann. 3rd rev. and enl. ed. Franz Muncker. 23 vols. Stuttgart and Leipzig, 1886-1924.

————. *Theatralische Bibliothek.* Berlin, 1754-1758.

————. *Werke.* Ed. Julius Petersen and Waldemar von Olshausen. 30 vols. Berlin, Leipzig, Vienna, Stuttgart, 1925-1935.

Lessing, Gotthold Ephraim; Moses Mendelssohn; Christoph Friedrich Nicolai et al. *Briefe, die neueste Literatur betreffend.* 24 pts. Berlin and Stettin, 1759-1765.

Lessing, Gotthold Ephraim and Christlob Mylius. *Beyträge zur Historie und Aufnahme des Theaters.* Stuttgart, 1750.

Löwen, Johann Friedrich. *Geschichte des deutschen Theaters (1766) und Flugschriften über das Hamburger Nationaltheater (1766 und 1767).* Ed. Heinrich Stümke. Neudrucke literarhistorischer Seltenheiten, 8. Berlin, 1905.

————. *Schriften.* 4 pts. Hamburg, 1765-1766.

Ludwig, Christian Gottlieb. "Versuch eines Beweises, dass ein Singespiel oder eine Oper nicht gut seyn könne." *Beyträge zur Critischen Historie.* Ed. J. C. Gottsched, II, 8 (1734), 648-661.

Marpurg, Friedrich Wilhelm. *Der Critische Musicus an der Spree.* Berlin, 1749-1750; rpt. Hildesheim and New York, 1970.

————, ed. *Historisch-Kritische Beyträge zur Aufnahme der Musik.* 5 vols. Berlin, 1754-1778; rpt. Hildesheim and New York, 1970.

Masenius, Jacob. "Theoretisches aus Jakob Masens Palaestra Eloquentiae Ligatae." 2d ed. 1664. *Das Ordensdrama, Barockdrama* II. Ed. Willi Flemming. Deutsche Literatur: Sammlung literarischer Kunst- und Kulturdenkmäler, in Entwicklungsreihen. 2d rev. ed. Hildesheim, 1965. Pp. 37-46.

Mattheson, Johann. *Critica Musica.* 2 vols. Hamburg, 1722-1725; rpt. Amsterdam, 1964.

————. *Grundlage einer Ehren-Pforte.* Hamburg, 1740; rpt. Berlin, 1910.

————. *Der Musikalische Patriot.* Hamburg, 1728.

————. *Das Neu-Eröffnete Orchestre.* Hamburg, 1713.

————. *Die neueste Untersuchung der Singspiele.* Hamburg, 1744; rpt. Leipzig and Kassel, 1975.

————. *Plus Ultra, ein Stückwerk von neuer und mancherley Art.* 3 pts. Hamburg, 1754-1756.

————. *Der Vernünfftler, Das ist: Ein teutscher Auszug/ Aus den*

Engeländischen Moral-Schrifften Des Tatler Und Spectator. Hamburg, 1713-1714.

————. *Der vollkommene Capellmeister.* Hamburg, 1739; rpt. Kassel and Basel, 1954.

Meier, Georg Friedrich. *Betrachtungen über den ersten Grundsatz aller schönen Künste und Wissenschaften.* Halle, 1757.

————. *Beurtheilung der Gottschedischen Dichtkunst.* Halle 1747-1748.

Mencke, Johann Burkhard. *Compendiöses Gelehrten-Lexicon.* Leipzig, 1715.

Mendelssohn, Moses. "Betrachtungen über das Erhabene und das Naive in den schönen Wissenschaften." *Bibliothek der schönen Wissenschaften und der freyen Künste,* II, 2 (1758), 229-267.

————. "Betrachtungen über die Quellen und die Verbindungen der schönen Künste und Wissenschaften." *Bibliothek der schönen Wissenschaften und der freyen Künste,* I, 2 (1757), 231-268.

————. *Gesammelte Schriften.* Ed. G. B. Mendelssohn. 7 vols. Leipzig, 1843-1845.

————. *Philosophische Schriften.* 2 pts. Berlin, 1761.

Menestrier, Claude-François. *Des ballets anciens et modernes selon les règles du théâtre.* Paris, 1682; rpt. Geneva, 1972.

————. *Des representations en musique anciennes et modernes.* Paris, 1684.

Mizler von Kolof, Lorenz Christoph, ed. *Neu-Eröffnete Musikalische Bibliothek, oder Gründliche Nachricht nebst unpartheyischem Urtheil von musikalischen Schriften und Büchern.* 4 vols. Leipzig, 1739-1754; rpt. Hilversum, 1966.

Möser, Justus. *Harlekin* (Rev. ed. Bremen, 1777). *Texte und Materialien mit einem Nachwort.* Ed. Henning Boetius. Ars Poetica: Texte und Studien zur Dichtungslehre und Dichtkunst, Texte 4. Bad Homburg, Berlin, Zurich, 1968.

————. *Sämmtliche Werke.* Ed. B. R. Abeken. 10 pts. Berlin, 1842-1843.

Morhof, Daniel Georg. *Unterricht von der Teutschen Sprache und Poesie* (Rev. and enl. ed. Lübeck and Frankfurt, 1700). Ed. Henning Boetius. Ars Poetica: Texte und Studien zur Dichtungslehre und Dichtkunst, Texte 1. Bad Homburg, Berlin, Zurich, 1969.

Mylius, Christlob and Johann Andreas Cramer, eds. *Bemühun-*

gen zur Beförderung der Critik und des guten Geschmacks. 2 vols. Halle, 1743-1746.

Nemeitz, Joachim Christoph. *Vernünfftige Gedancken Uber allerhand Historische/ Critische und Moralische Materien, Nebst verschiedenen dahin gehörigen Anmerckungen.* 6 pts. Frankfurt/M., 1739-1745.

Neumeister, Erdmann. *Die Allerneueste Art/ zur Reinen und Galanten Poesie zu gelangen.* Hamburg, 1707.

Nicolai, Christoph Friedrich. *Beschreibung einer Reise durch Deutschland und die Schweiz im Jahre 1781.* 10 vols. Berlin and Stettin, 1785-1795.

———. *Briefe über den itzigen Zustand der schönen Wissenschaften in Deutschland.* Ed. Georg Ellinger. Berliner Neudrucke, ser. 3, vol. 2. Berlin, 1894.

Niedersächsische Nachrichten von Gelehrten neuen Sachen. Ed. Christoph Friedrich Leissner. 6 vols. Hamburg, 1731-1736.

Noverre, Jean Georges. *Letters on Dancing and Ballets.* Tr. Cyril W. Beaumont. London, 1930; rpt. New York, 1966.

———. *Lettres sur la danse, et sur les ballets.* Stuttgart, 1760. Monuments of Music and Music Literature, ser. 2, 47. New York, 1967.

Opitz, Martin. *Buch von der Deutschen Poeterey (1624).* Ed. Wilhelm Braune. 2d ed. Richard Alewyn. Neudrucke deutscher Literaturwerke, N.S. 8. Tübingen, 1966.

———. *Judith.* Rev. ed. Rostock, 1646.

———. *Weltliche Poemata.* Pt. 1, 4th rev. ed. 1644. Deutsche Neudrucke: Barock. Ed. Erich Trunz. Tübingen, 1967.

Der Patriot. Ed. Michael Richey. 3 vols. New rev. ed. Hamburg, 1728-1729.

Paulli, Wilhelm Adolph. *Poesie und Prosa zum Nutzen und Vergnügen; Eine Wochenschrift.* 2 pts. Hamburg, 1755-1756.

———. *Poetische Gedanken von Politischen und Gelehrten Neuigkeiten.* 5 vols. Hamburg, 1750-1754.

Postel, Christian Heinrich. *Der Aus Hyperboreen nach Cymbrien übergebrachte Güldene Apfel.* Hamburg, 1698.

———. *Bajazeth und Tamerlan in einem Sing-Spiel.* Hamburg, 1690.

———. *Cain und Abel, Oder der verzweifelnde Brüder-Mörder In einem Sing-Spiel.* Hamburg, 1689.

———. *Der Durch Gross-Muth und Tapfferkeit besiegete Porus, In einem Singe-Spiel.* Hamburg, 1694.

———. *Die durch Wilhelm Den Grossen In Britannien/ Wieder eingeführte Irene, In einem Sing- und Tantz-Spiel.* Hamburg, 1698.

———. *Der Geliebte Adonis In einem Singe-Spiel.* Hamburg, 1697.

———. *Der Grosse König Der Africanischen Wenden Gensericus, Als Rom- und Carthagens Uberwinder/ In einem Singe-Spiel.* Hamburg, 1693.

———. *Die Gross-Müthige Thalestris, Oder Letzte Königin der Amazonen, In einem Sing-Spiel.* Hamburg, 1690.

———. *Der Königliche Printz Aus Pohlen Sigismundus, Oder Das Menschliche Leben wie ein Traum, In einem Singe-Spiel.* Hamburg, 1693.

———. *Die Listige Juno, Wie solche von dem Grossen Homer/ Im vierzehenden Buche Der Ilias Abgebildet.* Hamburg, 1700.

———. *Der Tapffere Kaiser Carolus Magnus, Und Dessen Erste Gemahlin Hermingardis, In einem Sing-Spiel.* Hamburg, 1692.

———. *Die Verstöhrung Jerusalem . . . Oder Die Eroberung Des Tempels, In einem Sing-Spiel.* 2 pts. Hamburg, 1692.

———. *Die Wunderbahr-errettete Iphigenia In einem Singe-Spiel.* Hamburg, 1699.

———. *Der Wunderbar-vergnügte Pygmalion, In einem Singe-Spiel.* Hamburg, 1694.

Praetorius, Johann Philipp. *Amphytrion, In einem Sing-Spiele.* Hamburg, 1725.

———. *Calypso Oder Sieg der Weissheit Ueber Die Liebe, In einem Sing-Spiele.* Hamburg, 1727.

———. *La capricciosa e il credulo, Intermezzi: Die geliebte Eigensinnige Und der Leicht-gläubige Liebhaber/ In einem Zwischen-Spiele.* Hamburg, 1725.

———. *Der Hamburger Jahr-Marckt Oder der Glückliche Betrug/ In einem schertzhafften Sing-Spiele.* Hamburg, 1725.

———. *Die Hamburger Schlacht-Zeit/ Oder Der Missgelungene Betrug/ In einem Singe-Spiel.* Hamburg, 1725.

———. *Das Jauchzende Gross-Brittannien . . . In einem musicalischen Divertissement Und einer vierfachen Prächtigen Illumination.* Hamburg, 1727.

Praetorius, Johann Philipp. *Tamerlan, In einem Sing-Spiele.* Hamburg, 1725.

Prologus der Musen/ . . . Oder Vor-Singe-Spiel. Hamburg, 1737.

Ramler, Carl Wilhelm. *Einleitung in die Schönen Wissenschaften, nach dem Französischen des Herrn Batteux, mit Zusätzen vermehret.* 4 vols. Leipzig, 1756-1758.

————. *Poëtische Werke.* 2 pts. Berlin, 1800-1801.

Raspe, Rudolf Erich. *Versuche über die Architectur, Mahlerey und musicalische Opera, aus dem Italiänischen des Grafen Algarotti.* Kassel, 1769.

Rauch, Christoph. *Theatrophania, Entgegen gesetzet Der so genanten Schrifft Theatromania.* Hannover, 1682.

Reiser, Anton. *Theatromania, oder die Werke der Finsternis in den öffentlichen Schau-Spielen, von den alten Kirchen-Lehrern und etlichen heidnischen Scribenten verdammet.* Ratzeburg, 1681.

Richter, Christian. *Der Erschaffene/ Gefallene Und Auffgerichtete Mensch, In einem Sing-Spiel.* Hamburg, 1678.

Saint Evremond, Charles de Marguetel de Saint-Denis. *Oeuvres en Prose.* Ed. René Ternois. 4 vols. Paris, 1962-1969.

————. *The Works Of Monsieur De St. Evremond.* Tr. Mr. Des Maizeaux. 3 vols. London, 1714.

Scaliger, Julius Caesar. *Select Translations from Scaliger's Poetics.* Tr. Frederick Morgan Padelford. Yale Studies in English. Ed. Albert S. Cook, 26. New York, 1905.

Scheibe, Johann Adolph. *Abhandlung vom Ursprunge und Alter der Musik.* Altona and Flensburg, 1754.

————. *Der Critische Musikus.* 4 pts. Hamburg, 1737-1740. Rev. and enl. ed. Leipzig, 1745; rpt. Hildesheim, New York, Wiesbaden, 1970.

————. *Thusnelde, ein Singspiel in vier Aufzügen, Mit einem Vorbericht von der Möglichkeit und Beschaffenheit guter Singspiele.* Leipzig, 1749.

Schiebeler, Daniel. "Anmerkung zu Lisuart und Dariolette." *Wöchentliche Nachrichten und Anmerkungen,* Ed. J. A. Hiller, II, 18 (2 November 1767), 135-139.

Schiller, Friedrich. *Briefe.* Ed. Fritz Jonas. 7 vols. Stuttgart, Leipzig, Berlin, Vienna, n.d.

————. *Sämmtliche Schriften.* Historisch-kritische Ausgabe. Ed. Karl Goedeke. 15 pts. Stuttgart, 1867-1876.

Schlegel, August Wilhelm and Friedrich Schlegel. *Athenaeum,*

Eine Zeitschrift (1798-1800). Neudrucke Romantischer Selten-heiten. 3 vols. Munich, 1924.

Schlegel, Friedrich. *Kritische Friedrich-Schlegel-Ausgabe.* Ed. Ernst Behler. Vol. 2: *Charakteristiken und Kritiken I (1796-1801).* Ed. Hans Eichner. Munich, Paderborn, Vienna, and Zurich, 1967.

————. *Literary Notebooks 1797-1801.* Ed. Hans Eichner. Toronto, 1957.

Schlegel, Johann Adolph. *Einschränkung der schönen Künste auf Einen einzigen Grundsatz, aus dem Französischen über-setzt, und mit einem Abhange einiger eignen Abhandlungen versehen.* Leipzig, 1751.

Schlegel, Johann Elias. *Aesthetische und Dramaturgische Schriff-ten.* Ed. Johann von Antoniewicz. Deutsche Litteraturdenk-male des 18. und 19. Jahrhunderts, 26. Heilbronn, 1887.

————. *Werke.* Ed. Johann Heinrich Schlegel. 5 pts. Copenhagen and Leipzig, 1761-1770.

Schmid, Christian Heinrich. *Chronologie des deutschen Theaters* (1775). Schriften der Gesellschaft für Theatergeschichte. Ed. Paul Legband, 1. Berlin, 1902.

Der Schutzgeist/ ein moralisches und satyrisches Wochenblatt. Ed. Johann Andreas Cramer. Hamburg, 1746-1747.

Spingarn, Joel E., ed. *Critical Essays of the Seventeenth Century.* 3 vols. Oxford, 1908-1909; reissued, Bloomington, Ind., 1957.

Stössel, Johann Christoph and Johann David Stössel. *Kurtzge-fasstes Musicalisches Lexicon.* Chemnitz, 1737.

Stolle, Gottlieb. *Anleitung zur Historie der Gelahrheit.* 3rd ed. Jena, 1727.

Strodtmann, Johann Christoph. *Beyträge zur Historie der Gelahrt-heit worinnen die Geschichte der Gelehrten unserer Zeiten beschrieben.* 5 pts. Hamburg, 1748-1750.

Strunk, Oliver, ed. *Source Readings in Music History.* 5 vols. New York, 1965.

Sulzer, Johann Georg. *Allgemeine Theorie der Schönen Künste.* 2 pts. Leipzig, 1773-1775.

Tieck, Ludwig. *Dramaturgische Blätter, Nebst einem Anhange noch ungedruckter Aufsätze über das deutsche Theater und Berichten über die englische Bühne geschrieben auf einer Reise im Jahre 1817.* 3 vols. Breslau, 1826 and Leipzig, 1852.

Uffenbach, Johann Friedrich von. *Gesammelte Neben-Arbeit in gebundenen Reden . . . nebst einer Vorrede von der Würde derer Singe-Gedichte.* Hamburg, 1733.

———. "Von der Würde derer Singgedichte, oder Vertheidigung der Opern." *Neu-Eröffnete Musikalische Bibliothek.* Ed. L. C. Mizler von Kolof, III, 3 (1747), 377-408.

"Von Opern und Comödien." *Braunschweigische Anzeigen,* I, 46 (9 June 1745), 750-753.

Walther, Johann Gottfried. *Musikalisches Lexicon oder Musikalische Bibliothec.* Leipzig, 1732.

Weckhrlin, Wilhelm Ludwig. *Chronologen, Ein periodisches Werk.* Frankfurt and Leipzig, 1779.

Weichmann, Christian Friedrich, ed. *Poesie der Nieder-Sachsen.* 3 pts. Hamburg, 1721, 1723, and 1726.

Weidemann. *Le bon Vivant oder Die Leipziger Messe / In einem Singe- und Lust-Spiel.* Hamburg, 1710.

Weisse, Christian Felix. *Komische Opern.* Karlsruhe, 1778.

Wend, Christoph Gottlieb. *Die aus der Einsamkeit in die Welt zurückgekehrte Opera, . . . In einem Vor-Spiele.* Hamburg, 1729.

———. *Die Last-tragende Liebe / Oder Emma und Eginhard, in einem Sing-Spiele.* Hamburg, 1728.

Wieland, Christoph Martin. *Ausgewählte Briefe von C. M. Wieland an verschiedene Freunde in den Jahren 1751 bis 1810 geschrieben.* 4 vols. Zurich, 1815-1816.

———. *Gesammelte Schriften.* Ed. Deutsche Kommission der Königlich Preussischen Akademie. Berlin, 1909-1939.

———. *Shakespeares Theatralische Werke.* 8 vols. Zurich, 1762-1766.

Winckelmann, Johann Joachim. *Briefe,* Ed. Walther Rehm and Hans Diepolder. 2 vols. Berlin, 1954.

———. *Gedancken über die Nachahmung der griechischen Wercke in der Mahlerey und Bildhauer-Kunst* (1755). Deutsche Litteraturdenkmale des 18. und 19. Jahrhunderts, 20. Heilbronn, 1885.

———. *Geschichte der Kunst des Alterthums nebst einer Auswahl seiner kleineren Schrifften.* Ed. Julius Lessing. Historisch-politische Bibliothek oder Sammlung von Hauptwerken aus dem Gebiete der Geschichte und Politik alter und neuer Zeit, 2. Berlin, 1870.

Wolf, Georg Friedrich. *Kurzgefasstes Musikalisches Lexikon.* Halle, 1787.

Zedler, Johann Heinrich. *Grosses vollständiges Universal Lexicon Aller Wissenschafften und Künste.* 64 vols. Halle and Leipzig, 1732-1750.

Zinck, Barthold Joachim. "Von gelehrten Sachen." *Staats- und Gelehrte Zeitung Des Hamburgischen unpartheyischen Correspondenten,* 124 (4 August 1745), cols. 5-8.

————. "Von gelehrten Sachen: Fortsetzung der Vertheidigung des Herrn Voltaire wegen seiner Oper." *Staats- und Gelehrte Zeitung Des Hamburgischen unpartheyischen Corresponden-ten,* 126 (7 August 1745), cols. 7-8.

SECONDARY SOURCES

Abert, Anna Amalie. "Die Barockoper: Ein Bericht über die Forschung seit 1945." *Acta Musicologica: Revue de la Société Internationale de Musicologie,* 41 (1969), 121-164.

Abert, Hermann Joseph. *Niccolo Jommelli als Opernkomponist.* Halle a.S., 1908.

Aden, John M. "Dryden and Saint Evremond." *Comparative Literature,* 6, 3 (Summer 1954), 232-239.

Aiken-Sneath, Betsy. *Comedy in Germany in the First Half of the Eighteenth Century.* Oxford, 1936.

Bäte, Ludwig. *Justus Möser,* Advocatus patriae. Frankfurt/M. and Bonn, 1961.

Bate, Walter Jackson, ed. *Criticism: The Major Texts.* New York, 1952.

Beare, Mary. *The German Popular Play "Atis" and the Venetian Opera: A Study of the Conversion of Operas into Popular Plays, 1675-1722.* Cambridge, 1938.

Behrens, Irene. *Die Lehre von der Einteilung der Dichtkunst vornehmlich vom 16. bis 19. Jahrhundert: Studien zur Geschichte der poetischen Gattungen.* Beihefte der Zeitschrift für Romanische Philologie, 92. Halle a.S., 1940.

Betz, Siegmund A. E. "The Operatic Criticism of the *Tatler* and *Spectator.*" *Musical Quarterly,* 31 (1945), 318-330.

Bolte, Joannes. *Die Singspiele der englischen Komödianten und ihrer Nachfolger in Deutschland, Holland und Skandinavien.*

Theatergeschichtliche Forschungen, 7. Hamburg and Leipzig, 1893.

Borchardt, Frank L. *German Antiquity in Renaissance Myth.* Baltimore and London, 1971.

Borcherdt, Hans Heinrich. "Geschichte des deutschen Theaters." *Deutsche Philologie im Aufriss.* Ed. Wolfgang Stammler. 2d rev. ed. Berlin, Bielfeld, Munich, n.d. Vol. 3, fasc. 29-30, cols. 1,099-1,238.

Borinski, Karl. *Die Antike in Poetik und Kunsttheorie von Ausgang des klassischen Altertums bis auf Goethe und Wilhelm von Humboldt.* 2 vols. Leipzig, 1914 and 1924; rpt. Darmstadt, 1965.

————. *Die Poetik der Renaissance und die Anfänge der literarischen Kritik in Deutschland.* Berlin, 1886; rpt. Hildesheim, 1967.

Brachmann, Friedrich. "Johann Hübner, Johannei Rector 1711-1731: Ein Beitrag zur Geschichte der deutschen Litteratur." *Gelehrtenschule des Johanneums* (1899), 1-32.

Braitmaier, Friedrich. *Geschichte der Poetischen Theorie und Kritik von den Diskursen der Maler bis auf Lessing.* 2 pts. Frauenfeld, 1888-1889; rpt. Hildesheim and New York, 1972.

Braun, Werner. "Die Musik in deutschen Gelehrtenbibliotheken des 17. und 18. Jahrhunderts." *Die Musikforschung,* 10, 2 (1957), 241-250.

Brockpähler, Renate. *Handbuch zur Geschichte der Barockoper in Deutschland.* Die Schaubühne, Quellen und Forschungen zur Theatergeschichte, 62. Emsdetten, Westphalia, 1964.

Brückner, Fritz. "Georg Benda und das deutsche Singspiel." *Sammelbände der Internationalen Musik-Gesellschaft,* 5 (1904), 571-621.

Bünemann, Hermann. *Elias Schlegel und Wieland als Bearbeiter antiker Tragödien: Studie zur Rezeption der Antike im 18. Jahrhundert.* Form und Geist: Arbeiten zur Germanischen Philologie, 3. Leipzig, 1928.

Bukofzer, Manfred. "The Baroque in Music History." *Journal of Aesthetics and Art Criticism,* 14, 2 (December 1955), 152-156.

————. *Music in the Baroque Era from Monteverdi to Bach.* New York, 1947.

Burdach, Konrad. "Schillers Chordrama und die Geburt des

tragischen Stils aus der Musik." *Deutsche Rundschau*, 142 (1910), 232-262, 400-433; 143 (1910), 91-112.

Calmus, Georgy. *Die ersten deutschen Singspiele von Standfuss und Hiller*. Publicationen der Internationalen Musik-Gesellschaft, Beihefte, ser. 2, no. 6. Leipzig, 1908.

Cannon, Beekman Cox. *Johann Mattheson, Spectator in Music*. New Haven, Conn., 1947.

Chrysander, Friedrich. "Geschichte der Hamburger Oper unter der Direktion von Reinhard Keiser (1703-1706)." *Allgemeine Musikalische Zeitung*, 15 (1880), cols. 17-25, 33-41, 49-55, 65-72, 81-88.

―――, ed. "Mattheson's Verzeichniss Hamburgischer Opern von 1678 bis 1728, gedruckt im 'Musikalischen Patrioten,' mit seinen handschriftlichen Fortsetzungen bis 1751, nebst Zusätzen und Berichtigungen." *Allgemeine Musikalische Zeitung*, 12 (1877), cols. 198-200, 215-220, 234-236, 245-254, 261-266, 280-282.

―――. "Ueber theatralische Maschinen: Zur Geschichte der Hamburgischen Oper." *Allgemeine Musikalische Zeitung*, 17 (1882), cols. 231-234 and 245-248.

―――. "Die zweite Periode der Hamburger Oper von 1682 bis 1694, oder vom Theaterstreit bis zur Direction Kusser's." *Allgemeine Musikalische Zeitung*, 13 (1878), 289-295, 304-311, 324-329, 340-346, 355-361, 371-376, 388-392, 405-410, 420-424, and 439-442.

Clark, Robert T., Jr. "The Union of the Arts in *Die Braut von Messina*." *PMLA*, 52 (1937), 1,135-1,146.

Clayton, Ellen Creathorne. *Queens of Song, Being Memoirs of Some of the Most Celebrated Female Vocalists*. London, 1863.

Cope, Jackson I. *The Theater and the Dream: From Metaphor to Form in Renaissance Drama*. Baltimore and London, 1973.

Danzel, Theodor Wilhelm. *Gottsched und seine Zeit: Auszüge aus seinem Briefwechsel*. 2d ed. Leipzig, 1855.

Davis, Garold N. *German Thought and Culture in England, 1700-1770: A Preliminary Survey Including a Chronological Bibliography of German Literature in English Translation*. University of North Carolina Studies in Comparative Literature, 47. Chapel Hill, 1969.

Deditius, Annemarie. *Theorien über die Verbindung von Poesie und Musik: Moses Mendelssohn, Lessing*. Liegnitz, 1918.

Degen, Heinz. *Friedrich Christian Bressand: Ein Beitrag zur Braunschweig-Wolfenbütteler Theatergeschichte.* Jahrbuch des Braunschweigischen Geschichtsvereins, N.S. 7. Braunschweig, 1935.

Deutsch, Otto Erich. *Handel, A Documentary Biography.* New York, 1955.

Döring, Paul. *Der nordische Dichterkreis und die Schleswiger Literaturbriefe.* Sonderburg, 1880.

Dyck, Joachim. *Ticht-Kunst: Deutsche Barockpoetik und rhetorische Tradition.* Ars Poetica: Texte und Beiträge zur Dichtungslehre und Dichtkunst, 1. Bad Homburg, Berlin, Zurich, 1966.

Eaton, John Wallace. *The German Influence in Danish Literature in the Eighteenth Century: The German Circle in Copenhagen, 1750-1770.* Cambridge, 1929.

Edelstein, Ludwig. "Wielands 'Abderiten' und der Deutsche Humanismus." *University of California Publications in Modern Philology,* 26, 5 (1950), 441-471.

Einstein, Alfred. *Gluck.* Tr. Eric Blom. London and New York, 1936.

Engländer, Richard. "The Struggle between German and Italian Opera at the Time of Weber." Tr. Erminie Huntress. *Musical Quarterly,* 31 (1945), 479-491.

Faber du Faur, Curt von. *German Baroque Literature: A Catalogue of the Collection in the Yale University Library.* 2 vols. New Haven, 1958 and 1969.

Fetting, Hugo. *Die Geschichte der Deutschen Staatsoper.* Berlin, 1955.

Finsler, Georg. *Homer in der Neuzeit von Dante bis Goethe: Italien, Frankreich, England, Deutschland.* Leipzig and Berlin, 1912.

Fischer, O. "Zum musikalischen Standpunkte des Nordischen Dichterkreises." *Sammelbände der Internationalen Musik-Gesellschaft,* 5 (1904), 245-252.

Flaherty, Marie Gloria. "Justus Möser: Pre-Romantic Literary Historian, Critic, and Theorist." *Traditions and Transitions: Studies in Honor of Harold Jantz.* Ed. Lieselotte E. Kurth, William H. McClain, and Holger Homann. Bad Windsheim, 1972. Pp. 87-104.

————. "Lessing and Opera: A Re-Evaluation," *Germanic Review*, 44, 2 (March 1969), 95-109.

Flemming, Willi. "Einführung." *Die Oper.* Barockdrama 5. Deutsche Literatur: Sammlung literarischer Kunst- und Kulturdenkmäler, in Entwicklungsreihen. 2d rev. ed. Hildesheim, 1965. Pp. 5-83.

————. "Einführung." *Das Ordensdrama.* Barockdrama 2. Deutsche Literatur: Sammlung literarischer Kunst- und Kulturdenkmäler, in Entwicklungsreihen. 2d rev. ed. Hildesheim, 1965. Pp. 5-36.

Freystätter, Wilhelm. *Die musicalischen Zeitschriften seit ihrer Entstehung bis zur Gegenwart: Chronologisches Verzeichnis der periodischen Schriften über Musik.* Munich, 1884.

Fuchs, Albert. *Geistiger Gehalt und Quellenfrage in Wielands Abderiten.* Paris, 1934.

————. "Wieland et l'esthétique de l'opéra." *Revue de Littérature Comparée*, 10 (1930), 608-633.

Garlington, Aubrey S., Jr. "*Le Merveilleux* and Operatic Reform in 18th-Century French Opera." *Musical Quarterly*, 49 (1963), 484-497.

Geffcken, Johannes. "Die ältesten Hamburgischen Opern, zunächst in Beziehung auf die in ihnen behandelte heilige Geschichte." *Zeitschrift des Vereins für hamburgische Geschichte*, 3 (1851), 34-55.

————. "Der Streit über die Sittlichkeit des Schauspiels im Jahre 1769 (Goeze, Schlosser, Nölting) ." *Zeitschrift des Vereins für hamburgische Geschichte*, 3 (1851), 55-77.

Gerth, Klaus. *Studien zu Gerstenbergs Poetik: Ein Beitrag zur Umschichtung der ästhetischen und poetischen Grundbegriffe im 18. Jahrhundert.* Palaestra, 231. Göttingen, 1960.

Goldschmidt, Hugo. *Die Musikästhetik des 18. Jahrhunderts und ihre Beziehungen zu seinem Kunstschaffen.* Zurich and Leipzig, 1915; rpt. Hildesheim, 1968.

Grasberger, Franz. "Zur Bibliographie und Katalogisierung der Textbücher." *Zentralblatt für Bibliothekswesen*, 66, 5-6 (Leipzig, 1952), 206-219.

Grout, Donald Jay. "German Baroque Opera." *Musical Quarterly*, 32 (1946), 574-587.

Grunsky, Karl. "Klassische Literatur und musikalisches Drama: Herder." *Bayreuther Blätter*, 22, 8-10 (1899), 230-265.

―――. "Klassische Literatur und musikalisches Drama: Lessing." *Bayreuther Blätter*, 22, 6-7 (1899), 172-193.

Guiet, René. *L'Évolution d'un genre: Le livret d'opéra en France de Gluck à la Révolution (1774-1793)*. Smith College Studies in Modern Languages, 18. Northampton, Mass., 1936-1937.

Haas, Robert. "Geschichtliche Opernbezeichnungen: Ein Überblick." *Festschrift Hermann Kretzschmar*. Leipzig, 1918. Pp. 43-45.

―――. "Wiener deutsche Parodieopern um 1730." *Zeitschrift für Musikwissenschaft*, 8 (1926), 201-225.

Haase, Rudolf. *Leibniz und die Musik: Ein Beitrag zur Geschichte der harmonikalen Symbolik*. Hommerich, 1963.

Hase, Hermann. "Johann Adam Hiller und Breitkopfs." *Zeitschrift für Musikwissenschaft*, 2 (1919), 1-22.

Heartz, Daniel. "The Genesis of Mozart's *Idomeneo*." *Musical Quarterly*, 55 (1969), 1-19.

Heitmüller, Ferdinand. *Hamburgische Dramatiker zur Zeit Gottscheds und Ihre Beziehungen zu ihm: Ein Beitrag zur Geschichte des Theaters und Dramas im 18. Jahrhundert*. Wandsbeck, 1890.

Herrick, Marvin T. *Tragicomedy: Its Origins and Development in Italy, France, and England*. Illinois Studies in Language and Literature, 39. Urbana, 1955.

Herrmann, Hans Peter. *Naturnachahmung und Einbildungskraft: Zur Entwicklung der deutschen Poetik von 1670 bis 1740*. Ars Poetica: Texte und Beiträge zur Dichtungslehre und Dichtkunst, Studien, 8. Bad Homburg, Berlin, Zurich, 1970.

Hövel, Ernst. *Der Kampf der Geistlichkeit gegen das Theater in Deutschland im 17. Jahrhundert*. Münster, 1912.

Holl, Karl. *Zur Geschichte der Lustspieltheorie*. Literarhistorische Forschungen, 44. Berlin, 1911.

Hope, Quentin M. *Saint Evremond: The* Honnête-Homme *as Critic*. Bloomington, Ind., 1962.

Huber, Wolfgang. "Das Textbuch der frühdeutschen Oper: Untersuchungen über literarische Voraussetzungen, stoffliche Grundlagen und Quellen." Diss. Munich, 1957.

Immerwahr, Raymond. *Romantisch: Genese und Tradition einer Denkform*. Respublica Literaria: Studienreihe zur europäischen Bildungstradition von Humanismus bis zur Romantik, 7. Frankfurt/M., 1972.

Jacoby, Karl. *Die ersten moralischen Wochenschriften Hamburgs am Anfange des achtzehnten Jahrhunderts.* Wilhelm-Gymnasium zu Hamburg, 7. Jahresbericht (1887-1888), 1-48.

Jantz, Harold. "German Baroque Literature." *MLN*, 77, 4 (October 1962), 337-367.

———. *German Baroque Literature: A Descriptive Catalogue of the Collection of Harold Jantz and a Guide to the Collection on Microfilm.* 2 vols. New Haven, Conn., 1974.

Jördens, Karl Heinrich. *Lexikon deutscher Dichter und Prosaisten.* 6 vols. Leipzig. 1806-1811.

Kettler, Hans Kuhnert. *Baroque Tradition in the Literature of the German Enlightenment, 1700-1750: Studies in the Determination of a Literary Period.* Cambridge, 1943.

Kindermann, Heinz. *Theatergeschichte Europas.* Vol. 3: *Das Theater der Barockzeit.* Salzburg, 1959. Vol. 4: *Von der Aufklärung zur Romantik,* pt. 1. Salzburg, 1961. Vol. 5: *Von der Aufklärung zur Romantik,* pt. 2. Salzburg, 1962.

Kleefeld, Wilhelm. "Das Orchester der Hamburger Oper, 1678-1738." *Sammelbände der Internationalen Musik-Gesellschaft,* 1 (1899-1900), 219-289.

Köster, Albert. "Das lyrische Drama im 18. Jahrhundert." *Preussische Jahrbücher,* 68 (1891), 188-201.

Kretzschmar, Hermann. "Das erste Jahrhundert der deutschen Oper." *Sammelbände der Internationalen Musik-Gesellschaft,* 3 (1901-1902), 270-293.

———. "Für und Gegen die Oper." *Jahrbuch der Musikbibliothek Peters für 1913,* 20 (Leipzig, 1914), 59-70.

Kristeller, Paul Oskar. "The Modern System of the Arts: A Study in the History of Aesthetics." *Journal of the History of Ideas,* 12, 4 (October 1951), 496-527; 13, 1 (January 1952), 17-46.

Krogh, Torben. *Zur Geschichte des dänischen Singspiels im 18. Jahrhundert.* Berlin, 1923.

Krome, Ferdinand. *Die Anfänge des musikalischen Journalismus in Deutschland.* Leipzig, 1897.

Kuehnemund, Richard. *Arminius or the Rise of a National Symbol in Literature (From Hutten to Grabbe).* University of North Carolina Studies in the Germanic Languages and Literatures, 8. Chapel Hill, 1953.

Kurth-Voigt, Lieselotte E. *Perspectives and Points of View: The Early Works of Wieland and Their Background.* Baltimore and London, 1974.

Lempicki, Sigmund von. *Geschichte der deutschen Literaturwissenschaft bis zum Ende des 18. Jahrhunderts.* 2d rev. and enl. ed. Göttingen, 1968.

Leo, Johannes Hermann. *Zur Entstehungsgeschichte der "Allgemeinen Theorie der Schönen Künste" J. G. Sulzers.* Diss. Heidelberg, 1906. Berlin, 1906.

Leysaht, Konrad. *Dubos et Lessing: "Réflexions critiques sur la poésie et sur la peinture" (1719), "Laocoon, ou traité des limites de la peinture et de la poésie" (1766).* Greifswald, 1874.

Lindner, Ernst Otto. *Die erste stehende Deutsche Oper.* Berlin, 1855.

"Listen der in Hamburg residirenden, wie der dasselbe vertretenden Diplomaten und Consuln." *Zeitschrift des Vereins für hamburgische Geschichte,* 3 (1851), 414-482.

Loewenberg, Alfred. *Annals of Opera: 1597-1940.* 2d rev. ed. Geneva, 1955.

Lombard, Alfred. *L'Abbé Du Bos: Un initiateur de la pensée moderne (1670-1742).* Paris, 1913.

Longyear, R. M. "Schiller and Opera." *Musical Quarterly,* 52 (1966), 171-182.

Loomis, C. Grant. "Erdmann Neumeister's Contribution to Seventeenth Century Bibliography." *Journal of English and Germanic Philology,* 42, 2 (April 1944), 222-241.

Lowens, Irving. "St. Evremond, Dryden, and the Theory of Opera." *Criticism,* 1, 3 (Summer 1959), 226-248.

Lucas, F. L. *Euripides and His Influence.* Boston, 1923.

Marks, Paul F. "Aesthetics of Music in the Philosophy of *Sturm und Drang*: Gerstenberg, Hamann and Herder." *Music Review,* 35 (1974), 247-259.

————. "The Rhetorical Element in Musical *Sturm und Drang*: Christian Gottfried Krause's *Von der musikalischen Poesie.*" *Music Review,* 30 (1972), 93-107.

Markwardt, Bruno. *Geschichte der deutschen Poetik.* Grundriss der germanischen Philologie, 13. Vol. 1: *Barock und Frühaufklärung.* 3rd ed. Berlin, 1964. Vol. 2: *Aufklärung, Rokoko, Sturm und Drang.* Berlin, 1956. Vol. 3: *Klassik und Romantik.* Berlin, 1958; rpt. Berlin and New York, 1971.

Martens, Wolfgang. *Die Botschaft der Tugend: Die Aufklärung im Spiegel der deutschen Moralischen Wochenschriften.* Stuttgart, 1968.

————. "Die Schriften wider und für den 'Patrioten': Bibliographie." *Archiv für Geschichte des Buchwesens,* 5 (1964), cols. 1,353-1,368.

Martini, Fritz. "C. M. Wieland und das 18. Jahrhundert." *Festschrift Paul Kluckhohn und Hermann Schneider.* Tübingen, 1948. Pp. 243-265.

Martino, Alberto. *Geschichte der dramatischen Theorie in Deutschland im 18. Jahrhundert.* Vol. 1: *Die Dramaturgie der Aufklärung (1730-1780).* Tr. Wolfgang Pross. Tübingen, 1972.

Marx, Emilie. *Wieland und das Drama.* Freie Forschungen zur deutschen Literaturgeschichte, 3. Strasbourg, 1914.

Mauser, Wolfram. "Wielands 'Geschichte der Abderiten,'" *Germanistische Studien: Innsbrucker Beiträge zur Kulturwissenschaft,* 15 (1969), 165-177.

Meinardus, Ludwig. *Rückblicke auf die Anfänge der deutschen Oper in Hamburg.* Hamburg, 1878.

Miller, Steven R. *Die Figur des Erzählers in Wielands Romanen.* Göppingen, 1970.

Minor, Jakob. *Christian Felix Weisse und seine Beziehungen zur deutschen Literatur des achtzehnten Jahrhunderts.* Innsbruck, 1880.

Montgomery, Franz. "Early Criticism of Italian Opera in England." *Musical Quarterly,* 15 (1929), 415-423.

Müller-Blattau, Josef. "Gluck und die deutsche Dichtung." *Jahrbuch der Musikbibliothek Peters für 1938,* 45 (1939), 30-52.

Nagel, Willibald. "Deutsche Musiker des 18. Jahrhunderts im Verkehr mit J. Fr. A. von Uffenbach." *Sammelbände der Internationalen Musik-Gesellschaft,* 13 (1911), 69-106.

Nessler, Nikolaus. *Dramaturgie der Jesuiten Pontanus, Donatus und Masenius: Ein Beitrag zur Technik des Schuldramas.* Brixen, 1905.

Neumann, Alfred Robert. "The Evolution of the Concept *Gesamtkunstwerk* in German Romanticism." Diss. University of Michigan, 1951.

————. "Gottsched versus the Opera," *Monatshefte,* 45, 5 (1953), 297-307.

Nivelle, Armand. *Kunst- und Dichtungstheorien zwischen Auf-*

klärung und Klassik. Berlin, 1960. Rev. translation of *Les théories esthétiques en Allemagne de Baumgarten à Kant.* Paris, 1955.

Nufer, Wolfgang. *Herders Ideen zur Verbindung von Poesie, Musik und Tanz.* Germanische Studien, 74. Berlin, 1929.

Oberländer, Hans. *Die geistige Entwicklung der deutschen Schauspielkunst im 18. Jahrhundert.* Theatergeschichtliche Forschungen, 15. Hamburg and Leipzig, 1898.

Olsen, Solveig. *Christian Heinrich Postels Beitrag zur deutschen Literatur: Versuch einer Darstellung.* Amsterdamer Publikationen zur Sprache und Literatur, 7. Amsterdam, 1973.

Orgel, Stephen. *The Illusion of Power: Political Theater in the English Renaissance.* Berkeley, Los Angeles, and London, 1975.

Parker, L. John. *Christoph Martin Wielands dramatische Tätigkeit.* Bern and Munich, 1961.

———. "Wieland's Musical Play 'Die Wahl des Herkules' and Goethe." *German Life and Letters,* 15 (1962), 175-180.

Pauly, Reinhard G. "Benedetto Marcello's Satire on Early 18th-Century Opera." *Musical Quarterly,* 34 (1948), 222-233.

Pechel, Rudolf. *Christian Wernickes Epigramme.* Palaestra, 71. Berlin, 1909.

Peiser, Karl. *Johann Adam Hiller: Ein Beitrag zur Musikgeschichte des 18. Jahrhunderts.* Leipzig, 1894.

Perry, Charles D. "Classical Myth in Grand Opera." *Classical Journal,* 53, 5 (February 1958), 207-213.

Petersen, Christian. "Die Teutschübende Gesellschaft in Hamburg." *Zeitschrift des Vereins für hamburgische Geschichte,* 2 (1847), 533-564.

Peucer, Alphons. "Die Hamburger Oper von 1678 bis 1728." *Allgemeine Theater-Revue,* 2 (1836), 3-43.

Pirrotta, Nino. "*Commedia dell' arte* and Opera." *Musical Quarterly,* 41 (1955), 305-324.

Popp, Georg. *Über den Begriff des Dramas in den deutschen Poetiken des 17. Jahrhunderts.* Diss. Leipzig, 1895.

Preisendanz, Wolfgang. "Mimesis und Poiesis in der deutschen Dichtungstheorie des 18. Jahrhunderts." *Rezeption und Produktion zwischen 1570 und 1730: Festschrift für Günther Weydt.* Ed. Wolfdietrich Rasch, Hans Geulen, and Klaus Haberkamm. Bern and Munich, 1972. Pp. 537-552.

Preussner, Eberhard. *Die musikalischen Reisen des Herrn von Uffenbach, Aus einem Reisetagebuch des Johann Friedrich A. von Uffenbach aus Frankfurt am Main, 1712-1716.* Kassel and Basel, 1949.

Reichel, Eugen. "Gottsched und Johann Adolph Scheibe." *Sammelbände der Internationalen Musik-Gesellschaft,* 2 (1900-1901), 654-668.

Reuter, Fritz. "Die Entwicklung der Leipziger, insbesondere italienischen Oper bis zum siebenjährigen Krieg." *Zeitschrift für Musikwissenschaft,* 5 (1922), 1-16.

Robertson, John George. *Lessing's Dramatic Theory.* Cambridge, 1939.

————. *Studies in the Genesis of Romantic Theory in the Eighteenth Century.* Cambridge, 1923.

Rogers, Francis. "Some Prima Donnas of the Latter Eighteenth Century." *Musical Quarterly,* 30 (1944), 147-162.

Rogerson, Brewster. "*Ut musica poesis*: The Parallel of Music and Poetry in Eighteenth Century Criticism." Diss. Princeton, 1945.

Rolland, Romain. *Goethe and Beethoven.* Tr. G. A. Pfister and E. S. Kemp. New York and London, 1968.

Rosenkamer, Eugen. *Johann Adolph Scheibe als Verfasser seines "Critischen Musicus."* Diss. Bonn, 1929.

Rosenmüller, Max. *Johann Ulrich König: Ein Beitrag zur Litteraturgeschichte des 18. Jahrhunderts.* Leipzig, 1896.

Rutledge, John. *The Dialogue of the Dead in Eighteenth-Century Germany.* German Studies in America, 17. Bern and Frankfurt/M., 1974.

Rutledge, Joyce S. *Johann Adolph Schlegel.* German Studies in America, 18. Bern and Frankfurt/M., 1974.

Sachs, Curt. *Musik und Oper am kurbrandenburgischen Hof.* Berlin, 1910.

Saintsbury, George. *A History of Criticism and Literary Taste in Europe from the Earliest Texts to the Present Day.* 3 vols. Edinburgh and London, 1900-1904.

Schaal, Richard. "Die vor 1801 gedruckten Libretti des Theatermuseums München." *Die Musikforschung,* 10 (1957), 388-396, 487-497; 11 (1958), 54-69, 168-177, 321-336, 462-477; 12 (1959), 60-75, 161-177, 299-306, 454-461; 13 (1960), 38-46, 164-172, 299-306, 441-448; 14 (1961), 36-43, 166-183.

Scheid, N. *Der Jesuit Jakob Masen, ein Schulmann und Schriftsteller des 17. Jahrhunderts.* Cologne, 1898.

Schenker, Manfred. *Charles Batteux und seine Nachahmungstheorie in Deutschland.* Untersuchungen zur neueren Sprach- und Literatur-Geschichte, N.S. 2. Leipzig, 1909.

Schering, Arnold. "Hugo Goldschmidt, *Die Musikästhetik des 18. Jahrhunderts und ihre Beziehungen zu seinem Kunstschaffen,* Zurich und Leipzig, 1915" (review). *Zeitschrift für Musikwissenschaft,* 1 (1918-1919), 298-309.

Scherle, Arthur. "Das deutsche Opernlibretto von Opitz bis Hofmannsthal." Diss. Munich, 1954.

Schiedermair, Ludwig. *Die Deutsche Oper: Grundzüge ihres Werdens und Wesens.* Leipzig, 1930.

Schild, K. A. "Die Bezeichnungen der deutschen Dramen von den Anfängen bis 1740." *Giessener Beiträge zur Deutschen Philologie,* 12 (1925), 30-33.

Schletterer, Hans Michael. *Das deutsche Singspiel von seinen ersten Anfängen bis auf die neueste Zeit.* Zur Geschichte dramatischer Musik und Poesie in Deutschland, 1. Augsburg, 1863.

Schmidt, Friedrich Adolf. "Maler Müllers Stellung in der Entwicklung des musikalischen Dramas." *Germanisch-Romanische Monatsschrift,* 28 (1940), 179-188.

Schmidt, Gustav Friedrich. "Die älteste deutsche Oper in Leipzig am Ende des 17. und Anfang des 18. Jahrhunderts." *Festschrift zum 50. Geburtstag: Adolf Sandberger.* Munich, 1918. Pp. 209-257.

————. *Die frühdeutsche Oper und die musikdramatische Kunst Georg Caspar Schürmanns.* 2 vols. Regensburg, 1933-1934.

————. "Zur Geschichte, Dramaturgie und Statistik der frühdeutschen Oper (1627-1750)." *Zeitschrift für Musikwissenschaft,* 5 (1922-1923), 582-597; 6 (1923-1924), 129-157, 496-530.

Schreiber, Irmtraud. *Dichtung und Musik der deutschen Opernarien, 1680-1700.* Diss. Berlin, 1934.

Schröder, Hans. *Lexikon der hamburgischen Schriftsteller bis zur Gegenwart.* 8 vols. Hamburg, 1851-1883.

Schueller, Herbert M. "Correspondences between Music and the Sister Arts according to 18th Century Aesthetic Theory." *Journal of Aesthetics and Art Criticism.* 11, 4 (June 1953), 334-359.

Schulze, Walther. *Die Quellen der Hamburger Oper (1678-1738):*

Eine bibliographisch-statistische Studie zur Geschichte der ersten stehenden deutschen Oper. Mitteilungen aus der Bibliothek der Hansestadt Hamburg, N.S. 4. Hamburg-Oldenburg, 1938.

Schuppenhauer, Claus. *Der Kampf um den Reim in der deutschen Literatur des 18. Jahrhunderts.* Abhandlungen zur Kunst-, Musik- und Literaturwissenschaft, 91. Bonn, 1970.

Schwan, Wilhelm Bernhard. *Die opernästhetischen Theorien der deutschen klassischen Dichter.* Diss. Bonn, 1926.

Sengle, Friedrich. *Wieland.* Stuttgart, 1949.

Serauky, Walter. *Die musikalische Nachahmungsästhetik im Zeitraum von 1700 bis 1850.* Universitas Archiv: Eine Sammlung wissenschaftlicher Untersuchungen und Abhandlungen, 17. Münster, 1929.

Seuffert, Bernhard. *Wielands Abderiten: Vortrag.* Berlin, 1878.

Silz, Walter. "Chorus and Choral Function in Schiller." *Schiller 1759/1959: Commemorative American Studies.* Ed. John R. Frey. Illinois Studies in Language and Literature, 46. Urbana, 1959. Pp. 147-170.

Smith, Patrick J. *The Tenth Muse: A Historical Study of the Opera Libretto.* New York, 1970.

Sonneck, Oscar George Theodore. *Library of Congress Catalogue of Opera Librettos Printed before 1800.* 2 vols. Washington, D.C., 1914.

Spitta, Phillipp. "Ueber die Beziehungen Sebastian Bachs zu Christian Friedrich Hunold und Mariane von Ziegler." *Historische und Philologische Aufsätze: Festgabe an Ernst Curtius.* Berlin, 1884.

Spitzer, Leo. *Classical and Christian Ideas of World Harmony: Prolegomena to an Interpretation of the Word "Stimmung."* Ed. Anna Granville Hatcher. Baltimore, 1963.

Stammler, Wolfgang. " 'Edle Einfalt,' Zur Geschichte eines kunsttheoretischen Topos." *Worte und Werte: Bruno Markwardt zum 60. Geburtstag.* Ed. Gustav Erdmann and Alfons Eichstaedt. Berlin, 1961. Pp. 359-382.

Stege, Fritz. "Die deutsche Musikkritik des 18. Jahrhunderts unter dem Einfluss der Affektenlehre." *Zeitschrift für Musikwissenschaft,* 10 (1927), 23-30.

Terras, Rita. *Wilhelm Heinses Ästhetik.* Munich, 1972.

Teuber, Eugen. "Die Kunstphilosophie des Abbé Dubos." *Zeit-*

schrift für Aesthetik und allgemeine Kunstwissenschaft, 17 (1924), 361-410.

Ullmann, Richard and Helene Gotthard. *Geschichte des Begriffes "Romantisch" in Deutschland.* Berlin, 1927.

Van der Bent, Ilse Marie. "Music in the Life and Works of Christoph Martin Wieland." Diss. University of Cincinnati, 1975.

Vogel, Hermann. *Christian Friedrich Hunold (Menantes): Sein Leben und seine Werke.* Lucka S.-A., 1897.

Wehl, Feodor. *Hamburgs Literaturleben im achtzehnten Jahrhundert.* Leipzig, 1856.

Weigand, Paul. "Schiller's Dramas as Opera Texts." *Monatshefte*, 46, 5 (1954), 249-259.

Weilen, Alexander von. *Zur Wiener Theatergeschichte: Die vom Jahre 1629 bis zum Jahre 1740 am Wiener Hofe zur Aufführung gelangten Werke theatralischen Charakters und Oratorien.* Vienna, 1901.

Weinberg, Bernard. *A History of Literary Criticism in the Italian Renaissance.* 2 vols. Chicago, 1961.

Weinkauf, Arnold Lewis. "The Literary Life of Hamburg during the Transition from the Baroque to the Enlightenment." Diss. Northwestern University, 1951.

Weisstein, Ulrich Werder. "Studies in the Libretto: Otello—Der Rosenkavalier, Prolegomena to a Poetics of Opera." Diss. Indiana University, 1954.

Wellek, René. *A History of Modern Criticism: 1750-1950.* Vol. 1: *The Later Eighteenth Century.* New Haven, Conn. and London, 1955.

Whitton, John. "Sacrifice and Society in Wieland's *Abderiten.*" *Lessing Yearbook*, 2 (1970), 213-234.

Wilkinson, Elizabeth M. *Johann Elias Schlegel: A German Pioneer in Aesthetics.* Oxford, 1945; 2d ed. Darmstadt, 1973.

Will, Frederic, Jr. "Cognition through Beauty in Moses Mendelssohn's Early Aesthetics." *Journal of Aesthetics and Art Criticism*, 14, 1 (September 1955), 97-105.

Wöhlke, Franz. *Lorenz Christoph Mizler: Ein Beitrag zur musikalischen Gelehrtengeschichte des 18. Jahrhunderts.* Würzburg-Anmühle, 1940.

Wolfenbüttel, Herzog-August-Bibliothek Kataloge. Vol. 14: *Li-*

bretti: Verzeichnis der bis 1800 erschienenen Textbücher. Ed. Eberhard Thiel and Gisela Rohr. Frankfurt/M., 1970.

Wolff, Hellmuth Christian. *Die Barockoper in Hamburg (1678-1738).* 2 vols. Wolfenbüttel, 1957.

Yuill, W.E. "Abderitis and Abderitism: Some Reflections on a Novel by Wieland." *Essays in German Literature,* 1. Ed. Frederick Norman. London, 1965. Pp. 72-91.

Zinar, Ruth. "The Use of Greek Tragedy in the History of Opera." *Current Musicology,* 12 (1971), 80-95.

Ziolkowski, Theodore. "Language and Mimetic Action in Lessing's *Miss Sara Sampson.*" *Germanic Review,* 40, 4 (November 1965), 261-276.

INDEX

Abschatz, Hans Assmann von, 50
acting, 15; academies, 129, 183-84,
222, 262; and dramatic structure, 57, 216, 226, 323-24 n. 5;
both simultaneous in space and
progressive in time, 224; Ekhof,
129; exaggerated style, 272;
juxtaposition of French and
English styles of, 57-59; Hamburg interest in, 129; Hamlet's
advice to players, 224; importance for living theater, 85, 89,
183-84; of singers, 80, 202-203;
views on ancient techniques of,
215; Weimar style, 300; Wieland, 277. *See also* non-verbal
communication; performance
actors: defense of, 21-22, 131;
Lessing and, 201; need technical training, 222; oppose public
criticism, 231; professional
pride of, 223
acts, 76; number of, 28, 62
adaptation, operatic, *see* ancient
drama, operatic adaptation of;
epics, operatic adaptation of;
Greek tragedies, operatic adaptation of; novels, operatic
adaptation of
Addison, Joseph, 83, 267
adiaphora, 21, 25
Aeschylus, 271
aesthetic reaction, 296; a basic
human desire, 197; broaching
the subject of, 113; genuine,
278; interest in psychology of,
190; mysterious inclinations as,
181-82
aesthetics: Baumgarten on, 3,
196; Dubos on, 188; ideas pre-

cede systems of, 5; music to be
included in theory of, 245; new
science of, 191; reduced to imitation of nature, 150 passim
Agricola, Johann Friedrich, 163,
164, 209, 226-27
Ahlefeldt, Benedikt von, 310 n.
15
Alamode, opposition to, 12. *See
also* foreign cultural domination; foreign fashions
alexandrines: inappropriate for
opera, 50
Algarotti, Francesco, 262, 265,
329 n. 10
America, 153-54
ancient and modern, 13-14, 106,
225, 274. *See also* Quarrel of
the Ancients and the Moderns
ancient drama: invalid as modern
critical standard, 125; operatic
adaptations of, 34-35, 56-57, 78,
116-17, 214; unnaturalness of,
112. *See also* Greek tragedy
Anna Amalia, 183, 257
another world, 59, 63, 88, 115,
181, 195, 230, 238, 247, 250, 290,
293, 295-97, 311 n. 20. *See also*
artificiality of art; artistic
reality; order, an artificial new;
truth, artistic
antiquity, *see* Greek antiquity;
Nordic antiquity
Anton Ulrich, 29
Arcadian Academy, 308-309 n. 3
aria, 203, 219, 265; coloratura, 249;
declamatory, 249; experimentation with, 283; importance in
early German opera, 19; religious song revitalized with,
50; "soul" of opera, 50

theater: clerical opposition to, 20-
25; diversity of early eighteenth-
century, 37; English, 212, 214,
216; French, 55, 66; history of
German, 279; Italian, 55, 214,
216; Spanish, 214
Theater am Gänsemarkt, 21, 42,
67, 72, 74, 82, 83, 102, 116, 119
Thirty Years' War, 10, 11, 13
Tieck, Ludwig, 180, 278, 292, 294-
95, 333 n. 7
time and space, imaginary, 33, 108,
113, 136, 298-99
Tirso de Molina, 6, 8
totality, work of art as, 47, 196,
206. See also performance
tragedy: Christian world view pre-
cludes pure, 16; lyrical, 154; a
make-believe fabrication like
opera, 156; opera as, 121; opera
destroys appreciation for, 40;
study of essence of, 188; super-
seded by opera, 45. See also
Greek tragedy
tragicomedy, 8, 11, 16, 45
travesties, 252
Triewald, Samuel, 73
truth, artistic: defense of, 62-63;
differs from actual, 28, 29, 30;
difficulties in explaining, 195;
necessitates changes in facts, 64;
not limited to nature and facts,
69, 295-96; opera's importance
in explaining, 296; to be understood figuratively rather than
literally, 87-88, 96. See also
another world; artificiality of
art; artistic reality

Uffenbach, Johann Friedrich, 97,
109-114, 126, 136, 138, 152,
156, 185, 262, 284, 290
unities, the three: as critical
standard, 99, 136, 142; contribute to simplicity, 172; dis-

pute over validity of, 27-28;
irrelevance of, 14, 15, 230, 237;
opera to observe, 76, 306 n. 12;
Renaissance origins of, 6; subordinate to music's needs, 199
unity: as opposed to unities, 237,
296; essence of great art, 241,
285
unity of action, 52; important for
simplicity, 33; only valid dramatic rule, 43. See also continuity of scenes
unity of place: irrelevance of, 33,
43, 108, 298; only incidental
rule, 151. See also time and
space, imaginary
unity of time: doubts about contribution to probability, 51-52;
irrelevance of, 33, 43, 108, 298;
much disputed, 61; only incidental rule, 151; rejection of,
46. See also time and space,
imaginary
utility, 137, 261; ethical, 23, 28,
81; spiritual, 25. See also moral
lesson
ut pictura poesis, 14-15, 28, 215,
323 n. 5

variety, 15, 30, 33, 59, 71, 103,
106, 196
verisimilitude: carried to extreme,
144, 210; formation of concept
of, 6; opera's lack of, 39, 70,
100; related to concept of poetic
fiction, 51; scrutiny of concept
of, 48-49, 69, 115, 134, 140, 289-
91, 314 n. 25; with a musical
medium, 64. See also artistic
media; comparisons; imitation
of nature; probability
verse, 26, 107, 132, 139, 143, 151,
298. See also metrics
Vienna, 128, 233, 243, 266
Villati, Leopoldo di, 202, 210

LIBRARY OF CONGRESS CATALOGING
IN PUBLICATION DATA

Flaherty, Gloria, 1938-
    Opera in the development of German critical thought

    Bibliography: p.
    Includes index.
    1. Opera—Germany—History and criticism.
2. Opera—History and criticism—18th century.
3. Germany—Intellectual life. I. Title.
ML1729.F6   782.1'0943   78-51163
ISBN 0-691-06370-2